Medieval History a

General Editors
JOHN BLAIR   HELENA HAMEROW

Perceptions of the Prehistoric in Anglo-Saxon England

Perceptions of the Prehistoric in Anglo-Saxon England represents an novel exploration of the place of prehistoric monuments in the Anglo-Saxon psyche, and examines how Anglo-Saxon communities perceived and used these monuments during the period AD 400–1100. Sarah Semple employs archaeological, historical, artistic, and literary sources to study the variety of ways in which the early medieval population of England used the prehistoric legacy in the landscape, exploring it from temporal and geographic perspectives. Key to the arguments and ideas presented is the premise that populations used these remains, intentionally and knowingly, in the articulation and manipulation of their identities: local, regional, political, and religious. They recognized them as ancient features, as human creations from a distant past. They used them as landmarks, battle sites, and estate markers, giving them new Old English names. Before, and even during, the conversion to Christianity, communities buried their dead in and around these monuments. After the conversion, several churches were built in their shadow and great assemblies were held at them, and felons executed and buried within their surrounds.

This volume covers the early to late Anglo-Saxon world, touching on funerary ritual, domestic and settlement evidence, ecclesiastical sites, place-names, written sources, and administrative and judicial geographies. Through a thematic and chronologically-structured examination of Anglo-Saxon uses and perceptions of the prehistoric, Semple demonstrates that populations were not only concerned with *Romanitas* (or Roman-ness), but that a similar curiosity and conscious reference to and use of the prehistoric existed within all strata of society.

Sarah Semple is Professor of Archaeology at Durham University.

MEDIEVAL HISTORY AND ARCHAEOLOGY

General Editors

John Blair   Helena Hamerow

The volumes in this series bring together archaeological, historical, and visual methods to offer new approaches to aspects of mediaeval society, economy, and material culture. The series seeks to present and interpret archaeological evidence in ways readily accessible to historians, while providing a historical perspective and context for the material culture of the period.

RECENTLY PUBLISHED IN THIS SERIES

PERCEPTIONS OF THE PREHISTORIC IN ANGLO-SAXON ENGLAND

Religion, Ritual, and Rulership in the Landscape

SARAH SEMPLE

OXFORD
UNIVERSITY PRESS

OXFORD
UNIVERSITY PRESS

Great Clarendon Street, Oxford, OX2 6DP,
United Kingdom

Oxford University Press is a department of the University of Oxford.
It furthers the University's objective of excellence in research, scholarship,
and education by publishing worldwide. Oxford is a registered trade mark of
Oxford University Press in the UK and in certain other countries

First published 2013
First published in paperback 2019

Published in the United States of America by Oxford University Press
198 Madison Avenue, New York, NY 10016, United States of America

British Library Cataloguing in Publication Data
Data available

Library of Congress Cataloging in Publication Data
Data available

ISBN 978–0–19–968310–9 (Hbk.)
ISBN 978–0–19–884411–2 (Pbk.)

For my parents

Praise for *Perceptions of the Prehistoric in Anglo-Saxon England*

Preface and Acknowledgements

The beginnings of this book lie in an undergraduate dissertation which investigated the medieval church and large prehistoric henge at Avebury in Wiltshire. This project, and a passion for early medieval archaeology, were nurtured at the Institute of Archaeology, University College London, encouraged by my excellent tutors especially James Graham Campbell. The main project, however, began life as doctoral research, funded by the AHRC and completed at The Queen's College, Oxford in 2003. After several revisions, the final manuscript was realized during research leave granted by my department at Durham University in 2010. Throughout its creation, I have benefited from the inspiring guidance of John Blair, who has provided advice on all forms of evidence for the Anglo-Saxon world, and to whom I remain indebted, for his continuing generosity with knowledge and good advice.

The resulting volume is, I hope, something a little different from the main stream literature on Anglo-Saxon England. We know that early medieval communities were intimately connected to the landscape that surrounded them through their daily lives and activities. This book reveals that ancient prehistoric monuments in those landscapes had as much meaning for early medieval communities as the natural world. They were not just places to bury the dead, but legendary locations and places of pre-Christian power and myth that continued to hold meaning after the conversion. To stand in a certain ancient hill fort was to stand where past heroes had fallen, where battles had been lost and won, at a place intimate to tales of the beginnings of Anglo-Saxon Society. An ancient barrow cemetery on the skyline could be claimed anew, and reworked into the fabric of a new mythology of descent, ownership, and territory. Monuments, therefore, rather than merely old features inspiring awe or fear, were used to mark out a potent terrain invested with power and myth. Far from fading away at the conversion, this meaningful landscape survived and was negotitated afresh by late Anglo-Saxon populations who populated its hills and pools with monstrous entities and beasts and used landscape to structure new rituals of power.

It is my hope that this book achieves a deeper understanding of this numinous landscape and reawakens the early medieval imagination in the modern eye. There is material here of interest for archaeologists working on funerary archaeology and landscapes, and working with concepts of power, monumentality, and place, and elements of the book may have appeal to those working in place-name studies, literary studies, and, of course, medieval history. Any book has its limitations and this one is no exception. On reflection the question of competing British traditions of reuse in the fifth and sixth centuries has received less attention than it should. The geographic focus is also skewed to the Anglo-Saxon kingdoms in the south, east, and north, and the west of England is not explored here fully. Finally the emphasis on landscape and prehistoric monuments could have been balanced with a deeper consideration of the use of Roman ruins and more detailed investigation of the recycling and circulation of prehistoric and Roman artefacts. I can only hope that what lies in these pages acts as a stimulus and incentive to others to press on and explore these gaps further.

The text has been seen by many on its journey and is much improved as a consequence. I am grateful to my examiners Helena Hamerow and Martin Carver; and to Richard Bradley, John Hines, Helen Geake, Sam Lucy, Howard Williams, and Victoria Whitworth for early comments on my thesis. More recently the revised script has benefited from input by Abby Antrobus, Gwen Bergius, Derek Craig, Rosemary Cramp, Vicky Crewe, Tom Moore, and Sam Turner. Specific chapters were read and commented on by Stuart Brookes, John Baker, and Alex Sanmark (Chapter 3), Alaric Hall and Richard Jones (Chapter 5), and Andrew Reynolds, Stuart Brookes, and John Blair (Chapter 6). Alaric Hall and John Baker deserve especial thanks for their close scrutiny of my use of Old English literary sources and Old English place-names in Chapter 5 and Appendix 4. Two anonymous reviewers also provided welcome advice which has served to strengthen the volume, and the text has been much improved by the hard work of Alejandra Gutierrez and the OUP team. I am grateful to Brian Buchanan and Alex Turner for producing the original illustrations in the volume and to John Blair, John Bleach, Bill Britnell, Stuart Brookes, Vicky Crewe, Paul Everson, Richard Green, Dawn Hadley, Sam Lucy, Dominic Powlesland, Andrew Reynolds, Daniel Smith, David Stocker, Paul Tubb, Alisdair Whittle, Mark Whyman, Howard Williams, and the British Museum, Cambridge University, Corpus for Anglo-Saxon Stone Sculpture, English Heritage, Oxford Archaeology Unit, the Society for Medieval Archaeology and the Victoria and Albert Museum for permission to reproduce illustrations.

The early research for this book was made possible by support from my parents, epecially when my son was younger. Its completion has been made all the more pleasurable by working with a fantastic group of colleagues at Durham, in Archaeology and in the Institute for Medieval and Early Modern Studies, not least my recent PhD students, Gwen Bergius, Lisa Brundle, Sira Dooley Fairchild, Celia Orsini, and Tudor Skinner. Family, close friends, and colleagues have all indirectly in one way or another contributed to the development of this book, but my final thanks are to those who lived with its creation, to Andrew, Alex, and Jacob.

Sarah Semple

Contents

List of Figures

List of Colour Plates

1 West Heslerton cemetery, North Yorkshire
2 Adam's Grave or *wodnesbeorh*, 'woden's barrow', Wiltshire
3 The early medieval settlement at Yeavering, Northumberland
4 Uffington hill fort, the White Horse, and Dragon Hill
5 Stonehenge, Wiltshire: a place of execution in the eighth century
6 Sinners at the mouth of hell with severed limbs
7 Sinners depicted as executed, beheaded victims
8 'Marvels of the East'

List of Tables

List of Abbreviations and Primary Sources

ASC	*Anglo-Saxon Chronicle* (Swanton 1996)
Ass	Asser, *Life of Alfred the Great* (Keynes and Lapidge 1983)
B	Anglo-Saxon charters cited by catalogue number from Birch 1885–93
BAR	British Archaeological Reports
BCS	Birch *Cartularium Saxonicum* (Birch, W. de Gray 1885–93)
CBA	Council for British Archaeology
DB	Domesday Book
EPNS	English Place-Name Society
Germania	Tacitus, *Germania*, ed. and trans. Mattingly 1970
HBMCE	Historic Buildings and Monuments Commission for England
HE	Bede, *Historia Ecclesiastica Gentis Anglorum* (Sherley-Price 1968)
HMSO	Her Majesty's Stationery Office
K	Anglo-Saxon charters cited by catalogue number from Kemble 1839–48
OE	Old English
ON	Old Norse
RCHME	Royal Commission on the Historical Monuments of England.
S	Anglo-Saxon charters cited by catalogue number from Sawyer 1968
SMR	Sites and Monuments Record, now Historic Environment Record
Vercelli	*The Vercelli Homilies* (Scragg 1992)
Vita Sancti Guthlaci	Felix's Life of St Guthlac (Colgrave 1956)
Vita Wilfridi	Stephen of Ripon, *The Life of Bishop Wilfrid by Eddius Stephanus* (Colgrave 1927)

County Abbreviations
(Counties are those that preceded the reorganization of 1974)

BDF Bedfordshire	MDX Middlesex
BRK Berkshire	NFK Norfolk
BUC Buckinghamshire	NTB Northumberland
CAM Cambridgeshire	NTH Northamptonshire

CHE Cheshire

CMB Cumberland

DEV Devon

DOR Dorset

DRB Derbyshire

DRH Durham

ESX Essex

GLO Gloucestershire

HMP Hampshire

HNT Huntingdonshire

HER Herefordshire

HRT Hertfordshire

KNT Kent

LEI Leicestershire

LIN Lincolnshire

LNC Lancashire

NTT Nottinghamshire

OXF Oxfordshire

RUT Rutland

SFK Suffolk

SHR Shropshire

SOM Somerset

SSX Sussex

STF Staffordshire

SUR Surrey

WAR Warwickshire

WLT Wiltshire

WML Westmorland

WOR Worcestershire

YOE Yorkshire East Riding

YON Yorkshire North Riding

YOW Yorkshire West Riding

1

The past in the past

Multidisciplinary perspectives on Anglo-Saxon 'reuse'

Introduction

In AD 1006 a challenge was made to the English by the Danish raiding army at *Cwicchelmes hlæwe [Cwichelmeshlæwe]* or the 'Mound of Cwichelm'. This site is known today as Scutchamer Knob, situated in East Hendred on the Oxfordshire and Berkshire border (Gelling 1974: 481–2). The raiding army camped and by so doing confronted local legend, awaiting in vain the 'boasted threats, because it had often been said that if they sought out Cwichelm's Barrow, they would never get to the sea' (*ASC* (E) 1006; Swanton 1996: 137, n. 20). They eventually turned homeward, achieving a safe return to the Hampshire coast. Today *Cwichelmeshlæwe* is recognized through fieldwork as a prominent tumulus, once over 60 metres in diameter and 7 metres in height (see Figure 1.1) (Semple: forthcoming (a)). Despite its creation in prehistory, this monument must have held a political significance for the late Anglo-Saxon communities and powers of this region. It was named after a member of the West Saxon royal family and is twice documented as the meeting place of the late Saxon shire assembly (Gelling 1974: 481–2; see also Robertson 1939). In 1006, the monument was described in relation to emotive and popular folklore, linking the safe defence of England to the security of the mound. Perhaps for this reason the raiding army chose it as a place for a theatrical and political statement designed to weaken English resolve.

Prehistoric monuments were important to early medieval populations. They recognized them as ancient features, as human creations from a distant past. They used them as landmarks, battle sites, and estate markers. They gave them new Old English names. Before and even during the conversion to Christianity, communities buried their dead in and around these relict features and placed elite graves within them. After the conversion, several churches were built in and on these monuments, great assemblies and meetings were held at them, and felons executed and buried within their surrounds.

This book examines how the communities of Anglo-Saxon England perceived and used prehistoric monuments across the period AD 400–1100. The early

Fig. 1.1 *Cwichelmeshlæwe*: Scutchmer's Knob, Hendred, Berkshire: the location of the Anglo-Saxon *scirgemote*. Author's image.

centuries are recognized here as a time when indigenous and incoming groups competed for resources and power. Prehistoric monuments were relevant to all sides in these negotiations, but they came to occupy a more central place in the forging of an Anglo-Saxon identity during the late sixth to eighth centuries. Using a range of sources including archaeological, historical, art historical, and literary, the variety of ways in which populations used the prehistoric legacy in the landscape is explored from temporal and geographic perspectives. Key to the arguments and ideas presented is the premiss that populations used these remains, intentionally and knowingly, in the articulation and manipulation of their identities: local, regional, political, and religious. It is argued that evidence for funerary reuse, well recognized in scholarship, is but one part of a more complex data set demonstrating that relationships between people and ancient monuments were widespread, varied, and long lived. Regional and local studies are employed to show this variety, and multidisciplinary research demonstrates changes across time, particularly within the period in which Christianity became widely accepted in England.

Past and contemporary studies

Before the aims and approaches of this book are developed further, it is necessary to offer a short summary of past scholarship to contextualize this study. Debates in early medieval archaeology on the recycling of the ancient landscape by past communities are relatively recent (initially stimulated by Lucy 1992 but taken forward by Williams in 1997). Discussions that attempt to characterize early medieval perceptions and cognitive relationships with landscape are even fresher in modern academic debate (Semple 1998, 2003b, 2009; Williams

2006a). The author's paper in *World Archaeology* in 1998 represented a first attempt in archaeological scholarship to characterize Anglo-Saxon emotions and thoughts in relation to place and landscape, establishing that the appreciation of natural features and human-made monuments from the distant prehistoric past could change over time. This paper, now twelve years old, inevitably has its flaws and limitations, as more recent studies and this volume identify (Hall 2006, 2007a; Halsall 2010). It remains, however, a turning point for early medieval scholarship, an encouragement for new research to re-engage with historical, literary, and place-name sources and, never to lose the primacy of archaeology within the debate. This book presents a considerable advance on this original paper, and while it is the first 'holistic' study of perceptions of the prehistoric in Anglo-Saxon England, the new arguments offered here are enhanced by the legacy of work engendered and influenced by the original publication in 1998, and by publications by Williams in 1997 and 1998 (Semple 2003a, 2003b, 2007, 2008, 2009, 2010; Williams 1998b, 1998c, 1999, 2001, 2002, 2006a; Holtorf and Williams 2006; see also Bell 1998, 2005; Petts 2002; Blair 2005; Thäte 2007; and more recently Devlin 2007; Chester-Kadwell 2009; Reynolds 2009a; Crewe 2010, 2012). This book embraces significant advances in prehistoric archaeology and is influenced too by new approaches in medieval archaeology, especially those developed in relation to the early medieval landscape (see Gardiner and Rippon 2007: 1–8; Reynolds 2009b). The narrative also draws on folklore, English literary studies, place-name research, and art-historical approaches.

In part the volume responds to an enduring problem: the topic has never been the domain of a single discipline. Prehistorians, historians, folklorists, place-name scholars, landscape historians, geographers, anthropologists, and archaeologists have all, over time, commented on the phenomenon of past societies recognizing and reworking the material remains of previous generations. Early medieval traditions receive mention in all these fields of study, but the discussion has often been a side order to the main thesis. This book seeks to redress this disparate background by bringing together many of these data sets and approaches and begins here with a short summary of previous relevant studies.

Antiquarian and nationalist landscapes in the early twentieth century

The origins and development of Anglo-Saxon studies lie in the period following the Dissolution, when the Saxons emerged in textual terms as the 'progenitors of the English church and nation' (Content and Williams 2010: 186; Dooley Fairchild 2012: 85–110). Interest in the ancient 'landscape' was confined to imagined concepts of pagan temples and holy groves (Dooley Fairchild 2012: 85–110). Real interest in the material remains of the Saxons, the weapons, jewellery, and urns recovered through barrow diggings, became widespread at the turn of the nineteenth century (Williams 2006b, 2006c; Young 2008;

Content and Williams 2010: 185–7). The Victorian barrow diggers, however, although keen on the treasure recovered from burials, showed a remarkable and marked disinterest in the frequent discovery of Anglo-Saxon graves as secondary burials within prehistoric barrows and monuments (Williams 1997: 2). Despite making such discoveries in all types of prehistoric monument, diggers like Faussett, Mortimer, Greenwell, and Bateman registered no surprise or excitement at the phenomenon (Bateman 1861: pp. x–xiv, xiii; Mortimer 1905: pp. lxxxiii–lxxxv). In the late nineteenth and early twentieth century, cemetery and grave exploration remained firmly tied into the processes of cataloguing artefact types, creating typologies, and establishing evidence for ethnic groupings (see Lucy 1998: 12, for a summary and reference to: Kemble 1855; Rolleston 1870; Leeds 1913, etc.). Landscape was relevant only as the canvas upon which the conquest of England was achieved (see Williams 1997 on Myres 1986). By the 1930s and 1940s, the Anglo-Saxons were conceived of as 'impoverished', 'primitive', and 'barbaric' (see Lucy 1998: 14–15; and then Leeds 1936: 20–2, 114; Kendrick 1938: 61), with little or no reflection on the complex patterns of engagement between people and landscape. These mentalities were not restricted to archaeology, of course. Extensive and ground-breaking work in the early to mid-twentieth century in place-name studies identified a wide range of terminologies and descriptive terms for barrows, hill forts and camps, linear earthworks, and dolmens (Cameron 1988: 33–62; Gelling 1988: 130–214). Scholars were still quick, however, to emphasize the limitations of the evidence, arguing that early medieval people conceived only of a crude and imprecise aesthetic sense of landscape (Gelling 1988: 130–1).

Despite many new excavated discoveries (see, e.g., Knocker 1957: 117–70; Musty 1969), secondary burial was acknowledged only as a kind of labour-saving device (Hawkes 1986: 81–2). Regional and county studies did little more than acknowledge the practice as frequent in certain areas such as Wiltshire, the Peak District, and the Yorkshire Wolds (Meaney 1964, particularly the summary on p. 18; Ozanne 1962–3).

The Making of the English Landscape, published in 1955 by Hoskins, is a pivotal publication for medieval archaeology, introducing the concept of the landscape as a palimpsest and encouraging archaeologists to view sites as constituents in a wider tapestry of contemporary and antecedent features (Gerrard 2003: 106; Johnson 2007: 34-69; see also Gardiner and Rippon 2007: 1–8). Churches, settlements, castles, and cemeteries are all now regularly studied in a landscape context. The publication of the excavations at Yeavering in 1977 provided for the first time absolute evidence for the intentional planning of an early medieval settlement in relation to prehistoric barrows, standing stones, and enclosures (Hope-Taylor 1977). Brian Hope-Taylor argued for the intentional use of the ancient in the creation of a seat of Northumbrian power. At the same time other areas of scholarship were recognizing the extensive recycling and use of classical and Roman material remains by early medieval populations. Michael Hunter, in an exploration of written sources and material culture, established that late Anglo-Saxon literate and Christian populations were profoundly influenced by Rome and the ancient classical world, borrowing its material remains as well as its customs, laws, and regalia (1974). A far greater subtlety to Anglo-Saxon 'reuse' began to emerge, influenced by the extensive Continental material and textual repertoire that recorded the ancient high classical past (Hunter 1974; Greenhalgh 1989: 145–201). Place-name scholarship became accepting of early medieval aesthetics too. Early medieval people were recognized as having the ability to distinguish the landscape around them with a degree of sophistication and aesthetic appreciation (see Hooke 1980–1; 1998: 3–5; Grinsell 1991b; Gelling 1998: 75 and 97). The naming of monuments was also taken up by folklorists. Names such as *drakenhorde*, 'dragon's hoard', at South Damerham, Hampshire (S513), and *welandes smidan*, 'Wayland's Smithy, Compton Beauchamp, Berkshire (S564) (see Grundy 1924: 69; Gelling 1976: 692–4) were recognized as testament to local imaginative responses to ancient physical remains (Grinsell 1976a). The association of monuments with myths, legends, and heroes suggested these ancient remains had a place in early stories and narratives. Folklore also indicated their use for gatherings, for retrieving relics, and even for healing (Grinsell 1939, 1967, 1973, 1976a, 1976b, 1991b). In studies of early medieval Ireland and Scandinavia, folklore was used alongside place-name evidence, literature, and archaeology (see, e.g., respectively, Ellis 1943; Ellis Davidson 1950, 1964; Charles-Edwards 1976; Wailes 1982; Warner 1988). These scholars were not working to an explicit theoretical agenda, but they were attempting to understand the beliefs and ideas of late prehistoric and early medieval populations. The systems of belief under discussion often involved landscapes: real, imagined, and mythical. Hilda Ellis Davidson, for example, argued that the pagan populations of northern Europe held commonplace beliefs in the inhabitation of natural features, standing stones, and burial mounds by the dead and supernatural beings (1964).

Recycled landscapes: landscape, memory, and identity

Cognitive archaeology, a forerunner to the postprocessual archaeologies emergent in the late twentieth century, explicitly aimed to investigate the 'minds' of past societies, particularly the religious behaviours, beliefs, and practices of past populations (see Johnson 1999: 89–90). Such approaches are now in the mainstream, but these have been slow to arrive in medieval archaeology (see considerations of this in Gerrard 2003; Williams 2006a: 5–13; Price 2002: 38–43). A stream of influential studies has debated the engagement and reception of landscape by past societies (e.g. Barrett 1994; Tilley 1994; Hingley 1996). But it is largely a single prehistorian who has been responsible for bringing such ideas to the attention of archaeologists dealing with historic periods (Bradley 1987a, 1993, 1998a, 2000, 2002). Richard Bradley's recognition that Roman and medieval populations and societies recycled ancient remains to create a sense of antiquity and legitimate ancestral descent created a wave of interest in early medieval studies (Bradley 1980: 173; 1984a, 1984b, 1987a). The physical presence of ancestors within ancient prehistoric barrows and monuments was argued as a means by which people might assert claims to land and territory (Bradley 1984a, 1984b, 1987a; see Parker Pearson 1982; Lucy 1992).

Concepts of long-term continuity have been current in early medieval studies since the last decades of the twentieth century, with arguments for the ritual or spiritual continuity of some Roman monuments, structures, or burials as holy places or cult-sites into the post-Roman era (see Chapter 5 for discussion, but also Biddle 1976: 65–6; Morris and Roxan 1980; Rodwell 1984: 1–23; Stocker with Everson 1990; Hase 1994; Morris 2011). The concept of long-term continuities from prehistory has also featured: Knowlton and Avebury, for example, are suggested to represent types of 'regenerative' cult-site at which religious or ceremonial activity has persisted over long time periods (Morris 1989: 57–74). The dignity and authority of ancient remains are also suggested as a motivation for the location of early church foundations (Blair 1988).

The recycling of prehistoric and Roman remains seems to reach a kind of intensity in the seventh and early eighth centuries. This is a time when elite or aristocratic families began to assert their power more widely in the landscape and when the new Christian Church was also establishing its visible presence and its place within secular elite ideologies (Blair 1994: 31–4). Richard Bradley's concept of elite power-strategies and hereditary myth creation has provided a highly relevant set of concepts for understanding this upsurge in monument reuse. Far from representing the long-term sacred continuity of such places, the evidence points instead to selective strategies employed by emergent elites to enhance claims to land, territory, and political primacy (Bradley 1987a, 1993; Blair 1988; Lucy 1992; Williams 1997; Bell 2005). Monuments, as timeless and visible survivals, are suggested to capture a subtle index of the deeper currents in society, through their adaption and alteration (Bradley 1993: 93). The growth in academic interest in monument creation and reuse, and the concepts of identity, memory, and landscape, has been exponential ever since. Successive publications have furthered our understanding of human interactions with the ancient past (e.g. Darvill 1997; Knapp and Ashmore 1999; Effros 2001; Williams 2003; Yoffee 2007; Aldrich and Wallis 2009; Halsall 2010). Criticisms have been few and conflicting ideas have not found popularity. For example, the discussion by Whitley of the problem of the 'omnipresent ancestor' and its relationship to a renaissance of nationalism in prehistoric studies, as well as his contrasting interpretation of funerary reuse representing the 'othering' of social outcasts from society, has not been as widely welcomed as Bradley's work in early medieval studies (see Whitley 2002). This may be because an emphasis on the ancestral value of ancient monuments reflects an extensive and complex array of social practices involving the selective valorization of the past, something that has been recognized in historical studies as well as archaeology (Geary 1994; Innes 2000; Janes 2000; Pohl 2000; Geary 2002a, 2002b).

Ancient monuments have not been considered solely as representative of 'ancestors' by early medievalists, and beliefs and perceptions are not conceived as static. Medievalists have been more engaged with ideas of selective and changing narratives: the 'remembering' and 'forgetting' of the past, and the knowledgeable re-creation of the past for the purposes of the present (e.g. Semple 1998; Williams 1998b, 2003). The use of ancient monuments for the purpose of 'othering' is thus bound up with arguments for ancestral importance, lineage, genealogy, power, and identity. When the 'reuse' of the prehistoric past is considered alongside the intentional usage of imperial narrative and terminologies in the ninth-century Carolingian court (Garipzanov 2008), or the harnessing of ancient cemeteries and monuments by elite powers as places of assembly and consensus in Viking Age Sweden (Sanmark and Semple 2008, 2011), it is impossible to consider funerary reuse or monument reuse in general to be entirely a product of ancestral concerns. Social identity at multiple scales, a sense of place, popular beliefs, memory and legends, selective creations of past, evocations of authority, and symbolic alienation are all potentially competing and contemporaneous possibilities (see Scull and Harding 1990: 24, for an early emphasis on different scales and acts of legitimation relevant to differing levels of society). This burgeoning of scholarship on landscape as memory, identity, social order, and transformation has, without question, pushed its way into early medieval archaeology, although the focus until now has generally been secondary burial practices (see pp. 13–16).

Landscapes of identity and landscapes of mind

Prehistoric studies can certainly be seen to have offered a stimulus, injecting ideas into the mainstream of early medieval archaeology, but these ideas have subsequently developed and engendered wholly new theoretical approaches and interpretations. Indeed, as a consequence, early medieval archaeologists have successfully cross-fertilized prehistory, with new approaches regarding identity (e.g. Lucy 2002; Hills 2003; Devlin 2007; Chester-Kadwell 2009; Sayer and Williams 2010); memory and mortuary ritual (Williams 2003, 2006a); ideology and belief (Semple 1998, 2009; Carver 2001, 2002). Martin Carver has developed and promoted the ideal of dynastic signalling and the relationship of monuments to power play, political defiance, and, at a broader level, a material signature that is generated in newly forming polities and early kingdoms (Carver 2002: 133, 138, 140). Rather than merely a conduit to a supernatural world (Barrett 1994: 72–7), barrows can be understood as components in a novel symbolic elite repertoire that experimented with new and recycled symbols of power (Geake 1997; Carver 2001, 2002, 2005; see also Edwards et al. 2010). The Roman material legacy played a crucial part in these sixth- and seventh-century processes. Elite families and kings were consciously using and drawing upon goods and traditions imported from a classical world as symbols of power and prestige (Wormald 1983; Geake 1997: 132–4).

Recent scholarship has also pointed to changing attitudes to the prehistoric during and after the conversion. The preponderance of Devil names and Devil myths associated with standing stones and earthworks is suggested, for example, as evidence of changing perceptions after the arrival of Christianity (Holtorf 1997). Barbara Bender has argued for the Church-driven destruction of prehistoric remains aimed at obliterating the old magic and popular importance of these 'pagan' sites (Bender 1998). This is now considered unlikely (see Chapter 5), but the basic premiss that perceptions are not static but subject to change over time is now a widely held position. Superstitions about landscape are regionally varied too. They reflect the effects of specific landscapes and features on local populations leading to perceptions and beliefs that are locally specific and are influenced too by the composite identity of the population (on megaliths in the Mecklenburg-Vorpommern region in Germany, see Holtorf 1997, 1998a, 1998b; for folklore and collective identities and archaeology, see Gazin-Schwartz and Holtorf 1999: 17). Simple motifs are, however, shared across north-west Europe, such as a belief in the inhabitation of standing stones by supernatural creatures (Holtorf 1998a). This suggests an underlying need in all human communities to rationalize the world around them, to share and borrow traditions, and to familiarize and embellish stories, giving them greater relevance and resonance to local people and places (Gazin-Schwartz and Holtorf 1999: 1–20). The ancient prehistoric landscape was something that communities needed to explain, and offered physical pegs from which to hang narratives about origins and identity (Champion and Cooney 1999; Green 1999: 48–62). Prehistoric monuments, if they survived the passage of time, retained meaning and value long after their original construction, but these varied temporally and spatially. Monuments were reinterpreted by successive generations and by incoming groups, and used and viewed differently from place to place (Gazin-Schwartz and Holtorf 1999: 18–19).

Interdisciplinary medieval landscapes

Archaeologists of the Anglo-Saxon period have increasingly found themselves working at an interface between prehistoric archaeology and history. The relationship between medieval archaeology and history is complex and has at times been difficult (see Gerrard 2003, 2009a, 2009b). In brief, advances in prehistoric studies may have loosened the constraints of a historical framework for early medieval archaeology, but the historical record remains an essential and integral source. The retention of this historical evidence as one strand within archaeological approaches has not, as was feared by some, resulted in the death of medieval archaeology or even in a narrowing of the study of the Anglo-Saxon material past (see papers in Gilchrist and Reynolds 2009). Multidisciplinary approaches have instead flowered in the postmodern academic scene. Martin Carver (2005) has related regional archaeological patterns to documented political events and shown that archaeology can offer a much richer source of evidence for these complex changes in a proto-historic society. John Blair has reignited debates on the material evidence for pre-Christian belief showing that archaeology can produce evidence for practices and beliefs that received only the barest mention in the historical record (see his discussion of shrines: Blair 1995). Another rich vein of research has emerged in Ireland and Scotland, which highlights the reuse of extensive prehistoric monumental sites as royal sites, all part of dynastic and royal attempts to legitimate familial and hereditary power. Complexes such as Tara, Co. Meath, Ireland, and Scone and Forteviot, Midlothian, Scotland, are documented in the traditions of early kingship as places of royal power, inauguration, and assembly (Wailes 1982; Warner 1988, 1994; Aitchson 1994: 310–11; Cooney and Grogan 1991; Newman 1997: 139; Driscoll 1998; Bradley 2000; FitzPatrick 2004a). These palimpsests were reused within the early historic period and drawn upon in the *dinschendas* or traditional 'lore' created to legitimate and celebrate early kings and war leaders (Aitchson 1994: 306).

There are indications that similar processes emerged in mid to late Anglo-Saxon England. Scholars working with place-name evidence have increasingly pointed to evidence for the location of late Anglo-Saxon assemblies, including the shire moot and the *witan*, at round and long barrows and within hill forts (Meaney 1995, 1997; Pantos 2002). Late Saxon palaces too, on occasion, may have been framed by mementoes of the prehistoric and Roman past (see Semple 2009). Judicial execution and the burial of executed felons at prehistoric monuments, particularly in the south of England, are now well recognized as well (Reynolds 1997, 1999, 2009a). A reworking of landscape seems possible, with the ancient prehistoric and Roman remains drawn upon to support and legitimize new administrative organizations and the extended royal power of the largest kingdoms. The folk beliefs and superstitions evident in literature and place-names suggest that popular beliefs were acknowledged and used within this elite reworking of the landscape (Semple 1998; and Chapter 5). Barrows and monuments that were once perceived as places connected to an ancestral past became feared as haunted places and physically appropriated as locales for the interment of the damned (Semple 1998, 2003a, 2003b; and see Chapters 5 and 6).

Such processes were not confined to Britain and Ireland. The reworking of the past to frame and legitimate the growing authority of elites can be found across early medieval Europe (see, for example the important work of Bonnie Effros (2001) and Guy Halsall (2010) on early medieval Gaul, discussed in more detail on pp. 55–62), but few studies have contextualized the Anglo-Saxon evidence with that from parallel European societies. This book reaches out to the European evidence at points to underline this, but a fully integrated European discourse is not attempted here.

The scope of the volume

This book responds to past research by bringing together evidence for the great variety of ways in which the monuments of the prehistoric past were recognized, referenced, and used by populations in pre- and post-conversion Anglo-Saxon England from AD 400 to 1100.

Anglo-Saxon England developed slowly from the small political units that appeared in the aftermath of Roman withdrawal. The archaeological record attests to populations and communities at this time representing a mix of ethnicities and identity as a diverse and fluid construct (Hills 2003; Härke 2011). By the seventh century, elite Anglo-Saxon overlordship had extended in certain regions—notably in the north-east for example, where Edwin and his successors successfully forged the greater kingdom of Northumbria from early smaller political units under British and Anglian control. It is in this century that an Anglo-Saxon identity seems to have emerged, signalled particularly in the material culture of the ruling elite (Härke 2011). During the eighth to eleventh centuries, Anglo-Saxon power fluctuated. The West Saxons pressed further west in the late seventh century, but complete rule of the west was achieved only much later by Æthelstan. It is clear as well from material culture, including metalwork and sculpture, that communities in southern Scotland, in the territories beyond Northumbria, were using Anglo-Saxon material culture in the seventh and eighth centuries. The story of Anglo-Saxon power is of course not all about expansion and conquest. Anglo-Scandinavia settlement and the creation of the Danelaw considerably restricted Anglo-Saxon power in central and northern England in the ninth and tenth centuries, and left its own distinct mark on the language and landscape of England at the eve of the Norman Conquest. The focus of this book is the use and perception of the prehistoric in England, but the approach is selective, drawing on different case studies and source analysis to achieve an overarching sense of change over time. The geographic scope reflects the slow and piecemeal emergence of an Anglo-Saxon elite identity and its long-term survival as a strong signature within certain core areas and kingdoms. The book begins with study of some of the early heartlands where British populations and Continental incomers were present and seeks to explore early medieval perceptions and localized responses to the ancient. Identities were fluid in this era, and landscape and monuments were used alongside material culture in a negotiation of identity and status by indigenous and incoming groups. The use of monuments by elite groups is picked up as a main theme, and this takes the discussion to some of the larger kingdoms, where Anglo-Saxon power was successfully expanded to incorporate previously British territory. Here the focus is often on the use of the ancient by these aspirant elite groups in the restructuring of power and therefore on these Anglo-Saxon royal and aristocratic families. In the last chapters of the book, the focus is largely on the core areas of Anglo-Saxon power and identity—the south, south-east, central, and north-east England—the kingdoms and heartlands of Anglo-Saxon control. Similarly the issue of whether Anglo-Scandinavian settlement changed perceptions and practice in the areas under their control is left for discussion by others in due course.

This book provides an overview of the full range of evidence, but it is also concerned with establishing variations in practice across regions and time, and, to facilitate this, traditional chronological parameters are employed. The discussion commences with consideration of the fifth century, widely conceived as a period of unrest, flux, and change, a period of migration following the decline of Roman authority in parts of England. It ends in the eleventh century, when Anglo-Saxon royal authority diminished, and networks of authority were replaced in parts of England, reorganized, and even erased (Hills 2003, 2009). This broad chronology allows us to explore changing modes and scales of engagement with prehistoric remains during times of political, ideological, and religious change. Evidence for perceptions and uses of the prehistoric is thus related to the wider social, political, and religious scene, and to the changing dynamics of society in terms of its fluid and shifting power structures and changing religious focus.

From Chapters 2 to 5, the reader will move through time, different themes, and data sets. The book takes the reader from the early to the late Anglo-Saxon world via funerary ritual, domestic, and settlement evidence, ecclesiastical sites, place-names, and written sources, administrative and judicial geographies. This is not an exhaustive account: such a study is inevitably selective. In each chapter, although the broader national picture is set out, regional and local case studies and selected texts and images are used. By the end, an overall sense of the changing conception of the ancient is established. Through a thematic and, in part, chronological examination of early medieval uses and perceptions of the prehistoric in England, this book will demonstrate that populations were not only concerned with *Romanitas*, but that a similar curiosity and conscious reference to and use of the prehistoric existed as well within all strata of society.

This book begins with a consideration of secondary burial and a critical appraisal of the advanced work in this area of study (Chapter 2). The chapter offers a case-study-led survey of regional variation in the uses of prehistoric monuments for burial in AD 400–800 and examines the practice at differing scales: intra-site, within the immediate locality, and at a local landscape and regional level, pointing to a complexity in the choices and uses of prehistoric remains for cemeteries and individual burials. Care is taken to recognize these practices as a reflection of a mixed and competitive population, composed of migrants and indigenous families, and later as signalling inherent to the emergence of elite rule over larger kingdoms. Chapter 3 draws on contemporary but wider data sets to explore the use of prehistoric monuments as foci in pre-Christian traditions and their possible role in the beliefs and practices of the early populations of Anglo-Saxon England. The concept of Christian attitudes to the prehistoric is critically appraised in Chapter 4, by examining in detail the evidence for 'church appropriations of ancient prehistoric remains' and scrutinizing what such juxtapositions may actually represent. A literate, Christian, Anglo-Saxon perception of the past is then investigated in Chapter 5, which explores how the prehistoric was referred to and used within poetic and prose texts. By introducing place-name evidence, Chapter 5 also explores the idea of a popular versus literate 'landscape of mind' within which surviving monuments were landmarks on which to hang local legends and stories. Finally, in Chapter 6, a variety of secular and elite uses of the prehistoric are discussed as components of the highly regularized systems of authority and power evident in the tenth and eleventh centuries. Concluding remarks follow in Chapter 7, where the relevance of the prehistoric to identity, belief, power, and sense of place is discussed and summarized.

This book is not envisaged as a final word on the topic. It is a first overview that reveals that this phenomenon was common, complex, and changing, and shared by many early medieval societies. One hopes therefore that the volume will, on the one hand, change current understanding, but also serve to stimulate new trajectories of research within the broad perimeters of the topic.

2

Burial, community, and identity and the prehistoric past

Anglo-Saxon England c. AD *400–800*

Then the Geat people began to construct
A mound on a headland, high and imposing,
a marker that sailors could see from afar.
(*Beowulf*, trans. Heaney 1999: 99, lines 3156–8)

Introduction

The early medieval passion for raising barrows over the dead, remembered and celebrated here in the poem *Beowulf*, must in part account for the recognition, and frequent reuse, of prehistoric barrows as places for burial. The Bronze Age round barrow was a common feature of the English early medieval landscape, attested in the many recorded uses of such features as late Anglo-Saxon estate boundary markers (O'Neill and Grinsell 1960; Hooke 1980–1; Grinsell 1991a). The reuse of these monuments as places for the burial of the dead was frequent throughout the fifth to eighth centuries and continued as a practice during and after the conversion. Howard Williams, in his first study of this phenomenon in 1997, argued that examples of the funerary reuse of prehistoric and Roman monumental remains potentially accounted for a fifth to a quarter of the entire corpus of mortuary sites (1997: 4). This was a figure broadly confirmed by Elizabeth O'Brien's later review of burial practices in Britain (1999: figs 2.1 and 2.2). Williams revealed the great diversity of monument types reused for burial. Barrows of all sizes were recycled alongside henges, stone circles and hill forts, Roman villas, linear ditches, and Roman temples. The round barrow was a preferred choice, but early medieval communities did not confine themselves to this type of monument (Williams 1997: 8). Williams took a national perspective, but identified that the selection of monument types might vary from place to place: for example, the reuse of round barrows occurred in significant concentrations in Wiltshire, East Yorkshire, and the Peak District. These are regions notable for a high frequency of surviving Bronze Age barrows (1997: 14), suggesting that communities may have had an affinity with what was most frequent and familiar to them in their immediate environment. Williams pointed in particular to the distribution of long barrows used for burial, arguing this reflected precisely the areas of England with a high ratio of surviving monuments of this type (Williams 1997: 10).

The practice of recycling of ancient monuments as places for burying the dead is evident, however, throughout north-west Europe in the early medieval era, and can be found in Romanized and non-Romanized areas. Early medieval populations in Wales and the west of England and Ireland used prehistoric barrows and enclosures as locations for burial as well as other types of ancient monument (Petts 2002: 35–9). Similar practices occurred in late Iron Age Denmark, Sweden, Norway, Northern Germany, and Gaul (Thäte 1993, 1996; 2007: 51–94; Williams 1996: 82–7; Härke and Williams 1997; Zadora-Rio 2003). The reuse of Roman structures for burial is also recognized as an aspect of the Anglo-Saxon funerary record (Williams 1997: 7–13 and fig. 7; Bell 2005: 38–127; Blair 2005: 53–4 and n. 172). This too is attested in France, Italy, and northern Spain from the fifth to the tenth centuries (Halsall 1995, 2006; 2010: 254–5; Keay 1988: 212; Arce 1997: 31–2; Effros 2001; Zadora-Rio 2003; Bell 2005: 28–35). This suggests that while such practices may well have had distinctive local or regional contexts, they were also products of greater social and political shifts at a European level (Halsall 2006: 231; 2010: 232–60). Post-Roman Western Europe in the fifth, sixth, and seventh centuries saw the fragmentation of political structures and social groupings, the migration and movement of communities, and dynamic changes in social and religious organization, alongside a remarkable persistence of Roman traditions in some regions (Wickham 2005: 153–258, 303–82). In this era, groups were forced to renegotiate their status, identity, and place in the world, and reshape the way they organized their lives (Halsall 1995; Härke 1997a, 1997b; Williams 2006a: 11–12; Williams and Sayer 2009: esp. 21–2). The treatment of the dead was central to these processes. The dead were a powerful and active group (Parker Pearson 1993), representing ancestry and belonging, and they could also provide evidence for claims to power and land. A relationship with ancestors and the dead was central to establishing a position among the living; indeed not creating such connections may have been considered dangerous (see Sanmark 2010: 167–74).

England was no exception. The transformation of the landscape after the withdrawal of Roman authority involved the arrival of settlers from Scandinavia and northern Germany, who established their homes alongside Romanized British populations, some of whom were displaced and themselves migrated west and south-west, and others who retained claims to their territory and landscape (Hills 2003: 109–15). The palimpsest of prehistoric and more recent Roman monuments provided a rich canvas on which to construct new identities and claims. The English data set thus offers an opportunity to explore processes that were at play more widely across Western Europe. New evidence of regional choices and preferences are offered here, taking our understanding of funerary reuse to a deeper level.

Current established trends

The tradition of secondary burial occurred in England in varying forms from the fifth to the eleventh centuries and seems to have increased in frequency in the seventh and eighth (Blair 1994: 32–3; 2005: 53–4, n. 172; Chester-Kadwell 2009: 131). Cemeteries of varying sizes were located at ancient monuments across England (Williams 1997: 16–17; *contra* Meaney 1964: 18–19; Lucy 1992: 97), but individual secondary burials were most common, and an increase in the number of centrally placed burials in ancient barrows is evident in the seventh century (Williams 1997: 22; 2006a: 181–5; Semple 2003a). Regional variations in practice are recognized (O'Brien 1999). Sam Lucy explored early medieval burial rites in East Yorkshire (Lucy 1998) and argued that the location of cemeteries changed over time. Cemeteries were more likely to lie close to a pre-existing linear earthwork in the fifth and sixth centuries, an Iron Age cemetery in the sixth and seventh, and a Bronze Age round barrow in the seventh and eighth (Lucy 1998: 88–9). Dawn Hadley later emphasized the distinctiveness of the northern funerary record, highlighting both regular occurrences of prehistoric 'reuse' and the possible late survival of these practices (Hadley 2001: 29–31; 2002, 212).

At an intra-site level, the selection at Yeavering, Northumberland, of certain types of prehistoric monument as foci for settlement and religious activity suggests that early medieval people had preferences and made choices in regards to the secondary use of older monuments (Bradley 1987a: 7). The cemetery layout at West Heslerton, North Yorkshire, is thought to be structured by the surviving prehistoric remains. Individuals under 12 years old were more likely to be buried in areas covered by barrows or encompassed by enclosure ditches, whilst prone burials were more likely to be found within the ditches (Lucy 2002: 85) (see Colour Plate1). The frequent positioning of early medieval burials around the eastern ends of long barrows, in the entrance or forecourt area, and the attested preference for secondary burial in the south and south-east portion of round barrows provide similar evidence for choices by those burying the dead (Williams 1996: 12–15). Preferences for burying the dead in the ramparts of Iron Age hill forts or for burying in relation to the largest ancient barrow on a site (Williams 1996: 45–7; 1998b: 101) suggest active selection by communities who were choosing to prioritize one type of monument or monumental feature over another. Such decisions were most likely rooted in community beliefs regarding these features and the wider landscape. In the words of Williams: 'communities were constructing and reproducing their idealized visions of the past and present, their mythical origins and their social identities' (1997: 25). To this we can add Halsall's assertion that communities were employing a precise *grammar of display* transmitting information about the deceased and their social sphere and position to a present audience to ensure a place in future memories, but at least part of that display was situated with firm reference to a perceived past (Halsall 2010: 253–4, 260).

The reuse of ancient monuments as places for early medieval burial is now acknowledged to continue after the onset of churchyard burial (Hadley 2001: 30). By the tenth and eleventh centuries, these ancient monuments were killing places for felons and locations for the burial of the socially excluded (Reynolds 1997, 1998, 1999, 2009a).

Aims of this chapter

Building on this considerable research, this chapter explores the diversity of monument reuse, regional trends, and patterns of chronological change from the fifth to ninth centuries. Three zones or regions are chosen here for closer inspection: West Sussex, East Yorkshire, and North Wiltshire. These share a comparable geology and topography. They are also regions that have produced a wealth of surviving material evidence of early medieval date and host a large number of prehistoric monuments (see Figure 2.1). Each region is also part of a different political entity, and all three witnessed contrasting trajectories of post-Roman development in terms of population mix, settlement, land use, and political structure. The cemeteries of East Yorkshire reviewed here lie within the early kingdom of *Deira*, the study area of North Wiltshire is situated in the kingdom of the *Gewisse*, and the cemeteries of West Sussex fall within the kingdom of the *Suthsaxa*. No restriction has been placed on chronology in order to capture information on the likely occurrence of secondary burial rites as late as the tenth and eleventh centuries, but specific discussion of criminal or deviant burial in relation to ancient monuments is left for more detailed discussion in Chapter 6.

The profile of 'reuse' within each study area is characterized, and considered in the context of the social, religious, and political development of each region. The regional variations in burial practice elicited are then considered in the context of evidence from other regions, including Kent and Norfolk. The chapter closes with a consideration of similar practices found elsewhere in Britain and in Europe, concluding that 'reuse' and secondary burial are distinctive rites within different regions, while elite burials at ancient monuments emerge as an overarching or supra-regional phenomenon, interlocking with the political and religious changes of the seventh and eighth centuries.

Regional landscapes of the living and the dead

West Sussex: from the Arun to the Adur

A summary review of the West Sussex funerary evidence provides a useful contrast with the funerary landscapes of East Yorkshire and North Wiltshire

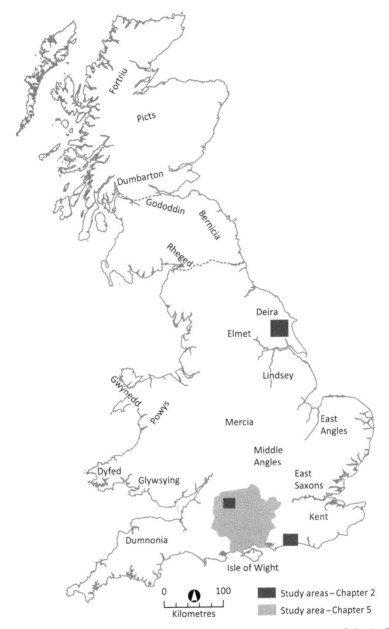

Fig. 2.1 The location of the study regions investigated in Chapters 2 and 5. © Crown Copyright/database right 2012. An Ordnance Survey/EDINA supplied service.

(see Semple 2008 for full discussion). The South Saxon kingdom is referred to in the early written sources as a territory defined by bloodshed and slaughter (*ASC* (A) 477 and 491), with fierce inhabitants and a persistent 'pagan' culture (*Vita Wilfridi* 13; Colgrave 1927: 28; *HE* II, 5). Although its presence and power had diminished by the seventh century, written records imply that the South Saxon kingdom held some prominence in the sixth century through the authority of an individual named as Aelle, described as a king by Bede (*HE* II, 5). By 800, the South Saxons had been absorbed into the larger political unit of Kent (Yorke 1990: 157–9). The archaeological record for the fifth and sixth centuries suggests a core area of control with a Saxon identity in the east, and strong political and social affinities, if not alliances, with Kent (Welch 1983: i. 278; Drewett et al. 1988: 256 and fig. 7.2). The western region gradually came under Saxon influence and control by the sixth century, and thus initially comprised a tract of landscape protected by the large, established woodlands to the west and north that separated an east Saxon heartland from core areas of Saxon identity and power in Wessex, Hampshire and the Isle of Wight, Salisbury, and the Upper Thames Valley. Surviving charters and witness lists (see pp. 25–6) reveal a system of petty kings as late as the end of the seventh century, in conflict with the West Saxons over tracts of territory and on occasion fighting in alliance with the *Gewisse* when threatened by the 'West Welsh' of Devon and Cornwall (*ASC* (A) 710).

The area of landscape under study centres on the historic town of Steyning and encompasses *c.*20 square kilometres of land stretching from the River Arun in the west to the River Adur in the east (see Figure 2.2). This region lay outside the core of Saxon military control to the east. The topography is defined by the wide and meandering rivers of the Adur and Arun, which offer a fertile lowland zone for cultivation and settlement, shadowed by the steep rise of the chalk downland. This was once a wooded landscape cleared extensively in prehistory (Drewett 1978: 27; Sheldon 1978: 6; Scaife and Burrin 1983: 7). By the fifth to seventh centuries, a combination of environmental, archaeological, and historical evidence suggests the reversion of portions of the landscape to woodland, interspersed by open pasture (see Bell 1977: 271; Waton 1982: 85–6; Drewett et al. 1988: 292–3; Gardiner 2003: 152; and Bede's description of Bosham, *HE* IV, 13). A relatively high number of prehistoric round barrows survives and traces of field systems, several hill forts and enclosures, and occasional traces of prehistoric house platforms and huts (Drewett et al. 1988: 24–177).

In the fifth to eighth centuries, inhumation seems to have been the dominant visible rite (Welch 1983). Cemeteries and isolated burials are present, for example at South Heighton, as well as reasonably sized inhumation cemeteries, such as Alfriston and Appledown. Although generally accompanied by weapons, jewellery, or personal items (for Alfriston see Griffith and Salzmann 1914; Griffith 1915; Welch 1983: ii. 347–87, no. 12), the assemblages are often far from remarkable or diagnostic (O'Brien 1999: 142–9). Most discoveries are

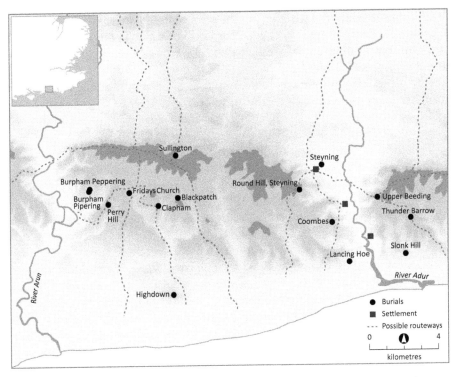

Fig. 2.2 Burials and settlements of fifth- to eighth-century date in the West Sussex study area. © Crown Copyright/database right 2012. An Ordnance Survey/EDINA supplied service.

antiquarian in date and the information they provide is often partial and brief and many burials remain undated.

On occasion, burial rites in terms of assemblage and location are argued to be symptomatic of some continuity of population from the Roman to early medieval period (O'Brien 1999: 142–9; Petts 2000), for example, the co-location of Romano-British and early Anglo-Saxon burials at places such as Stonepound, Sandpit, or Hassocks (O'Brien 1999: 145). The cluster of fifth-century Germanic-style burials between the Ouse and Cuckmere valleys, by contrast, is argued to indicate the cession of this portion of landscape to new Saxon settlers in the immediate post-Roman era (Welch 1983: i. 278; Drewett et al. 1988: 256 and fig. 7.2). Specific densities of funerary activity in this area, even when sited in the uplands, can be seen to cluster in the immediate geographic vicinity of the river valleys (Drewett et al. 1988: fig. 7.2; Welch 1989: fig. 5.321). Burials are usually situated on the crest of the downland, easily accessible and perhaps sometimes visible from the valley floor. By the sixth century, Saxon settlement and material culture had spread along the entire length of the South Downs (Drewett et al. 1988: fig. 7.2; Welch 1989, 83). The spread of funerary evidence by this date is far more extensive, but the river-centred pattern remains obvious. Cemeteries cluster around the upper escarpment of the downland along the Adur and Ouse river valleys and to a lesser extent along the east side of the Arun Valley too (Drewett et al. 1988: fig. 7.2).

Along the Adur in particular, the burial at Slonk Hill and the cemetery at Lancing mark the entrance to the wide estuary. A series of cemeteries and individual burials mark the upper edges of the chalk escarpment flanking the river valley (Figure 2.3) (see also Semple 2008: fig. 1).

The fifth- to early eighth-century populations of the region consciously integrated the physical remains of the prehistoric past in this funerary geography. The occurrence of secondary burial in this region of Sussex was frequent, accounting for broadly 60 per cent of the record (Tables 2.1(a) and (b)).

Of the sixteen possible funerary locations, eleven were associated with some form of ancient monument and a wide variety of monument types were reused (see Table 2.1(b)): several intrusive burials were recovered from prehistoric barrows or mounds, one burial reused a long barrow, four cemeteries comprising clusters of primary barrow burials were situated around one or more Bronze Age barrows, and one extensive cemetery was located within and outside an Iron Age hill fort. In addition, the reused barrow at Thundersbarrow lay close to an Iron Age/Romano-British circular enclosure and one clutch of primary barrow burials were situated around the earthworks of a Bronze Age settlement at Clapham.

The early medieval population used what was available and although ancient round barrows were preferred, when present, ancient settlement remains or enclosures were brought into use. The evidence implies that although burial took place throughout the landscape in the fifth to eighth centuries, a wide variety of prehistoric monument types were used. Intrusive and isolated secondary burials cut into prehistoric monuments were difficult to discern owing to poor antiquarian records, but are infrequent in the record. Inhumations and cremations were present and most often these were surmounted by small, primary barrows, usually *c.*9 or 10 metres in diameter. In several cases, large prehistoric barrows ranging between 17 and 80 metres in diameter provided a focus for clusters of these smaller barrows, for example, Perry Hill, Clapham, and Blackpatch. These prehistoric mounds must have had a considerable visual presence over their later and more diminutive companions (see Semple 2008, 8 for discussion). The frequency of these *associative* groupings—clusters of primary barrow burials placed around larger prehistoric monuments—is a striking feature of the Sussex record. This is a practice unparalleled in the regions of North Wiltshire and East Yorkshire (see pp. 26–45 and Williams 1996; Lucy 1999; Semple 2003a), but can be found on the Isle of Wight, and, on occasion, also in Hampshire, Kent, and East Anglia. At least five possible instances were identified (Blackpatch, Sullington, Friday's Church,

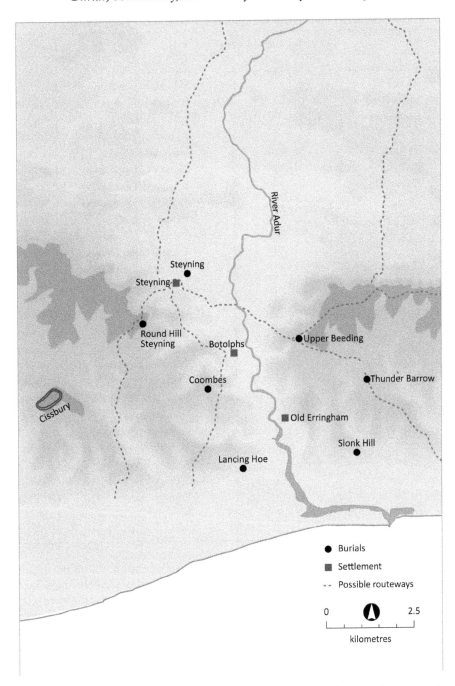

Fig. 2.3 Burials and settlement of fifth- to seventh-century date located along the Adur Valley. © Crown Copyright/database right 2012. An Ordnance Survey/EDINA supplied service.

Table 2.1(a) Cemeteries and burials identified in the West Sussex study region

	Site	No. burials	Sex*	Type	Date†
1	Thundersbarrow	Multiple	?	Secondary cremations	C5th/6th?
2	Slonk Hill	1	F	Secondary inhumation	C7th/8th?
3	Upper Beeding	2	M & ?	Primary barrow burials	C7th/8th?
4	Lancing Hoe	7	?	Inhumations	C6th
5	Coombes	1	?	Secondary inhumation	C7th/8th?
6	Steyning	Multiple	?	Inhumations	Late AS
7	Round Hill, Steyning	Multiple	?	Secondary inhumations	Late AS?
8	Blackpatch	5	M	Secondary inhumation	C5th–8th?
			M	Secondary inhumation?	C5th–8th?
			?	Secondary inhumation	C5th–8th?
			?	Secondary inhumation	C5th–8th?
			?	Secondary inhumation	C5th–8th?
9	Highdown	186	M & F	Secondary inhumations	C5th–7th
10	Clapham New Barn Down	2 +	?	Primary barrow burial	?
			M	Primary barrow burial	C7th/8th
11	Sullington	9 +	?	Inhumation burial	C5th–8th?
			?	Secondary cremation	C5th–8th?
			?	Secondary cremation	C5th–8th?
			?	Un-urned cremation	?
			?	6 barrow burials	C5th–8th?
			M	Secondary inhumation	C5th–8th?
12	Friday's Church	2?	?	Secondary/primary?	?
13	Perry Hill	4	F	Primary barrow burial	C5th–8th?
			M	Primary barrow burial	C5th–8th?
			M	Primary barrow burial	C5th–8th?
			F	Primary barrow burial	C5th–8th?
14	Burpham Pipering	1	M	Primary barrow burial	C7th/8th?
15	Burpham Peppering	13	M	Secondary inhumations	Late
16	Burpham	11?	?	Primary barrow burials	?

* M = male, F = female.

† Chronological ranges of burials and cemeteries used here are based on the detailed dating undertaken by Martin Welch, published in his gazetteer of possible Anglo-Saxon funerary sites in Sussex (1983). These have been altered to acknowledge the more recent presumption that many inhumation and cremation rites once thought to be restricted to the fifth to seventh centuries are now also attested in the early part of the eighth century in many regions (see Geake 1997 for discussion of the burial rites of the conversion period).

Table 2.1(b) Sussex burials and their topographic associations

Thundersbarrow (C5th/6th?)	Cremations intrusive and associated with a prehistoric barrow, circular enclosure and extensive field system
Slonk Hill (C7th/8th?)	Inhumation adjacent to a square structure imposed upon a prehistoric round barrow, close to a deserted Romano-British settlement
Upper Beeding (C7th/8th?)	Primary barrow burials placed at the edge of the chalk escarpment
Lancing Hoe (C6th)	Inhumation cemetery without barrows positioned on a natural spur
Coombes (C7th/8th?)	Intrusive inhumation within a single prehistoric barrow
Steyning (undated)	Inhumation cemetery, no barrows, no apparent topographic associations
Steyning Round Hill (undated)	Inhumations positioned around a prehistoric barrow
Blackpatch (C5th–8th?)	Inhumation graves without barrows and a primary barrow burial associated with Neolithic and Bronze Age mine shafts and spoil heaps
Highdown (C5th–7th)	Inhumation cemetery within hill fort
Clapham New Barn Down (C7th/8th)	Primary barrow burials positioned around Bronze Age settlement earthworks comprising platforms and enclosures
Sullington (C5th–8th?)	Cremation and inhumation burials and primary barrow burials associated with prehistoric barrows
Perry Hill (C5th–8th?)	Primary barrow burials associated with Bronze Age barrows
Burpham Pipering (C7th/8th?)	Primary barrow burial
Burpham Peppering (undated/ late Anglo-Saxon?)	Burials positioned around a possible prehistoric long barrow

Perry Hill, and Clapham). At each site, one or more smaller barrows had been built around or next to a larger prehistoric monument (see Welch 1983: ii. 490–2, no. 105; 484, no. 96; 488, no. 101 for Perry Hill and Clapham; for Blackpatch, see Pull 1929; 1932: 67–9, 72–4, 82–7; Welch 1983: ii. 459–60, no. 94). These associative cemeteries in West Sussex cannot be dated more closely than some-time between the fifth and seventh or eighth centuries. Outside the study area at Bishopstone in Sussex and at Bowcombe Down on the Isle of Wight, cemeteries of this type are more securely dated to the fifth and sixth centuries (Hillier 1855: pl. 4; Arnold 1982: 89–96). If the examples identified in West Sussex represent funerary ritual of a similar date, then these burials might signal the activities of dislocated or newly forming communities, seeking to assimilate with the land-scape (see Semple 2008, citing Lucy 1992, 93–105; see also Williams 1997). Indeed the predominance of associative burial practices in West Sussex might reflect the acknowledged absence of a single dominant authority in this era. In the vacuum created by the collapse of Roman rule, many different groups were seeking to define themselves in new ways and struggling to retain or acquire land and territory (Harrington and Welch 2014). By associating burials with visible ancient monuments, populations may have sought to claim or signal continuity of landownership and control of local resources.

The spatial patterning of burials within the study region, and a consideration of the choice and use of prehistoric monuments as part of this pattern, presents some interesting anomalies. Burials of the fifth to eighth centuries cluster around the Adur Valley (Figure 2.3), in positions exploiting wide panoramic views of the Channel or the river valley. The positioning of barrow burials in relation to rivers is something exemplified, of course, by the Sutton Hoo cemetery, where barrow burials marked a dynastic cemetery and created an impressive landmark visible to any vessel entering the East Anglian kingdom via the River Deben (Carver 1998: 107). The premiss of visibility or inter-visibility of funerary sites relies on the burial or cemetery being marked in some substantial manner and on the nature of the vegetation and cover in the region in question. As argued elsewhere, environmental evidence suggests that although some of the downland was wooded in this era, much of the lower slopes were covered by wood pasture, and thus visibility between the valley bottom and the upper edge of the chalk escarpment seems likely (Semple 2008). On this basis, it is possible to suggest that the large prehistoric barrows at Thundersbarrow Hill, Slonk Hill, Upper Beeding, and Coombe were chosen for their prominent visibility from the coast, estuary, and river and would have provided impressive landmarks to those entering the estuary and moving inland.[1] Such large monuments, physically situated at the top of the chalk escarpment may also have appealed because of their liminal position separating the seasonally used uplands and the fertile and settled river valleys (see Roymans 1995). Settlement evidence, although limited, does seem to support this, attesting to settlement *c.*5–15 metres above the flood-plain (Drewett et al. 1988: 274; Gardiner 1988: 55, 59; 1990, 241; 2003: 152, citing Wilkinson et al. 2002). A withdrawal of settlement from the slopes and hilltops into the fertile lowland valleys in the post-Roman era is generally accepted, with the higher land utilized as pasture (Welch 1985: 21–3; Gardiner 2003: 152). The monuments chosen as sites for secondary burial marked the interface between these zones, and some lay next to the natural routes on which people would have moved between them. The position of the early medieval burials along coast, estuary, and river, with some taking advantage of the crest of the escarpment, may have been intentional in terms of relating cemetery and settlement by means of visibility. Their position next to large and prominent older monuments, although liminal in several ways, also served to ensure at least some of these burials and cemeteries were visually integrated with the immediate world view of these communities. Flanking the mouth of the Adur are the burial sites of Lancing to the west and Slonk Hill to the

---

[1] Thundersbarrow: Curwen 1933; Oakley 1933; Meaney 1964: 256; Welch 1983: ii. 449, no. 81. Slonk Hill: Hartridge 1977–8: 72, 87, 100, no. 16, 141, figs 2 and 11.16; Welch 1983: ii. 450, no. 82. Upper Beeding: Meaney 1964: 247; Welch 1983: i. 111, 453, no. 86. Coombes: Dixon 1849: 269; Grinsell 1934: 236, 254; Meaney 1964: 248; Welch 1983: ii. 457, no. 90.

east. Lancing, a sixth-century cemetery, does not seem to have been marked in any way (Dixon 1849: 269; Grinsell 1934: 236, 254; Meaney 1964: 248; Welch 1983: ii. 457, no. 90), but Slonk Hill, where a seventh-century female burial was placed next to a large Bronze Age barrow, was marked by a square post-built structure erected encompassing the prehistoric monument (Hartridge 1977–8: 72, 87, 100, no. 16, 141, figs 2 and 11.16; Blair 1995). The barrow had a prominent position, but the additional enclosure would have increased its visibility. The Slonk Hill burial and its adjacent square enclosure, which has been identified as a kind of early Anglo-Saxon shrine (Blair 1995), are also positioned next to evidence of Romano-British settlement activity (Hartridge 1977–8). The Slonk Hill burial site may have been visible to those entering the estuary and river valley by boat, and, as they moved inland, other burials marked by prehistoric monuments could have been visible along the way.

Everitt has argued that the underlying geography and topography, particularly watercourses, were integral to the colonization and settlement of the neighbouring Kentish landscape from prehistory to the late medieval period (see Everitt 1986: 46). The rivers in Sussex may similarly have acted as the major unifying resource, interlinking coastal, estuary, and riverside communities and providing a form of local identity too in the early medieval period. Such themes have been strongly reinforced by the work of Stuart Brookes on Kent, where river and land routes were shown to shape the very earliest patterns of settlement and burial in the fifth and sixth centuries (Brookes 2007a, 2007b, 2011; Brookes and Harrington 2010). The pattern of settlement and burials along the Adur river valley is echoed also by the distribution pattern of fifth- to seventh-century material along the Ouse, Arun, and Cuckmere rivers (see Semple 2008). This corroborates the idea that the patterning reflects a kind of local 'world view'—a way of shaping the topography using burial to reflect local territorial control and identity.

The South Saxon kingdom remains one of the most obscure of Anglo-Saxon polities, with no surviving king-list or genealogy (Kelly 1998: p. lxxiii). A pattern of local territories, with their own rulers, many of whom called themselves 'king', is implied (Kelly 1998: pp. lxxiii–lxxx). There does not seem to have been a stable tradition of centralized rule in the South Saxon kingdom. Susan Kelly argues instead that 'political authority appears often to have been fragmented, and it may have been the case that independent tribal "kingships" persisted for longer than was generally the case in early England' (Kelly 1998: p. lxxvi). This is often used to explain the late conversion of the South Saxons: with several local rulers, conversion would have been especially difficult (Kelly 1998: p. lxxvi). Mark Gardiner similarly emphasizes that the lack of any centralized power in Sussex, comparable to Winchester or Canterbury, may result from the absence of any powerful lords, lay or religious, who were able to connect with major centres of power and commerce (Gardiner 2003: 158–9). The funerary record seems to reflect this kind of political scene, symptomatic perhaps of land claims and competitions between the rulers of small political units or polities. The South Saxons did not coalesce with the same degree of success as other political units emergent in the late fifth to seventh centuries such as Wessex. Perhaps for this reason West Sussex lacks precisely the kind of dramatic symbolism evident elsewhere in the seventh-century burial record (see also pp. 48–51; Semple 2003a, 2008). The absence of rich, isolated, prestigious burials, and, in contrast, the presence of associative burials in the late fifth, sixth, and seventh centuries, signals the absence of a single cohesive political identity in these centuries. Instead communities defined themselves by funerary acts that tied them to visible symbols of the ancestral past, and by so doing claimed small blocks of territory with major river valleys at their heart. Such river-centred polities or units would, of course, concur with arguments for the ancient origins of the Sussex hundreds, which, in contrast to the Rapes, are defined by the major river valleys at their centre (Salzman 1931: 20–9).

East Yorkshire: Goodmanham to Rudston region

The funerary record in East Yorkshire provides a marked contrast. The area under study here is in the East Riding of Yorkshire on the Wolds, which lay within the documented early Anglo-Saxon kingdom of Deira, established early in the fifth century (Yorke 1990: 74–7). The name is British, as is the name of the neighbouring kingdom of Bernicia (Yorke 1990: 24). Within the early kingdom of Deira, David Rollason (2003: 46–7) has argued for three cores or heartlands of activity: from York east across the Wolds to the Driffield Basin; the fringes of North Yorkshire and Whitby; and the Vale of York. The archaeological evidence for fifth- to eighth-century activity is rich but scattered and does not wholly support such clear-cut divisions. It does suggest, however, that an active core of burgeoning power lay within and around the Driffield Basin in the fifth and sixth centuries (Eagles 1979: 427–8; Loveluck 1996; Lucy 1999; Rollason 2003: 46–7).

The Driffield 'heartland' may reflect a much earlier territory or locality. The region is naturally encompassed by the rising Wolds to the west and north coast on the east and the Humber to the south. It is argued, based on concentrations of elite burials, that this naturally defined territory may have emerged as a power centre in the Iron Age (Parker Pearson 1999). Chris Loveluck (1996) has argued that the extraordinarily rich array of fifth- and sixth-century Anglo-Saxon graves and cemeteries within the Driffield Basin, and the numerous iron artefacts represented in the assemblages, point to the control of iron-working resources and technology by Anglo-Saxon elites.

The area under study encompasses the upper Wolds dividing the Driffield Basin from the Vale of York and the Vale of Pickering. It broadly lies within an area of royal interest stretching from York eastwards. The kings of Deira are recorded in action (or in death) at the royal vill at York and at another vill elsewhere on the River Derwent, at a cult-complex at Goodmanham and later at Driffield too, suggesting a further royal vill near Driffield (see Rollason 2003: 46–7). Movement between these royal estate centres, dictated by the need for kings to travel to maintain authority, suggests the area under consideration might be considered to lie *between* early core areas, dividing the naturally defined, populated lowland regions, but representing a kind of buffer zone that was seasonally exploited and traversed. The Wolds are notable for an array of fifth- to eighth-century burials and these concentrate particularly around the routeways that linked the Vale of York to the Driffield Basin (see pp. 36–8).

The populations of Deira in the fifth century represented a mix of British communities and incomers of 'Germanic' origin. Continuities in population presence, the layout of field divisions and agricultural systems and boundaries, alongside evidence from sites such as West Heslerton, where later Anglian settlement can be seen to focus around a Romano-British ritual complex (Powlesland 1999; Rollason 2003: 94), all strongly suggest that populations of mixed ethnicity existed and indigenous communities and families persisted. By the late sixth and seventh centuries, Bernicia and Deira had been brought under a single rule, and the kingdom of Northumbria was formed (Yorke 1990: 77–81). It is striking, however, and relevant to the archaeological signature for the region, that even when firmly a sub-kingdom of Bernicia, the royal house of Deira and the kingdom retained a separatist and independent identity that persisted into the eighth century, featuring strongly in the writings of Bede (Yorke 1990: 78–80).

The Wolds was once a wooded environment, and even today the landscape is distinctive for its rolling chalk and narrow and sudden dips and valleys marked by thick stands of woodland. The region has seen relatively intense archaeological investigation. J. R. Mortimer (1905), for example, famously carried out extensive investigations in the nineteenth and early twentieth centuries. Detailed assessment of the early medieval record has been undertaken by Margaret Faull (1979) and Bruce Eagles (1979), who both focused on relationships between British and Saxon. More recently, Sam Lucy (1998) has undertaken analysis of the funerary evidence of fifth- to eighth-century date in the region, taking particular account of the spatial placement of cemeteries. The publication in 1997 by the Royal Commission (RCHME) of a full transcription and primary analysis of crop marks in this region revealed a vast array of lost monuments of prehistoric and historic date adding an additional layer of data (Stoertz 1997). The Wolds share with North Wiltshire and West Sussex a similar chalk geology. They are also rich in surviving prehistoric remains, including numerous round barrows, linear earthworks, and enclosures, and more unusual features such as square barrows, monoliths, and cist graves. The region discussed here extends from Market Weighton to Rudston (see Figure 2.4). Early medieval burials located in the study area are listed in Table 2.2, and more detailed information can be found in Appendix 1.

Over 70 per cent of identified burials were positioned in relation to surviving and upstanding monuments of an earlier date. Bronze Age round barrows were reused frequently, perhaps reflecting the rarity of long barrows and hill forts in

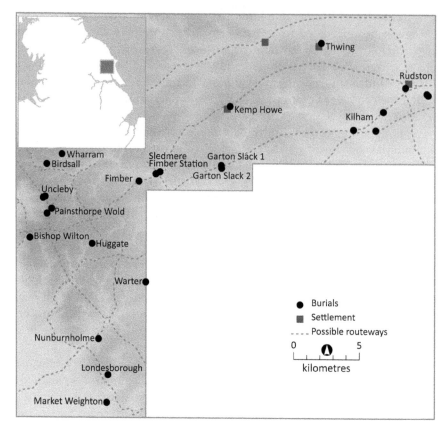

Fig 2.4 Burials and settlement of fifth- to eighth-century date in the East Yorkshire study area. © Crown Copyright/database right 2012. An Ordnance Survey/EDINA supplied service.

this region (Stoertz 1997: 22–3, fig. 8). Indeed monuments of this kind in the study area showed no signs of secondary burial. Instead the ditches and banks of linear earthworks were occasionally reused as locations for burials. Although unusual on a national scale, it is a distinct feature here. Two new correspondences were identified, raising the number of cemeteries associated with linear earthworks in this area to four (see Figure 2.5; Appendix 1). The use of a single ancient enclosure, in this case a substantial prehistoric enclosure remodelled in the Bronze Age as a ringfort, occurred at Thwing. This monument was the location of a seventh- to ninth-century settlement and an associated Christian cemetery. The enclosure would have been large and visually impressive.

Although much of the recorded evidence is from antiquarian accounts, chronological evidence is more frequent and reliable in this data set. Secondary burial occurred throughout the fifth to eighth centuries with evidence for an increased frequency in practice in the fifth and sixth, and again in the seventh and eighth. Notably, there was more evidence for secondary burial in the eighth

Table 2.2 Cemeteries and burials identified in the East Yorkshire study region

Site	No. of burials	Sex*	Type	Date
Birdsall	1	?	Secondary cremation	
Bishop Wilton	1	?	Secondary inhumation	C5th–7th (7th?)
Huggate	1	?	Secondary cremation	C5th–6th
Kilham	1	?	Inhumation	C5th–6th
	?	?	Multiple inhumations	C5th–6th
Kilham	1	J	Inhumation	C5th–6th
Kilham	6	?	Inhumations	C8th +
Painsthorpe Wold 4	6	?	Secondary inhumation **A**	C7th?
		?	Secondary inhumation **B**	C7th?
		?	Secondary inhumation 1	C7th?
		?	Secondary inhumation **C**	C7th?
		M	Secondary inhumation 1*a*, *b*	C7th?
		F	Secondary inhumation **D**	C7th
Painsthorpe Wold 102	1	?	Secondary inhumation	C5th–7th
Painsthorpe Wold 200	1	?	Secondary Inhumation	C5th–7th?
Londesborough	?	M and F	Multiple inhumations	C5th–6th
Uncleby	76	M and F	Secondary inhumations	C7th
Market Weighton	2	F	Inhumation	C6th
		M	Inhumation	C7th
Nunburnholme	3	?	Inhumations	C5th–6th
Rudston	2	?	Inhumation	C5th–9th
		?	Inhumation	C5th–9th
Rudston	?	?	Multiple burials	C5th–6th
Rudston	5	M	Secondary inhumation	?
		M	Secondary inhumation	?
		M	Secondary inhumation	?
		M	Secondary inhumation	?
		?	Disturbed inhumation	?
Sledmere (Fimber Station)	?	?	Multiple inhumations	C5th–7th?
Garton Slack I	52–4 +	M and F	Multiple inhumations	C8th
Garton Slack II	4	j	Secondary inhumation	?
		?	Secondary inhumation	?
		?	Secondary inhumation	?
		?	Secondary inhumation	C5th–7th?
Warter	1	?	Secondary inhumation	C5th–7th

(continued)

Table 2.2 Continued

Site	No. of burials	Sex*	Type	Date
Wharram	2	?	Secondary inhumation	Late AS?
		?	Secondary inhumation	
Fimber	2	?	Inhumation	C7th?
		?	Inhumation	?
	6 +	?	Multiple inhumations	?
Kemp Howe	5	?	Secondary inhumations	?
	1	?	Secondary inhumation	?
	10	?	Secondary inhumations	C8th
Thwing	132	M and F	Inhumations	C7th–9th

* M = male, F = female, J = juvenile.

century in the East Yorkshire study area than in any other region under consideration. The use of Bronze Age round barrows for burial became more popular in the seventh century and continued in favour in the eighth, supporting Sam Lucy's claim that prehistoric round barrows were most likely to be selected for funerary activity in the seventh and eighth centuries (1998: 88–9). The choice of old linear earthworks occurred within the same time frame. Garton Slack I is dated to the eighth century and Garton II to the seventh/eighth centuries (Lucy 1999: 40, 36). A new example at Rudston cannot be placed more closely than between the fifth to ninth centuries (Eagles 1979: 214, 445), but the burial at Fimber Station is likely to date to the sixth or seventh century (see Appendix 1). The cremation from Huggate is probably of fifth- or sixth-century date (Lucy 1999: 26).

The small group of individual secondary barrow burials in the region—Birdsall, Bishop Wilton, Painsthorpe Wold 102, Painsthorpe Wold 200, and Warter, all intrusive in Bronze Age round barrows, have all been dated previously to the fifth and sixth centuries (Lucy 1999). This contrasts with the vast majority of burials of this type that usually fall within the late sixth and seventh centuries (Shephard 1979b; see also Blair 1994: 32, n. 4; Williams 1997). All five burials may in fact be later in date. That at Bishop Wilton Beacon contained a spear-head that could be classed as a type with good seventh-century associations (see Mortimer 1905: 144–5, Barrow no. 69, and fig. 387; Swanton 1974: 13–14). The Warter burial was accompanied by a lost and unrecorded iron sword that could easily be dated to the sixth or seventh century. Painsthorpe Wold 200 contained a 'thin bronze bowl' of a type found at Dover Buckland and elsewhere in fifth- to seventh-century contexts (Evison 1987: 103–4, 327, Grave 137, 1, dated to Phase 5 (650–75); Geake 1997; 85–8, esp. 87). Painsthorpe 102 was accompanied by an iron knife that although

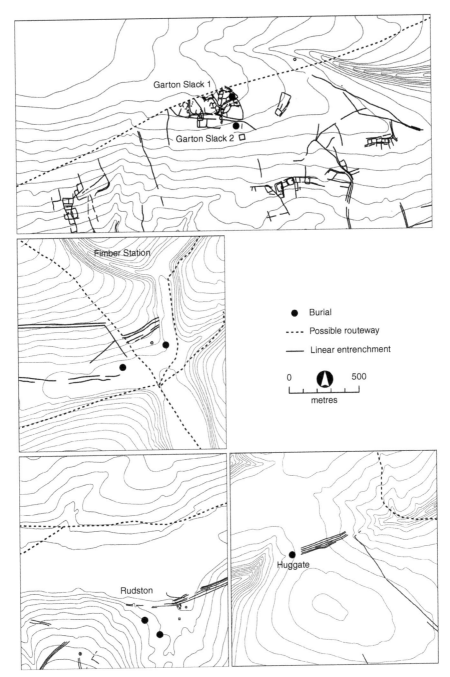

Fig. 2.5 Cemeteries and burials located on or near linear entrenchments in East Yorkshire. © Crown Copyright/database right 2012. An Ordnance Survey/EDINA supplied service.

corroded, suggests a sixth- or-seventh century date (Mortimer 1905: fig. 305; Evison 1987: 113, 115, fig. 22). Thus, with the exception of the anomalous Birdsall cremation, all of these isolated secondary burials are plausible as products of the sixth and seventh centuries in line with traditions elsewhere in England (Welch 1992: 88–96; Blair 1994: 30–1).

The redating of these burials is significant because it would support the suggestion by Sam Lucy that the size of cemeteries was decreasing over time (1998: 99), perhaps reflecting an increasing restriction on certain types of rite, location, or cemetery type. Nevertheless, although cemetery size may have been decreasing, *increasing* numbers of funerary acts were taking place at prehistoric sites in this time period. By the seventh and eighth centuries, ancient barrows and other antecedent features were increasingly in use as locations for more than one burial (recognized by Lucy 1998: 88–9). As funerary rites involving prehistoric monuments grew in popularity, the size of cemeteries decreased, implying that, as a diminishing number of people chose to situate cemeteries or burials in the wider landscape, they were more frequently choosing ancient barrows, old ditches, and enclosures as markers. These practices continued in use after the arrival of Christianity.

The position of cemeteries was relatively varied, but a position on the chalk escarpment overlooking the vales and lowlands was more likely by the seventh and eighth centuries. Such locations were marginal, away from low-land settlement, and perhaps more inaccessible and restricted in terms of access (Lucy 1998: 99). As this marginal zone was increasingly exploited, the size of cemeteries decreased, which implies that smaller numbers of people were choosing or were allowed to bury their dead in this zone. These families or communities also frequently chose a prehistoric monument as a location for the cemetery. These were often large monuments and situated close to major thoroughfares. For example, Kemp Howe, a long barrow modified into a round barrow in the Bronze Age (Mortimer 1905: 336–8; Geake 1997: 158), was reused as a site for a small eighth-century cemetery. The barrow is located within 500 metres of two Bronze Age barrows, still visible and upstanding in Mortimer's day (Mortimer 1905: see Barrows 277 and 210). Kemp Howe, with a modified diameter of *c*.30 metres, thus distinctly larger than its neighbours (*c*.17 and 15 metres in diameter), was chosen at the expense of the barrows nearby. As Figure 2.6 reveals, the diameters of barrows selected as funerary locations in the seventh and eighth centuries were significantly larger than the barrows reused in the fifth and sixth centuries. Substantially sized barrows were also favoured if situated particularly close to land routes.

On Painsthorpe Wold, where four cemeteries were established in close prox-imity, the prehistoric monuments selected were those monuments closest to the Roman road (see Figure 2.7). Proximity to routeways is a consistent and important feature of cemetery location throughout the fifth to eighth centuries

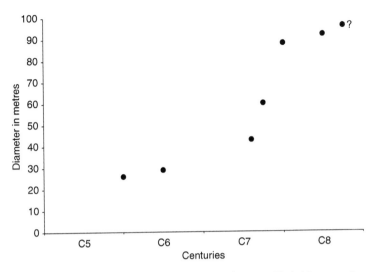

Fig. 2.6 The changing size of barrows reused for burial in East Yorkshire over time.

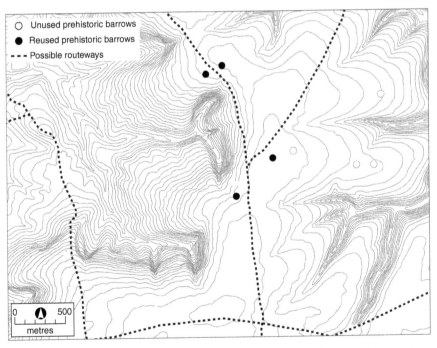

Fig. 2.7 Burials reusing prehistoric barrows at Painsthorpe Wold, East Yorkshire. © Crown Copyright/database right 2012. An Ordnance Survey/EDINA supplied service.

(Figure 2.4). River courses too may have been influential factors in cemetery placement, with the Gypsey Race attracting a density of activity.

Painsthorpe Wold 102 is generally treated as an isolated phenomenon (Meaney 1964; Geake 1997; Lucy 1998), but in fact this is one of a group positioned in a closely defined area of the landscape. This group comprises evidence of numerous funerary events, most of them secondary in prehistoric barrows situated close to the Roman road. The proximity of Uncleby and Painsthorpe Wold 4 alone argues for some form of interrelationship between the cemeteries. These are close in date (Appendix 1), but the wider group more broadly falls between the fifth and seventh centuries. This cluster may represent a politically or ideologically significant block of landscape or, given the spatial relationship to the Roman road, a corridor of power across the upland linking York to Driffield in the sixth and seventh centuries.

Cemeteries and settlements

Alongside an increasing preference for locating burials around prehistoric monuments in the upland marginal zone, a handful of sites also suggest funerary sites were occasionally established in close arrangements with early medieval settlement remains. The Gypsey Race, a major river cutting through the Wolds, attracted settlement and funerary activity in an arrangement similar to that in West Sussex. At Rudston, evidence suggests settlement followed the valley bottom, while cemeteries or burials were situated at a slight remove on the upper slopes of the escarpment overlooking the river. At several sites, however, an even closer spatial relationships can be discerned. At Kemp Howe, excavation revealed evidence for structures, including sunken-featured buildings, immediately along-side the prehistoric monument and the eighth-century cemetery. A cemetery and settlement also appear in close spatial conjunction at Garton Slack I. The burials at this cemetery are aligned on a large linear earthwork (Mortimer 1905: fig. 731) (see Figure 2.8) and were unaccompanied by weapons or dress fittings, but add-itional burials discovered in 1959 suggest an eighth-century date. Burial 2 was associated with a group of sceattas deposited after *c.*720–5 (Geake 1997: 158). Pottery and animal bone were present in the graves, but may represent residual domestic debris from a neighbouring settlement (Geake 1997: 158; Lucy 1998: 119). An extensive curvilinear complex, comparable to those identified at West Heslerton and Boynton, is present on aerial photographs at this location (Figure 2.8) (Stoertz 1997: 59, fig. 30 (6)). Indeed, Mortimer remarked on Anglo-Saxon pottery, buckles, and traces of 'primitive dwellings' (1905: 269). Garton Slack II is suggested to lie on the southern periphery of this complex (see Appendix 1). Given the absence of grave goods and the suggested eighth-century date for those recovered in 1959, it is possible that these burials post-date the settlement or an earlier part of an extensive settlement complex still active in the eighth century. The discovery of early medieval pottery some 300 metres east of a cemetery at Rudston (see Rudston RB (6), Eagles 1979: 445) might also indicate a relatively close spatial relationship between settlement and funerary activity.

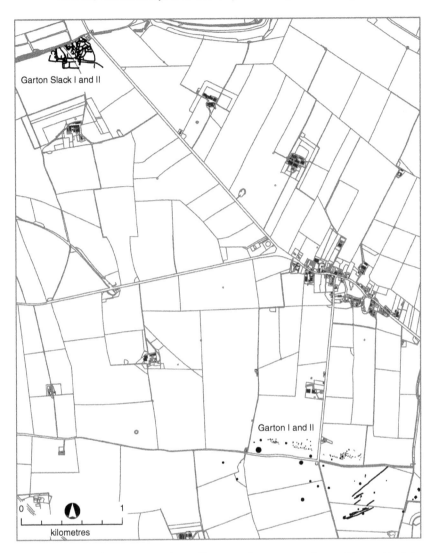

Fig. 2.8 Proximity of cemetery and curvilinear settlement complex at Garton Slack I and relationship of Garton Slack I and II to Garton I and II. © Crown Copyright/database right 2012. An Ordnance Survey/EDINA supplied service.

The burials here are also associated with a linear entrenchment (Eagles 1979, 214; see now Stoertz 1997, Map 3, SE 113 672). Small finds indicate activity here as late as the ninth century, with a coin of Eanred (810–41) retrieved in the same place as burials with assemblages of earlier date (Eagles 1979, 214).

These sites require further exploration, but the relationships are interesting. Investigation of early medieval settlements in Yorkshire, such as Cottam, have underlined the presence of settlement mobility over time (Richards 1999), whereas the recent broader scale assessments by means of geo-prospection in the Vale of Pickering have raised the possibility of seasonal settlement patterns and settlement functions (Powesland et al. 2006). At West Heslerton, however, there is unquestionable evidence for continuity of population at a fixed place, and evidence that community was keen to invest in physical relationships with the Roman and prehistoric landscape. The location of the settlement and neighbouring cemetery appears to be dictated by the presence of antecedent monuments: the settlement is established around a Roman-period ritual focus and the cemetery within, and by a Neolithic henge (see Colour Plate 1) (Powlesland 1999; Powlesland with Haughton 1999). The examples of cemetery and settlement congruence identified in this study are less clear-cut. These could represent retrospective relationships, where abandoned settlement sites have been 'reused' as places of burial. It is also possible that the settlements were relatively large and long-lived, perhaps mobile and multifocal, with funerary activity taking place in abandoned zones or areas of older activity away from core living areas. It is notable that three of these sites were located in relation to linear entrenchments, at crossing places, or thoroughfares across the landscape. This might suggest that their placement, in relation to these linear divisions and routes, signalled a new kind of geography, overwriting an older pattern of activity, aligned to movement across the Wolds from one royal heartland to another (see Loveluck 1996, and discussion at pp. 36–8).

Ditches and boundaries

The reuse of linear earthworks is acknowledged here as a distinctive trend (Figure 2.5). The cremation burial from Huggate is fifth or sixth century in date, the Sledmere–Fimber burials are suggested as sixth century, the cemetery at Garton Slack I was active as late as the eighth century, and close by at Garton Slack II four intrusive inhumations discovered in a round barrow can be placed broadly in the sixth to seventh centuries. The burials at Rudston cannot be more precisely dated than the fifth to ninth centuries, but burial was taking place here in the sixth. Outside the study area, a well-known additional example is Garton II, where the dead were inhumed in a linear earthwork, either side of a prehistoric round barrow. This cemetery is dated to the seventh and eighth centuries and lies some 800 metres east of Garton I, a seventh-century cemetery that reuses a cluster of Iron Age square barrows (Figure 2.8). Chris Loveluck has suggested the cemeteries at Garton Slack and Garton lie on the periphery of the intense sixth- to eighth-century activity at Driffield (1996: fig. 11). He has argued too that these burials were placed on earlier divisions or ditches that may have been adopted as territorial or political boundaries. The cemeteries are also located at points where the entrenchments are broken by tracks and routes and thus perhaps at crossing points between territories. These cemeteries and their position could reflect the tense politics of the redrawing of political territory. The kingdom of Northumbria was certainly not created with ease—written sources indicate the Deiran Royal house retained its independent identity as late as the eighth century. Such cemeteries might thus represent, despite the embrace by wealthy Driffield families of a new and greater political order, a need on the part of these Deiran elites to articulate a separate political identity linked to the long-term inhabitation and ownership of the Driffield Basin and its resources. Such acts imply families may have been nominally Christian but engaged in funerary events that valorized perceived ancestral places, including earlier settlement sites. The use of linear earthworks for funerary ritual and the recycling of square barrow cemeteries may have been prompted by a combination of reasons, but could reflect an emerging seventh-century interest in reactivating 'ancestral' claims at a time when Bernicia and Deira were being brought under a single rule (Yorke 1990: 78–80). The chronological evidence is not precise enough to take this argument further, but the cluster of cemeteries in the area of Garton broadly fits within this time frame.

In the mid-sixth century the Driffield area was densely populated and rich (Loveluck 1996: 32). The material wealth may have stemmed from the inheritance of a strong Romano-British iron-working tradition, combined with the exploitation of the available expanse of high-quality arable land. Prosperous centres of craft specialization and, latterly, the political stability in Deira, granted by the rule of a single unbroken dynasty in the seventh and early eighth centuries, may have greatly assisted the Driffield population (Higham 1993: 144). The funerary practices identified in the study area to the north and west of the Driffield heartland may in part reflect the benefits of this increase in wealth and stability (see Geake 1992; 1997: 127), and the determined signalling of a Deiran identity. The positioning of burials during the sixth to eighth centuries next to routes crossing the upland, exploiting ancient monuments and old land divisions and earlier settlements, suggests an increasing interest by a minority in signalling a particularly distinctive identity via the funerary rites. Indeed, the selection and reuse of the prehistoric palimpsest on the Wolds for the purposes of burial can be suggested to exemplify an increasing investment over time in interments that created visible statements of ownership and identity. If better dating evidence were available, the handful of isolated secondary burials using prehistoric barrows could be tied to the very beginnings of the emergence of aristocratic ruling groups in Deira, and the absence of any super rich seventh-century examples to the cessation of Deira as a politically distinct and active unit. The continued interest in using round barrows, square barrows, and linear earthworks suggests that the use of burial to maintain claims to land and a distinct regional identity was a fashion that persisted and that drew upon a distinctively prehistoric repertoire. It is worth considering here as well the striking reintroduction of crouched burial as a seventh-century tradition (Lucy 2000: 14, 16–17).

The emergence of the greater Northumbria presumably forced a restructuring and realignment of power, and the populations of what had been Deira were by the seventh to eighth centuries looking towards the Vale of York as the major centre of Northumbrian authority. The increased preference for the use of prehistoric monuments and old barrows for burial in the seventh and eighth centuries occurred within a Christian era. It is possible that this represented a form of ideological and political opposition to the power centre of York (see Carver 1992, 2002). Given the clear Christian burial practices evident at some sites, this preponderance of seventh- and eighth-century funerary activity, arguably available only to a restricted minority situated on the crossing places across the Wolds, may represent the actions of an elite looking towards the main sphere of power and authority governed by Oswald and his successors at York. These burials and cemeteries reflect a hybrid mixture of traditional practice, retrospective innovations, and new fashions, and could be considered symptomatic of a group seeking both to curate their past power and to establish themselves firmly within the new political geography for the future.

In simple summary, the record offers strong contrasts in the ways in which the populations of East Yorkshire disposed of the dead compared to the populations of Sussex and North Wiltshire (see pp. 38–44). This supports the argument that at regional and local levels ancient monuments were selectively reused in the creation of new and distinct social and political identities. The suggestion has also been made that the landscape offered a stage in which, in the face of the creation of the larger kingdom of Northumbria, communities or families articulated their claims by creating new rites that meshed perceived ancient traditions and activities, and drew on the physical remnants of the distinctive regional past that surrounded them.

North Wiltshire: Avebury region

The development of the kingdom of Wessex as a political force and entity is equally as complex as the development of Northumbria. It is argued to have grown from a nucleus of Saxon settlement controlling the Upper Thames Valley in the late sixth century (Yorke 1990: 132). By the seventh century, the sources describe repeated skirmish and conflict between Mercia and Wessex along a frontier corridor in North Wiltshire. By the seventh century, Wessex was in part defined by its resistance to Mercia's expansion on the east and south (Yorke 1990, 136–7). The area chosen for investigation comprises a rolling expanse of chalk downland (*c.*20 square kilometres in size) centred on the village of Avebury (see Figure 2.9). In the late sixth century this region lay outside the heartlands defined by the rich and princely burials of the Upper Thames Valley and the Salisbury area to the south. By the seventh century, it lay within the northern border regions of Wessex: an area that faced repeated threat and contestation by the growing power of the Mercian kingdom (Yorke 1990: 128–94, esp. 132–42).

In the Roman to post-Roman period this was a populated landscape (Corney 2001; Eagles 2001; Pollard and Reynolds 2002). Place-names, cartographic evidence, and environmental sequences testify to the regeneration of and

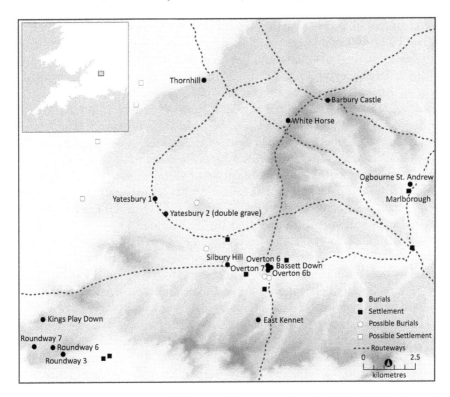

Fig. 2.9 Burials and settlements of fifth- to eighth-century date in the North Wiltshire study area. © Crown Copyright/database right 2012. An Ordnance Survey/EDINA supplied service.

presence of woodland, alongside arable land and chalk grassland (Fowler and Blackwell 1998: 13–30; Fowler 2000: 3–11). The resources of the chalk and clay (or the chalk and the cheese) in North Wiltshire seem to have underpinned the range of subsistence and agricultural practices that sustained a medieval economy built on arable and mixed farming (Draper 2006: 4–5). The richness of the landscape and its resources supported a population that persisted into the fifth and sixth centuries, despite the abandonment of Roman villa estates at Cherhill and Avebury Trusloe, and planned settlements such as Waden Hill (Corney 1997; 2001: 26–9; Pollard and Reynolds 2002: 149–238, esp. figs 63 and 78; Draper 2006: 27–35, esp. 35). The archaeological record for the fourth and fifth centuries indicates a populated region with scattered farming communities (Draper 2006: 36–55). There is little, if any, securely dated evidence for the disposal of the dead at this time, although a number of unaccompanied inhumations and cemeteries might easily account for the absence of fourth- and fifth-century graves and cemeteries (Eagles 2001; Foster 2001: 174). Crop marks in combination with recognized small-find scatters suggest that a series of Romano-British settlements survived into the fourth and fifth centuries AD. A cluster of timber post-built structures at the 'Headlands' are argued by Fowler and later Reynolds as late fourth- to fifth-century settlement (Fowler 2000: 59–60; Pollard and Reynolds 2002: 160–6) and pottery scatters south of Yatesbury provide a third- to fourth-century date for a small-scale farming settlement revealed by combined geo-prospection (Pollard and Reynolds 2002: 157–8). An unusual cluster of Roman barrows at the crossroads of the London to Bath Roman road and the prehistoric Ridgeway offers the first material signs of funerary ritual. These contained cremations dating to the first and second centuries *and* evidence of funerary reuse in the fifth century. The fifth-century material is the first indication of Germanic-style influence or presence in this landscape (Eagles 1986: 103–19). Not far from this, to the south-west of the great henge at Avebury, a settlement existed in the fifth century, attested by a scatter of postholes and sunken-featured buildings (Pollard and Reynolds 2002: 192–8). This may represent the creep of post-Roman settlement across the slopes of Waden Hill. A Roman settlement situated here was abandoned by the fourth century. Occupation seems to have moved north-west and by the fifth century concentrated around the south-west exterior of the henge (Pollard and Reynolds 2002: figs 63 and 78).

The region is, of course, notable for its concentration of surviving prehistoric monuments. The henge and stone circle and standing stone avenues at Avebury are surrounded by round barrows, and linked to the great monument of Silbury Hill and its lesser companion, the chamber barrow at West Kennet. The causewayed enclosure at Windmill Hill lies to the east, and the downs are overshadowed by the ramparts of the Iron Age hill fort, Oldbury Castle. The modern landscape is full of surviving prehistoric monuments, and the place-name record provides a rich catalogue of Old English names that make reference to upstanding prehistoric and Roman remains (see Grundy 1919 and 1920 for terminologies used in OE bounds in Wiltshire). Amid this palimpsest, the position of the medieval church at Avebury, at the western entrance to the great henge, attests to the medieval communities that have lived among these ancient remains since the acceptance of Christianity (see Chapter 4; Semple 1994; Pollard and Reynolds 2002: 235–8).

A detailed analysis of all evidence for post-Roman burials in this immediate region has already been published, together with a gazetteer of all possible burials of early medieval date (Semple 2003a). What follows is a summary of findings, outlining the ways in which the ancient monuments of the Avebury region were used by post-Roman and Anglo-Saxon communities.

A large number of sites or burials of early medieval date that make use of prehistoric remains can be found in this landscape. Burials associated with prehistoric monuments account for around 80 per cent of the known funerary record, with secondary burial or reuse postulated at ten prehistoric round barrows, two long barrows, and a cemetery located in the ramparts of a hill fort. No incidences of burials or cemeteries using relict or ancient Roman remains or ruins were discovered. The frequency here of 'reuse' is thus far higher than the national average (see Williams 1997), although any such comparison is coarse grained and must be treated with considerable caution. The exceptionally large number of surviving prehistoric monuments within this region may account for the abnormally high percentage of early medieval intrusive burials: more dense distributions of prehistoric monuments could result in higher numbers of reused sites. This density of prehistoric monuments also attracted substantial antiquarian interest as early as the sixteenth century, and prolific exploration may have resulted in the recovery of particularly high numbers of early medieval secondary burials (Semple 2003a: appendix Ai and ii).

With these provisos in mind, it is still possible to assert that this region was one in which communities made wide and varied use of the prehistoric in their funerary rites in the fifth to eighth centuries. The monuments used were diverse, but, as one might expect, round barrows were the general preference (Williams 1997, 6). Close regional study offers some additional and interesting contrasts. Despite the survival of numerous megalithic monuments in this landscape, no burial has been recovered in association with the stone circle at Avebury, the stone rows, or individual standing stones (see review of past discoveries by Gillings and Pollard 2004; papers in Brown et al. 2005; and published excavations by Gillings et al. 2008). The great henge at Avebury, although now substantially reconstituted, survived with some cohesion before restoration (Ucko et al. 1991: 244–5).

The place-name record and notably the *OE* bounds surviving for the North Wiltshire landscape include numerous examples of named individual and multiple standing stones, although whether natural or raised by humans is uncertain (for example, *micelne stan*, 'the big stone', S272/S1403; *dunnan stanwith foan stān dunnan tham burg gete*, 'the stone in front of the fortification', S784; *tha twegen stanes*, 'the two stones', S312). Large, unusually sized stones, paired stones, or stones of certain colours or attributes were certainly visible and used as boundary markers. It is tempting to dismiss the absence of burial in association with these features as a product of the neglect of such monuments by antiquarians who largely favoured barrows over megaliths. The use of stone circles or standing stones as early medieval funerary foci is rare across England, however, and possible examples such as Mount Pleasant in Dorset are considerably less convincing on closer inspection (Schweiso 1979). The ambivalence of the North Wiltshire communities towards upstanding megalithic monuments may therefore fit with a broader lack of concern for this type of monument (see Chapter 4, p. 110). Another monument type that received limited attention is the long barrow. Only one of a potential thirty or so examples had indications of secondary burial (Barker 1984: fig. 1; see Semple 2003a). This contrasts with the recognizably high frequency of secondary burials in long barrows in Wessex as a whole (Williams 1997: 7, fig. 3). Of four hill forts and two Neolithic enclosures in the study area, only Barbury Castle provided evidence for secondary burial, although several other prehistoric enclosures produced evidence for early medieval activity: a fifth-century brooch was discovered at Oldbury and a sixth-century sword was located during excavation of the earthworks adjacent to Knap Hill (see Chapter 3, p. 78, for discussion and Appendix 2). The modes of reuse are thus highly varied and in some instances even unique. The possible burial from Silbury Hill and the secondary burials apparently made in stone-chambered round barrows at East Kennet and Overton are all quite unusual examples (see Semple 2003a). Communities in the North Wiltshire chalk uplands were, it seems, making explicit choices, selecting monuments in the landscape with special attributes.

Close dating of many of these burials is almost impossible, but secondary burial is recognizable as a predominant and constant aspect of funerary practice from the sixth through to the eighth centuries, with the very late and unusual example of a male secondary burial at Ogbourne St Andrew, potentially dating as late as the ninth or tenth century on the basis of the surviving coffin fittings (see Figure 2.10) (Semple 2003a: 79). The persistence with which the communities of this landscape recycled the prehistoric remains for burial across such a long time frame, alongside the high frequency of the practice in this area, has been argued elsewhere as evidence for a strong regional predilection or preference for burying the dead in and around prehistoric remains. There is a notable incidence of isolated barrow burials which, where datable, fall in sixth and seventh centuries. Although imprecise dating means any detailed interrogation of choice or preference over time is difficult, it can be asserted that, in contrast to other regions, use of the prehistoric for cemeteries here was rare and limited to the fifth and sixth centuries. Over time increasing numbers of single, isolated secondary interments were made in individual prehistoric monuments, predominantly ancient barrows (Semple 2003a: 72–91). Particularly large barrows were preferred, and over time visibility from lowland settlements and proximity to routeways became important factors.

The burial record for North Wiltshire has been argued to reflect the role of this region in the political dynamics of the sixth to seventh centuries (Semple 2003a). This was a landscape marked by single funerary events, comprising mainly male burials that mostly reutilized ancient prehistoric remains. Some burials could be described as elite, accompanied by items indicating prestige and perhaps aristocratic connections (for example, at Yatesbury and Roundway 7). During the sixth to eighth centuries it seems that monument size, visibility, and route proximity all increased in importance. At the same time there was a growing ostentation in the assemblage, the burial location, and the method of interment.

These burials are situated within a landscape in which there is comparatively little evidence for other contemporary activity. Cemetery and funerary evidence of fifth- to sixth-century dates predominates in South Wiltshire and to the east of the Avebury region, around and to the north-east of *Cunetio* (Hawkes 1989:

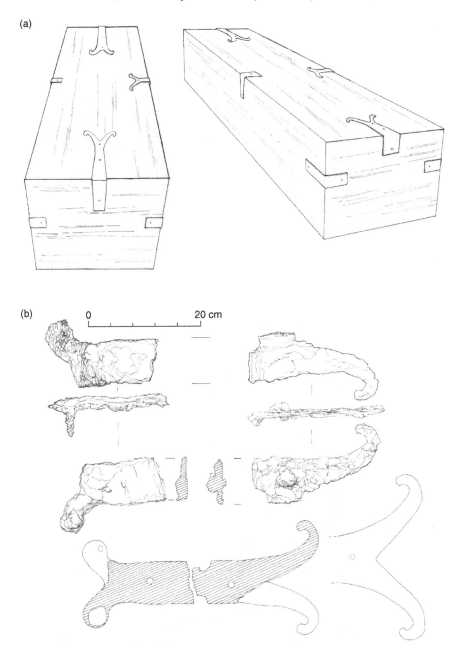

Fig. 2.10 Ogbourne St Andrew, Wiltshire: (a) A reconstruction of the iron-bound coffin; (b) The coffin fittings. Author's image.

fig. 27; Yorke 1995: fig. 4). This landscape is discussed in documentary sources that record battles against the British in AD 556 and 592: the former at Barbury Castle (*ASC* (A) 556), the latter at Adam's Grave (*ASC* (A) 592). Such early chronicle entries are untrustworthy (Yorke 1995: 32–4), but, broadly speaking, they suggest this was a region defended by the British and an area of conflict— an interface between British and Anglo-Saxon communities in the sixth century (Eagles 1994: 26–8; 2001). This region came under an increasing Anglo-Saxon influence from the south, and possibly the east too, in the sixth and seventh centuries (Eagles 2001), and remained contested as late as the seventh century, when it was disputed between the expanding kingdoms of Wessex and Mercia (Yorke 1995: 61–2). The granting of land within this region by both Mercian and West Saxon kings demonstrates how rapidly the control of the region fluctuated throughout the late seventh to eighth centuries (Yorke 1995: 61). Even more revelatory is a late-seventh-century grant of privileges to Aldhelm, abbot of Malmesbury, from Pope Sergius I, which was ratified by both Ine of Wessex and Aethelred of Mercia, and used to secure their agreement that Malmesbury should not suffer in the wars between these two kingdoms (Edwards 1986). By AD 715 Woden's Barrow, now Adam's Grave, was the setting for a battle between Wessex and Mercia (*ASC* (A) 715), and in 802 control of North Wiltshire was ceded to Wessex after a decisive battle at Kempsford (Yorke 1995: 61–4; *ASC* (A) 802). The funerary record in this region is dominated by a handful of male burials, exploiting topographic positions no less impressive than the large funerary monuments used, and comprising funerary events that without exception purposely reused major prehistoric monuments. This implies the kind of aggressive posturing that may well have taken place in a contested landscape in which emerging West Saxon dominance was being played out (Eagles 2001). The predominant use of the ancient prehistoric monuments and the high number of individual, isolated interments of the sixth and seventh centuries may well reflect an intensely contentious, political climate and the role of the region as a borderland.

These impressive funerary events are likely to have survived on in memory, perhaps as witness of the legitimate secular jurisdiction and authority over the localities (Williams 2006a: 215–21). The funerals and their lasting monumental legacy could signal the actions of communities under pressure (as in Deira), keen to designate land ownership and power. Or they may have resulted from the kind of aristocratic competition indicative of supra-regional power play and claims. It is possible that the rich male and female graves of the chalk upland around Avebury are members of either Mercian or West Saxon aristocratic families; however, political labels taken from documentary accounts are potentially unnecessary. The archaeological evidence is more helpful. Reuse was one component in a package of funerary rituals, of which many elements strongly suggest display and competition, and may reflect the uncertainties of populations vocalizing claims within a contested and embattled region.

Regional preferences—wider perspectives

Mortuary archaeology as a means of understanding social identity has moved on considerably from the twentieth-century fixations with ethnic affinities (Hills 2003; Williams and Sayer 2009). Funerary evidence is now frequently viewed as an arena within which 'syncretic processes' took place (Lucy 2002); a theatre within which mourners moulded and combined differing strands of influence into regionally distinctive identities (Lucy 2000, 2005; Hills 2003; see also Williams and Sayer 2009). Lucy and Hills envisage this in material terms, particularly concerning grave assemblages, dress fittings, modes, and styles of burial and interment. The landscape setting or the geography of burial is, however, shown here to be equally distinctive and diverse, in terms of natural settings and the adoption of ancient palimpsests of monumental remains. The underlying pattern of the natural and antecedent landscape served to shape the activities of the early medieval population, rendering quite distinct differences in the ways in which landscape was used in funerary ritual. While processes of legitimating ownership, land claims, or power are without question at play in these varied choices (Bradley 1987a; Williams 1996, 1998b), we have perhaps underestimated the complexity and individualism of the messages being created.

The burial habits of the populations in North Wiltshire, West Sussex, and East Yorkshire exemplify how the underlying landscape and natural geography formed a significant facet of mortuary theatre. It influenced people's choices of site and monument when establishing a burial ground. Cemeteries and individual graves were placed with reference to inter-visibility, accessibility, proximity to land and coastal routes, settlements, the edges of the cultivated lowland, places frequently traversed or passed or visible to travellers, crossroads, and borders. The choice of an ancient barrow or Roman site was informed by a wide variety of geographic and aesthetic aspects. It is this multiplicity of influences—natural and historic—that informed the imagination of communities, allowing them to build narratives about their origins, place in the world, and relationship with the landscape in which they lived. In combination, such influences resulted in the regionally and locally distinctive ways of using the landscape that we see in the Wessex, South Saxon, and Deiran case studies.

The 'identities' created by people were also multiscalar. Dress fittings and weaponry, or the disposal rites of cremation or inhumation, could be used to signal affinity with a much broader cultural construct aligned to perceived Continental origins, as demonstrated here in the fifth-century burials accompanied by imported objects at West Overton in Wiltshire (see p. 40 and for a broader discussion of this idea see Chester-Kadwell 2009). Landscape positioning, however, could reflect more local, community-driven aspirations. The variety of experimentation in the use of prehistoric remains strongly suggests local traditions symptomatic of the instability and competition between micro-territories, as indigenous populations and incomers struggled to consolidate power. The river valleys of West Sussex offered geographic and territorial definition for the fifth-, sixth-, and seventh-century populations, with ancient prehistoric monuments appropriated and new burials created, in a physical process used to describe a continued sense of place and belonging, related to this underlying geography.

The relevance of geography to the shaping of political identities, flagged by Mark Gardiner in his published research on Sussex and Kent, has seen recent emphasis in the work of Stuart Brookes on the cemeteries of Kent. This study revealed a close correlation between early medieval cemeteries and the principle routes of movement by land or sea. The relevance of the underlying geography and the main coastal route of communication to the identity of these communities is exemplified further by the inclusion of clinker boat fragments in late-sixth- to seventh-century graves (Brookes 2007a: 125, 148; 2007b: 1–18). These reinforce the concept that the funerary arena—grave location, landscape positioning, and assemblage—might represent an interweaving of choices, signalling the strong relationships and affinities between community, landscape, and resource. Just as the West Saxon record points to the choice and selection of particular prehistoric monuments within the landscape, influenced by their position in relation to river and land routes and patterns of settlement, Brookes has argued that, in Kent too, choices of 'monuments were used to visibly differentiate community territories' (Brookes 2007a, 2007b). Ancient remains—prehistoric and Roman—were tied into this reworking of the landscape to define group associations and claims.

The funerary record for East Yorkshire offers evidence for the use of the natural and antecedent landscape. The proximity of monuments selected for funerary reuse to lowland-to-upland routeways and watercourses, and the use of the edge of the Wold escarpment in the fifth and sixth centuries for the siting of cemeteries where such tracks allowed movement on to the Wolds, suggest a similar process of cemetery placement relating to settlement patterns and seasonal subsistence activities in this environment. Local and regional preferences and ideas can also be discerned in the cluster of cemeteries reusing linear earthworks in the fifth, sixth, and seventh centuries (Figure 2.5) and the increasing preference for particularly large, old barrows close to routeways as communal cemeteries (Figure 2.4). While the underlying geography and the ways in which the living interacted with it informed the placing of the dead in the landscape, the choice of antecedent historic features involved choices by mourners, family, and groups or communities.

A recent study of the funerary landscape of Norfolk by Mary Chester-Kadwell provides a particularly valuable insight into the complexities of the regional funerary scene. She demonstrates correlations with subtle attributes such as soil types, soil drainage, watercourses, and watersheds and argues that differences in topography and in resource exploitation may have influenced the creation of communities with varied characters that shaped their burial geography (Chester-Kadwell 2009: 150–2). Her findings strongly concur with the ideas presented here and Brookes's work on Kentish cemeteries. Roman and Romano-British sites are also shown to be important factors in the positioning of early medieval activities. Although spatial associations with prehistoric barrows and ring-ditches were higher than expected (Chester-Kadwell 2009: 127–31, figs 7.64–72), significantly more cemeteries were found within 100 metres of a Roman site (2009: 131–42, figs 7.80–93). At Oxborough, for example, cemeteries were established in the fifth and sixth centuries in direct relation to prehistoric barrows, and spatially close to Romano-British sites and structures, including a Romano-British cemetery. Oxborough developed over time as an extensive, multifocal funerary site with groups of burials arranged around prehistoric barrows or ring-ditches, with small clusters of burials added in different locations (2009: 147–51). Through broader statistical study and close intra-site interrogation, Chester-Kadwell argued that the fifth- to sixth-century population in Norfolk was immersed in a complex process of creating, maintaining, and contesting identity at local scales (2009: 146–65, 147, 162). Choices of ancient monument involved consideration of a variety of attributes: position, visibility, topographic proximity to antecedent landscape features, and aesthetics. As in Wessex, Deira, Kent, and the South Saxon kingdom, differences can also be discerned in the ways in which landscape and ancient monuments were used for burial in Norfolk. Alongside this regionally distinctive mortuary terrain, the varied uses of ancient remains reveal local preferences and choices as well. It is the combination of individual, local, and community narratives that drew upon natural geography *and* the antecedent landscape to construct concepts of ancestry, place, and identity that result in the regional differences we can perceive in the recycling of ancient remains.

The affinity with a prehistoric or Roman past could also be affirmed with more than just physical reference in spatial terms between burial, cemetery, and ancient monument. There are incidences in the funerary record for the fifth and sixth centuries where items of the assemblage accompanying an inhumation or cremation both echo and reinforce the relationship of cemetery to landscape. The recycling of Roman building material in the graves of the dead, for example, is a feature of several cemeteries in north Norfolk that lie in proximity to Roman sites and monuments. Chester-Kadwell argued that the populations of Norfolk showed in their cemetery placement an affinity with Roman and Romano-British sites. It is interesting to note, therefore, that at some of these Norfolk cemeteries Roman tiles were used deliberately to cover or to contain the inhumation or cremation, and burials were specifically inserted into Roman features (see Eckart and Williams 2003: 163–4). At Caistor-on-Sea, the cemetery to the north-west is associated with a kiln site and that to the south-east with an extra mural settlement to the Roman town. (Darling and Gurney 1993). Such evidence supports Chester-Kadwell's arguments that fifth- and sixth-century communities had a particular affinity with Roman material remains and the wider argument presented above that at a local scale, mourners were engaged in the conscious creation of individual narratives about people and place using old places and antique things.

Barrows and elite graves

The use of prehistoric monuments, and most commonly round barrows, for single furnished burials is a well-recognized feature of the late sixth- and seventh-century funerary records (Welch 1992: 88–96; Blair 1994: 30–1). They are termed 'princely' or elite barrow burials and can be found within cemeteries and in isolation; they are generally inhumation burials, although there are occasional cremations such as that at Asthall in Oxfordshire. Both men and women were buried in this way. The male graves are generally placed in the late sixth and seventh centuries and female graves in the seventh and early eighth (Geake 1997: 2002). Male graves tend to be primary barrow burials, while female graves are often secondary interments in prehistoric barrows (see Blair 2005 for discussion of female elite graves). They have been considered as defiantly pagan and as ambiguously Christian and are often cited as evidence for the emergence of social differentiation and stratification in early Anglo-Saxon society (Shephard 1979a, 1979b), as a manifestation of competition (Arnold 1982), and even resistance (Carver 2001). They may have encompassed all of these possibilities and more, representing commemorative monuments that activated and curated experiential and collective memory: fields of discourse for the living and the dead (Barrett 1994; but see Williams 2006a, 145–7, for an excellent summary on 'theorizing monuments'). Between the late sixth and early eighth centuries, the burial of richly endowed individual interments in or under barrow mounds became a rare but repeated feature of the funerary ritual in south, east, and central England. The cemetery at Sutton Hoo encompasses a sequence of primary barrow burials of considerable wealth and status. These burials are also indicative of an impressive and theatrical funerary display. This has been termed a dynastic cemetery: a place where the pagan kings of East Anglia in the last decades of their power and supremacy signalled their role as a powerful, pagan family with hereditary, legitimate, and sacral rights over the land of East Anglia and its people (Carver 2005). Similar isolated burials occurred elsewhere in the same time period. The male buried in a chamber grave at Taplow (Berkshire), the cremated individual at Asthall (Oxfordshire), and the more sparsely furnished grave of a male at Laverstock (Wiltshire) are all examples of this genre of prestige interments (Webster 1992). Female isolated barrow burials usually comprised bed burials, where the deceased was laid out within a chamber or grave on a low, wooden bed, dressed and accompanied by a range of dress fittings, jewellery, and some goods. Although usually isolated, exceptions include the bed-burial from Edix Hill, Cambridgeshire, and the more recent discovery of a female bed-burial at Street House Farm, North Yorkshire, neither of which was placed in or beneath an earth mound (Sherlock and Simmons 2008). These burials have seen a significant amount of enquiry already. They are a diagnostic of the conversion period: a time of experimentation and use of exotic ideas as well as goods (Geake 1997). They seem to tie neatly into our understanding of the seventh century as a period of kingdom formation and expansion, and to the emergence of kings, laws, lineages, and the idea of royal descent and hereditary rights to power. These graves are often situated on hilltops and high places commanding extensive views (Williams 1999). They may reflect the emergence of ideas of ancestry and legitimate claims to territory, land, and power (Williams 1996) (see Figure 2.11). The female graves are sometimes associated with assemblages containing amulets or items of magical or religious value (Meaney 1981; Petts 2011: 110–14).

These types of grave do feature within the study areas mentioned here but not in equal measure. There are virtually no examples from West Sussex. At Coombes a large and low spread mound probably of Bronze Age date produced an 'Anglo-Saxon' knife and spear-head but no further evidence at all of a burial or associated goods or finds (Meaney 1964: 248; Swanton 1973: 81–3). The burial of a male beneath the now lost 'Pipering Barrow', Burpham, described as having an iron sword below the hand on the left side and an iron fragment, suggested to be a part of a spear-head, above the head on the right (Collyer 1895–6), may have been an isolated male barrow burial but can hardly be described as rich or distinctive. In East Yorkshire, five apparently individual

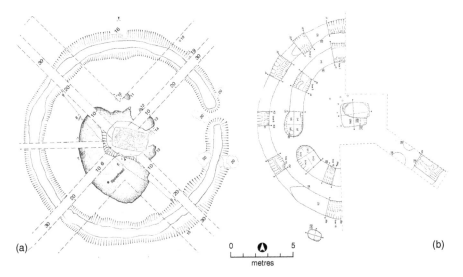

0   5
metres

(a)   (b)

Fig. 2.11 Excavation plans of (a) the secondary female burial at Swallowcliffe Down, Wiltshire; (b) the possible location of the female burial at Roundway Down, Wiltshire. Author's image.

and isolated male barrow burials were identified. All represented individual mortuary acts with burials placed intrusively in Bronze Age round barrows. A reappraisal of the evidence suggests these could all be placed comfortably in the sixth or seventh centuries (pp. 30–2). In East Yorkshire this type of burial did not increase in frequency at the expense of other established funerary traditions, but the use of prehistoric barrows did increase in popularity and the numbers of individuals interred in such locations also seems to have increased. In sharp contrast to East Yorkshire and West Sussex, isolated individual interments using prehistoric monuments dominated the funerary record in North Wiltshire. These too were not richly endowed, but they did frequently contain items that placed them firmly within the genre of isolated graves datable to the seventh century.

A range of summary observations can be made. In general, the funerary evidence of all three areas reveals that a general movement towards the interments of individuals beneath newly built barrows or in reused prehistoric barrows began in the sixth century and continued into the seventh century. These were not always richly endowed in terms of metalwork and dress items, but they were monumentalized and covered by large barrows or sited to take advantage of large prehistoric barrows; they were frequently situated in highly visible locations, close to river and land routes. The use of prehistoric monuments—round barrows—was common. Although a slowly increasing interest in associating the dead with prehistoric barrows in all three regions can be discerned, it is only in North Wiltshire that the inhumation rite seems to have focused entirely around individual monumentalized interments. It is clear that the creation of prestige or elite barrow burials was something regionally distinctive. It did not happen everywhere and, when it did, it could differ considerably in terms of date, prestige, and complexity. The burials of North Wiltshire have been argued by the author to fit with the emerging political competition between the growing kingdoms of Mercia and Wessex (Semple 2003a). This is an interpretation admittedly reliant to an extent on Arnold's old assertions of barrow burials as evidence of competition within early Anglo-Saxon societies (1980) and Bonney's suggestions that burials might mark the boundaries of polities or territories (1966). The absence of isolated rich prestige graves in primary or prehistoric barrows in West Sussex broadly concurs with this. The absence of a single unified kingship until the mid-seventh century seems to have both impeded conversion and prevented the development of any single dynastic family signalled through associated prestige burial grounds.

We are left then with an interesting conundrum. At the broadest level, the richest graves of the seventh century, those we might associate with an emerging kingly class, were frequently monumentalized, often experimental and ostentatious, and harnessed the apparent prestige or value of prehistoric monuments, mostly large barrows. Other people and communities were using prehistoric remains too, however, for less wealthy individual interments and for cemeteries.

The use of the prehistoric in the seventh century was thus not solely about status and prestige and legitimate power. It certainly lent itself to this kind of use and was increasingly harnessed for elite purposes in this and later centuries (see Chapters 3 and 6), but it also continued to hold potency and meaning for ordinary people and communities too. Ancient monuments were asserted earlier in this chapter as ideal physical and visible places for the forging of narratives of belonging and ownership. They were places that activated, stimulated, and curated discourse and memory relating to identity, place, and belonging. These ideas persisted into the seventh century, even as emerging elite or aristocratic groups began more consciously to harness such beliefs and the monuments themselves, to the purpose of securing their hold over nascent kingdoms.

The variety and diversity of fifth- and sixth-century 'reuse' points to highly divergent and locally specific traditions of burial that wove narratives about people and place. The spiritual power and meaning of prehistoric monuments are discussed in more detail in Chapter 3, but the evidence suggests that ancient monuments endured as potent features, synonymous perhaps with the past and past generations, continuing to hold an important place in the belief systems of local communities and populations. These widely held, yet diverse, beliefs provided an ideal pool from which emerging elite families could draw in order to forge new personalized narratives of lineage and rightful power. The ways in which these groups began to use the power of monuments differed considerably, but the local flavour of earlier beliefs gave shape to a regionally diverse array of emerging individual and personally driven narratives of the new supra-local elites.

Burials, monuments, and identity beyond Anglo-Saxon England

Similar changes in the use and recycling of the ancient in the landscape can be discerned in other areas of Britain and Europe. Although beyond the scope of this volume, the use of prehistoric and Roman monuments as places of burial by early medieval communities is a practice attested far more widely than England alone. At the most cursory level, this indicates that the topic is in need of study at a much wider scale. It also signals that the emphasis on the local and regional discussed here is not the sole way in which to examine and interpret the reuse of ancient and antecedent monuments in English landscape. This section cannot be comprehensive and by necessity is reliant on secondary literature, but it serves to show that parallels exist beyond the narrow confines of England for the exploitation and use of ancient places and monuments by early medieval communities.

Britain and Ireland

The use of the prehistoric by other medieval societies in Western and Northern Britain is acknowledged in the first chapter of this book and will reappear at times throughout. With specific regard to funerary reuse, there are subtle trajectories of practice, but a paucity of information on well-dated burials and cemeteries at present hampers any grand overview of the British evidence. In Ireland, while the great royal centres attest to the valorization of the past and tend to dominate the debate, there are certainly indications of funerary reuse too in the fifth to seventh centuries. At Ardsallagh I (Meath) some thirty inhumations of the fifth to seventh centuries were found in association with a pennanular ring-ditch in an area with Bronze Age and Iron Age cremation burials (Clarke and Carlin 2009). Another possible early medieval example can be found at Farta, Kiltullagh, Galway, where a female accompanied by antler remains and horse bone (perhaps a whole horse) was buried in the upper levels of a Bronze Age burial mound (Coffey 1904). The new online initiative, *Mapping Death, People, Boundaries and Territories in Ireland, 1st to 8th Centuries* AD, will without question open the Irish early medieval cemetery evidence to further scrutiny, but for now it is sufficient to recognize that the funerary reuse of earlier prehistoric monuments is most certainly present within the Irish corpus (see also O'Brien 1999). The use of boundaries and liminal places for burial and especially barrow burial is an acknowledged feature in Ireland and in neighbouring Wales (see Charles-Edwards 1976; James 1992; O'Brien 1999). Indeed, in Wales, proximity to Bronze Age structures is suggested to have been motivated by the use of these ancient features as the markers of boundaries and divisions (James 1992). A scarcity of well-dated funerary evidence makes clear statements difficult for these areas, but numerous examples exist (Petts 2000, 2002). At Tandderwen in Clwyd, Wales, a prehistoric monument seems to have been turned to a Christian funerary purpose, while at Plas Gogerddan, Powys, an early medieval cemetery lies adjacent to Bronze Age ring-ditches (Brassil et al. 1991; Petts 2000: 115–16; Petts 2002: 195–209, 199). Such evidence has been used to emphasize that a British tradition of 'reuse' may have existed with its roots in Romano-British practice (Williams 1998c; Petts 2000: 88–9). The creation of a new monumentality within western and Welsh funerary practice is also recognized. Standing stones and inscribed stone markers are not, as once suggested, reused prehistoric standing stones. Instead these are now recognized as a tradition inspired by late antique prototypes and ogham-inscribed stones common to southern and western Ireland (Petts 2002, 195–209, 196). There is certainly an Irish and western and Welsh context for the funerary reuse of ancient monuments for burial, and it does seem at least on cursory inspection to be related to concepts of monumentality, commemoration, and the marking of territory.

A recent detailed survey of funerary evidence in Scotland offers additional corroboration for similar early medieval traditions. New research has exploited the limited numbers of well-dated cemeteries and the cemetery corpus as whole, to reveal scarce but convincing evidence for the reuse of prehistoric monuments as places for burial from the first to the eighth centuries AD (Maldonado 2011). The tradition in Scotland differs from England, lacking ostentation and sometimes appearing ambiguous or coincidental. Regional variations in practice are evident, however, as well as changes in emphasis across time relating to conversion and the development of more complex, hierarchical social structures (Maldonado 2011: 152–5). Only rarely are burials positioned in direct 'intrusive' relationships with monuments, for example, at the henges of Cairnpapple in the West Lothians (Piggott 1948) and North Mains of Strathallan, Perthshire (Barclay 1983, cited by Maldonado 2011: 153). Associative practices are more common at Garbeg, Inverness (Wedderburn and Grime 1984), and Newton, Islay, Aberdeenshire (McCullagh 1989), for example, where burials are associated with large prehistoric settlements; or Forteviot Perthshire, where square barrows seem to cluster around prehistoric foci in the landscape (Driscoll 1998, 2010; Halliday 2006; but see also Maldonado 2011: 153 and fig. 6.10; and section 6.4.3). With the proviso that attempts to see continuity are hazardous (Cowley 2003), Maldonado does identify differing and perhaps competing traditions: correlations with Iron Age settlements in Atlantic Scotland, with upstanding brochs in Caithness, and the use of prehistoric enclosures in the south-west (2011: 153–4). Not only does this bring into question the tendency to see funerary reuse as a distinctively strong tradition in Anglo-Saxon England, perhaps connected to traditions on the Continent in the migration period (Härke and Williams 1997; Williams 1998b: 103; Thäte 2007: 47); it also challenges the idea of a competing monolithic British tradition of burial practice and 'reuse' (Petts 2000; but see Petts 2004 for *contra* arguments and Thäte 2007: 46–9). Maldonado's work sets the evidence for Scotland clearly within the theoretical compass of this chapter. He concludes that approaches to burial including monument reuse were locally varied, perhaps regionally distinctive, but certainly diverse and changing. These practices were used by communities and groups to serve particular local or regional agendas and articulate specific types of identity by means of complex engagement with the remains of the distant and more recent past (Maldonado 2011: 155–6, 264).

Germany and Scandinavia

Eva Thäte has undertaken a valuable European survey that offers evidence for similar practices and traditions involving burial at earlier antecedent monuments beyond Britain. In Germany old prehistoric barrows were again used as places of burial, and in some areas reuse is suggested to be prolific (e.g. Capelle 1971: 106; Tempel 1982: 317–18; Thäte 2007: 94–7; see also response by Härke and Williams 1997). Thäte has identified what she considers are strong similarities to the English evidence, and as a consequence has argued for a continuance or even resurgence of tradition in England caused by incoming Germanic groups. Older monuments were not always chosen as the initial point of focus in these Continental cemeteries, and other types of topographic feature were frequently brought into use. Further study on the burial grounds of northern Germany and Scandinavian and Slavonic evidence by Thäte (2007) and Sopp (1999) has led to arguments for the presence of ancestor cults for German communities and the Germanic settlers in England. Both studies show that the reuse of earlier or antecedent monuments from prehistory for burial by early historic communities was present in Germany and Scandinavian and Slavonic areas. Thäte reviewed some 160 sites with evidence for reuse in Denmark, southern Sweden, and south-west Norway. The tradition generally featured across the Viking Age but seems to have been more intensely practised in Denmark in the tenth century and perhaps in Sweden and Norway as well. In a similar pattern to the Scottish evidence, burials were more commonly placed next to ancient monuments, rather than in intrusive relationships cutting into earlier structures (Thäte 2007: 275). There was also little evidence of extensive reuse of barrow cemeteries: the Viking communities preferred to use individual ancient monuments and on occasion stone cists or earth graves inside barrows or cairns. There were also differences between regions: large Iron Age monuments were imposed on ancient flat grave cemeteries in Sweden; and flat graves of the late Iron Age deliberately reused flat graves of the early Iron Age mainly in Denmark. Thäte also noted late Iron Age monuments aligned on ancient structures, and though barrows and cairns were the most common focus for secondary funerary activity, other kinds of monument and natural features also exerted influence over the living. Thäte noted the reuse of house ruins, particularly dense in Rogaland in south-west Norway. The houses were structures abandoned in the Migration period; for example, at Ullanhaug three houses burned to the ground in the sixth century were reused for later burials, some of Viking Age (Thäte 2007: 101–7). Thäte also points to the evidence for a tradition of establishing settlements around earlier monuments, citing Galstead and Langvang in Denmark in the late Iron Age (Thäte 2007: 109). Some of the most significant conclusions of this study include indications that, in different places or regions, these traditions may have been the preserve of only certain sectors or groups within late Iron Age society. A virtual absence of child and deviant burials at reused monuments can be contrasted, for example, with a high proportion of female adults in secondary burials in barrows in Sweden and Denmark (Thäte 2007: 276). Another important contribution is her observation that the patterns of reuse imply a concept of time and ancestry rooted in the recent rather than distant past: in the later early Iron Age in Norway. Monuments and structures dating to earlier periods were ignored in favour of monuments or graves of the Roman Iron Age or Migration periods. This contrasts with Denmark and Sweden, where the frequency of Neolithic and Bronze Age monuments used for burial was significantly higher (Thäte 2007: 276). Thäte has produced a rich study that offers far more than this mere summary, but in conclusion it is worth emphasizing that strong regional variations in tradition existed.

For Thäte, ancestry and legitimation were major provocations for these practices: the past was selectively chosen by the living to play a part in tightly defined genealogical constructs. She has also asserted that the types of ancient monuments used needed to be familiar rather than 'other', and finally she has pointed to the ideas of repopulation and colonization as potential motivating forces, arguing that resettlement required a negotiation of existing and older 'ancestral' monuments (Thäte 2007: 279). Thäte concludes by stating that, although 'legitimation' is a useful catch-all, the use of ancient monuments was part of a far more complex concept of the afterlife displayed in a highly varied array of funerary practices. Ancestors and their legitimating functions were important, but so were topographic attributes (see also Maldonaldo 2011: 142–54). In other words, as in Scotland and England, the patterns of reuse were situated within and shaped by the underlying geography and topography and the praxis of communities. In sum, such processes served to facilitate the creation by groups and individuals of competing and successive intellectual narratives of being, identity, and place signalled through funerary theatre.

France

The topographic placement of cemeteries in Gaul in the sixth and seventh centuries is well rehearsed (see, e.g., Halsall 1992, 1995, 2006, 2010), but the available literature makes slim acknowledgement of the use of ancient prehistoric monuments for early medieval burial. By contrast, the density of evidence and thus the discussion by these and other authors has largely focused on the relationship between cemeteries of the sixth and seventh centuries and Roman remains and ruins. 'Reuse' in sixth- and seventh-century Gaul involved a variety of differing strands of activity. The 'past' was appropriated, for the purposes of living families and groups, in what is described by Halsall as a fiercely competitive, community-based society (2010: 259–60; see also Effros 2003: 178–9 for discussion of local family competition involving revived epigraphic memorialization at Neuvicq-Montguyon, citing Maurin 1971 and Pietri 1983: 516). Another characteristic identified by Effros (2003: 191) is the development of cemeteries close to or within 'the ruins of abandoned structures such as prehistoric dolmens, villas, baths, civic buildings, temples and fortresses'. This occurred within urban centres alongside a wide range of other activities that transformed the late antique towns and cities of Gaul, but also within the rural landscape. Effros and Halsall both point to a distinct change in mortuary practices around *c.*600: most notably the emergence of a tradition of placing cemeteries actually *in* ancient ruins rather than *close* to them (Effros 2003: 191; Halsall 2010: 254). A classic exemplar cited by both is represented by Berthelming (Moselle), where a Gallo-Roman villa provided a focus for a small, seventh-century cemetery (Halsall 1995: 96–8; 2010: 254; Effros 2003: 191; both citing Lutz 1950). A larger example, where the prehistoric rather than the Gallo-Roman past is referenced, can be found at Sublaines (Indre-ed-Lore). Here a dolmen and ritual focus of the Neolithic and Bronze Ages attracted the establishment of a cemetery of some 200 graves during the mid-seventh to the late eighth centuries (Cordier 1985; Billard et al. 1996, 279–80). Halsall and Effros emphasize in particular the significance of Gallo-Roman ruins and structures for the communities of sixth- and seventh-century Gaul (Halsall 1995: 96–8; 2010: 254–60; Effros 2001; 2003: 175–217). Cemeteries were indeed frequently established near and later in abandoned villas and other Roman structures including *fanum* (see Halsall 1995: 96–8; 2006; 2010: 254, citing Ennery and Lavoye for the former sixth-century practice and Audun-le-Tiche as representative of seventh-century changes in cemetery and burial placement). As Sublaines indicates, however, the prehistoric too played a role in determining and shaping the identity of communities in the sixth and seventh centuries. A recent publication outlining the early medieval use of a series of three prehistoric monuments at Val-de-Reuil et Porte Joie (Eure) is compelling in its discussion and collation of further examples of cemeteries founded next to menhirs and dolmens, barrows, and ring-ditches (Carré and Treffort 2010). At Val-de-Reuil, dolmens and chambered tombs of the Neolithic provided a focus for later prehistoric, Gallo-Roman, and Merovingian activity. This cluster of sites lies close to the confluence of the Seine and Eure. Three chambered tombs, associated with standing stones at Butte Saint-Cyr, Fosse XIV, and Beausoleil, provided foci for early medieval funerary activity in the seventh and eighth centuries. The excavators have argued that each monument was reused in different ways. The construction of an early seventh- or eighth-century church on the site is also conjectured by the excavators from posthole evidence and the correspondence of the plan of the later medieval church. The final 'reuse' or robbing of stones from the Neolithic monument in the ninth century is argued to have been for the purpose of laying foundations for the Carolingian church (Carré and Treffort 2010: 350). The excavators stopped short of attempting an in-depth wider survey of evidence for the appropriation of prehistoric sites and complexes but do point to a number of other examples and list over thirty sites where cemeteries sit next to dolmen, menhirs, barrows, ring-ditches, Iron Age graves, and cemeteries. There is room for significant additional research here, not only to expand this corpus but also to distinguish and investigate the local and regional contexts of this activity. It is sufficient, however, here, in providing clear evidence for the use of ancient prehistoric monuments in Gaul for burial alongside the more extensive appropriation of Gallo-Roman structural ruins. The frequency of activity at these sites in the seventh century is also useful in its corroboration of a seventh-century context for such funerary innovation (as cited by Halsall 1995: 162–3, 246–7, 263–6, 271–2; 2010: 255–6; Effros 2003: 200–1). It is useful to end by noting that la Butte Saint-Cyr is one of a group of sites where a church was constructed on, or by, prehistoric remains. The pre-Romanesque church at the Priory of St Mary, Ecrehous, Jersey, built over a cairn covering a megalithic tomb, is a more widely known and recognized example (Rodwell 1986: fig. 57). In addition, however, Carré lists examples at Aizier, Giverny, Saint-Just and Saint-Marcel, Les Guimbets (Eure), Belin-Beliet, Blasimon, Saint-Aubin-de-Brane and Saint-Ciers-d'Abzac (Gironde), Roye-sur-Matz (Oise), Confolens (Charante), and Médeyrolles, Viverols (Puy-de-Dôme) (Carré and Treffort 2010). Carré and his collaborators acknowledge an important point that is relevant to these examples and the discussion later in this volume of churches and prehistoric monuments in England (see Chapter 4). At Butte Saint-Cyr, while the placement of the cemetery was driven by the presence of the megalithic monument, the placement of the church was determined by the presence of the cemetery (Carré and Treffort 2010: 350). This list may thus include additional potential sites where prehistoric megalithic monuments inspired the foundation of new early medieval cemeteries that in turn drew the attention of the early Christian Church.

There are interesting analogies and tensions in this comparative evidence from Gaul. Halsall (2010: 253) has acutely observed that the appropriation of the Roman or Gallo-Roman past by Merovingian communities, which entered into a rather novel and direct phase of engagement in the seventh century, attests to a new forward-looking society, in which groups and families were seeking new ways to establish claims, lineage, and status. Such encounters with the prehistoric or Gallo-Roman past were sought, it seems, particularly in this century and especially in the words of Bonnie Effros, by elite families 'regardless of ethnic identity' who 'co-opted Roman symbols and customs in their daily activities and then incorporated them into their mortuary rituals' (Halsall 2000: 269–73; Effros 2003: 195). At the same time, the separation of elite burial from the normal mortuary sphere increased in practice and 'exclusive interments occupied smaller, more restricted rural sites' (Effros 2003: 197). Effros has argued that a kind of authenticity could be obtained from reused late antique ruins and *spolia*, whether for those interring their dead in these seventh-century cemeteries or for those using and inhabiting new buildings, edifices, and, of course, churches wrought from ruins and *spolia* (2001, 111–12). Thus, for Effros (2001: 118), ancient ruins, including reused prehistoric monuments, offered a fluid principle for ordering and reorientating the cultural landscape and increasingly became a focus of clerical and lay elite activity. For Halsall (2010: 253, 257–8) such activity was integral to the process of signalling status in the present and future—and thus knowledgeable, informed, and creative—a means by which new authority might be inscribed selectively, utilizing and overwriting past material narratives. As we have seen in England, regional, local variations, and trends in the fifth and sixth centuries, suggest that the ancient here too was a means of shaping identity and distinguishing and ordering social and spatial divisions. By the seventh century, the use of the ancient prehistoric at least was increasing within the ambit of an elite, keen to differentiate and project a sense of identity and power that drew upon the past (both the ancient and more recent), but selectively, using it to set an agenda for the future for the few and not the many.

Identity, people, and place

English traditions thus sit within a broad panoply of evidence for similar processes around the North Sea and the North Atlantic in the same early medieval time frame. These regions and areas of Europe, whether previously under Roman rule or not, were populated by communities who were coming to terms with the aftermath of the fall of the Roman Empire. The dramatic political and social changes that ensued, that shaped the emergence of new early medieval societies, seem to have promoted an allegiance between people, place, and landscape, and old monuments seem to have found an especially evocative function as a medium for articulating a sense of identity and connection to place.

Within Anglo-Saxon and early medieval archaeology, the fifth and sixth centuries have been extensively debated from a national perspective that has focused on questions of migration, ethnicity, and settlement by incoming Continental groups. The written accounts of the invasion of England in the fifth century have long been considered works of propaganda: texts designed to legitimize power via tales of ancestry, lineage and descent, battles and conquest—written to valorize specific peoples, figureheads, and families (Amory 1994; Geary 2002a: 41–62). The material changes in settlement and funerary traditions, the emergence of a new language, and the renaming of the landscape do, however, suggest that England, like the neighbouring provinces of Europe, witnessed a great period of fragmentation, dispersal, and change in the fifth and sixth centuries.

The evidence presented in this chapter for the creation of a sense of place and belonging by means of constructed funerary landscapes argues for negotiated and created identities that existed at a range of local to supra-regional scales. This reflects processes that were at play across large parts of post-Imperial and late Iron Age Europe within the first millennium. The works of John Hines (1984) and Tania Dickinson (1991, 2005), Helen Geake (1997), and more recently Aleks Pluskowski (2006a, 2006b, 2010) and Chris Fern (2010) have all shown how material culture might be used to create and manipulate symbolic 'cultural' relationships and identities that spanned the North Sea or borrowed from and aligned with late Roman and late antique symbolism and expression. Sam Lucy and Catherine Hills have moved the debate towards understanding funerary archaeology as a complex process of identity creation in a post-Roman scene characterized by fragmented structures and social collapse (Lucy 2002; Hills 2003). Within this time frame, the archaeological record is emphatic in its testimony of the use and material culture to signal perceived ethnicities and new identities—at least at the funeral (Halsall 1995, 2006, 2010; Williams 2006a; Sayer and Williams 2010).

At one level, the recycling of prehistoric and Roman monuments for burial can be interpreted as an expression of the interest by populations—migrant or indigenous—in forging links to the landscape and signalling legitimate ownership of land and resource (Lucy 1992). With further interrogation it is clear that these actions can be interpreted as expressions of emergent and competing, regional and local community identities (Semple 2003a, 2008, 2010). Populations were looking to consolidate their place in the present, and specific groups within those populations were looking to secure their power and status for the future by manipulating monuments that were visible physical reminders of an earlier time (see also Halsall 2010: 232–60). With geography as a strong and underlying force, the ways in which people lived and how they buried their dead in their landscape can be argued as a vibrant window on the first stages of consolidation of power in a post-Roman landscape, centred initially on families and community. The uses of the antecedent monumental landscape, via the funeral, to establish a sense of place and belonging point to highly complex and localized processes within post-Roman society, in which individual families and communities sought to create a mythology around their origins, their lineage, ancestry, and connection to place. It is precisely this lack of a fixed sense of national or even regional identity, mingled with a loss of roots and stability, that seems to have led to a remarkable burgeoning of funerary rites and traditions around England (and indeed elsewhere). These processes used material culture in diverse ways to articulate precise ideas of origins, lineage, descent, identity and social place, and status. Populations were locked into a pattern of funerary activity that was, on the one hand, deeply conservative in terms of gender and age, but, on the other, the costume and theatricalities of death, including the funerary landscape, were open for extraordinary experimentation.

The case studies here, alongside complementary discussion, show that the communities of the fifth and sixth centuries shaped their identity through funerary rites and theatre with an individualistic and local outlook. As the funerary records of all these regions reveal, however, more conformity can be discerned in the ways in which antecedent landscapes were used as individual families developed control over larger landscapes. The increasing interest in single, isolated secondary burials in prehistoric barrows in Wessex and the growing interest in placing the dead in large and prominent prehistoric barrows in East Yorkshire in the seventh century reflect similar emerging interests in Kent. In Gaul too cemeteries were being situated by and notably *in* ancient monuments in the seventh century.

In England these changes in preference and increasing interest in recycling ancient monuments by more specific sectors of society can be argued to reflect the emergence of supra-local and supra-regional strategies by elite groups. A need to signal new narratives of authority and power on the part of the elite led to increasing ostentation through selective reworking of the past, and more recent landscape, and its monuments. These changes may reflect in England new emergent aristocratic groups seeking to create narratives of ancestry and power. Perhaps, as Halsall has argued for Gaul, such creative strategies involved an overwriting of the past, but I would add that they also involved selective discrimination, choice, and valorization of ancient monuments and past practice in order to shape a new intellectual territory from the old. Bringing elements of the past under their personal control enabled elite families to set themselves apart, distinct from local and regional allegiances and affiliations. The creation of a new intellectual territory, situated within the landscape and cosmology of the old, facilitated an entirely new and extensive reach of power over landscape and people: shared by the few, looking towards the future, but retaining the legitimacy of the past (see Carver 2011, for discussion of developing intellectual territories).

Summary

The use of ancient monuments for funerary activity in the fifth to seventh centuries was far removed from being a merely labour-saving device and was driven by far more complex processes than the need to create legitimate claims over land and resource. The selective use of the landscape—natural and manufactured—in funerary ritual represented the intentional symbolic construction of individualized notions of identity by the indigenous and incoming communities of the post-Roman landscape. As one moved from region to region and locality to locality in the fifth and sixth centuries, one would have discerned differences in how communities disposed of their dead in terms of the places they chose to do this; but fluidity and variation in practice remained wide-ranging. Communities made use of the landscape and monuments most familiar to them and most relevant to their sense of who they were and their place in the world. The recycling and reuse of prehistoric and Roman monuments were varied and experimental, reflecting the creation of narratives of descent and origin at both a group and a family level. Large-scale, repeated use of sites by numerous groups or communities over time, such as the establishment and use of the vast cremation cemetery around a 'barrow-shaped' knoll at Loveden Hill, Lincolnshire (Williams 2004), or the successive and repeated funerary activity around several monuments at Saltwood, Kent (Glass et al. 2011), demonstrate the creation of a sense of identity as a group, with a common narrative of ancestry and claim. Indeed, both sites may well have served to shape early territorial claims and collective identities and later still administrative geographies (see pp. 92–4). The communities of the Arun and Adur river valleys chose to use small-scale funerary events alongside the establishment of larger cemeteries, as a way of defining their place in the landscape and a sense of their communities' claim to that geographically defined territory or space. The populations of the Wolds chose things familiar to that landscape: square barrows, henges, prehistoric ring works, and, of course, barrows. Each reused site may have signalled the writing of a legend or claim—or at least represent one strand in the creation of a complex story of ancestry, heroes, and origins. These processes signal a growing interest in theatricality too, with explicit sites chosen for activities and rituals that reaffirmed identity and presumably kin-group relations and also a sense of origin and place.

This chapter offers merely a beginning. Comparative evidence reveals the potential of further study. The teasing out of these landscape narratives at a variety of scales, geographic and temporal, requires interrogation and cross-referencing with material assemblages, from the grave, the settlement, and in broader material culture terms. The uses of the ancient and natural landscape point to a poetic subtlety and deep imagination in how the populations of the fifth and sixth centuries perceived themselves and their ancestry and past, something that the material record and artistic repertoires of the period already attest to (Dickinson 2005, 2009; Pluskowski 2010). Future research that tests out the 'geographic and topographic' identities of communities with the 'material' identities represented in dress items, weaponry, ceramics, and building styles may provide an even closer view of the emotions and mentalities of these early communities, casting light perhaps on the conflict and convergence of indigenous 'British' and incoming 'Germanic' myths and traditions.

The individual acts of reuse in the borders of Wessex and the increasing interest in using barrows for burial in East Yorkshire both represent a distinct shift away from these early complex localized responses towards strategies that were the preserve of a few elite families. These changes, when compared to the preceding varieties of funerary activity in relation to ancient remains, may signal a move by certain sectors of society to a more conservative and supra-regional fashion: one that prioritized the use of Bronze Age barrows and particularly large prehistoric monuments and that involved rich, individual burials as well as ostentatious acts of 'reuse'. The use of prehistoric barrows for elite burial in the Peak District in the sixth to seventh centuries, and the emergence of distinctive settlement-cemetery complexes in the north of Northumbria in the same time frame, are also signals of a changing scene dominated by the actions of an elite class. This emergence of what could be described as innovative supra-regional rites involving prehistoric remains can be aligned with competing dynastic claims and the contests over ownership and territory by elite families described in written sources from the late seventh century onwards. Similar processes can be seen in seventh-century Gaul involving the direct usage of ancient monuments (but more frequently Gallo-Roman structures and ruins), but comparisons have yet to be fully discerned in other areas. It is also evident in England (and in the studies of Scotland and Scandinavia) that routeways and Roman remains, as well as prehistoric and later burials and cemeteries, could be drawn upon in the shaping of districts, central places, and political heartlands in the earliest Anglo-Saxon era (Brookes 2007a, 2007b, 2011; Dickinson et al. 2011; Dickinson 2012). It seems that similar processes were at work across north-west Europe, and geographical, topo-graphical, and antecedent features all served as a means of ordering and reorientating the post-Imperial cultural landscape, within and beyond its borders (see Effros 2001: 118, for comments on Gaul). Equally, more ex-tensive interrogation and comparison of the trajectories of 'reuse' in Britain, the Continent, and the North are likely to bear fruit.

The next chapter explores the exploitation of ancient monuments in the early Anglo-Saxon period for purposes other than burial, and argues that the ancient played a significant part in the spiritual repertoires of early medieval commu-nities in England alongside the natural world and landscape. Just as burial at ancient monuments may have provided a security and focus for the populations inhabiting the post-Roman landscape, so rituals at ancient monuments may have secured connections between the living and the local landscape, and may have provoked and provided a forum for both conflict and discourse relating to anxieties over possession and place.

After *c.*600 distinct changes are also apparent in non-funerary usage. Along-side the use of prehistoric monuments for isolated elite burial, documentary sources as well as archaeological evidence suggest that such features were chosen as places for elite settlement, as locations for battles, mustering, and for assembly. The perceived ancestral importance of such features may well have shaped elite interest, but remembered or invented activity at these places may also have rendered such sites iconic, mythical, and powerful. Their real plenipotency may, however, have developed from their place and role within the competitive local scenes of the fifth and sixth centuries. It is in this time that concepts of origin, ancestry, and heritage slowly developed within communities and served to tie families to larger units of territory. Monuments formed a medium by which such narratives could be situated, and signalled, and offered communities nodal places that linked past and present worlds. Certain monu-ments, through local status and repeated activity, seem to have acquired suffi-cient meaning to sustain their later exploitation and usage by elite families before, during, and after the conversion, while others, previously untouched, perhaps provided a means of signalling the emergence of a new order, shaped by a forward-looking aristocratic elite.

3

Ancestral, spiritual, and magical?

Pre-Christian attitudes to the prehistoric

> My howe shall stand beside the forth. And there shall be but a short
> distance between mine and Þorsteinn's, for it is well that we should
> call to one another.
>
> Friþófs Saga I (Ellis-Davidson 1943: 90–6)

Interest and reverence for older monuments, especially their use as places of
burial, are considered by many a signal of ancestral concerns in early medieval
societies (e.g. Semple 1998; Williams 1998a; Williams 2006a: 100, 121;
Theuws 2009; Sanmark 2010, etc.). Indeed the existence of ancestor cults in
early medieval Scandinavia and Iceland is asserted on the basis of literary and
documentary evidence including the *sagas* which, as this excerpt demonstrates,
point to popular belief in a life after death within the burial mound and to
practices and activities related to the veneration and appeasement of these dead
mound-dwellers (Sanmark 2010: 158–76). The use of ancestral as a catch-all
explanation for mortuary rituals in past societies has been sharply criticized
(Whitley 2002; Halsall 2010: 245–6), but it is difficult to disassociate ideas of
ancestry completely from the wide variety of early medieval funerary rituals
that so readily embraced and made use of material culture of a more ancient
age. Ancestors and their veneration was a single but powerful strand within a
large and complex network of ideas and rhetoric about the remembered and
invented past (see Williams 2006a: 22). The powerful dead—whether remembered or imagined, commemorated as ancestors or as mythical heroes—provided
unrivalled opportunities for creating a sense of place and importance in early
medieval societies.

Ancient monuments were, however, just one element of a wider numinous
natural world. The supernatural opportunities of the grave, the barrow, and
ancient monuments existed as components in a landscape within which all
things could be potent to greater and lesser extents (asserted by Stefan Brink
for late Iron Age societies in southern Scandinavia; see Brink 2001; also Semple
2010). The Norse literary legacy, for example, attests to medieval beliefs in the

continued presence of the dead within the landscapes of the living, but also places emphasis on the spiritual potency of other beings, often connected to specific places and types of feature (Hellström 1996; see also Sanmark 2004, 2010). A broader spiritual landscape existed within which older monuments and places of burial helped shape and fix a sense of identity, but the natural world was crucial too, moulding the world view of these communities: supporting their existence, connecting and separating them, and facilitating their movement and travel (see, for example, discussions by Howe 2000, 2002, 2004).

This chapter moves beyond mortuary practices and examines other pre-Christian activities that exploited prehistoric monuments as a setting. It begins by setting the mortuary scene outlined in Chapter 2 within a broader pre-Christian 'spiritual' canvas before moving on to consider a wider variety of evidence for what can be classed as *non-funerary* activity at ancient sites and monuments. The use of the prehistoric by communities is argued as a component within the large and complex network of ideas, rhetoric, and rituals, which the communities of the fifth and sixth centuries used to define and situate themselves. The aim here is to show just how 'creative a medium' the ancient was for shaping and signalling identity, belief, ideology, and politics at the most local of levels, perhaps leading to its special role in later Anglo-Saxon elite narratives.

The pre-Christian landscape

The work of Stefan Brink on the late Iron Age and Viking pre-Christian landscapes of Sweden and Norway has been highly influential in its demonstration of how settlements, monuments, burial sites, sacred natural locations, and assemblies might all represent components in a landscape in which there was a multiplicity of potency. Layers of meaning, invested in particular features, activities, or sites, overlapped so that a traveller through a landscape would encounter a world within which all aspects were sacred to greater and lesser extents (Brink 2001). Similar themes have been raised by David Stocker and Paul Everson (2003), in a regional exploration of the siting of churches and monasteries along the Witham Valley, Lincolnshire. Natural features—the River Witham and its natural crossing places—are argued as topographic elements that became resonant and meaningful over a long period of time.

Both papers are significant for their emphasis on the importance of natural geography alongside the powerful nature of antecedent and ancient features (see also Gardiner 2003; Brookes 2007a, 2007b), and the relevance of human interaction with both natural and the human-altered features in the landscape. It is not the rivers, hills, or ancient barrows in isolation that were momentous: human encountering and traversing of the landscape rendered natural and ancient places intermittently special over long time frames (see Ingold 2000: chapter 3 and p. 155 for arguments on the importance of human movement and interaction with the environment). Monuments may have held meaning because of their setting and the aesthetics of their location, and because of the particular ways in which people interacted with them (see Tilley 1994, 1996, 2004; Bradley 2000: 35; Bender et al. 2007; Scarre 2007, 2011). In prehistoric studies, authors have made strong arguments for the relevance of natural places and features to the spirituality of people in the past, arguing that natural places may acquire an archaeology, attracting activity and developing into places revered and physically enhanced over millennia particularly through visual and physical encounter. Monuments, through their construction, could also magnify the special nature and spectacle of place (Bradley 2000). Henges in southern England, for example, exploited naturally rounded, theatre-like spaces, whereas megalithic monuments in Brittany were often situated on prominent coastal positions, visually dominating seascapes and seaways (Scarre 2011). At Durrington Walls, Wiltshire, the river and watercourse provided the main route of connection between this monument and Stonehenge, linking the rituals at both sites and serving to restrict access, both physical and visual, to the monument (Parker Pearson 2005). The natural world and ancient monuments were frequently used together to shape people's experience and to structure how people viewed and encountered the landscape.

These concepts are also relevant to early medieval archaeology. The importance of the natural world and how it was encountered, has been argued as central to how cemeteries and burials were situated by early medieval communities (see, e.g., Semple 2003a, 2008; Williams 2006a: 179–214; Brookes 2007a, 2007b). What is less well researched but increasingly acknowledged is the power of natural places themselves and their place in real and imagined spiritual topographies (see Semple 2010, 2011). The natural might be important in ritual terms not just because of accessible, visual, or aesthetic qualities, but also because of its value to populations in terms of subsistence, seasonality, and survival. The seasonality of life and reliance on the natural world has always shaped the belief systems of populations—whether prehistoric or medieval, ancient or modern, Christian or pagan. Thus, to fully understand how prehistoric and Roman remains may have been perceived or viewed as a part of the pre-Christian spiritual compass, an examination of their importance within the wider natural and numinous setting is required, in order fully to conceptualize how the natural and ancient was experienced and valued in pre-conversion England.

The natural world

Recent studies have made clear that the early Anglo-Saxon population had a synergic relationship with the natural world. Evidence that religious practice was temporally organized can be found in chapter XV of *De Temporum Ratione* by Bede (*c.*672–735). As John Hines notes, the survey 'reveals a pattern of regular feasting and rites closely connected with the cycle of fertility and the agricultural year' (1997: 379). The surviving Old English names of the months of the year relay an annual cycle of living and spirituality that was bedded in the rhythm of the seasons, for example, *thrimilchi*, the month when cows could be milked three times; *weodmonath*, the month of weeds; *blotmonath*, the month of blood-letting or sacrifice (Stenton 1941: 97–8; Hines 1997). The animal and plant kingdoms were not merely a resource, but components of the early medieval spiritual repertoire. In the fifth to eighth centuries, animals were used in artistic designs as protective as well as powerful devices that might shield the wearer from danger or even allow access to the attributes of the animal (Dickinson 2005, 2009). Particularly within the designs used to decorate military kit, animal designs representing both real and mythical creatures— dragons, biting beasts, wolves, bears—were often emblematic of the kinds of predatory and marshal powers the protagonist and wearer were seeking to draw from the spiritual world (Pluskowski 2006a, 2006b, 2010). Plants are harder to isolate within the preliterate and Christian evidence, but special plants and herbs are present within male and female grave assemblages, in pouches and work boxes (Meaney 1981; Semple forthcoming c). Plants and trees were also resources used extensively within the mortuary arena: for bedding, packing, and covering the corpse and for cremation pyres, for coffins, for chambers, and of course for numerous objects within furnished burials, for example, beds, spear shafts, and buckets (for plants as soft furnishing, see Harrington 2006; Annable and Eagles 2010; for a broad array of papers on plants and trees, see Biggam 2003). Trees and wood were also used in the building of structures thought to be shrines (Blair 1995), and for standing posts used in these shrines, but more commonly within cemeteries too, perhaps functioning as memorials or markers and probably once carved with decoration (Blair 2005: 185–7; 2013). The place of plants and trees within pre-Christian spiritual beliefs is powerfully attested in written sources. Anglo-Saxon runes include several named from specific tree species: the names of ash and oak for individual runes were added to the already existing yew and birch runes (Halsall 1981: 152, 154; Hooke 2003: 17). From Tacitus to Bald's leechbook, the power and efficacy of wood and plants, plant parts, leaves, bark, and trees in symbolic ritual and in healing are emphasized (see Bintley 2010; but also Hooke 2003, 2010). The seeking of auguries from the animal world and the creation of charms and spells that made use of plants and animal parts were loudly condemned in Christian sources, and the powerful animal repertoires represented on dress fittings and military kit were considerably altered in terms of form and use by the conversion (Pluskowski 2006a, 2006b, 2010; Carver 2010). Plants, however, remained a firm element of the motif repertoire in sculpture, metalwork, textiles, and manuscript art, and continued in use in magic and healing into the eleventh century (Hawkes 2003b; Bintley 2010). Alongside animals and plants, the earth and land were also potentially venerated: in the *Æcerbot Charm*, *Erce* or 'earth' is invoked as a deity or spiritual entity that could help ensure fertility from the land and good crops (Jolly 1996; Pollington 2000). Soil was prescribed as ingredients for charms—notably the charm against a stillbirth in which soil from a grave was considered efficacious in preventing miscarriage (Jolly 1996; Pollington 2000). The description by Bede (*HE* III, 9) of pilgrimage to Oswald's place of slaughter at *Maserfelth* is also relevant here:

Many people took away the very dust from the place where his body fell, and put it in water, from which the sick folk who drank it received great benefit. This practice became so popular that, as the earth was gradually removed, a pit was left in which a man could stand.

Water and watery places, perhaps especially places where the waters had significant qualities, for example, intertidal zones, places with seasonal surges, or water sources with a high mineral content or unusual colouration are all suggested to have provoked interest, and in some instances, veneration (Lund 2005, 2008; Semple 2010, Reynolds and Semple 2011). Alongside the purely natural, what might be described as 'human-altered natural places' were also imbued with specific value perhaps as liminal and thus especially charged environments where humans were encountering raw nature (this, for example, is not unlike the potential potency of crossing places and intertidal zones where the power or danger of the natural location lies in the human need to safely interact with it). As argued elsewhere, the *feld* (field) and *lēah* (grove) occur in a small number of instances in combination with theophoric names such as *woden*, *thunor*, and *tiw* (Hines 1997: 386, see also table 12–1). It is uncertain how these sites functioned, and most are unidentifiable in today's landscape (for example, *Thunresfelda*, 'field of Thunor' (Wiltshire) and *Tislea*, 'clearing of Tiw' (Hampshire) (but see Figure 3.1: Heavenfield, place of muster and prayer before Oswald's defeat of Cadwalla in AD 634 (*HE* III, 2)). *Feld* is generally interpreted now as a term used regularly in the sixth and seventh centuries for unencumbered land with unrestricted access and essential communal rough pasture (Gelling and Cole 2000, 269–71). The *feld* was thus peripheral but visited, accessible, even commonly used and owned by communities. Some of the earliest mentions of *feld* place-names refer to battle sites and meeting places or councils, which enforces the idea of the *feld* being particularly liminal and thus suitable for decision-making events (Gelling and Cole 2000: 272). *Lēah*, in recent research, is now interpreted as an active term applied to areas of actively managed or maintained and grazed wood pasture (Gelling and Cole 2000: 220; Hooke 2010). These types of place, on occasion ascribed to deities and also considered suitable as sites for battles and major assemblies, were thus partially

Fig. 3.1 Heavenfield, Northumberland: the place where Oswald prayed for victory over Cadwalla (*HE* II, 2) in AD 634. Author's image.

managed habitats, in other words, human-altered natural places that in spatial terms were used and visited, indeed communally owned in some instances, but were situated away from the core areas of habitation and cultivation (Gelling and Cole 2000: 220; Hooke 2010).

Natural features

Within this landscape, a range of natural features was sufficiently valued to have caused later Christian writers to stipulate against their worship or veneration. Late laws occasionally mention the worship of springs, stones, or trees: II Cnut V (1020–1: Wormald 1999: 345), and in one rare instance the setting-up of sanctuaries at such places: 'if there is on anyone's land a sanctuary [*friþgeard*] round a stone or a tree or a well [= spring] or any such nonsense' (Northumbrian Priests Law; Whitelock et al. 1981: 463). Trees have already been noted above, but it is worth underlining that individual sacred trees as well as specific tree species were assimilated into Christian traditions too. The ash is found in association with several accounts of early saintly activity (Blair 2005: 476–7). Trees and shrubs could be described as holy or sacred (Hooke 2003: 18), and at Taunton the charter-bounds, probably pre-Conquest in origin, record the 'ash tree which the ignorant call sacred' (Smith 1956: i; see also Blair 2005: 277). The importance of sacred trees and standing posts or pillars as individual features or markers of 'holy zones' implies their potency may well have stemmed not just from their individual qualities but also from their wider landscape context (Blair 2013). Thus, we might conclude that only some types of species were special, and, of these, only some trees offered the kinds of qualities that made them spiritually important. The reception of trees within Anglo-Saxon Christianity is profoundly interesting and informative. As Tolley (2009, 2013) believes, there are good reasons to accept that the concepts of a 'World Tree' were familiar to Anglo-Saxon pre-Christian communities and that it was absorbed into and used extensively within Christian contexts as an allegory and symbol. As Bintley has so cogently argued within his work, the Christian Anglo-Saxons were able to rationalize and continue their veneration of their sacred trees and pillars, by seeing these as precursors of the cross (2010, 2013). Indeed, early high crosses of the north, such as Ruthwell and Bewcastle, as well as the plant-rich vine scroll decoration, may well reflect the rendering in stone, within Christian monumental repertoires, of monuments and motifs once created in wood by pre-Christian populations (Hawkes 2003b).

Standing stones or boulders, although mentioned alongside trees in the laws quoted above, are far less conspicuous in all other written sources. In sharp contrast to evidence for early folk beliefs across the North Sea that suggests natural stones or boulders were considered to house spirits and supernatural creatures, there are few pre-Conquest references in England to animate or inhabited stones, to their veneration, or indeed to the felling of sacred stones by Christian saints. English folklore of a much later era is rich, however, in its reference to standing stones and stone circles. The Rollright Stones in Oxfordshire, for example, a Neolithic complex which provided a focus for several successive periods of activity and which attracted burial of early Anglo-Saxon date (see Beesley 1855; Dryden 1897; Lambrick 1988: 17 and fig. 2), became the subject of an extensive collection of stories regarding the creation of the monument and its magical and devilish properties (see Evans 1895). First mentioned by Camden (1610), the tale describes the thwarting of an ambitious king and his followers by a witch, who causes the long mound to be raised up and turns the king and his followers to stone (Evans 1895). Such monuments were more frequently attributed, however, to the work of a higher power, rationalized as punishments meted out by God for heathenry such as dancing or playing music on the Sabbath, or as creations of the Devil (Simpson 1987; Hutton 1993; Walsham 2011). Whilst such sources are likely the result of both the emergence of intense antiquarian interest in the sixteenth and seventeenth centuries in these newly recognized monuments and the arrival of radical Protestantism after the Reformation (Walsham 2011: 178), they also hint at popular activities perhaps of longer origin: fairs, dancing, gatherings, revels, and midsummer rituals involving drink, youths, and maidens. Other motifs that can be found in popular folklore and that may have arisen within a similar era include the association of such monuments with the activities of witches and with the hiding and discovery of treasure (see Grinsell 1973, 1976a). It seems likely that the populations of England prior to the enlightenment did not readily distinguish between natural stones or boulders and human-raised megaliths. The few attestations we have for the early medieval era, from written and archaeological sources, in fact imply that, when standing stones or megalithic monuments did attract attention, it was precisely because they had acquired a 'specialness' resulting from their apparent artificial rather than natural qualities.

Hilltops can, however, be regarded as an indisputable element of the pre-Christian spiritual topography. Although theophoric place-names tying gods to hills are rare (cited examples include Tishoe, Surrey, and Tysoe, Warwickshire, both 'Tiw's spur'; Gelling 1988; Wilson 1992: 13; and Easole, Kent, interpreted by Wilson as 'the god's spur'; Wilson 1992: 21), Frank Stenton firmly believed the place-name term *OE hearg*, 'temple/shrine', referred in many instances to some form of hilltop sanctuary (1941: 10–11). Where place-names containing the element *hearg* can be identified with confidence and precision, the association with distinctive hilltops, prominent knolls, or whalebacks is comprehensive (see Figure 3.2). What types of physical structure or activity were once associated with these hilltops are lost in the passage of time, but it is possible to argue that visually distinct hilltops and spurs with additional special attributes

Fig. 3.2 Harrow-on-the-Hill, Middlesex. Reproduced from Lysons 1792–96: ii, pt 3, 150.

were the types that acquired special meaning. Hilltops with prominent outlines and forms (Harrow-on-the-Hill, Middlesex; Tysoe, Warwickshire); spring-lines (Goodmanham, Yorkshire); ancient monuments and features of prehistoric and Roman and Romano-British date and manufacture (for example, Wood Eaton, Oxfordshire); hidden and concealed qualities (Harrow Hill, Sussex); and unusual or prominent colouration (the blood red sandstone of Harrowedone Hill, Thurstaston, Wirral) are all attested (see Semple 2007, 2010). High places also seem to have drawn specific types of activity: prior to the conversion, cemeteries and individual burials were commonly positioned in high and prominent topographic positions, for example, Lowbury (Berkshire) and Cuddesdon (Oxfordshire) (see Lucy 1998; Williams 1999). Assembly-places too are recorded and attested on hilltop positions with extensive views (Meaney 1995; Pantos 2002: 147–52). Adam's Grave (Wiltshire), known in Old English as *wodnesbeorh* 'woden's barrow', is recorded as the location for two early battles (*ASC* (A) 592 and (A) 715). The prehistoric barrow sits on a prominent knoll or hilltop, a landmark visible for miles across the downs to the north and the Vale of Pewsey to the south (see Colour Plate 2). It seems inevitable that such visually prominent landmarks would have established a place within the consciousness of local communities, especially those with the marks of earlier activity or distinctive sensorial aspects such as colour, shape, or even perhaps types of vegetation or acoustic properties.[1]

Caves, pits, fissures, and hollows were also significant places (Semple 2003b, 2010, 2011). Openings in the earth and rock were dangerous places in the minds of late Saxon Christian communities, topographic locations perhaps, that fitted their conceptions of hell as a form of living death, trapped within the fissures and cracks of the hellish underworld. Such conceptual ideas are from wholly late Anglo-Saxon sources. St Cuthman in Sussex is remembered for having caused an old woman to be picked up by the wind and blown across the downs before being swallowed into the earth at a place later known as Fippa's pit (Blair 1997). The sinners drowned in *Andreas* are swallowed by an awesome fissure in the earth (*Vercelli* XIV), a motif that occurs again in the foundation myth for Minster-in-Thanet, in which the wicked councillor Thunor was swallowed into the ground (Hollis 1998: 41). Later written sources attest to place-names that suggest localized folk superstitions surrounding these kinds of

---

[1] The sacred or holy hill of Zebrene in Semigallia, Latvia, acted as a natural pharmacy: its outstanding natural fertility led to the collection and use of plants from this site as medicinal remedies, with local communities revisiting the site to 'garden' and pick plants for medicinal remedies in the nineteenth century (Urtāns 2008). The acoustic qualities of natural locations were certainly taken into account too in the choice of assembly places (Sanmark and Semple 2010).

features: a *þyrs pytt* in Marlcliffe, Worcestershire (AD 883; [38] S222), for example, and Grimes Graves in Norfolk are both place-names that suggest pits; shafts and hollows might be suspected of hosting particularly nasty and malevolent creatures (see Chapter 5, pp. 172–86). There is virtually no archaeological evidence, however, for activity at caves, fissures, pits, or prehistoric mineshafts before the conversion to Christianity, with the exception of one instance of a sixth-century burial made in association with the spoil heaps from prehistoric flint mines at Blackpatch, Sussex (see Chapter 2, p. 23, Table 2.1 (b)).[2] It is possible that these types of features were as feared and avoided by early pre-Christian populations as they were by their Christian descendants, and the terrors associated with such sites easily translated into the Christian conceptions and horror of hell. It is also possible that late Anglo-Saxon fears and superstitions surrounding such features were products of an entirely new Christian conception of landscape (see pp. 188–92).

Watery features and locations are less debatable as places of import within the spiritual landscape (see Lund 2005, 2010; Semple 2010, 2011). Springs, wells, rivers, and lakes attracted activity of a ritual or religious nature in the pre-Christian and conversion period, as attested by finds of metalwork retrieved from rivers and the establishment of churches, standing crosses, and the application of Christian dedications to river crossings, springs, and wells (see Rattue 2001; Blair 2005: 477–8). Excavations in 1981 at Fiskerton, Lincolnshire, produced evidence for late prehistoric and Roman deposition of metalwork and organic material around a timber causeway crossing a wetland and tributary leading to the River Witham (Field and Parker Pearson 2003). Stocker and Everson (2003, table 17.1) have tracked these ritual practices along the Witham Valley into the late medieval period, identifying several items of late medieval weaponry from six further causeways along the river. Early medieval metalwork deposited before and after the conversion is now known from the Witham, the Rivers Thames, Kennet, Cherwell, Avon, Lea, Way and Nene (see Blair 1994: 99; Hines 1997: 381; Halsall 2000: 267–8; Lund 2005; 2010: Reynolds and Semple 2011). Wider survey is needed, alongside a critical assessment of patterns of deposition in relation to tidal regimes and river activity: not only could some material have eroded from *in situ* dry land deposits, but the types of activities associated with major rivers such as the Thames were significantly varied, for example, fairs, fishing, rogation-tide rituals, trading, domestic disposal, riverside churches, and burials (Cohen 2003). The recovery of a variety of objects of varying date, if intentionally deposited, implies, however, a much wider and

---

[2] Early medieval coin finds are known from: Merlewood Cave (Lancashire) and Attemire Cave (Yorkshire) (Rigold and Metcalf 1984: 262); both, however, date to the conversion period or later. The find from Merlewood (Lancashire) of seven, ninth-century coins was made in a very inaccessible cave in the face of a cliff.

complex set of traditions that may have varied between regions as well as over time (Reynolds and Semple 2011). Finds broadly indicate that crossing places and fording points, as well as bridges, were areas likely to attract such activity (see Lund 2010). Other watery locations with liminal status and subject to seasonal inundations, such as seasonal islands, tidal islands, intertidal zones, marshes, and fens, also held a special place in the minds of past communities in the prehistoric and historic periods (see, for example, the discussion of the ritual or spiritual importance in prehistory of intertidal zones and islands in Scarre 2002a, 2002b; see also Wickham-Crowley 2006; Flatman 2010). Islands, bridges, rivers, and streams often functioned as territorial divisions and boundaries in early medieval England (Cohen 2003). They were natural barriers, crossing places, and routes of communication. These 'liminal' and contrastingly 'accessible' qualities may have been particularly valued for assembly locations (see Semple and Sanmark 2013). Rivers, wet places, islands, or tidal confluences will have held different meanings for local, regional, and visiting populations. A deep-running, common concern, however, is with the liminal qualities of particular watery features. Perhaps fords, bridging points, tidal inlets, and river boundaries were particularly potent because if crossed or travelled upon there was a risk of moving from the real and present world into another supernatural world, even from the living to the dead. Julie Lund has argued for similar concerns and beliefs in Old Norse sources and has linked the deposited artefacts found at bridges and fords in Viking Age Scandinavia to the liminal concept of the bridge in the cognitive landscape (2005, 2008).[3]

Springs and wells are somewhat more complicated. John Blair has outlined how such natural water sources might have existed as pre-Christian cult-foci, surviving as cult-sites into the Christian period, representing an aspect of continuing popular belief (Blair 2005: 226–7, 472–3; Turner 2006: 132–3; Whitfield 2007). This appropriation could certainly happen at minster level (Rattue 2001: 55–61), but John Blair also postulates a 'much humbler level' of adoption, taking account of less formally developed landmarks (Blair 2005: 226, see also 477–8). Barton-on-Humber, where the tenth-century church is aligned on a group of wells, the alignment pointing to the pre-minster importance of the springs, is often cited as an exemplar (Rodwell and Rodwell 1982: fig. 6). There is, however, a strong possibility that, at Barton-on-Humber and at many other sites in the west of Britain, rather as clefts, hollows, and fissures became important elements within the Christian mental landscape, so springs and wells emerged as types of site that offered a spiritual legitimacy to new

---

[3] The positioning of major monasteries at river mouths or estuaries along the north-east coast of England implies a concern on the part of the Christian Church to take control of crossing places or important nodes in communication. It also perhaps permitted these communities to make symbolic statements regarding the subjugation of dangerous liminal places and the power of the Church to render them safe (Turner et al. 2013).

Christian foundations, irrelevant of any pre-Christian spiritual meaning (see Turner 2006: 132–3).

For our purposes here, it is sufficient to state that watery sites, especially rivers and notably crossing places and other liminal bodies of water and watery features, were likely important in a pre-Christian spiritual landscape. Their significance may have lain in a need to ensure a safe passage when travelling along or across them or their role as boundary markers. Their potency as places survived the conversion to Christianity and they attracted Christian markers including crosses, churches, shrines, Christian names and saintly associations, as well as rituals designed to draw on the power of these places or subdue it.[4]

Ancient monuments

The pre-Christian and Christian populations of England had a strong aesthetic awareness of their environment. Significant places were designated through their unusual attributes, their prominent visibility, shape, form, and even colour. Not all rivers and hills, fields, or groves were picked out as meaningful: it depended on how they were encountered visually or physically, as well as a myriad of different sensory attributes: colour, light, fresh or salt water, crossable, hidden, etc. Human-altered places, ancient monuments, and ruins were also important. Chapter 2 has shown already how the antecedent landscape shaped the funerary rituals of early medieval pre-Christian populations and how different varieties of monument were used from region to region. This alone suggests that monuments had more than a generic meaning to the pre-Christian population and that early communities were involved in carving out new ideas of connection to place and even ancestry. What is less well rehearsed is evidence of their use for purposes other than burial. We know that some early settlements were established in relation to prehistoric monument complexes, and that votive activity may on occasion have taken place in their environs too. Documentary sources suggest the association of some monuments with deities and heroes, and also indicate that on occasion prominent ancient monuments were the locations of battles, assemblies, and major meetings. This insinuates that some monuments accrued meaning as seminal places within the landscape and psyche of early Anglo-Saxon England. The local, it seems, began to give way to more selective legends and myths, perhaps rooted in real or invented memories that valorized some features and places over others.

---

[4] For example, the rites described in the Abingdon Chronicle that were used to decide upon the bounds of the monastic estate at Abingdon: 'they commit[ed] the shield with the sheaf and taper to the river which runs by the church, with a few brothers following in a boat. Thus the shield preceded them, and as if with a finger pointing out the lawful possessions of the House of Abingdon which lay close by, turning one moment here, one moment there; one moment to the right-hand side, the other to the left, the shield went faithfully before them until it came to the bank near the meadow which is called Beri . . .' (translation from North 1997: 190).

Gods and heroes

Although rare, monuments and sometimes identifiably prehistoric monuments did carry *theophoric* place-names. These are well known and offer several difficulties, including the problem of actually dating these names to an era before Christianity. Such names could stem from later literate and Christian traditions (Hines 1997). The Anglo-Saxon genealogies, for example, reveal exactly the kinds of process whereby kings established a lineage that enhanced their authenticity by the incorporation of mythical ancestors, including pagan gods, ancient heroes, and Christian biblical characters (see Sisam 1953; Dumville 1974, 1977). Bede, for example, lists the Hengist and Horsa as the ancestors of the Angles, citing them as 'the sons of Wictgils, whose father was Witta, whose father was Wecta, son of Woden, from whose stock sprang the royal house of many provinces' (*HE* I, 15). Later in this book, I argue that the association of prehistoric monuments with evil and heathen connotations formed a component within popular late Anglo-Saxon tradition (see Chapter 5). The association of barrows, linear earthworks, and other features with deities or mythical figures such as Woden, Tiw, or Freyr might fit this type of post-conversion perception too: connecting monuments with the imaginary, mythic, and supernatural as well as the malevolent and hellish. Such naming might also signal the emerging ambiguity of these important but heathen ancestral characters in the late Anglo-Saxon Christian mentality. Despite these concerns and putative late contexts, it is also possible, as suggested in past scholarship, that such names attest to pre-Christian activity of a spiritual nature (Stenton 1941; Gelling 1988; Hines 1997). These names, reviewed here, mainly reference natural places (see p. 67; Hines 1997: 385–6, table 12–1). Only a few reference monuments. Adam's Grave in Wiltshire is recorded as *wodnesbeorg*, 'hill or barrow', in the *Anglo-Saxon Chronicle* (E) in 592 and 715. To this can be added Wenslow, 'Woden's mound', Bedfordshire; Wednesbury, 'Woden's fort', Shropshire; Thunderlow, *Thunor's hlaw* (Essex), *Thunreslau* (Suffolk) and the lost *thunoreshlæw*, mentioned in the foundation myth for Minster-in-Thanet, Kent (see Hollis 1998). None of these can be identified with prehistoric features, but associations are made in these names with the *OE* terms for barrow, *hlāw*, and fortification, *burh*. Wansdyke in Wiltshire, named, as *wodnes dīc*, in the bounds of a late Anglo-Saxon charter, is a name that certainly includes a mention of Woden. This large earthwork is argued to be an early medieval construction, built perhaps as late as the eighth century (Reynolds and Langlands 2006). The name is suggested by these authors to reference the importance of this political division to the well-established, power base of Wessex—the royal line of which traced descent from Woden (see also Dumville 1974)—and the immediate presence of the important landmark of *wodnesbeorh* (See p. 71). Other less convincing examples, often cited, include Friday's Church, Sussex, where the twin prehistoric barrows could have had an association with Freyr (Coates 1982; Welch 1983).

These theophoric names are not certain references to pre-Christian sacred sites, but they are consistent in their reference to barrows, the occasional fortified enclosure, and two male gods: Woden and Thor. We know that Christian elite dynastic groups engaged in creative processes that used landmarks and important features as a means of giving more reality to the stories and claims of their ascent (Dumville 1974, 1977). Such myth-making processes may have been conscious or unconscious, but could have resulted in the ascription of mythical names and seminal events to major landmarks and important places. For example, can we be sure that when Cynric and Ceawlin fought against the Britons at *Bera's Stronghold* or Barbury Castle in Wiltshire they actually met and fought at the hill fort? The use of such features in stories, even when ideally placed as a location of conflict, could easily represent tropes. Hill forts and barrows were ideal landmarks for creating a sense of reality that linked legends to landscape and underpinned late Anglo-Saxon royal claims and power. The ascription of monuments to gods and heroes may thus have been part of a similar 'rewriting' of elite narrative and embedding of legend within the contemporary landscape, and, of course, places of pre-Christian importance may also have been subject to narratives aimed at discrediting their power and symbolism. Such associations must therefore be treated with caution: they may have developed from the pre-Christian importance of the ancient to local identity and beliefs but equally could represent the imaginings of a Christian age.

Terms for temple and shrine

This category of evidence poses similar problems. The *OE* term *hearg*, 'temple', occurs in an eighth-century charter (S106) and in ninth-century texts (Meaney 1995, 31), while the word *weoh*, 'holy place, idol, altar', features in an authentic late-seventh-century charter (S235, Whitelock 1955: 484, no. 58). These place-name terms have long been accepted as references to locations where pre-Christian 'temples' or 'altars' once existed, but recent research has raised the question of whether such associations could also be considered later, imaginative naming of unusual and prominent places marked by ruins and monuments (Semple 2007). Specially dedicated pre-Christian ritual buildings such as shrines or halls existed in Scandinavia and possibly England too (Walker 2010), but no correspondence has yet been identified between a place-name containing the *OE* element *hearg* or *weōh* and any physical evidence for a timber- or stone-built structure, or indeed settlement evidence of any kind. It has been suggested that places with names incorporating the term *hearg* were naturally distinctive locations with material evidence for long-lived activity from prehistory through to the Romano-British and early medieval periods. In particular, when identified on the ground, such places offered particularly strong evidence for Roman or Romano-British religious activity (e.g. Wood Eaton, Oxfordshire, and Thurstaston, Cheshire) (Semple 2007). These sites may thus have been active as spiritual places in the fifth to seventh centuries, but the naming could equally represent the ascription of the term 'temple' to sites perceived through ruins and ancient activity as old places of worship. Such naming might even represent the kind of re-imagined late Anglo-Saxon landscape in which heroes and gods and ancient events were instilled in the landscape through new stories built around the dynastic families that had come to rule the larger major kingdoms.

Very few examples can be identified in the modern landscape. Post-medieval and modern place-names that appear to contain these elements are not sufficiently robust as sources of evidence. 'Harrow' place-names, for example, are assumed to develop from the *OE* term for temple: *hearg*. New arguments have been made, however, for a separate genre of 'harrow' place-names that could originate out of reference to agricultural and farming practices of the pre- and post-Conquest period (Briggs 2010). Until a thorough revision is undertaken combining a new linguistic interrogation with archaeological and historical data within a landscape framework, it is difficult to say much beyond the fact that current preliminary research suggests that places with place-names containing the terms *hearg* and *weoh* frequently show signs of being closely associated in spatial terms with upstanding prehistoric monuments or monument complexes (for example, Waden Hill, Wiltshire), or Roman/Romano-British structural remains or ruins (for example, Thurstaston, Cheshire, and Wood Eaton, Oxfordshire).

Monuments and 'special deposits'

The potency of old burial mounds, ruined walls, and ancient forts certainly led to such sites being visited and used for burial. A more ephemeral class of material evidence suggests that other types of activity may have been taking place at some of these sites too. Visiting places and leaving objects or artefacts are things that even modern populations engage in. The deposition of coins at wishing wells, flowers and candles at prehistoric monuments, and rags at old 'sacred sites' or living trees are all small traditions pursued by some in the twenty-first century. Such practices imply an element of veneration, belief in the potency or efficacy of such features, and a sense that interaction with these sites can facilitate a beneficial connection with the 'other'. Such activities are common to most cultures and occur throughout human history. The Neolithic passage grave at Newgrange, Co. Meath, is well known for one of the largest collection of Roman material in Ireland including coins and jewellery (Edwards 1990: 3).

Fig. 3.3 Knap Hill, Wiltshire. Reproduced by permission of Paul Tubb. All rights reserved.

Such items attest to visitation, curiosity, and veneration of these ancient remains in the first to fourth centuries, and current interpretations even suggest the presence of a Roman temple at the site (Edwards 1990: 3). A more recent example can be found in the offerings by modern visitors at Chaco Canyon, Mexico. This ancient archaeological site now holds meaning for the Native Americans of the region and is the focus of new age rituals that include the deposition of objects such as the burial of crystals (Finn 1997: 169–78).

During excavations of the Neolithic causewayed enclosure at Knap Hill, Wiltshire, by the Cunningtons (experienced excavators for their time), a sixth-century iron sword was recovered from a long mound that on excavation was revealed as a late prehistoric midden (Cunnington 1911–12; Robinson 2002). Bone preservation is usually excellent on the North Wiltshire downs, but the sword is an entirely isolated find (see Figure 3.3). Again, on the chalk, this time in the north-west of Wiltshire, an isolated sixth- to seventh-century weapon group was recovered from within the hill fort at Barbury Castle (see Figure 3.4) (Meaney 1964: 265; Cunliffe 1978: 418, fig. 34; Swanton 1973: 81–3). These two instances are representative of a small collection of finds—all iron weapons—that may represent isolated 'special deposits' at prehistoric monuments (see Table 3.1 and Appendix 2).

In the corpus of ancient monuments reused as places for disposal of the dead, there are numerous instances of artefactual discoveries made without accompanying human remains. The reasons often lie in the underlying geology. The acid soils formed on sands and gravels devour the flesh and bones of the corpse, leaving only the artefacts that once accompanied the burial. In addition, where the finds are from antiquarian excavations, the discolouration that suggests human remains in acid soil conditions will often have been missed entirely. The finds and their contexts may also be badly disturbed, resulting in little if any evidence of the original funerary context. Even with these provisos firmly in mind, there still exists a small number of finds of weapons, like the Knap Hill sword and Barbury hoard, discovered at prehistoric and Roman

Fig. 3.4 Barbury Castle, Wiltshire. Reproduced by permission of Cambridge University.

monuments, without any discernible, immediate funerary context. In a number of instances, the finds are at monuments that have evidence for burial activity in the fifth to eighth centuries, but the artefacts have been recovered separately. For example, an iron spear-head recovered in the matrix of the reformed Bronze Age mound at Swallowcliffe Down (Wiltshire), may have been a redeposited find from an earlier disturbed grave, or a disturbed find from the robbed female burial, but it could also constitute a later deposit, struck into or buried in the mound after the female burial was interred. At Llandysilio, on the English–Welsh border, a comparable find constituted the discovery of a fifth- or sixth-century spear-head and javelin in the upper ditch fill on the north side of a large prehistoric round barrow (see Figure 3.5). The provenance of the spear-head and javelin from Llandysilio is given as the Germanic areas north of the Rhine (Barford et al. 1986). The excavators were able to show that the weapons were serviceable when deposited and probably complete with shafts. There were secondary burials present: a series of poorly dated inhumation graves, ascribed

Table 3.1 Weaponry found at prehistoric monuments in possible non-funerary contexts

Location	Find	Date	Monument type
Cherbury Camp, BRK	E1 spear-head	C6th or earlier	Hill fort
Devil's Dyke, CBM	Collection of weaponry, spur, and stirrup	C5–7th?	Linear earthwork
Badbury Rings, DOR	E1 spear-head	C6th or earlier	Hill fort
Hardown Hill, DOR	Collection of weaponry, brooches	Early Anglo-Saxon	Low barrow
Spettisbury Rings, DOR	Spear-heads	C5–7th?	Surface finds at hill fort
Wendens Ambo, ESX	Iron work, spears	C5–7th?	Mutlow Hill, mound and assembly-place
Preston Candover, HMP	Spear-head and seax	As late as C7–8th	Barrow in 'Long Barrow Field'
Whitchurch, HMP	Sword	C6–7th?	Long barrow/round barrow
Ditton, KNT	Spear-head	C5–6th?	Natural knoll/barrow
Langham, NFK	Iron spear-head and boss	C5–7th	Bronze Age round barrow
Poningland, NFK	5–6 spear-heads	C6–7th	Barrow
Barrasford, NTB	Boss, silver discs from shield, broad two-edged sword, and knife	C6–7th	Bronze Age cairn
Chinnor, OXF	Spear-heads and scabbard chape	Undated	Pair of barrows
Lyneham, OXF	Boss, seax, spear-heads	As late as C7–8th	Shield-boss by long barrow, spear-heads to north-east edge of camp
Ramshorn, STF	Iron spear-head	C5–7th?	Large old barrow
Coombes, SSX	Knife and spear	C11th?	Bronze Age barrow
Barbury Castle, WLT	Seax, knives, iron spear-heads	C6–8th?	Found in two places within hill fort
Swallowcliffe Down, WLT	Spear-head	C7th?	In top of mound material to southern edge of Bronze Age barrow containing C7th female secondary burial
Knap Hill, WLT	Iron sword	C6th?	Long mound
Fimber, YOE	Spear-head	Undated	Prehistoric barrows
Severus's Hills, YOW	Spear-head	C10th	Glacial mounds
Four Crosses, Llandysilio	Spear-heads	C5–7th	Bronze Age mound

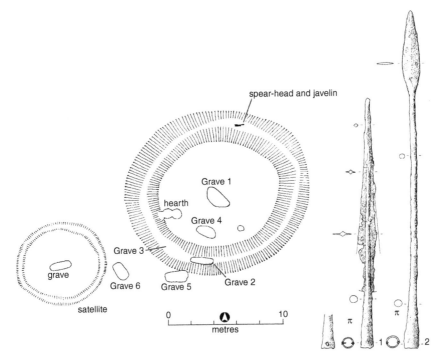

Fig. 3.5 Early medieval burials situated at a cluster of prehistoric barrows at Llandysilio in Wales, with evidence for the separate deposition of several spear-heads. After Barford, Owen and Britnell 1986: fig 7. Reproduced by permission of Bill Britnell.

to the early medieval period, lay on the opposite side of the ring-ditch, but the weapons were regarded by the excavators as a separate stage of activity: 'they were at an angle of about 15° from the horizontal, sockets uppermost, and points towards the east. About half their length fell within the upper humic filling of the ditch (layer 2), and the lower half within a more gravelly secondary fill (layer 3), as though they had been thrust right into the ground' (Barford et al. 1986: 10). The excavators argued that these were deposited separately from the inhumations, the shafts left jutting out above the surface. At Wredon Hill in Staffordshire, an iron spear-head and knife were located some considerable distance from two centrally placed, extended inhumations in a prehistoric mound (Bateman 1861: 122–3). The weaponry is not dated, but is described as an iron spear-head with shaft remaining, and a narrow iron knife some 8 inches (c.20 centimetres) long, which suggests a seax.

   All the examples presented must be treated with extreme caution, but particularly Wredon and its like, which represent finds recovered by antiquarian excavators. Another tantalizing example is listed by Bateman at Vincent Knoll, Derbyshire: a Bronze Age barrow reused for a series of early medieval secondary burials. A small iron spear-head of fifth- to sixth-century date (type E1) was recorded as a separate find, not belonging to any interment (Bateman 1861: 49–50; Swanton 1974: 87). A spear-head and seax were retrieved from a prehistoric barrow at Preston Candover, Hampshire—the spear-head in the barrow and the seax from the edge—although the barrow may have been part ploughed, resulting in disturbed finds (Shore 1893: 285–6). If these represent intentional deposits, they can be grouped into two broad categories: weaponry left in isolation or thrust into prehistoric monuments, mainly barrows; and groups of iron weapons or weapon hoards deposited at hill forts and linear entrenchments. The discovery at Barbury Castle is described as a collection of spear-heads, knives, and a seax (suggestive of a seventh-century date) positioned inside the hill fort (Cunnington 1933–4: 174); whereas at Devil's Dyke, Cambridgeshire, again on the chalk, a collection of weapons described as a pair of throwing axes, a spur, stirrup, and a lance head with a long slender blade were recovered during the levelling of a portion of the dyke (Fox 1923: 263, 292, pl. 35). To this we can add single iron spear-heads of sixth-century date from Cherbury hill fort (Berkshire), from Badbury hill fort (Dorset), and a group, also broadly of the sixth century, from Spettisbury Rings (Dorset) (for all see Swanton 1973: 37–9, 49–51, 77–83; 1974, 40, 30, 83) (although these latter three finds would fit in either category).

The majority of items deposited are spear-heads, although swords and seaxes also feature. In most instances the objects cannot be closely dated, but the chronological range of the weaponry listed in Appendix 2 stretches from the fifth to the tenth and eleventh centuries, with the majority falling into the sixth- to seventh-century range. The finds of tenth- to eleventh-century date at Combes, Sussex, and Severus's Hills, Yorkshire, both of spear-heads attributed in terms of form and decoration as Scandinavian in manufacture, are particularly important as they demonstrate the placement of weaponry at prehistoric monuments in an era when burial at prehistoric monuments accompanied by weapons and dress fittings had ceased to occur (see Dixon 1849: 269; Grinsell 1934: 236; Lang 1981: 159–60).

The explanation of these finds as 'special' deposits is clearly contentious—it relies on problematic source material and disputable secondary accounts. It is worth considering, however, that this limited evidence compares favourably with that for an analogous rite: the deposition of weaponry and tools in rivers at crossing places (see pp. 72–3). Despite considerable doubt, this is now accepted as an activity taking place along several major and minor English rivers, both before and after the conversion to Christianity and long after the end of Anglo-Saxon power (Wilson 1965; Fitzpatrick 1984; Blair 1994: 99; Hines 1997: 380–1; Halsall 2000: 268; Lund 2005, 2010; Semple 2010; Reynolds and Semple 2011). In a recent article by Julie Lund (2010: 58), deposits of weaponry and other items from English rivers are discussed alongside evidence for the deposition of smith's tool chests or tool hoards from similar watery locations, for example, the Hurbuck Hoard from Shalbrook

Burn, Lanchester (Hodges 1905, 215) and the Nazeing Hoard from the bank of the River Lea (Morris 1983). More investigation is needed, but weapons and weapon hoards deposited at prehistoric monuments, particularly spears cast or thrust into monuments, might be considered to fit a similar repertoire of activity as the weaponry and tool hoards recovered from wet contexts. A final point of note is that the votive deposition of weapons has long been recognized as a facet of prehistoric ritual practice (Bradley 1998b: 1–42) and watery contexts, *and* ancient monuments—notably burial mounds—are suggested and proven as typical locations at which such ritualized hoarding or deposition might occur (Levy 1982; Bradley 1987b: 354). An interesting combination of ancient monument and watery site is represented by the find of an isolated fifth-century sword concealed in a ruinous Roman bath-house in a villa at Feltwell, Thetford, in Norfolk.

Other object types can also be included in this discussion. Again, with the same provisos in mind, we might reconsider some of the following finds. The metalwork recovered at Lilla Howe in Yorkshire (Wilson 1964: 19–20; Hinton 1978: 152; Watkin and Mann 1981) was thought to represent a burial, but is now suggested as a possible hoard (Halsall 2000: 267). Other isolated dress items and jewellery of early Anglo-Saxon date are known from ancient monuments, but are difficult to interpret as special deposits with any kind of certainty; for example, a hanging bowl and escutcheon from a Bronze Age round barrow at Garrett Piece, Derbyshire (Ozanne 1962–3: 22); a silver-gilt mount with *niello* decoration and an inset garnet used as an early seventh-century fitting for a sword scabbard from Adam's Grave, Wiltshire (Robinson 2002: 3); or a copper-alloy brooch and bracelet from the lynchets at Woolbury Ring, Hampshire (Anon. 1932–4: 208). Although these all could easily represent casual losses or disturbed funerary assemblages, they may also point to the purposeful deposition at prehistoric sites of additional types of artefacts besides weapons. Coins too are also retrieved on occasion at prehistoric monuments and usually considered casual losses and evidence of marketing or fairs. Seventh- to eighth-century sceattas have been located at the hill forts of Hod Hill, Dorset (Metcalf 1984: coin no. 5; Rigold and Metcalf 1984: 252); Hunsbury, Northamptonshire (Meaney 1964: 189; Webster and Cherry 1972; Rigold and Metcalf 1984: 253; Metcalf 1993–4: pl. 6, no. 109); St Catherine's Hill, Hampshire (Rigold and Metcalf 1984: 261), and Walbury, Inkpen, Berkshire (Rigold and Metcalf 1984: 264; Gunstone 1992: coin nos 480 and 482; Metcalf 1993–4: pl. 18, no. 313; pl. 20, no. 344; pl. 20, no. 349; pl. 21, no. 364; pl. 27, no. 452). A group of ninth-century coins was discovered at Castle Head, Penwortham, in Lancashire (Stockdale 1978 [1872]: 5, 203; Baines 1836: 628, 64) and a small tenth-century coin hoard at Spettisbury Rings (Dorset), where a single, sixth-century iron spear-head was also recovered (Metcalf and Jonsson 1980). A single tenth-century coin was even found at Stonehenge, Wiltshire (Gunstone 1992: coin no. 536). Coins are usually interpreted as evidence of productive sites but such locations are notable for hundreds if not thousands of coins (Ulmschneider 2000: 11). These casual losses or small groups of coins may reflect markets and fairs, but votive practices should not be dismissed out of hand. Roman votive activity at temples and sometimes at monuments of early and late prehistoric date often involved the deposition of coins and items of jewellery. Prehistoric barrows, for example, may yield significant quantities of Roman coins, suggesting that they were venerated sites during the Roman era, such as Walkington Wold, Yorkshire (Bailey 1985; Buckberry and Hadley 2007).

The holding of medieval and late medieval fairs at prehistoric monuments offers an alternative interpretation. Stonehenge, for example, is recorded as a market site in the twelfth century (Grinsell 1976b), and fairs situated in hill forts in western England are documented as late as the nineteenth century. Another type of gathering recorded on occasion at prehistoric monuments is the outdoor assembly or moot (see pp. 89–94). Assemblies may have involved marketing activities and the carrying of and the deposition of weapons: John Blair has previously suggested a connection between weapon-finds in rivers and the use of fords and bridges as late Anglo-Saxon meeting places (1994: 99). Monuments were also used for mustering military forces: when Alfred called the men of Somerset, Wiltshire, and Hampshire to him at Egbert's Stone in 878, he called a military muster and an assembly (*ASC* (A) 878). The significance of prehistoric monuments as battle locations, is considered next (pp. 89–94). Barbury Castle, Knap Hill, and Adam's Grave, all sites with isolated weapon or weapon-related finds, are also recorded as early battle sites. Perhaps such places served a variety of activities that could account for both intentional deposition and casual loss of weapons, coins, and other artefacts.

Monuments and battles

This book opened with the unusual entry in the *Anglo-Saxon Chronicle* for the year 1006 (E) which described a show of bravado by the Viking raiding party at the large barrow known as *Cwicchelmes hlæwe [Cwichelmeshlæwe]*. Early medieval warfare is argued as a ritualized form of encounter that involved small armies and designated and chosen places of both muster and combat (Halsall 1989). Several battles are recorded between AD 600 and 850 at locations marked by ancient remains (see Table 3.2). Cynric and Ceawlin fought the British at Bera's stronghold in 556 (*ASC* (E)). Bera's stronghold or *Beran byrg* is Barbury Castle, an Iron Age hill fort in North Wiltshire (Figure 3.4). Ceawlin was later defeated by the British, resulting in 'great carnage' at *Wodnesbeorg* in AD 592 (*ASC* (E)). Woden's barrow, a chambered long barrow in North Wiltshire, is now known as Adam's Grave. A second major battle is recorded here in 715 between Ine of Wessex and Ceolred of Mercia (*ASC* (E)). Additional possibilities include

Table 3.2 Battles AD 450–850 recorded in both the *Anglo-Saxon Chronicle (ASC)* (E) and Bede, *HE*

Date	Battle	Location
455	Hengist and Horsa versus Vortigern	*Agelesford*, Aylesford, ford on River Medway, KNT
456	Hengist and Æsc versus the Britons	Crayford, a river crossing, KNT
465	Hengist and Æsc versus the Welsh	*Wippedesfleot*, unidentified
477	Ælle and companions fought on landing	*Cymenes ora*, The Owers, sandbanks at Selsey, SSX
485	Ælle versus the Welsh	*Mearcrædes burnan*, unidentified
491	Ælle and Cissa besiege the British	*Anderitum, Andredes cester*, Pevensey, SSX
495	Cerdic and Cynric versus the Welsh	*Cerdices Ora*, Cerdic's shore
501	Port and sons versus the British	Portsmouth, possibly Portchester, HMP
508	Cerdic and Cynric versus the British	*Cerdices ford*, Charford, HMP
514	Stuf and Wihtgar versus the British	*Cerdices Ora*, Cerdic's shore
519	Cerdic and Cynric versus the British	*Cerdices ford*, Charford, HMP
552	Cynric versus the Britons	*Searo byrig*, Old Sarum, WLT
556	Cynric and Ceawlin versus the British	*Beran byrg*, Barbury Castle, WLT
568	Ceawlin and Cutha versus Æthelbert	*Wibbandun*, unidentified hill
571	Cutha versus Britons	*Biedcanford*, unidentified ford
577	Cuthwine and Ceawlin versus Britons	*Dyrham*, Avon River crossing, Bath, SOM
584	Ceawlin and Cutha versus British	*Fethanleag*, lost near Stoke Lyne, OXF
592	Ceawlin versus British?	*Wodnesbeorg*, long barrow, WLT
605	Æthelfrith versus Welsh	Chester, CHE
614	Cynegils versus Cwichelm	*Beandun*, unidentified
617	Æthelfrith versus Rædwald	River Idle, NTT
641	Oswald versus Penda	*Maserfeld* (Oswestry?), SHR
654	Oswy versus Penda	*Winwidfeld*, near flooded River Winwæd near the Humber
658	Cenwalh versus Welsh	*Peonnum*, Penselwood, WLT
661	Cenwalh	*Posentes byrig*, unidentified
675	Wulfhere versus Æscwine	*Biedan heafde*, unidentified
685	Ecgfrith killed	Firth of Forth, Anglian–Scots border
710	Beorhtfrith versus Picts	Between Avon and Carron, Anglian–Scots border
715	Ine versus Ceolred	*Wodnesbeorg* long borrow, WLT
716	Osred killed	Northumbrian and Mercian border
752	Cuthred versus Aethelbald	*Beorhford*, unidentified
761	Moll versus Oswine	*Ædwines clif*, unidentified, possibly Eildon Hills, Roxburghshire
777	Cynewulf and Offa	Benson/*Bensington*, OXF
778	Æthelbald and Heardberht	*Cininges clife*, Coniscliffe, and *Helathyrne*, unidentified
798	Alric and others killed	Whalley, on the River Ribble, LNC

(Continued)

Table 3.2 Continued

Date	Battle	Location
800	Hwicce and the Wiltshire men	Kempsford, GLO–WLT border
823	Britons versus Devon men	*Gafol-ford*, 'tax ford', Galford on the River Lew, DEV
823/5	Egbert versus Beornwulf	*Ellendun*, Elderbush Down near Wroughton, WLT
833	Egbert versus Danes	Carhampton, royal estate on the Bristol channel, SOM
837	Ealdorman Wulfheard versus Danes	Southampton, HMP
840	King Æthelwulf versus Danes	Carhampton, SOM
848	Dorset and Somerset men versus Danes	Mouth of the River Parrett, SOM

Cenwalh's challenge to the Welsh at Penselwood in 658 (*ASC* (E)), supposedly close to Keniwilkin's Castle (Kenwalch's Castle, Somerset; Swanton 1996, 32, n. 1), and two years later a second confrontation involving Cenwalh at *Posentes byrg* (*ASC* 661 (A), *byrig* (E)), a name that means a fortified stronghold but is still unidentified at present. Another interesting entry for 552 records a battle between Cynric and the British at *Searo byrig*: Old Sarum, Salisbury, Wiltshire (Hill 1962, 51–3). The remaining battle locations listed in the *Anglo-Saxon Chronicle* include mainly fording places and crossing points on rivers, with the occasional ridge and hill, cliff, and island and mentions of the *feld* and even a *leāh* (see Table 3.2). Three entries record battles at Roman settlements: at *Anderitum* (491), Portchester (501), and Chester (605). Just as Sarum is suspected to be an occupied rather than abandoned earthwork defended by the British against the West Saxons, so these Roman sites are considered to be occupied and defended places. *Anderitum* and Portchester are third- and fourth-century Saxon shore forts. Chester, a Roman fort and town, lies on the River Dee looking out over the Welsh border. By the late fifth and early sixth centuries, these sites may have been landmarks and reminders of a Romano-British and British past. Some were certainly occupied and defended. Whether reoccupied as strategic military locations or simply iconic, on occasion such sites were used for battle. It is possible that some old monuments may have been intentionally chosen as landmarks for ritualized encounters between small groups of forces.

These battles feature in the *Anglo-Saxon Chronicle*, which survives as a late-tenth-century manuscript with its origins in the late ninth century. This archetype was a composite document, drawing on several earlier sources for its information (Swanton 1996: pp. xi–xxxv, esp. pp. xviii–xix). The reporting of the pre-ninth-century battles and their locations thus relies on already ancient tales and folk memory. The dates and details of battles and their locations is therefore best treated with caution as an accurate record, although it remains equally important that the composers of the ninth- and tenth-century chronicles chose to correlate these events to specific types of location. They selected legends, folk tales, and information from older documents in their creation of the chronicles, and what they produced, even if an invention in part, shows that they envisaged and believed the key battles that created an English kingdom and identity took place at iconic sites: major ancient monuments, ancient forts, and significant natural landmarks. There is no reason to assume that the list of battle locations relayed in the chronicle is entirely creative. The entry for 1006 is informative in its suggestion that a force or army might encamp as a challenge at a particular place, inviting the opposition to meet them at a specific landmark. It is interesting to note that the contemporary account for 1006 records the raiding army, still unchallenged, abandoned *Cwicchelmes hlæwe [Cwichelmeshlæwe]*, moving south on the Ridgeway pushing down into the heart of the West Saxon landscape. The English were awaiting them, assembled at the River Kennet (*ASC* 1006 (E)). The Ridgeway crosses the River Kennet at East Kennett, a fording place overlooked by numerous large prehistoric barrows, including two chambered long barrows (see Figure 3.6). It is the site of The Sanctuary, a timber henge that, although long gone by the eleventh century, lay at the end of an avenue of standing stones connected to the great henge at Avebury. The site was in view of Silbury Hill as well as Avebury. It was overlooked by Waden Hill (*OE weoh + dun*, 'idol' or 'shrine' on the 'hill'), and situated at the natural entrance to a corridor of land marked by places dedicated to Woden (see pp. 75–6), the sites of past battles (see pp. 44, 84), *and* the ancestral graves of seventh-century elites (see Chapter 3, pp. 43–4, Figure 2.9). The Danish chose to challenge the English at an emotive and important monument. The English could not have selected a more intimidating locale, or one vested with so much ancestral value, at which to attempt a vengeful rout of the Danish army.

If a late Anglo-Saxon Christian military favoured encounters at auspicious and propitious places, then perhaps the British and pre-Christian Anglo-Saxons did so too in earlier centuries. The locations listed are sites that may have been significant in the mentalities and ideologies of either of the combative sides. In the mid-sixth century, the West Saxon king Cynric and his son Ceawlin faced the British at *Beran byrig*, the Iron Age hill fort of Barbury Castle in Wiltshire, having previously defeated them at *Searo byrig*, Old Sarum by Salisbury (*ASC* 552 (E)). Both ancient forts were located at crucial locales, overlooking significant crossroads and routes that gave access to the Thames Valley to the north and the Avon flood plains to the south and the south coast. Neither monument has provided significant material evidence for fifth- or sixth-century settlement or re-fortification, although other western hill forts were reoccupied and re-fortified in the fifth century (see Dark 1994a, 1994b; Yorke 1995: 19–24, 26–7). Both sites are iconic landmarks and may have been emblematic of the diminished Romano-British authority and power in this region in a bygone era, or perhaps represented legendary sites, redolent with the tales of the pre-Roman past and legends of long distant acts of heroism and resistance to a Roman invasion.

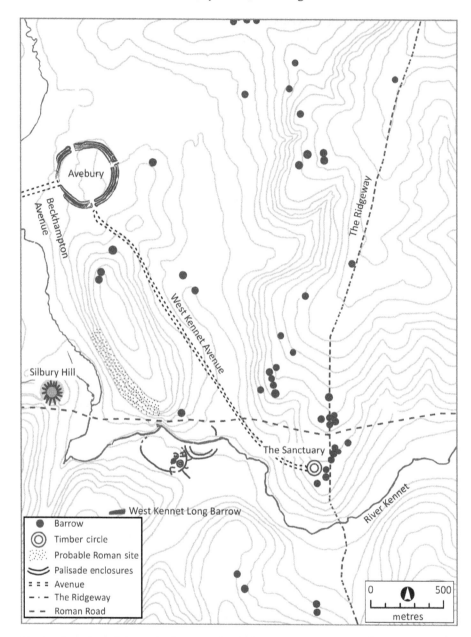

Fig. 3.6 Location of the ambush site at the fording place on the River Kennet, Wiltshire, where Anglo-Saxon military forces failed to stem the return of the Danish raiding army to the south coast (*ASC* 1006 (E)). © Crown Copyright/database right 2012. An Ordnance Survey/EDINA supplied service.

Such emotional investments in place can only be imagined. Archaeologists and historians are left solely with the brief chronicle entries and the sites themselves. From this, a tentative conclusion can be proffered. Ancient encampments and barrows may have been chosen as battle sites in the pre-Christian centuries and after. They were also remembered and later recorded as landmarks that signalled places of decisive engagements: conflicts that were crucial to a late Anglo-Saxon sense of identity rooted in stories of the successful conquest and colonization of a British land by Germanic invaders. The late Anglo-Saxon populations certainly remembered these places and perhaps treated sites such as Adam's Grave (*wodnesbeorh*) with the same kind of reverence and curiosity that modern populations display for medieval and post-medieval battle sites such as Flodden and Bosworth Field. Before moving on it is worth re-emphasizing that two of the early battle sites marked by ancient forts or barrows are monuments where fifth- to seventh-century weaponry was recovered without a burial context and one is recorded as a late Anglo-Saxon shire assembly.

Monuments and assemblies

It seems natural to discuss the evidence for early assemblies at prehistoric sites next, although, in the last chapter of this book, assemblies, meeting places, and late Anglo-Saxon administrative arrangements are returned to in a discussion of the role of ancient monuments in the late Anglo-Saxon legal landscape. The summary here is therefore brief, and relates particularly to evidence that might imply the use of monuments as meeting places in the pre-Christian and conversion era.

Assembly occurred within late Anglo-Saxon society at a range of scales, and royal *witans* or councils were very specific events. Alongside these major meetings recorded at courts, palaces, hunting lodges, estates, and towns, assemblies were held at shire and also hundredal levels. Shires, at least in the south-west, are considered of seventh- or eighth-century origin, and their existence becomes explicit in the eighth century (Reynolds 1999: 72–3). Equivalent units can be found in the lathes in Kent and Bede's description of *regiones*, resulting in the reconstruction of possible regions or 'shires' in the north (see O'Brien 2011). The hundred is accepted as a basic unit of local governance 'from at least the tenth century, when it is first mentioned explicitly in a document of King Edgar's reign (AD 957–75), known as the "Hundred Ordinance" (Reynolds 1999: 75–81). There are good reasons to suspect these local units have their origins in a much earlier time, although there is evidence that local divisions were tightened or tidied up by late Anglo-Saxon kings in a more uniform system of local management (Reynolds 1999: 76). The meeting places themselves have been considered by some as archaic and ancient, and, again, there are reasons to believe at least some hundred meeting sites do reflect places of early political and perhaps even cultic importance for small polities and 'tribal' groupings. Places of assembly and inauguration are in evidence in several late prehistoric societies in northern Europe, and this has provided a basis for some scholars to assert a pre-Christian origin for assembly in England, suggesting that such gatherings may have had both religious and legal functions like their European counterparts (Meaney 1995, 1997). In these analogous early systems of power, for example, in Scandinavia and Ireland, ancient monuments played a prominent part (see respectively Newman 1997; Brink 2001). The earliest English evidence, drawn from written accounts and place-names, is, however, quite ambiguous, and seems to underline the great importance of outdoor meetings in 'untouched' natural places.

When Augustine and his mission set foot in Kent in 597, Bede described (some 135 years later) how Æthelbert met with the priest in the open air: 'he took precautions that they should not approach him in a house; for he held an ancient superstition that, if they were practisers of magical arts, they might have opportunity to deceive and master him' (*HE* I, 25; Sherley-Price 1968, 69). This extract is regularly cited as evidence for early traditions of outdoor assembly alongside the more problematic account in *Germania* of outdoor judicial assemblies (*Germania* 11 and 12). The early emphasis on outdoor meetings, however, has recently been underlined by the identification of a series of place-names that contain two Old English words that seemed to have had an archaic usage as assembly terms in England (see Pantos 2004a for a full discussion). The *OE* term *þing* seems to have had the meaning 'to hold a meeting' (Stanley 1979; Pantos 2004a: 183) but is not found outside poetic texts. It does, however, appear in the laws of Hlothere and Eadric and is argued to be an antique and archaic term, inherited from Old Frisian (Stanley 1979: 179–84). *Mæðel* meaning 'assembly' exists almost exclusively in poetry but is used twice in early law codes (Pantos 2004b: 183). Both are argued to have disappeared from general use, replaced by other terminologies in the law codes by the late seventh century. They remained in use in poetry, however, as literary terms for assemblies and meetings (Pantos 2004b: 4). Old English *þing* place-names are hard to distinguish from *þing*-names that derive from Old Norse and can be attributed to the Scandinavian settlement of England. Of the few that lie outside of areas of Scandinavian settlement and influence—Thinghill (Hereford), Tinhale (Sussex), Thingley and Tinkfield (Wiltshire)—none has a name that implies a meeting associated with a prehistoric monument; only hills, wood pasture, and the *feld* are referred to. Where place-names containing the element *mæðel* can be identified, five are combined with words for trees or stands of trees, for example, Madehurst (Sussex) and Malehurst (Shropshire), 'wooded hill', and Matlock (Derbyshire), 'oak tree'. Other documented early assemblies include one of the first Christian synods in 603. Augustine met with the British bishops at a conference called by Æthelbert at a place that in Bede's time was remembered by the name 'Augustine's Oak' and that lay on the border between the

Hwiccas and the West Saxons (*HE* II, 2; Sherley-Price 1968: 101). These sources suggest that early meetings took place in open and wooded landscapes, at natural sites, *away* from the influences of the living in settlements and the dead in ancient barrows and monuments. This provides a sharp contrast to activities evident in Ireland and in parts of Scandinavia. Moving later in time, when the system of meeting sites serving the late Anglo-Saxon hundredal system is examined, the preponderance of natural locations as chosen hundred meeting sites is also noticeable (see pp. 213–21).

The hundred meeting was essentially a place for the resolution of local dispute (Liebermann 1913; Loyn 1984; Wormald 1999). It is within this category of assembly that the use of open air meeting sites is most common. In contrast to the *witan*, which was frequently situated as we have seen in settlements, palaces, and churches, the hundred assembly seems to have taken place at a wide range of physical, visual landmarks (such as stones, trees, fording places, thorn bushes) and at ancient monuments too. Sometimes the named features were ephemeral and seasonal, for instance, Hemlingford Hundred, Warwickshire: *Humilieford* 1162, 'ford by the wild hops' (Mawer and Stenton 1936: 12–13). Others were natural meeting places and landmarks, such as Barlichway Hundred, Warwickshire: *Barlicheweihund* 1174, 'road along which barley was carried' (Mawer and Stenton 1936: 193). Dugdale (1656) recorded the location of this hundred meeting place as a 'plot of ground about eight yards square, now enclosed with a hedge and situated upon the top of a Hill in the way between Haseler and Binton and about half a mile from Temple Grafton, which is reported to be the very place where these three parishes do meet'. Other hundred names do, however, suggest the use of ancient monuments, for example, Knightlow Hundred, Warwickshire: *Cnichtelawav* 1169, 'hill or barrow of the young warriors or knights' (Mawer and Stenton 1936: 95).

It has been rather uncritically assumed, since Liebermann (1913) and Anderson (1934–9), that the named place or feature referenced in hundred names must represent the place of the assembly. It is clear, however, that local geographies changed, that multiple assembly sites existed in some hundreds, and that some documented assembly places were not apparently situated at the place indicated by the hundred name (see Pantos 2002 for an extensive and critical survey). This suggests some caution in accepting that every site, monument, or feature listed in surviving hundred names represented a location of late Anglo-Saxon assembly. The assembly site for Tremelau Hundred, Warwickshire, for example, is identified with the surviving field-name Moot Hill (*Mutt Hill*) in Lightbourne 'to the east of the church on a well-marked hill', but *not* with an alternative site marked with one or more surviving tumuli (see Mawer and Stenton 1936: 247–8). Another interesting case is the hundred of Hormer in Berkshire, the name of which implies a lake or mere as a focus for the assembly, but the hundred meeting place, which is recorded specifically several times, is the ancient wood of Bagley. It is a difficult topic and a full revision of the evidence led by the *Landscapes of Governance* project at UCL is much antici-pated. It is clear, however, that the planned hundredal administrative system rolled out in the tenth and eleventh centuries formalized and drew upon some pre-existing, less structured, fragmentary, and localized systems of assembly, and as a consequence some old assembly sites were certainly retained, although others were replaced.

Some archaic places of assembly that may have been retained include the monuments apparently referenced in the hundred names of Thunderlow, Essex (*Thunres hlāw*): 'the mound of Thunor'; and Wenslow, Bedfordshire (*Wōdnes hlāw*): 'Woden's mound' (Meaney 1997: 198). Such names are more of a rarity than a norm, and Audrey Meaney has pointed to Margaret Gelling's assertion that 'pagan names' reflect areas where heathenism was persistent into Christian times (Meaney 1997: 198–9; Gelling 1961: 20). By this argument, these meeting places associated with 'pagan' deities as well as mounds or barrows were late survivals: last vestiges of persistent pagan belief in a newly Christian world that survived within the late Anglo-Saxon administrative system. Neither mound can now be identified nor their origin or date. It is entirely possible that these were early Anglo-Saxon, Romano-British, Roman, prehistoric, or simply nat-ural features. Correlations between named hundred meeting places and sites or features of early Anglo-Saxon date or earlier monumental features are, in fact, quite rare in some areas. In Meaney's study of the Cambridge region, of the fifty-seven hundred meeting places listed, only three or four prehistoric barrows and one Roman site can be identified. Of the potential 'Anglo-Saxon features', we can include plenty of bridges, a brushwood causeway, a *hlōse* or shed, a *stoc* or secondary settlement, a single barrow, a *stapol* or pillar, two crosses, and one *worþ* or settlement. The seventh-century Anglo-Saxon burial mound at Mutlow Hill, Uttlesford, and perhaps Wenslow, Thunderlow, and Staploe, are the only sites that might be associated with early Anglo-Saxon monumental features. There are, however, ten undated mounds mentioned, including Wenslow and Thunder-low (Meaney 1997: 234–9). Thus natural features and places are the most com-monly recorded meeting foci in the hundred names. A handful of features of Anglo-Saxon date are attested, and an even smaller number may refer to markers of pre-Christian significance, but a significant proportion refers to undated mounds—perhaps natural or man-made. In some instances, such as at Secklow, meeting mounds have been argued to be purpose-built in the late Anglo-Saxon era as places for assembly (Adkins and Petchey 1984).

The rarity of associations between known places of early Anglo-Saxon activ-ity, especially burial, is reflected more widely in the national record, although a small but highly informative group of hundred meeting places that are excep-tional in their apparent relationship with pre-Christian cemeteries does exist. This has recently prompted an extensive survey of eastern and southern England, which has provided some evidence for the use of ancient monuments and palimpsests, and early Anglo-Saxon 'folk' cemeteries (Brookes in press). Loveden Hill is widely acknowledged as a late Anglo-Saxon hundred meeting place and an extensive early Anglo-Saxon cremation cemetery situated around a natural barrow-shaped knoll (Williams 2002: 355–7; 2004: 119–24); the cemetery at Bowcombe Down, Isle of Wight, became a hundred meeting place, as did a barrow or barrow-shaped knoll at Mutlow Hill (*(ge)mōt-hlāw* or 'meeting mound') at Wendens Ambo, Uttlesford, Essex; and finally the recently excavated cemetery complex at Saltwood, near Folkestone in East Kent, emerged as the site of the hundred assembly in the late Anglo-Saxon era (Glass et al. 2011).

At Wendens Ambo in Essex, Mutlow Hill lies just to the north of Uttlesford Bridge, which preserves the name of Uttlesford Hundred. Mutlow Hill is identified as the hundred meeting place. This is a natural prominence, but accounts indicate that discoveries of early medieval spear-heads, a shield-boss, pots, and other bits of iron were made in the nineteenth century, but no evidence of burials was forthcoming (Fox 1925: 265). To the south-west of Mutlow Hill is an important large villa complex with preceding activity of Iron Age date (Powell 1963: 199, pl. XXIX B; Scott 1993: 66).

Across the border in Cambridgeshire, another Mutlow can be found, marking a break in the Fleam Dyke. Here, excavations in 1852 identified a Bronze Age barrow and a Roman 'temple' comprising a circular structure associated with finds of brooches of the first to fourth century AD as well as coins and bracelets (Neville 1852: 226–30; Fox 1923: 35–6, 187). This complex is directly positioned on the Bronze Age barrow. It also lies close to an important villa complex. The ditch is thought to be an early medieval construction, and by the late Anglo-Saxon era the barrow served as a meeting place (Reaney 1943: 138). This example is discussed by Brookes, who also notes that the location indicates the meeting mound may have operated on a nodal boundary, serving all three neighbouring hundreds, and may thus intimate the existence of a larger territorial grouping, pre-dating the hundredal system (Brookes in press). Mutlow Hill in Uttlesford seems to have served only this unit, but it would have provided a highly accessible and central location situated next to a fording place, a river course, and a major land route.

This emerging evidence corroborates some of the arguments made separately by Williams and Semple for cemeteries, particularly those situated at prominent landmarks, reusing ancient monuments and with new monumental additions such as mounds and posts, or structures as likely places of early gathering and assembly (Semple 2004; Williams 2004). It also ties into the suggestions posed at the end of Chapter 2 and the beginning of this chapter regarding the role of burial sites and barrows as features that connected people to landscape and helped shape identity and local power structures at an early stage. This small handful of sites, all situated within south-east England, suggests that the ancestral dead were relevant, at least in some regions, to emerging localized power structures.

The evidence therefore suggests that a mix of natural places and features, ancient and contemporary monuments, and occasional sites of pre-Christian religious significance all feature in the later patterns of assembly. This concurs well with the arguments put forward earlier in this chapter for a pre-Christian spirituality that embraced many natural aspects of the landscape, flora, and fauna as well as older features and monuments. The regularized hundredal system may have been a late Anglo-Saxon development, but the types of location are an interestingly accurate reflection of the localized affinities and beliefs glimpsed in the fifth to seventh centuries. Prehistoric monuments and mounds of all kinds and dates might have developed as meeting places at this early stage, but they represented only one type of feature amid a myriad of other possibilities. This concurs with the assertion that the dead or the ancestors may have represented only one strand in the evolving belief systems of these early populations. Many natural and ancient things were numinous and significant too, in a vast and locally varying spiritual repertoire that encompassed ancient monuments and the dead alongside rivers, pools, trees, and many other natural phenomenon and features. What is attested here is that burial places in some regions were integral to the shaping of early territories, and on occasion can be shown to have played a part in the development of places of collective identity and debate.

Monuments and settlements

Ancient burial mounds and other monument types were therefore certainly visited and used both as places of burial and perhaps in some instances as locations for consolidating and signalling collective identity through assembly and ritual by the populations of early Anglo-Saxon England. It is unsurprising therefore that new research has begun to reveal that settlements were also established in proximity to individual monuments and palimpsests (Crewe 2010; 2012). This category of evidence is much neglected and has generally been considered problematic because associations between prehistoric monuments and later settlements are difficult to prove.

Certain sites have provoked academic comment in the past. At Barrow Hills, Radley, in Oxfordshire, for example, a settlement of the fifth to seventh centuries was found through excavation to overlie a series of seven prehistoric ring-ditches (see Blair 1994; Barclay and Halpin 1999; Chambers and McAdam 2007; see Crewe 2010: 275–307; 2012: 136–45) (see Figure 3.7). Several of these were especially large, and the monuments would once have represented a striking cluster of barrows of varying sizes. A range of sunken-featured buildings,

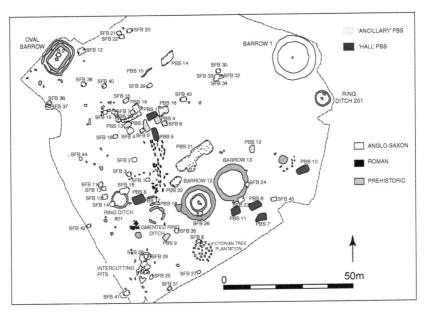

Fig. 3.7 The Anglo-Saxon settlement at Barrow Hills, Radley, Oxfordshire (PBS = post-built structure). Crewe 2010: fig. 6.6. Reproduced by permission of Vicky Crewe.

discovered at the southern edge of the settlement, respected the monument grouping and a single sunken-featured building (Building 9), in the north-west of the site, is central to a Neolithic oval long barrow (Crewe 2012: 137). This barrow grouping seems to have been instrumental in dictating the placement of the settlement and affected its spatial layout and development. The Neolithic barrow can be shown to have survived as a low mound (Bradley et al. 1984: 5, fig. 2) and the place-name Barrow Hills provides a further indication of the visibility of the prehistoric monuments long past the post-Roman era. A similar arrangement may be evident near Hough-on-the-Hill, Lincolnshire (identified by Crewe 2010: 158–9; 2012: 48, 243–4). A Bronze Age ring-ditch excavated at Frieston Road, found to have a sunken-featured building constructed across its south-west quadrant, proffers an interesting and similar instance to Barrow Hills. Late sixth- to seventh-century pottery was recovered from the sunken-featured building; the upper layer of the prehistoric ring-ditch contained similar sherds. In reference to Hough, Vicky Crewe suggests that the monument could have been visible when the sunken-featured building was constructed and that the building is likely to have formed a component of a larger settlement, located around one or more barrows. The geophysical survey suggests further ring-ditches and buildings to the north and south-west of the excavated area (Crewe 2012: 48, fig. 4.20).

Barrow Hills is certainly convincing, but at Hough-on-the-Hill, whether the monuments were actually upstanding and visible as features when the buildings were constructed remains unresolved. Other notable, well-known instances include Hatton Rock, a settlement of sixth- to seventh-century date situated by a large ring-ditch. The buildings seem to have respected the barrow, but the monument cannot be assumed with any certainty to have survived as a physical feature when the settlement was active (Rahtz 1970).[5] Certain identification of relationships between ancient monuments and settlements remain contentious. At New Wintles, Eynsham (Clayton 1973: fig. 2) the sixth- to seventh-century settlement situated next to several large ring-ditches is considered to have been constructed after the prehistoric features were ploughed away (Blair 1994). Similarly, the seventh-century hall-complex at Cowdery's Down, Hampshire, is situated amid a series of ring-ditches, but the excavators considered them to have been ploughed or levelled by the late Iron Age (Millett and James 1983: 163, fig. 5). A more compelling and well-accepted example, analogous to Cowdery's Down, is of course the settlement complex at Yeavering, Northumberland (see Colour Plate 3). This site is reviewed later in this chapter and again in Chapters 4 and 6 and so comment here is kept to a minimum. A crucial element of the findings at Yeavering is the establishment of the settlement in the sixth century and the clear reference of the first simple arrangement of hall structures to the pre-existing or antecedent monuments (Hope-Taylor 1977; Scull 1991). The prominent gravel plateau overlooking the River Glen hosts a range of upstanding prehistoric remains: a large barrow, a circle of standing stones (possibly removed before the sixth century but leaving a circular bank and ditch as visible features), and at least one henge monument (Harding 1981: 119–29). In addition, the Great Enclosure dominated the site, which is considered a later feature, but one that pre-dated the Anglian settlement (see Colour Plate 3). The settlement was not isolated; new discoveries suggest that other less elaborate and yet prominently situated settlements existed along the course of the Glen and Till rivers and were active during this early time (Anon. 2007, 2009; Passmore and Waddington 2009). According to historical accounts, in the sixth century this settlement lay within the British kingdom of *Goddodin* (Driscoll 1998: 143; O'Brien 1999: 63). The settlement developed significantly in the seventh century after the expansion of Anglian control in the north. In these more elaborate phases, when the settlement is considered to have developed as an estate centre and site of Anglo-Saxon royal power and assembly, the earlier monumental remains continued to structure activity on the site, as well as influencing the layout of the settlement itself (Hope-Taylor 1977).

---

[5] At Cowage Farm in Wiltshire, a large palatial complex of timber halls revealed as crop marks through aerial photographic survey also lie close to probable Bronze Age ring-ditches (Hinchcliffe 1986).

Thus a number of convincing examples exist that describe direct relation-ships between settlement, building, and monument. To this we can add several more sites where the underlying antecedent features, barrows, enclosures, banks, or field divisions appear to have helped shape the layout of early settlement sites. The early medieval settlement at Bishopstone, Sussex, already mentioned in Chapter 2, dates to the fifth and sixth centuries. An unusually shaped, trapezoidal, timber building (LI) was discovered some 60 metres from the main area of settlement and adjacent to the contemporary Anglo-Saxon cemetery. The settlement at Bishopstone is, it seems, positioned in reference to an earlier, late prehistoric or Romano-British rectilinear enclosure (Bell 1977: fig. 86). The outlying structure LI lies within the cemetery, aligned on a large Bronze Age ring-ditch. The burials envelop the land curving around the barrow and are inserted into the mound, confirming the barrow was upstand-ing during the life span of the cemetery. The function of the structure is unknown, but a range of features served to situate the early settlement and funerary activity (Bell 1977; Nick Stoodley: pers. comm.). At Mucking in Essex, pre-existing prehistoric and Roman field ditches and enclosures dic-tated the position of a sunken-featured building (Hamerow 1993: 86, fig. 51). The early medieval settlement at West Heslerton in Yorkshire makes an even more persuasive case. Here the late Roman system of enclosures and struc-tures, with a suspected ritual function, shaped an Anglian settlement dated to the fifth to seventh centuries (Powlesland 1999: 57–8, fig. 3). There are problems in assuming direct continuity at the site. The fifth- to sixth-century settlement was extensive and highly zoned, and the layout was established quickly; in many respects the strong architectural styles, individual house plots, and enclosures on the site suggest a strong discontinuity with the preceding activity. To the north, however, the cemetery that served the settle-ment makes use of a prehistoric complex consisting of henges and ring-ditches (Lucy 1998; Powlesland 1999) (Colour Plate 1). The ancient monuments, Roman and prehistoric, were visible in the fifth to seventh centuries and seem to have structured the patterns of settlement and burial. Similar influ-ences may also be evident at Bishopstone, Sussex.

Of course, relationships with Roman and Romano-British sites and monu-ments and even Iron Age citadels are widely accepted in current studies. In the north and west of Britain, the continuing occupation of a site or its hinterlands, or a continued reverence and knowledge of the place, is well accepted as a feature of post-Roman life (see Alcock 1988; Dark 1994a, 1994b, for the reoccupation of hill forts in the west). In England, fifth- and sixth-century settlement activity is, in some instances, located close to evidence of Roman or Romano-British settlement activity, as at Heslerton (examples are numerous, but see Godmanchester, Cambridgeshire; Gibson and Murray 2003; and

Bloodmoor Hill, Carlton Colville, Suffolk; Lucy et al. 2009). Such incidences may reflect coincidence or the establishment of new settlements in fresh ground close to, but separate from, abandoned settlements. The fourth to fifth centuries are almost wholly characterized in the south and east of England in terms of a break in settlement pattern, form, and tradition, but increasingly researchers are pointing to continuities as well as changes, implying the persistence of Romano-British populations and traditions (see, e.g., Woolf 2003). In summary, at present English medieval archaeologists have little problem with fifth- and sixth-century communities in England having a knowledge or memory of Roman and Romano-British settlements and Roman monuments, living close to them, and in some instances gathering things from them, or undertaking new types of activity within them (such as processing and storage). In particular but rare instances, direct occupation of the same site is also attested. It seems strange, therefore, that the use of prehistoric monuments has so frequently been dismissed as pure coincidence.

The evidence, now bolstered through Crewe's study of the Midlands, is increasingly compelling. The list of sites is nowhere near as extensive as that for funerary reuse, and although further study might increase the numbers of convincing examples, it seems likely that it was not a widespread practice. However, not only were populations willing to establish settlements within close proximity of upstanding remains, but the monuments in some instances were crucial in the design, layout, and shape of these settlements, defining where structures were built, and shaping the plan of settlements over time. The few examples of early Anglo-Saxon date identified do not offer any evidence for specialized activity or particular functions that might set them apart from other settlements of the same era. In several instances, buildings— usually sunken-featured buildings—are constructed directly on barrows. In at least two instances, including Barrow Hills, Radley, the monuments were already a focus for Romano-British activity. Here, a cemetery of Romano-British date was established within the enceinte of prehistoric features (Bradley et al. 1984; Chambers and McAdam 2007). There may be room to investigate such associations further in terms of real or perceived ethnicities and affinities versus the adaptation or overwriting of claims by migrant settlers.

The use of prehistoric remains as locations for settlement activity continued in the seventh to early eighth centuries, and examples can be found that even date to the ninth (see Crewe 2012). This developing phase of activity is discussed in Chapters 6 and 7, where arguments are put forward for an increasing and more widescale use of the prehistoric by the elite families. For now, it is interesting to note that such practices had their origins in the fifth and sixth centuries. Such activity fits well with suggestions in Chapter 2 of early funerary reuse as a means of shaping local identity. At several of these early medieval settlements, such as Bishopstone in Sussex and West Heslerton in Yorkshire, burial evidence of the same date is also present. It seems plausible that this combination of activity was aimed at shaping and confirming identity and signalling territorial power at small scales. The integration of the living, the dead, and the old and ancestral at these sites represents something quite distinctive and potentially powerful that deserves further closer attention.

There are other possibilities too that only future research and fieldwork can truly elucidate, but are worth mentioning here. It is possible, despite a current absence of evidence, that these were specialized settlements with particular mediating functions related to the ritual or spiritual negotiation of the ancestral (asserted by Crewe 2012: 196–220). Such sites would be analogous to and echo the kinds of rural Roman temple complex where ancient prehistoric monuments were foci for temple structures, associated buildings, and for visitation and votive depositions of coins and other personal items (e.g. Motlow, Fleam Dyke, Cambridgeshire, p. 93; and consider too West Heslerton, Yorkshire). Another related possibility is that such sites were territorial centres *and* cult-sites—places of emergent power where connections were being made with the supernatural or ancestral and where access to this powerful resource was managed.

It would be foolish not to acknowledge that such relationships could be far more mundane, attesting, for example, to the use of unused space for settlement that could not be usefully cultivated. The placing and orientation of buildings in relation to monuments could thus be more pragmatic in terms of labour and suitable terrain for the siting and construction of buildings. Either way, such evidence provides an important lesson. The communities inhabiting these early Anglo-Saxon sites were not afraid to live alongside monuments that as ancient burial places may have been perceived to have connections to the dead, the supernatural, and the other world, even if their contemporaries were also choosing to use such places as cemeteries and sites of burial.

Monuments and structures

One class of associated evidence comprises individual structures of varying kinds found in direct archaeological relationships with prehistoric remains. These comprise individual buildings, enclosures, and standing posts that mark ancient barrows and monuments. These could, of course, represent elements of more extensive but undiscovered settlements, and, as this section will show, several examples exist within excavated settlements. The structures and features discussed here may therefore reference modes of venerating and marking prehistoric monuments in isolation or within settlement and cemetery contexts *or both*. The earlier section has already introduced some of these features: the sunken-featured building at Barrow Hills, Radley, the square enclosure and standing posts at Yeavering, and the unusual timber-built structure at the cemetery at Bishopstone.

Posts

At Yeavering, the square enclosure in all its phases encompassed a single standing post or pillar (see p. 103, 105). This post and its successor formed an axial arrangement with another post implanted in a large Bronze Age barrow to the south-east of the site, within the lip of the Great Enclosure (Colour Plate 3). The earliest phase of settlement at Yeavering aligned to this arrangement. Single standing posts are present at other sites. Single posts are, of course, extremely common as funerary markers of primary Anglo-Saxon ring-ditches and barrows. In Sussex and Kent they are often positioned at the small break in the surrounding ring-ditch (see Welch 1992; Lucy 2000). On occasion they are found in relation to burial sites that make use of prehistoric monuments. An odd example can be found at Roche Court Down, Wiltshire, where a small cemetery was found to have been positioned in relation to three barrows within an Iron Age enclosure (Stone 1932). Barrow 3, to the south-east, was prehistoric, with evidence of an undated, central secondary burial. Barrow 1 to the north-west was non-sepulchral and remains undated, but excavation revealed a large central posthole and an internal concentric ditch. Barrow 2 comprised a burial mound containing a primary, Anglo-Saxon, male inhumation burial. Although not wealthy in material terms, the large grave chamber implies an interment of some prestige, and a sixth- or seventh-century date can be assumed. Barrow 2 was similar in size and form to Barrow 1, and the male grave aligned with the central post in Barrow 1. At Tandderwen on the Welsh border, a Bronze Age barrow was encompassed by a square enclosure whose entrances gave access to a large standing central post and a single grave (Blair 1995: 11–13).

At Bampton, Oxfordshire, John Blair has revealed through excavation a series of seventh-century graves apparently reusing prehistoric barrows later appropriated by an early minster church (see Chapter 4, pp. 117–18). The name Bampton (*OE bēam + tūn*) refers to a standing post or monolith of some kind at the site, which has been interpreted by Blair (2013) as a kind of ritual post, totem, or marker. There exists a range of complementary evidence for standing orthostats or pillars functioning as cultic foci. Several place-names include the OE element *stapol* 'post or standing pole' and *bēam* 'beam or post'. These may evidence sacred trees, tree trunks, wooden posts, or stone pillars (see Gelling 1988; Blair 1995, 2013; Meaney 1995). Among these can be found the hundred name of Staploe (Cambridgeshire) *stapol + hlaw*, which indicates that the meeting place of the hundred was a barrow marked by a standing post

(Meaney 1997: 211). To this can be added *Thurstaple,* Kent: a lost hundred meeting place apparently associated with the *stapol* or post of Thor (Meaney 1995). John Blair has recently undertaken a thorough examination of place-names containing the element *beam* and *stapol,* concluding that place-name and charter boundary material suggests these terms were used particularly for individual trees or posts with some local intrinsic significance (Blair 2013). A detailed assessment of the locational aspects of *bēamas* is informative, revealing further links between these markers and barrows, Anglo-Saxon burials, blood-letting or sacrifice, *Grim, Thunor,* standing stones, and *stapols,* leading Blair to conclude that the *beam* was a ritual focus, perhaps a living tree or wooden pillar or post. They were accessible, locally distinctive in terms of their settings, and may have marked larger ritual complexes within more than one ritual foci (Blair 2013).

The *beam* and *stapol* were monuments with an extensive repertoire of uses: as markers for graves, barrows, cemeteries, as foci on settlements, and as elements used to structure the orientation of both burials and buildings on cemeteries and settlements. It is difficult to speculate on the meaning of these monuments, particularly as the wide variety of contexts implies differing ritual uses and highly localized significance. Some no doubt were grave markers that commemorated the dead and their kin group, some may have signalled kin-based or group identities, marking territory, crossing places, places of assembly, and sacred sites. Just as posts were used on settlements to structure the layout and perhaps activity and at cemeteries to mark graves and mounds, so posts in the landscape may have served to structure the movement of people and signal territory or mark places of inter-action. Some, as we have seen, were raised on and by prehistoric barrows.

Two crosses erected on barrows are worth noting briefly here. The first, the *Pillar of Eliseg,* an eighth-century monument, was erected to celebrate the lineage and kingship of Eliseg and was placed on a prehistoric barrow; it is thought to mark a place of assembly (see Figure 3.8). The second is Lilla Howe, an excavated Bronze Age barrow used as a marker for the early monastic bounds of Whitby Abbey surmounted by a stone cross that bears a strong resemblance to Norse crosses of the North Atlantic (Woodwark 1924; Fisher 2005) (see Figure 3.9).[6] There is no indication of assembly here, but the name of the monument seems to commemorate the heroic seventh-century figure Lilla, the thegn of Edwin, recorded by Bede as forfeiting his life to save the king from an assassin in AD 626 (*ASC* (E) 626; *HE* II, 9). These and other examples perhaps suggest posts, markers, and later perhaps stone pillars and monuments served as monumental features aimed at evoking

---

[6] Although not situated on a mound, another example for consideration is the late-tenth-century cross at *Maen Achwyfan* in Flintshire, which seems likely to occupy its original position within an oval/circular enclosure and is argued to lie within an enceinte of ancient barrows and barrow-like natural knolls that mark the surrounding hills (Griffiths 2006).

Fig. 3.8 The Pillar of Eliseg, Llangollen, Wales. Reproduced by permission of Howard Williams. All rights reserved.

Fig. 3.9 Lilla Cross at Lilla Howe, North Yorkshire. © Reproduced by permission of Daniel Smith. All rights reserved.

multifaceted statements of power and sacral authority (see discussions of Eliseg by Edwards 2009b; Edwards et al. 2010; Williams 2011). Perhaps the *beam* and *stapol* were not merely commemorative, but more potent: markers denoting important places conceived as significant in local identity, myth and legend and connected with lineage, royal power, and authority.

Shrines

A second, equally ephemeral type of structure is the timber-built, square-fenced enclosure that occasionally accompanied and encompassed prehistoric features. They are found sometimes in association with single standing posts. The best known and well-dated example is the sixth-century square, post-built, fenced enclosure or stockade imposed upon the western ring-ditch (WR-DC) at Yeavering, Northumberland. The square structure and its central sequence of standing wooden posts or pillars replaced a circle of standing stones with a central stone monolith and associated cremation. This first megalithic monument was certainly prehistoric and may have had a low external bank. The removal of the stones left an embanked ring-ditch of some 14.5 metres in diameter. This must have been visible—even if ephemeral—when the central post was inserted and the square post-built enclosure constructed. The square setting of posts lies symmetrically within the circle of stone settings. The structure was some 9 metres square, post-built with walls of 'wattle-laced' cob (Blair 1995: 18). The date and sequence of the timber building and associated posts is complicated. The central post was replaced several times and it provided a focus for thirty-one inhumation graves, nearly all of which are argued to lie within the compass of the timber 'mortuary enclosure or shrine' (Hope-Taylor 1977: 113–14, fig. 52). Dated by the presence of iron knives in two graves, as well as arguments based on the sequence of the structure in relation to buildings A1–A3 on the site, the square 'shrine' with its central post is placed by Hope-Taylor in the sixth century, and by others in the late sixth to seventh centuries (Scull 1991; Blair 1995: 16–18).

A range of examples has been put forward and reviewed by John Blair in his argument for the existence of a type of Anglo-Saxon square, timber-built shrine that had its origins in late Iron Age antecedents. The Slonk Hill enclosure, mentioned already in Chapter 2 (pp. 24–5), is some 12.5 metres square with a single entrance on its west side; it is post-built and superimposed on a Bronze Age ring-ditch (Hartridge 1977–8). It is undated, but a seventh-century female burial was within the threshold or entrance. It is thought by the excavators to have post-dated several adjacent square post-built enclosures that are assumed to be Romano-British in origin; however, the structure could easily represent a related elaborate yet additional enclosure of the same period. What distinguishes it as a feature from the rest of the square structures is that it and the barrow it was constructed on provided a focus for burial in the seventh century.

Arguments have been made for connections between Iron Age square enclosures and square structures, Continental Iron Age temples and shrines and
Romano-British shrines, and these timber-built square structures in England
(Blair 1995; Carver 2010). These structures emerge, however, broadly in the
same period as princely burials, in John Blair's words 'not the last gasp of an old
order but...an ostentatious short-lived phase of monumental display in the
transformative decades of *c.*590–630' (Blair 2005: 51–7; 2013). Square enclosures do, however, feature in sixth-century funerary traditions in the south and
south-east and, of course, in the funerary rites of northern populations too in
the first to eighth centuries (see Maldonado 2011) and to a lesser extent in
Western cemetery traditions (Petts 2002). In Anglo-Saxon contexts, they were
used as grave houses, shrines, or simply markers for cremation and inhumation
graves: for example, the pair of possible square structures or enclosures at
Lyminge (Kent) (Warhurst 1955), and similar square structures from the cemeteries at Spong Hill (Norfolk) (Hills et al. 1984), Morning Thorpe (Norfolk)
(Green et al. 1987), Alton (Hampshire) (Evison 1988), and Appledown (Sussex)
(Down and Welch 1990). Even an apparently non-funerary example discovered
at Friar's Oak in Sussex (a small burned rectangular structure encompassing a
square arrangement of postholes, with clusters at each corner) seems likely
now to have related to some form of funerary activity, especially given the
absence of a wider archaeological context (Butler 1998: 465). This evidence
strongly indicates that in early medieval societies an association did exist
between square structures and funerary rites, notably graves or burials, in a
variety of regions and cultural zones. It is interesting then that the creation
of square structures underwent a resurgence in the seventh century but was
more commonly associated with cult features, ancient monuments, early
medieval burials, or groups of burials. This reinforces the idea that it had
some form of status as a ritual structure or shrine and perhaps some commemorative purpose too.

Whether a shrine, temple, house for the dead, or simply a grave marker, the
square shrine was a standard type of structure that varied in meaning and
function from place to place, and over time. For our purposes here, however,
it is sufficient to note that, in Britain, examples can be found imposed on or
next to Bronze Age barrows and on occasion other prehistoric monuments
(for example, an undated example lies at the eastern entrance to the Neolithic
causewayed enclosure at Windmill Hill, notably close to several Bronze Age
barrows that reference the enclosure). This tradition can be traced at sites of
sixth- and seventh-century date, where prehistoric monuments, in particular
barrows, were referenced by square post-built enclosures or square-fenced
enclosures, with one or more burials evident, relating both to the mound and
the associated square building. Given the very common association of this
form of enclosure or building—or type of architecture—with graves and
cemeteries, it can be assumed that, when positioned in relation to ancient

form lines at 15cm
vertical intervals

0 — 5

metres

Fig. 3.10 The square building or enclosure superimposed upon the Western ring-ditch, excavated at the early medieval settlement at Yeavering, Northumberland. After Hope Taylor 1977: fig 51. Reproduced by permission of English Heritage. All rights reserved.

barrows, such structures were performing similar functions, acting as houses for the dead or ancestral shrines. It would be incorrect to separate the 'square shrine' from square mortuary markers or funerary enclosures. Instead perhaps in a pre-Christian English context, such features are all best interpreted as simple types of ritual structure raised to provide a more formal and controlled focus for the kinds of veneration of ancestral graves and places of burial that are hinted at by later prohibitions and laws (for example, feasting; raising the dead; communicating with the dead, etc.).

It is interesting to note that in the early Christian written sources there are occasional intimations that barrows with added structures or platforms existed and were powerful as ancestral sites. An excerpt from the *Vita Wilfridi* describes the use of a barrow on the South Saxon shore as a platform from which to conduct magic either to repel or to ensure the capture of trespassers and ensure the safety of the land from intruders (see Chapter 2). Bede's famous description of the heathen temple at Godmundingham (Goodmanham, East Yorkshire) also referred to sacred enclosures (*HE* I, 30 (completed in AD 731)): 'the temple with all its fences/hedges' (translation from Blair 1995: 2); even the occasional law cites prohibitions against sanctuaries around stones, trees, or wells (Whitelock et al. 1981: 463).

Summary

Any exploration of pre-Christian belief and practice involves considerable speculation, rests upon a range of difficult and partial sources, and as a consequence is likely to reflect directly and indirectly the contemporary concerns and milieu of the writer (see Cantor 1991: 28, 37; and papers in Carver et al. 2010, especially Content and Williams 2010). Numerous sites and examples mentioned here are certainly open to reinterpretation. This chapter is intended as a stimulus for new thinking and more refined critical studies, and is not envisaged as the last word on the subject. The body of data introduced here, however, does imply a diversity of secondary uses of ancient monuments that is both interesting and compelling. This chapter started out by reviewing the evidence for the numinous and sacred natural landscape in order to situate monuments within the wider spiritual repertoires that existed in early Anglo-Saxon England. While the evidence is ephemeral and direct associations often difficult to pin down, a strong argument is made for the potency of monuments of the ancient past in this spiritual canvas. In some instances, these ancient sites may have held qualities now lost to us: associations with mythical ancestors, importance as ancestral places, connections to legends about origins, landownership, and identity. Bronze Age round barrows were more commonly referenced than any other monument types, but examples of forts, ditches, long barrows, and stones can be found within all categories of activity discussed. The uses varied. Burial, votive activity, posts, shrines, battle sites, places of assembly, and settlement activity, all argue against a common meaning or purpose. The evidence also suggests an intensely localized response to monuments, and that such responses may have had little to do with real or perceived ethnic affiliations or differences. Individual communities, perhaps even families, were negotiating their own contemporary narratives in relation to the landscape and pre-existing features. Although prehistoric monuments, especially barrows, were frequently a part of this, how they were reused was multifarious.

By the seventh century, prehistoric monuments seem to have come increasingly within the ambit of elite groups or families. Of particular note here is the emerging evidence for the formalization of relationships between activity and monument such as planned settlements and shrines. At the same time, burial practices involving ancient monuments seem to have become the preserve of fewer, wealthier people; traditions of imposing square structure or shrines in relation to prehistoric monuments seem to have arrived as well (Blair 2005, 2013), together with more formal relationships between buildings and monuments within settlement contexts (Crewe 2010; 2012). Not only does this fit with the ideas of experimentation and ostentation asserted for seventh-century elites (Geake 1997; Carver 2002); it implies that the localized and even individual interest in making 'ancestral' connections with older monuments may have informed and shaped elite choices. Such changes fit with wider interpretations of the seventh century as a time when small elite groups were securing greater regional power while manufacturing dynastic traditions and linkages between the living and dead. One might argue that, in the evidence reviewed here, the sense of investment by elite groups and their exploitation of local tradition, are increasingly evident from the late sixth century. At one site in particular, the harnessing of a full range of old and new monument types by a new dynastic power base is all too evident. Yeavering very clearly attests to the ways in which a new Anglo-Saxon elite sought to manipulate an existing site to create a theatrical environment that specifically embedded and valorized their new and future authority.

It seems possible that 'ancestors', or more likely the creation of *ancestry*, became particularly important to these emerging elite groups. As later discussions will argue, it is possible to discern during and after the seventh to eighth centuries an increased awareness of the past and the value of the ancient as a tool for creating a theatrical display of power and legitimating authority.

Although not all monument types were special, not all types of activity were funerary, and some of the discussion here is speculative to say the least, the evidence does attest to an early respect for these features. It is clear that they were considered powerful places: points of reference for communities seeking to establish a sense of place and authority in the post-Roman landscape. The evidence also suggests an intensely localized response to individual monuments and complexes in the fifth, sixth, and early seventh centuries, but changes are evident in the seventh century when an increase in the exploitation of such features by Anglo-Saxon elite families implies that prehistoric monuments, especially barrows, were progressively becoming the preserve of an exclusive group.

4

The circle and the cross

Medieval churches and prehistoric monuments

the site of this ruined Christian Church, standing within an earthen circle that seems to belong to the unknown religion of the Early Britons ... marks the strange changes and chances that have happened during the lapse of 2,000 years ...

(Sumner 1913: p. x)

Introduction

The reintroduction of Christianity into England created numerous material changes, not least the introduction of stone-built structures and decorated sculpture. Early medieval Christianity is increasingly rejected as a monolithic construct. There is now widespread acknowledgement of a variety in practice, architecture, and cult, and evidence of regional differences in beliefs, as well as acknowledgement of differing intellectual and political strategies in terms of conversion (see Petts 2011: 17–29 for useful critical summary; and Carver 2003, 2011; Pluskowski and Patrick 2003; Urbańczyk 2003). This chapter considers how the arrival of Roman and Irish Christianity and the conversion of the population in the seventh and eighth centuries impacted upon the local English scene, and how the pre-existing landscape shaped Christianity into something that in its earliest stages was also regionally and locally varied. At the core of this chapter are the remarkable and striking juxtapositions of ancient Christian Church and prehistoric monuments—recalled above by Sumner in reference to Stanton Drew—which have long provoked popular and scholarly debate (see Figure 4.1) (see also Allcroft 1927–30). For some, like Aubrey Burl, the burying of prehistoric monoliths at Avebury represented church-incited acts of suppression and destruction of symbols of an old and still venerated (pagan) religion (Burl 1979: 322; Bender 1998: 100–4, esp. 102). By contrast, others have seen such places as evidence of 'ritual' continuity (Morris 1989: 46–92). This chapter re-examines the evidence for churches built on or by

Fig. 4.1 Stanton Drew, Somerset. The church tower can be seen in the middle of the picture. Reproduced by permission of English Heritage. All rights reserved.

ancient prehistoric monuments. The data set used as a basis for this discussion is not comprehensive, but is presented in the appendices to this book as a handlist of examples of possible early medieval churches that seems to coexist with the remains of prehistoric monuments (Appendix 3). Many potential sites were visited and discarded in the process of defining this catalogue. Even so, the eighty or so remaining examples remain problematic. Many have been neither surveyed nor excavated. The most significant difficulty for interpreting church and monument relationships is the chronological disparity between the date of the prehistoric monument and its last known use, together with the earliest documented or structural date for the existence of a Christian church on the site. Well-established church and monument relationships are rare, but actual cases of datable pre-Conquest churches in the immediate vicinity of prehistoric structures are fewer still. Nevertheless, just over eighty sites have been identified in England where medieval churches may be intentionally constructed in, on, or by upstanding prehistoric remains. A critical archaeological examination of these places, taken as far as possible without extensive fieldwork, suggests that the oft-cited explanations of 'converted monuments' will not suffice. The motivations for the establishment of churches in the vicinity of enclosures, barrows, and megaliths are varied and of diverse dates.

The arrival of Roman Christianity in England in AD 597 following the coming of the Irish Christian Church certainly initiated a process of religious change that affected the English landscape in numerous ways, but the spiritual and ideological potency of ancient prehistoric monuments appears to have survived. In the seventh and early eighth centuries, when mourners continued to bury the dead in Bronze Age barrows in Northumbria and Wessex, old monuments began to be appropriated as locations for some of the first minster churches. What has yet to be discovered, and thus forms the basis of the research presented here, is whether such actions had political, spiritual, or ideological motives, or represent no more than functional usance, or if a combination of all served to drive the placement of churches within prehistoric palimpsests in the eighth to eleventh centuries.

Churches and megaliths (listed in Appendix 3)

It is asserted that no single example exists of an early medieval church that through its construction purposely destroyed a prehistoric monument (Hutton 1993: 253). Ronald Hutton qualifies this by adding that surviving superstitions and beliefs do, however, seem to have led to the Christianization of some monuments by the erection of crosses or churches in the vicinity (Hutton 1993). Megalithic monuments may not have been recognized as human constructions by medieval societies, but instead were conceived as natural phenomena. In this sense, they may have been venerated or imbued with local superstition as remarkable, natural, and powerful phenomena, but they were not a prime focus for pre-Christian worship and thus did not attract Christian aggression. This contravenes the assertions made by Holtorf (1997: 80–8) and later Bender (1998: 100–4) of church-incited destruction of megaliths in the early Christian era. The destruction of stones and naming associated with the Devil fit much more comfortably within the rhetoric of the Reformation and the years that followed. Indeed, the diabolical naming of stones has been argued to stem, at least in part, from the pulpit oratory of the post-Reformation era (Simpson 1986). Walsham (2011) argues that the burgeoning antiquarian interest in prehistoric monuments and the common interpretation of these as ancient temples by the first antiquarians may well have promoted the kinds of destructive fervour that resulted in the demolition of standing stones, such as those at Avebury (recorded by Stukeley in 1743). Examples of fifth- to seventh-century burials associated with standing stones or stone circles are also virtually non-existent (see Chapter 2, pp. 41, 69–70), perhaps underlining the limited spiritual value of such features to pre-Christian communities. There are, however, a handful of sites where a medieval church can be found situated by standing stones, although in all instances the chronology or the spatial relationship is open to question, making this small yet important category of sites difficult to interpret or discuss.

Rudston in East Yorkshire (see Figure 4.2) is an iconic site, much used in academic and public literature as a symbol of the appropriation of pagan and

Fig. 4.2 Rudston, East Yorkshire: the church and standing stone. Author's image.

ancient sites by the early Christian Church (see, e.g., Morris 1989: 81–4). The large standing stone situated in the churchyard is smooth, has a worked appearance, and tapers towards its summit. It lies on a high spur at the centre of an area with a complex array of prehistoric remains, including four (or five) cursus (Stoertz 1997: 28, fig. 10). The spur is a striking natural feature, overlooking the Gypsey Race River and a series of natural spring-lines. A Roman site, perhaps a villa, lies to the south-west below the spur (see Rudston in Appendices 1 and 2). A pair of fifth-century Anglo-Saxon brooches was discovered close by. A curvilinear complex has been identified to the north of the spur and church and is considered to be an early medieval settlement complex akin to Heslerton and Butterwick to the north (Stoertz 1997). The church and monument are thus just two surviving visible symbols of a longer and more complex sequence of activity on and around the natural spur. It is worth noting that the curvilinear complex itself overlies the intersection of several cursus and lies close to a feature called Maidens Grave, identified as a Class II henge and speculatively identified as the meeting place of the Wapentake (NMR 79850; McInnes 1964: 217–18; Allison 1974: 119). Prehistoric cist graves have also been uncovered on the summit of the spur, within the current churchyard (Stoertz 1997, 28, fig. 10). Rudston lies in an area with a significant number of burials and cemeteries considered to be of early medieval date. The church, however, has no fabric or sculptural evidence earlier than its Anglo-Norman tower. The All Saints dedication could, of course, corroborate a pre-Conquest date, but this is insufficient evidence alone. The place-name Rudston, *OE* terms *rod*, 'rood/cross', + *stān*, 'stone', is argued to refer to the remarkable menhir that still stands today within the churchyard of All Saints (Rodestan 1086 DB: see Smith 1937: 98–9). This perhaps offers some evidence for a Christian presence on the site before the Conquest but remains inconclusive.

A second site that echoes the difficulties and the distinctiveness of Rudston is the church of St Barnabus in Alphamstone, Essex. It is discussed here because it is popularly believed to be the site of a stone circle. The structure of the church is predominantly Norman, but remnants of Roman brick quoins suggest that a late Saxon building is partially fossilized within the structure standing on the site today. A scatter of large Sarsen stones lie in the churchyard, one of which was recovered at a depth of several feet below ground during grave digging. Despite claims of a stone circle, these large and unshaped stones could easily be natural erratics. However, Bronze Age cremations and fragments of Bronze Age pottery have been found inside and outside the churchyard. The HER records numerous multiperiod finds in the fields to the south and west, including evidence of a Roman structure, perhaps a villa, immediately south of the churchyard. The probable late Saxon church at Alphamstone thus sits within a complex multi-period site, but one that has no real archaeological evidence for upstanding prehistoric remains, and the church appears to be built next to and partially from the fabric from a Roman building (SMR 9317; Brooks and Dennis 2005).

The archaeological biography of each of these complexes is more long-lived and complicated than hitherto allowed. No single monument is a driving factor in church placement at either site. Instead these medieval buildings are situated in relation to places rich in multiperiod evidence with distinctive natural geographic elements and physical features: water courses, spurs, and large stones. These sites alone almost immediately dispose of the concept of the conversion of individual monuments. A mixture of Roman and prehistoric monuments, as well as evidence of burial and settlement of the pre-Christian era, provided a density of activity and probably reflect the presence of a local population. Both of these may have prompted the interest of the Christian Church, leading eventually to the construction of a Christian monument at each site.

Avebury—probably the most famous example of a church amid standing stones—is equally difficult to interpret (see Figure 4.3). The medieval church of St James is sited within a vast complex of upstanding prehistoric remains (Semple 1994; Pollard and Reynolds 2002). It lies a short distance from the western entrance to the great Neolithic henge and stone circle, but upstanding round barrows, field systems, enclosures, long barrows, standing stone rows, and considerably more monuments, now eroded by the plough, have been identified in the environs, including the spectacular West Kennet Long Barrow and Silbury Hill. The church has surviving Anglo-Saxon fabric of *c.*1000, but a single fragment of ninth-century sculpture and two pieces of early tenth-century date are visible in the build, hinting at an earlier ecclesiastical focus (Cramp 2006). It is easy to see how this visual spectacle has led to discussions of a 'de-paganizing act' (Bender 1998: 102), but the process of Christian appropriation is far removed from such a triumphant conversion narrative. As outlined in Chapter 2 (p. 40; Pollard and Reynolds 2002: 204–7), settlement evidence of fifth-century date exists around the south-west of the henge. By the eighth century, activity had intensified around the western entrance (see Pollard and Reynolds 2002: 198–9, for overview), and, by the ninth, a planned and enclosed rectilinear settlement, postulated as a *burh*, had been created—almost certainly one of the fortified settlements established across southern England in response to the Viking threat (Reynolds 2001; 2002: 204–7). All Saints Church sits within this planned,

Fig. 4.3 The church of St James, Avebury, set next to the great prehistoric monument complex. Reproduced by permission of English Heritage. All rights reserved.

fortified enclosure, neatly within one of the regular plots of land laid out perpendicular to the east–west route way but also in a position that could place it at the heart of any eighth-century activity too (Pollard and Reynolds 2002: 204–5 and colour plate 17). The ninth- and tenth-century sculptural fragments strongly suggest that a first ecclesiastical focus may have been created at the same time as the *burh*. The church at Avebury, rather than a 'de-paganizing' statement, seems instead to represent just one element of a complex development of activity in and around the henge spanning the fifth to eleventh centuries. The building of the church was almost certainly a consequence of the settlement of a population and the probable focus of the local elite rather than a direct challenge to an active site of pagan veneration within the henge complex.

One suspects that the remaining site to be discussed, if investigated further, will eventually offer a similar wealth of evidence for activity across the late prehistoric to early medieval periods. Stanton Drew, Somerset, represents an emotive juxtaposition of church and monument, but one that remains significantly underexplored (Figure 4.1). A geophysical survey has shown the large-scale complex of circles was once as impressive as Avebury, with concentric rings of timber posts lying within the largest ring of stones. An inhumation burial was recovered from the site close to a standing stone, accompanied by a large iron bell-shaped object, and whilst a sugarloaf shield-boss may be implied by this description, early medieval funerary activity remains only conjecture. The current church of St Mary's is no earlier than the thirteenth century in terms of surviving structural remains, although a Norman font survives. Little further is known about this unusual combination of church and megalithic complex. Stanton Drew encapsulates all the frustrations presented by this category of sites: a remarkable coincidence of church and monument but an absence of any real evidence for an early pre-Conquest church, limited exploration of the relationship between monuments, and intimations of a more complex pre-Christian archaeology at the site.

The paucity of examples suggests that megaliths and stone circles were generally of less interest than ancient earthworks, both to early medieval populations and to the Christian Church as well, but all four sites hint that complexes of monuments of varying kinds may have provided a focus for settlement, and the population that developed there over subsequent centuries may have provided the attraction for the early church. Direct Christian reference to monuments, as at Rudston, may hint at a kind of longitudinal local history at certain places that compelled the church to make reference to such places with early foundations or crosses (Morris 2011: 187–91; Stocker and Everson 2003).

Churches, earthen mounds, and barrows

Relationships between medieval churches and tumuli or barrow-like features are far more prevalent. Prehistoric long and round barrows are common in many regions as upstanding visible features, but only some provoked early ecclesiastical interest. On occasion barrows were used as platforms for pre-

and post-Conquest churches, and more frequently churches were built next to barrows or groups of barrows. These are discussed next as two related categories of activity, although again the archaeological quality of the evidence is poor and at many sites it is simply impossible to verify real pre-Conquest relationships between church and barrow.

Churches on barrows (listed in Appendix 3)

Allcroft published a reproduction of a nineteenth-century watercolour of St Michael's Church, Winwick (Northamptonshire), that shows the church perched on the summit of a large and bulbous mound. He argued that this provided evidence of an early church appropriating an ancient tumulus and place of burial (Allcroft 1927–30: i. 1–15, fig. 3). Today archaeologists are more cautious in their interpretations. It is widely recognized that the intensive use of cemeteries over a thousand years can create a marked build-up in the ground surface (Morris 1989: 240–1, fig. 65). If the churchyard was extended in the post-medieval and later periods, the original cemetery would survive as a visible, raised, mounded earthwork just like the hummock represented in this watercolour. Secondly, it is common for medieval churches to be positioned on hills, spurs, and small knolls (Morris 1989; Blair 1992: 227); this type of positioning in addition to cemetry build-up could give a church the appearance of sitting on a man-made mound or tumulus. Without archaeological intervention or investigation, such correspondences remain speculative.

Seventeen possible examples listed in Appendix 3 represent precisely this kind of untested and unproven association. The shape and size of the 'mounds' are highly varied. At Corhampton, Hampshire, the eleventh-century church is positioned astride a prominent oblong or oval rise, perhaps a natural spur, although within the churchyard earthworks are clearly visible, describing some form of sub-rectangular enclosure or platform (see Figure 4.4(a)). A Roman sarcophagus lies in the churchyard too (Brough 1908: 246; Taylor and Taylor 1965: 176–9; Pevsner and Lloyd 1967: 182). Pre-Conquest sculpture and surviving fabric at St Michael and All Angels, Edenham (Lincolnshire), attest to an Anglo-Saxon foundation as early as the ninth century, and the present church surmounts a raised earthwork platform bounded by earthworks (Taylor and Taylor 1965: 227; Everson and Stocker 1999: 157–62). The intact eleventh-century church of St Mary's at Chithurst, Sussex, is also situated on a large sub-rectangular/oval platform which has an artificial appearance (see Figure 4.4(b)) (Manwaring 1912: 98–107; Allcroft 1927–30: ii. 312–13, fig. 1; Nairn and Pevsner 1965: 186–7; Taylor and Taylor 1965: 157–8). The eleventh-century church at Ford, Sussex, occupies a low, circular mound. Pre-eleventh-century sculptural fragments suggest an earlier date (Tweddle et al. 1995: 144) and antiquarian excavation in the churchyard recovered six radially placed burials (see Figure 4.4 (c)) (Manwaring 1900: 106; Nairn and Pevsner 1965: 225–6).

Fig. 4.4 (a) Corhampton, Hampshire; (b) St Mary's at Chithurst, Sussex; (c) the eleventh-century church at Ford, Sussex. Author's images.

Several post-Conquest foundations exemplify similarly impressive relationships with artificial structures. A nineteenth-century illustration of Alfriston in Sussex depicts the churchyard as a large circular rise (Nairn and Pevsner 1965: ii. 396–7, pl. IV, no. 1). At Edlesborough, Buckinghamshire, the thirteenth-century church of St Mary the Virgin overlies an oval, but irregular, earthwork (Jennings 1925; Allcroft 1927–30: ii, pl. III, no. 2; Lipscomb 1831–47: iii. 349).

Although some of these are plausible as churches built astride prehistoric earthworks, without further intervention these remain unproven associations. In four instances, however, archaeological investigation has verified that a medieval church was built on top of an ancient barrow. These sites provide more extensive detail on the relationship between church and mound but are not without ambiguity. The only entirely convincing example is at Bampton, Oxfordshire, excavated by John Blair. On this site, the Deanery, an early Norman two-story chapel, was found to overlie a Bronze Age ring-ditch, and Bampton church, with a possible early Norman, or late Anglo-Saxon, core overlay a second smaller ring-ditch. A third barrow is suggested on the south side of the church, within the churchyard (see Figure 4.5) (Blair 1998). Three fragmentary, *in situ* burials cut the inner lip of the smaller ring-ditch beneath the church, and can be placed as early as *c*.700 (radiocarbon dates of AD 640–890; Blair 1999: 29). This evidence suggests that the prehistoric barrows, or barrow, provided a focus for funerary activity before the first documented reference to the Christian community and minster in the 950s. The place-name Bampton and the place-name of the location of the twelfth-century chapel of St Andrew's to the east, 'The Beam', both contain the

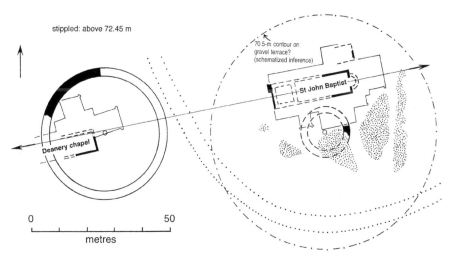

Fig. 4.5 The church and prehistoric ring-ditches at Bampton in Oxfordshire. Reproduced by permission of John Blair.

OE element *beam* 'post or obelisk'; this suggests that the barrows were further complemented by a post to the east later replaced by the chapel (Blair 1994: 64). A further group of burials, one with a seventh-century pin, was located between church and chapel (Blair 1994: 63–4, fig. 44), and to the west of the Deanery is the Lady Well, a medieval holy-well that survives today. The tenth-century or earlier minster was therefore situated in relation to a collection of cult-foci, including ancient barrows, pre-Christian or conversion period cemeteries, a standing post, and perhaps a spring or well. A crucial observation here in relation to this, the first and only irrefutable example of a church founded amid and over Bronze Age barrows, is that the ring-ditches may not have been the sole or even primary focus of the ecclesiastical interest and activity: they were one aspect of a varied collection of special natural, antecedent, and contemporary features, including burials of sixth- and seventh-century date situated around the barrows, pre-dating the minster.

Less conclusive case studies are represented by Fimber in East Yorkshire, Yatesbury in Wiltshire, and Wervin in Cheshire. At Fimber the findings rely on the observations of Mortimer, who identified prehistoric burials and what he thought to be an 'artificial, oval mound' (Mortimer 1905: 189–93) beneath the remains of the medieval church. At Yatesbury geophysical survey combined with survey and excavation identified a series of two or more Bronze Age barrows in the village (Reynolds 1999: 93–4), and an unpublished geophysical survey suggests that the twelfth-century church also sits on an oval rise defined by an oval ditch. At least one of these barrows was used for secondary burial, and one primary Anglo-Saxon barrow burial was positioned adjacent to a Bronze Age mound on the outskirts of the village. A final instance at Chapel House Farm, Wervin, also comprises an example of a post-Conquest church, in this case a thirteenth-century chapel, standing on an artificial mound. A geophysical survey is purported to have identified a substantial linear ditch running the length of the south side of the mound (Nenk et al. 1995).

In summary, then, of the twenty-one sites collected, only a single well-corroborated example of an Anglo-Saxon church or minster established on a prehistoric mound exists. At Bampton, however, other foci existed and pre-Christian funerary activity was present. We must ask ourselves this: is it the prehistoric barrow, the burials, or the entire multifocal complex that drew the foundation of a pre-Conquest church at this location? The overwhelming absence of good complementary evidence is striking. Bampton is a unique find, and thus one begins to suspect that the relationship of church and barrow here is just one element of the 'conversion' of an important and much more complex pre-Christian site that was certainly marked by barrow burials and funerary activity. Fimber, when considered with Bampton, provides examples of prehistoric barrows used for pre-Christian burial, thus perhaps providing a link between tumulus and church. Burials placed in and around prehistoric barrows are, as Chapter 2 and 3 have emphasized, well attested before and during the conversion to Christianity. Cemeteries such as Winwick in Cheshire,

Kemp Howe in Yorkshire, or Bevis Grave in Hampshire show extensive cemeteries focused around prehistoric barrows actively continuing as sites of burial across the conversion period.

Finally, Yatesbury and Wervin cut across the common assumption that these kinds of spatial relationships are pre-Conquest. The vast majority of the sites discussed, in terms of their physical evidence, like these examples, actually attest to post-Conquest churches and may potentially signal evidence of Norman-English and medieval habits rather than conversion-period practices.

Churches by barrows (listed in Appendix 3)

Despite the obvious overlap with 'churches *on* barrows', churches by barrows are treated here as a related but separate category chiefly because they present a contrastingly richer and more plausible data set. Twenty-three possible sites exist, and it is worth noting that Bampton and Yatesbury fit in this category as well.

These sites fall into two groups. In the first, early Christian churches and monasteries were founded within enceintes of prehistoric monuments, including prominent barrows or barrow-like features. In the second, medieval churches, some with pre-Conquest origins, lie next to large individual barrows.

Four sites have reasonable archaeological and topographic evidence for the establishment of pre-Conquest churches in close proximity to prehistoric barrows. They share several attributes with other sites such as Bampton and Avebury, where churches lie close to extensive ancient monumental landscapes and pre-Christian activity in the form of burial or settlement.

Yeavering in Northumberland, already discussed in Chapter 3, is a sixth- to seventh-century settlement placed within a landscape rich in prehistoric remains (see p. 96) (Colour Plate 3). A presumed timber church (building B) appeared in the penultimate phases of activity in the seventh century (Phase IV). It followed a new layout that rendered the western ring-ditch defunct as a ritual and funerary focus (Hope-Taylor 1977: 164–9; Blair 2005: fig. 7). This structure was also situated next to a prehistoric barrow marked by a standing post (BX). This had already attracted string-graves and formed a nodal point in the layout and orientation of buildings throughout the lifespan of the site (Hope-Taylor 1977: 278–9; Blair 2005: figs 7 and 8). Yeavering offers a significant archetype against which to match Woodnesborough in Kent. Eastry has seen recent intensive investigation (Dickinson, Fern, and Richardson 2011; Dickinson 2012). Until relatively recently Woodnesborough was recognized only through vague antiquarian accounts that mentioned a high and conical mound near the church and the discovery of a glass vessel, fibula, and spearhead, and, infamously, an earlier and separate find of thirty ancient glass claw-beakers (Akerman 1855: 34–6). In a close assessment of the archaeology and topographic placement of the surrounding cemeteries of Eastry I and II, Dickinson et al. have argued for a territory of the Eastringas, delimited by a circuit of cemeteries. By the seventh century, the place-name had ceased to refer to the loose, bounded territory, and instead referred to a royal centre at Eastry. A Roman road joined Eastry to Woodnesborough, flanked by sporadic burials and cemeteries. The elite and rich grave at Coombe and the finds at Woodnesborough imply a royal cult centre. Woodnesborough is a place-name considered to mean 'Woden's barrow'. It is here that a church was built, next to the large conical *wodnesbeorh*. Unlike Yeavering, we cannot discern associated cult structures, shrines, and halls in relation to a wider panoply of prehistoric monuments, but evidence does suggest the focus of Christianization by the church was the developing royal cult-site at the heart of a territory or unit of early origin. The church, however, has no pre-Conquest fabric, nor any documentary evidence of a pre-Conquest foundation (Akerman 1855: 34–6; Meaney 1964: 141; Ellis Davidson and Webster 1967: 7–8).

St John sub Castro in Lewes, Sussex, offers an equally ambiguous but interesting case. The evidence here is not only for at least one Saxon church near prehistoric barrows, but also for a larger, extensive Christianized 'landscape' of other prehistoric remains (Bleach 1997) (see Figure 4.6). The mottes of Brack Mount and Castle Mound are suggested to overlie earlier tumuli. To the north of Brack Mount four further barrows or mounds are recorded, two of which lie within the churchyard of St John sub Castro, one of which is certainly Bronze Age. To the south-east, on the site of All Saints Church, a well, a monolith, and a possible mound are recorded. To the south-west, burial mounds of prehistoric date were investigated lying adjacent to the church of St Anne (Bleach 1997). St John's Church has late Saxon fabric and lies at the corner of the late Saxon *burh*. A relationship between one or more Anglo-Saxon ecclesiastical foundations and a landscape of prehistoric barrows is evident at Lewes, but it is difficult to unpick the placement of the churches from the establishment of the late Anglo-Saxon *burh*. If St John's, All Saints, and St Anne's were established before the planned, defensive town, then they may represent the Christianizing of a pre-Christian 'numinous' landscape with multiple special or sacred places. The potency of groupings of upstanding monuments may be evident here, and the successive placement of churches over time offers the possibility that Christianization of 'prehistoric' landscapes might take place cumulatively over several centuries, in a stream of successive foundations that maintained that reference to the ancient remains.

An analogous example is provided by Ripon in North Yorkshire (see Figure 4.7). Richard Hall and Mark Whyman have described a poly-focal Christian monastic topography which incorporates a series of natural hills and spurs, and an isolated, conical, barrow-shaped natural hill (Ailcy) (Hall and Whyman 1996: fig. 36). The first phases of burial using Ailcy Hill occurred before

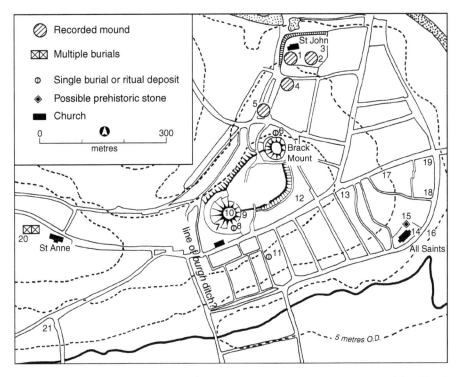

Fig. 4.6 A Christianized 'landscape' of prehistoric remains at Lewes in Sussex? After Bleach 1997. Reproduced by permission of John Bleach and John Blair.

Eata's or Wilfrid's monasteries were established. A series of sixth- to seventh-century, north–south burials are inferred. This natural arena, with its spurs, hills, barrow-shaped mound and pre-Christian burial site, is argued to have provided a theatre for a developing monastic complex of Christian churches, chapels, and cemeteries from the seventh century. While this example offers little evidence for the conversion of a royal cult-centre or central place, as at Yeavering, it seems that a landscape of natural features, perhaps perceived ancient features, were slowly 'converted' as a setting for a multifocal Christian landscape. There are pre-Christian burials at Ripon too, poorly preserved but attested through excavation at Ailcy Hill. This again offers a possibility that pre-Christian cemeteries and burials may provide a link between church and prehistoric monument.

These four sites attest to ecclesiastical interest in relatively large-scale, busy, multifocal landscapes, where single or numerous prehistoric remains or, in the case of Ripon, unusual natural features were referenced or acknowledged through secondary or associative burials, multifocal burial, timber-built structures, and single standing posts. There are unequivocal similarities with Avebury, Bampton, and Rudston. At Yeavering the Christian Church was proactive in establishing a presence at a major royal site and assembly-place framed by

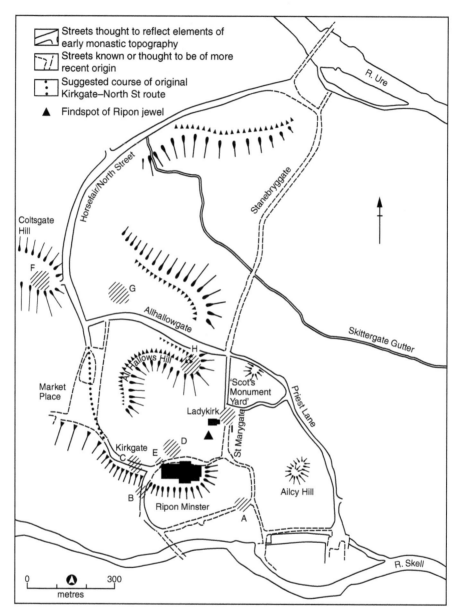

Fig. 4.7 The early medieval monastic landscape at Ripon, North Yorkshire. After Hall and Whyman 1996, fig. 36. Reproduced by permission of Mark Whyman.

mementoes of the prehistoric past (Semple 2009); the same process may be evident at Woodnesborough in Kent. Perhaps at Avebury, Bampton, and Rudston too, churches were established in relation to small 'meaningful' clusters of prehistoric monuments that had already played a part in shaping early to middle Anglo-Saxon funerary and settlement activity. At Ripon and possibly Lewes, a cumulative process of 'conversion' can be discerned, in which natural and antecedent features offered a theatre within which over time churches and chapels were established to denote an extensive Christian landscape.

Funerary activity and burial again provide the link between 'mound' and church in the second category of 'churches by barrows'. This group of sites shows, at least on surviving evidence, Christian or ecclesiastical interest in individual barrows. The majority represent undated, recognizably artificial mounds situated in churchyards close to the medieval or later church structure. However, a small group, subject to archaeological investigation, can be shown to be tumuli covering elite or aristocratic burials of the late sixth to seventh centuries. The nineteenth-century excavation of the large, isolated flat-topped mound at Taplow resulted in the discovery of a high-status male burial in a timber-built chamber, accompanied by an extensive aristocratic kit. There is no indication in the antiquarian report of any evidence to support a prehistoric date for the monument, although a large Iron Age hill fort and indications of further prehistoric features have been found in recent excavations in the vicinity of the barrow (Williams 2006a: 202–4; Pollington 2008: 168–9). The barrow would have sat near the entrance to the fortification at the highest natural point. Geophysical prospection in the mid-1990s revealed what may be a pre-Conquest and perhaps pre-Viking church in the immediate vicinity (Stocker et al. 1995) (see Figure 4.8). The authors of the short report have assumed a Christian appropriation of a pagan burial and again pointed to Pope Gregory's instruction to convert the temples of the pagan English. The evidence, although the postulated church is untested archaeologically, suggests the appropriation, absorption, and reworking of a possible pre-Christian princely burial into a Christian cult-site. The power of the deceased as an ancestral force was perhaps being harnessed by the church, or, more plausibly, the living relatives and family were ensuring their significant 'pre-Christian' ancestor was not being written out of history by the conversion.

The less well-known site of Ogbourne St Andrew, Wiltshire, offers a remarkably similar, although chronologically later, scenario. Ogbourne is recorded as a late Saxon estate centre before Domesday. After the Conquest, it became divided into Ogbourne St Andrew and Ogbourne St George. The former is considered the core of the archaic unit. Although the church standing today is no earlier than the eleventh century and there are no records to indicate the existence of a pre-Conquest church, a collection of finds from the vicinity of the modern village attest to mid to late Anglo-Saxon activity. A large, conical barrow covered in trees in the churchyard was excavated in the 1880s and

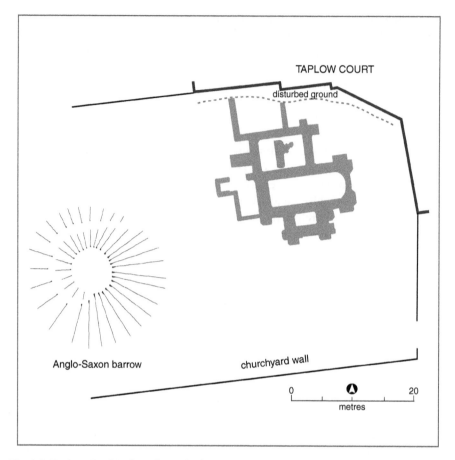

TAPLOW COURT

disturbed ground

Anglo-Saxon barrow   churchyard wall

0   ⬥   20

metres

Fig. 4.8 Taplow, Buckinghamshire: the barrow and the plan of the putative chapel. After Stocker, Went, and Farley 1995: fig. 6. Reproduced by permission of David Stocker.

identified as a Bronze Age barrow. This was reused for a male interment, placed in a wooden coffin with ornate iron fittings, which can be no earlier than the eighth century and may date as late as the ninth or tenth (see Chapter 2, pp. 42–3, and Figure 2.10) (Semple 2003a). The current road plan fossilizes what appears to be a rectilinear enclosure that encompasses the church, churchyard, and barrow, with the barrow situated at the north-east corner. This rich and elite Christian burial, secondary in a prehistoric barrow, represents a highly unusual event in late Anglo-Saxon England. The similarities with Taplow are palpable, but the chronology is frustratingly at odds, placing the Ogbourne St Andrew male firmly and irrefutably within a Christian time frame.

A final site for consideration is High Wycombe, Buckinghamshire, where another seventh-century elite barrow burial was identified some 30 metres from the medieval church. There is no archaeological evidence for a pre-Conquest foundation here, and the barrow is not considered a reused prehistoric monument, but the similarities demand that this is at least considered alongside Taplow and Ogbourne as another potential example of an elite barrow burial exerting influence in the siting of a church.

Although good archaeological and chronological corroborative evidence is absent, analogous sites can be suggested. An undated and unexcavated mound lies a short distance west-north-west of the late Saxon church of All Saints at Hinton Ampner, Hampshire. Another undated and unexcavated barrow lies within the churchyard of the undedicated church at Berwick in East Sussex, which contains thirteenth-century fabric (see Figure 4.9). A large and again unexplored mound is a central feature at the churchyard of All Saints in Wickham, Essex. An artificial mound some 300 metres south-south-west of the church at Stoneleigh, Warwickshire, is presently named Motslow Hill, thought to mean *OE (ge)mot* + *stow* 'moot place' (Gover et al. 1936, 184).

These sites pose more questions than answers. It is possible they do not even represent a distinct category of site. Not all of the mounds may be barrows, and, even if they are, some may be prehistoric, some Anglo-Saxon, and some a conflation of the two. Many of the churches are post-Conquest and later. The 'reuse' of these monuments may have taken place for different reasons according to the age of the barrow and the changing religious temperaments of the time. In light of Chapter 2, where prehistoric barrows were confirmed as monuments frequently used by Anglo-Saxons for pre-Christian burial, and

Fig. 4.9 Undated, flat-topped mound in the churchyard at Berwick in Sussex. Author's image.

given the appearance of pre-Christian graves and cemeteries at some of the sites discussed in this chapter (pp. 123–4), it is possible that one or two of these sites represent prehistoric barrows that attracted funerary activity in the fifth to seventh centuries. Some if not all of these mounds may also represent elite, primary barrow burials of the late sixth and seventh centuries.

There are, however, less dramatic possibilities. A notable cluster of sites lie in the border counties: Beckford (Gloucestershire), Thruxton (Herefordshire), Aston (Herefordshire), Kings Capel (Herefordshire), and Brinklow (Warwickshire). A sixth example, St Weonards (Herefordshire), serves as an informative case study. A thirteenth-century church stands some 100 metres from a large flat-topped conical mound (see Figure 4.10). The mound has the appearance of a Norman motte. Mottes of all sizes frequently occur in this region. Examples of post-Conquest churches and chapels founded within motte-and-bailey constructions are ubiquitous. Excavations in the nineteenth century at St Weonard's, however, revealed a prehistoric burial beneath the mound, showing that the motte was constructed over a prehistoric round barrow. The mound at Brinklow was certainly used as a motte, but the place-name suggests the mound might have an earlier origin. Recorded as *Brinchelau, -lawa* in the twelfth-century, the name seems to combine *OE brinc* 'slope/hill' or a personal name, and *hlaw* 'hill or barrow' (see Gover et al. 1936: 98–9). The mound also gives its name to the hundred. Not all the border mounds have evidence of a pre-Conquest or prehistoric origin, and many may comprise no more than small Norman mottes. Churches and chapels were frequently established within motte-and-baileys, and this would easily explain these church and mound combinations along the Welsh and English borders.

Appropriation of pre-existing mounds could have been a functional and labour-saving tactic, but Norman authorities may also have recognized the

Fig. 4.10 St Weonard's Church, Herefordshire. Reproduced from Wright 1855.

power of ancient barrows and their important place in the psyche of the English and Welsh populations. These prehistoric or pre-Christian tumuli, as at Brinklow, may have been actively used as places of assembly or have been emblematic of local identity or administrative and political borders (see O'Brien 1999 on barrows and frontiers), serving as places of resistance, resonant of indigenous identity and ancestry. Although speculative, where Norman engineers subsumed existing burial mounds under their mottes, they could have been attempting to eradicate those places of potent value to local identity.

A further possibility is suggested by two documentary accounts that attest to interest in ancient barrows by the post-Conquest Church. A written account of activities in 1199 in the Welsh borders describes how the monks at Ludlow removed a large barrow and discovered three burials while enlarging their church. The monks identified the bones as those of Irish saints, and they were translated and interred in the new church (Wright 1841: 14, 28). A rather similar tale describes how in *c.*1148 the Abbot of St Albans was visited in his dreams by a St Amphibalus, who indicated that his remains could be found close by in the barrows called the Hills of Banners. His monks duly opened up the prehistoric barrows near Redbourn and found the bones and remains of the saint, which were brought back to St Albans for translation (Page 1902: 256–8; Grinsell 1953: 110; 1986). The clear recognition that tumuli contained relics of the ancient dead might provide a reason for the post-Conquest appropriation of large mounds as the setting for churches. Such features may have been perceived or indeed invented as the graves of saintly founders. The potential value of grave mounds as a means of creating ancient legitimacy even after the Conquest should thus not be underestimated. The twelfth-century account of the barrow robbing at Ludlow incidentally also preserves evidence of yet another example of a pre-Conquest minster situated next to a large ancient burial mound: perhaps even the *hlaw* that gave Ludlow its name.

In summary, a range of differing potential motivations and processes are possible here. Several sites are places that may have exerted influence because of an existing elite presence. The prehistoric or pre-Christian mounds at these sites were already acting as enceinte and foci for settlement or burial. Other locations can be tentatively suggested as pre-Christian cult-sites with royal or elite connections, although it should be underlined again that the numbers of finds from churchyards that attest to pre-Christian burial at these sites are extremely rare. Sites that appear to show church appropriation of an elite grave or burial are thus especially interesting and anomalous, and, at one or two, sound archaeological evidence suggests what seems to be the translation of individual pre-Christian elite graves into Christian cult-foci. At many other sites there remains little or no evidence to explain when, how, or why the relationship between church and monument was forged. A final point of consideration is that the post-Conquest appropriation of some barrows, through the placement of churches or via the enlargement of the barrows as mottes, indicates a Norman and later interest in the prehistoric and pre-Christian sepulchres of the dead.

Churches and earthwork enclosures

In the seventh and eighth centuries, a number of early minster churches were also established and built within prehistoric enclosures, particularly hill forts. One of the earliest examples is the early seventh-century foundation of a monastic community at Malmesbury, North Wiltshire, within an Iron Age fortification. Twenty-three examples of churches of Anglo-Saxon and medieval date lie at the entrance to prehistoric enclosures or within them. Of all the data in this chapter, this category contains the largest proportion of churches confirmed by documentary or architectural evidence as Anglo-Saxon foundations. In many instances, excavation verifies the identification of an enclosure as prehistoric, usually Iron Age hill forts, which were reused for monastic foundations, such as at Aylesbury in Buckinghamshire, Tetbury in Gloucestershire, at Breedon-on-the-Hill in Leicestershire (see Figure 4.11), and Hanbury in Worcestershire. Two additional possibilities include St Buryan in Cornwall and Eynsham in Oxfordshire, where Bronze Age enclosures seem to have been used as enceintes for monastic communities. These types of site have been discussed several times by John Blair (1988, 2005), who has argued that they represented both 'a need for enclosure and an urge to reclaim the past' (Blair 2005: 190) and that relict forts and enclosures played little part in English life before the mid-eighth century with the exception of the northern citadels in

Fig. 4.11 Breedon-on-the-Hill, Leicestershire. © Reproduced by permission of Richard Green. All rights reserved.

'semi-British' Bernicia (Blair 2005: 168–9). This distinctive regional difference in the reworking of elements of the landscape is argued to have arisen from the difference in economic regimes between Anglo-Saxon and British territories (based on arguments put forward by Charles-Edwards 1989: i. 28–39). The reoccupation and re-fortification of prehistoric hill forts is well recognized as a feature of western and northern Britain. These sites functioned as elite, secular centres (Dark 1994a: 67–116; 1994b). Some were residences with large and elaborate structures, such as South Cadbury and Dinas Powys, where evidence indicated that prestige activities took place such as high-status metalworking. Citadels in the north, such as Dunadd, functioned as high-status residences, places of production for elite metalwork, and centres of administrative power used for the inauguration of kings (Alcock 1988; Thomas 1993). Occupied and re-fortified sites around the western coasts and Irish Sea basin housed consumers of Mediterranean imports who were linked to the trade networks that existed between the western Atlantic and the late Antique world (Thomas 1993; Campbell 2007). In the fifth and sixth centuries, some hill forts were reoccupied or were never completely abandoned. An entry in the *Anglo-Saxon Chronicle* for 571 records the taking of four settlements from the British by Cutha: Limbury, Aylesbury, Benson, and Eynsham (*ASC* (E) 571), suggesting the presence of British populations at at least two hill forts and perhaps one Bronze Age enclosure. It is a single written source, but it does suggest that in the post-Roman English landscape some hill forts were occupied by the British and fought over; and it may be no coincidence that early minsters were established at two of these reclaimed ancient monuments.

Many hill forts have no signs of reoccupation, but, as Chapters 2 and 3 established, the early Anglo-Saxons did not ignore them entirely. Although relatively rare, examples have been found of cemeteries of the fifth, sixth, and seventh centuries established within prehistoric forts. At Highdown in Sussex, a relatively large fifth- to seventh-century inhumation cemetery was laid out within the hill fort. Burials were accompanied by weapons sets and dress fittings (Welch 1983: ii. 219–27; Geake 1997: 184). By the late sixth and seventh centuries, some elite, high-status barrow burials (secondary and primary) were being constructed next to large hill fort and earthwork enclosures too, for example, at Taplow and Lowbury in Berkshire. This evidence suggests that hill forts and earthwork enclosures remained valued, and invested with some kind of meaning long after the fifth century. Hill forts were also places of conflict. Cynric fought the British at Old Sarum or *Searo byrig* in 552 and again at Barbury Castle or *Beran byrg* in 556 (*ASC* (E) 552 and 556) (see Chapter 3, pp. 85–90). These sites and events were remembered and recorded in the Anglo-Saxon histories. They were affiliated to the legends and stories of the conquest of the British, and thus important to the identities of both British and Saxon and crucial to the emerging narratives of the origins of the English.

Whilst no category existed in England of royal or princely citadels that acted as 'parent foci for seventh- and eighth-century monastic foundations' (Blair 2005: 270), at least some hill fort enclosures seem to have retained a symbolic value to local and regional populations (perhaps as the abandoned *urbs*, citadels, or regional capitals), attracting the interest of early populations, and by the seventh century, aristocratic or elite families. Hill forts may have offered a dignified surrounding—an easily reused enclosure fitting to the wider monastic concerns with bounding space in the seventh and eighth centuries. Some, like Aylesbury, may have already housed a settlement or have symbolized the political identity of a particular family and region. Others may have been emblematic of a British identity and past. Again, the evidence suggests that the use of hill forts and old earthwork enclosures for ecclesiastical sites is not a simple and readily interpretable pattern. In each case a set of individual reasons seems likely to have caused the early church to establish a new minster within a prehistoric enclosure.

A second group of churches associated with earthwork enclosures comprise tenth-century or later foundations within and at the entrances to hill forts and other prehistoric enclosures. Old Sarum (see Figure 4.12), an Iron Age circular fortification, later adjacent to the Roman town of *Sorviodunum*, was re-fortified in the tenth century as an emergency *burh* and mint. Two churches were established: one in the centre and one at the entrance. Similarly, at South Cadbury, the hilltop enclosure was re-fortified and a town laid out, including the foundations for a cruciform church, in the early eleventh century. Reoccupation of the hill fort was short-lived and it appears that the church was never actually completed. At Chisbury, the twelfth-century chapel at the eastern entrance to the small hill fort almost certainly became associated with the monument via an identical process, as the hill fort may be the *Cissanbyrig* referred to in the Burghal Hidage list (Hill and Rumble 1996: 197–8). Cholesbury, Great Kimble, and West Wycombe, all in Buckinghamshire, could reflect similar processes, together with the twelfth-century chapel on St Catherine's Hill in Winchester. Of all the examples discussed, Knowlton is perhaps the most difficult to categorize, primarily through a lack of evidence or context for the establishment of the church within the henge. The site could easily fit all of the models presented in this chapter: the de-paganization of a site of pre-Christian veneration, a middle Anglo-Saxon, ecclesiastical adoption of an unused enclosure, or the establishment of a church within a fortified settlement reusing a prehistoric earthwork, a process which might account for the establishment of a possible church next to the cemetery, within the prehistoric enclosure at Thwing, East Yorkshire.

The use of prehistoric enclosures as ecclesiastical sites became a recognized aspect of church practice in Anglo-Saxon England between the eighth and eleventh centuries but had widely differing motivations. Iconic and emblematic sites, memory of British affiliations and identity, natural enclosing qualities,

Fig. 4.12 Old Sarum, Wiltshire, from the air. © Cambridge University.

existing settlement, and royal presence are all possible motivations. The reoccupation and re-fortification of earthwork enclosures were also a clear driving factor in the ninth and tenth centuries.

Discussion

A number of the churches found in close spatial arrangements with prehistoric monuments cannot be discounted as mere coincidences in the landscape. The variety argues, however, against the simple interpretation that these represent evidence of the 'conversion' of monuments with a pre-Christian value. There are intimations that some prehistoric monuments had become venerated foci (for example, aligned burials, single elite graves, posts, square enclosures, etc.).

The post-Roman reoccupation of some ancient enclosures, the siting of settlements next to, in, and on monuments before and during the conversion period, and the re-fortification and military use of some ancient monuments all present alternative reasons, however, for the establishment of churches within the shadow of prehistoric remains. The written sources and accounts that describe the first foundations of churches and monasteries in the English landscape are oddly quiet in regards to any widespread process of adopting and adapting prehistoric monuments; indeed they are far more fulsome in their description of the establishment of churches within the ruins of Roman towns and buildings. This fits with the larger body of evidence for the reuse of old Roman sites and structures by the new Christian Church in Anglo-Saxon England. This odd collection of sites cannot therefore be discussed further without some reflection on early church locations in the written sources and the widespread archaeological and architectural evidence for the appropriation of Roman sites by the early Christian Church.

Romanitas

Richard Morris included the reuse of Roman sites by the Church within his class of regenerative cult-sites, pointing to the appropriation in some instances of temples and bath-houses as evidence of their ritual or religious significance before the arrival of the Augustinian mission (Morris and Roxan 1980; Morris 1989: 6–45, esp. 17–45). In more recent discussions the appropriation of a wide range of Roman ruins and sites for the establishment of churches, alongside the recycling of Roman building material in Anglo-Saxon church structures, has been interpreted as evidence for the value of Roman buildings as quarries for building materials and features, and as indicative of an ideological drive to 'rebuild Rome' by the Augustinian mission and the Roman Church on its arrival and re-establishment in England (Stocker with Everson 1990; Eaton 2000; Bell 2005). Archaeological research centred on other areas of the late antique world has also argued for the harnessing of Roman buildings and *spolia* by the Church, and has emphasized both economic and symbolic purpose, pointing to the role of the new Christian elite in the re-monumentalizing of urban centres (see Deichmann 1975; Brenk 1987; Moralee 2006; but especially Leone 2007: 180–7; 2013, chapters 3 and 4). A comprehensive study by Tyler Bell of the reuse of Roman structures in England identified over 250 medieval churches associated with Roman buildings and over 100 early medieval burial sites (Bell 2005: 152–3). Although Bell offers neither a definitive economic nor a symbolic explanation, his study does propose the existence of local and regional practices. Bell plots churches associated with Roman buildings against a background density of Roman buildings and Roman roads, and although a concentration of sites can be seen in those areas where the presence and survival of Roman buildings are common, there are a considerable number of outliers in Wales and north-west and far north-east of England (Bell 2005: fig. 35). This stands in contrast to Bell's plot of burials associated with Roman buildings against the same background density (Bell 2005: fig. 9). There are certainly some distinct geographic variations in his data. For example, the cluster of sites with very certain associations between a Roman villa, inhumations of post-Roman date, and evidence for an early medieval church all lie to the west, reaching from Oxford to the Severn and Exeter (Bell 2005: 129, table 10). Another well-known distinctive group, not in fact covered in Bell's thesis, are the Anglo-Saxon churches of the Tyne Valley, all largely constructed from recycled Roman stone (Cambridge 1984; Cramp 2005). We might consider too the particular nature of the early Kentish churches in the south-east, which were constructed on occasion using a whole Roman building as a basis (for example, St Martin's, Canterbury, and Reculver) or Roman building materials including stone, brick, and tile (for example, Bradwell-on-Sea and Lyminge). We are seeing perhaps, in the words of Martin Carver, 'intellectual territories': areas where people thought alike and where the antecedent landscape and monuments were an intrinsic inherited element of the fabric of their lives and their perceived identity (Carver 2011). Christianity in these areas was potentially being shaped by a rich pre-Christian inheritance that not only informed the adaptation of Christianity at regional and local scales but also provided political agendas with much needed narratives of ancient, ancestral, and legitimate authority.

Sam Turner in his work on the Christian landscape of Cornwall has shown how the distinctive underlying geography, the antecedent landscape, and the lifestyles of those who dwelled within it helped shape the distinctive Christian monumental repertoires of the far west (2006). Regionally distinctive Christian architectures have been revealed in Ireland too by Tomás Ó'Carragáin (2010: fig. 1, 45–9), and the whole concept of a 'Celtic' church has been deconstructed by the extensive works brought together by Nancy Edwards in her edited work on the churches of the west (Edwards 2009a), and by individual studies such as David Petts's examination of the Church in Wales (2009). Increasing numbers of studies focusing upon monumentality have thus begun to 'map' Christian investment and by so doing have revealed a complex dialogue enacted in monumental repertoires that is argued to offer insight into the social identities of different groups as well as political agendas at a variety of differing scales (see Howe 1997; Ó'Carragáin 2010: 49–45 and 57–85; Toop 2011: 87–8). Recent research on late antique and Byzantine townscapes has argued that architectural and epigraphic legacies of the Roman world were deliberately recycled and consciously harnessed by Christian elites for their narratives of sanctity and power. This proposition offers credence to the idea that *Romanitas* was a conscious component in elite strategy, one that was equivalent to the literary narratives of power and conversion being used to align a new Christian authority with the material legacy of *imperium* (Moralee 2006: 214; Leone 2007: 180–7; 2013: chapters 3 and 4).

Just as practices involving prehistoric monuments are shown here to be highly varied, so the appropriation of Roman sites and building fabric is equally diverse. These 'intellectual territories' are further complicated by the strong influences of Christian fashion and liturgical influences from elsewhere in Christian Europe on the local Christian scene in England. When Benedict Biscop brought masons of Gaulish origin to build his churches after the Roman manner, his choice was about wealth, position, status, connections, aligning to a Continental mode of Christian monument, and harnessing the power of the surviving monumental Roman remains of the Tyne Valley (Turner et al. 2013). We have to remember too that the establishment of churches and monasteries was not purely the whim of Roman or Irish missionaries; it was often dictated by the desires of kings. Kings were influenced by their subjects and sought to impress them. Biscop was given land by Ecgfrith and repaid him by bringing the grandeur of the Continent to the gateway of his kingdom, reinforcing the message already relayed by the visually impressive, albeit ruined magnificence, of the Roman ruins along the Tyne (Turner et al. 2013). Ecgfrith too, perhaps under encouragement from Biscop, was also aligning himself to elites in the Christian east, by patronizing the creation of a monumental symbolic narrative of sanctity and power that used, rather than townscapes, the Roman fabric available along the Tyne: forts, bridges, and monuments (see Leone 2007: 18–7; 2013: chapter 3).

The intellectual agenda for monument building could therefore be set by kings and their needs, informed by the political climate and aspirations of the ruling group, but also by the locality itself and the physical remains of the past therein and the local sense of identity shaped by this landscape. There are indications that agendas could be set by an individual or group. Was the appropriation of Roman towns and monuments in the south-east set for example by Augustine and his mission or by the Francophile aspirations and allegiances of Æthelbert? More likely, as at Monkwearmouth and Jarrow, such decisions were mutually beneficial, each site a suitably significant location chosen to enhance aspects of Christian ideology, but also meeting the desire of the patron for some form of political statement and signalling, and situated to the best economic advantage (Turner et al. 2013). Gwen Bergius has recently researched the Continental connections evident in Mercian sculpture and concluded that royal and ecclesiastical powers shared an interest in the late antique, which served to create a repertoire of art distinctive in its connections to late antique models and designs (Bergius 2011: 192–200). This reworking of late antique motifs was different in the sculpture of the Mercian heartland and of that created and erected along its peripheries. Bergius has argued for scales of influence, with lesser aristocratic landholders emulating the power of the Mercian heartland with their own particular, local variation of late antique influenced sculptural design (Bergius 2011: 192–200). The ancient was thus valuable to kings and to the Church, but also to lesser ranks of aspirants seeking to consolidate local power and landholding and to use the Christian faith and its materiality to enhance those claims.

The few examples of prehistoric and Roman monuments embellished with the erection of new sculptural additions are relevant here. Jane Hawkes notes that occasionally Anglo-Saxon sculptures lie within several kilometres of old Roman centres (for example, Otley, Yorkshire, and Hoddam, Dumfriesshire) (see Hawkes 2003a: 83); Wroxeter represents another important example (White and Barker 1995). Similarly, bodies of early medieval sculptural fragments including whole and partial crosses can be found at Roman towns and forts where a monastic or church presence is already attested, for example, at St John's Church, Chester (Bailey 2010), or York Minster (Lang 1991), Winchester (Tweddle et al. 1995), and Bath (Cramp 2006). Of the few crosses or stone sculptures found at or in Roman sites (see Hawkes 2003a: 80–7),[1] Bewcastle is perhaps the most famous of all. This sculpture is identified by the *Corpus of Anglo-Saxon Stone Sculpture* as a cross-shaft and base, dating to the eighth century (Bailey and Cramp 1988: 71, no. 162), and stands in the middle of a Roman fort in Cumbria, to the north of Hadrian's Wall (Cramp 1961; Mercer 1964; Newman 1984: 165–72; Bailey and Cramp 1988: 71, no. 162). It has been argued to represent a Rome-inspired column or obelisk rather than a cross (Orton 1999; Mitchell 2001) and to have a predominantly secular, rather than monastic purpose or context, raised perhaps in commemoration of a secular aristocrat (Orton 1999, 2003, 2006; Orton et al. 2007). Jane Hawkes offers a more spiritually orthodox motivation, suggesting that this and other crosses placed on Roman sites, in parallel to the first stone-built churches in Anglo-Saxon England, were positioned intentionally by those 'deliberately claiming and appropriating that which was Rome in order to establish it as part of the new Rome of Christ' (Hawkes 2003a: 82). This parallels Hawkes's arguments for the appropriation of Roman and late Imperial form and imagery at Masham, Rothbury, and Repton, as means of creating monuments that would have served as highly visible and permanent expressions of the power of the Roman Church (Hawkes 2003a: 69–100, esp. 76–9). Perhaps neither argument is wrong. The widespread adoption and reworking of Roman sites, structures, and building materials in the new architecture of the Christian Church might fit 'the empire-wide recreation of *Romanitas*' (Blair 2005: 189–90), but the *variety* of ways in which 'Rome' was harnessed implies that major royal or ecclesiastical figures and lesser aristocratic families had individual effects on these processes. The varied emphasis of local communities on immediate monuments

---

[1] Ilkley, West Yorkshire, Aldborough, North Yorkshire, and of course Wroxeter.

in their landscapes relating to local narratives of origin and identity may also have had a role in the development of strong regional variations on practice. The variety of prehistoric monuments adopted and used by the Church and the highly varied reasons for their use may thus be *less* at odds with this evidence for the use of the Roman past, once the scale and variety of recycling are unpicked.

Early medieval sources and written accounts

In light of this, it is interesting to review some of the early written sources that describe the conversion of the English landscape and the foundation of the first monasteries, minsters, and churches. Anglo-Saxon written accounts of prehistoric remains are hard to find, and often quite ambiguous, as Chapter 5 will show. Accounts of the Christian usage of prehistoric sites are even more elusive. By contrast, some of the earliest written sources mention the Christian recycling of Roman ruins. Following the arrival of Augustine in Kent in AD 597 with the Roman Christian mission, Bede lists repeated reclamations of Roman remains. According to Bede, Bertha, Æthelbert's Christian queen, was already using an old Roman church on the east side of the Roman city of Canterbury for Christian worship, 'built in honour of St Martin during the Roman occupation of Britain' (*HE* I, 26). After Augustine was granted his episcopal see in Canterbury, he proceeded 'with the King's help to repair a church, which he was informed had been built long ago by Roman Christians' (*HE* I, 33). These are just some of the more explicit descriptions of the recycling of Roman structures for Christian usage: many more references exist to the establishment of churches in the remains of deserted and partially inhabited Roman towns; for example, churches were built in the Roman cities of London, York, and Rochester (see *HE* II, 3 and 14). The adoption of prehistoric sites by the Christian Church is entirely absent as a comparable theme in Bede's narrative of the English conversion. Even in the description of Paulinus instructing and baptizing at Yeavering, Northumberland, Bede makes no mention of the prehistoric hill fort, barrows, or standing stones that influenced the positioning and layout of the site (*HE* II, 14). Bede was, of course, an incumbent of Jarrow, a monastery that even in its physical fabric resonated with *Romanitas*. Bede's account may be a verification for a general preference for Roman buildings and sites as locales for the first Christian churches, but may also signal a regionally distinctive vision of power created by Ecgfrith and Biscop, built around the latent and ruined symbolism of the Romanized Tyne Valley. In other words, Bede potentially was again working to a propaganda specific to his own Northumbrian intellectual territory.

   The *Vitae*—the individual stories that describe the evangelizing of the English landscape—are more varied in their description of the appropriation of places, landscapes, and monuments. Most notable among these sources is the *Life of St Guthlac*; written by a monk called Felix, it records the inhabitation of a burial mound on a haunted island by a holy man and the subsequent enshrinement of his relics at the same location (Colgrave 1956). A date between AD 730 and 740 is suggested for the composition of the *Vita*, although the earliest surviving manuscript is British Library Royal 4 A xiv, composed in the late eighth or early ninth centuries (Colgrave 1956: 18–19, 26). As Audrey Meaney and others have explained, many motifs within the *Vita* derive from biblical narratives and accounts of the Desert Fathers (Meaney 2001, 2005). The *Life of Guthlac* is no exception, as Meaney has argued with clear references to the life of both St Bartholomew and St Anthony (Meaney 2001, 2005). The *Vita* provided legitimation for the ancient sanctity of monastic houses, recounting the spiritual endeavours of their founders and saintly incumbents. These accounts draw on a wide range of biblical motifs but also attempt to set them within a vernacular scene. There is thus a reality to them, perhaps in the actions of these saintly founders, but also in the introduction of local detail to render these accounts more plausible and valid. Thus Guthlac's wilderness became the wet and noisome fens of Crowland: almost impassable, uninhabited, and inhospitable. His dwelling, instead of an ancient tomb, fort, or urn, is apparently a grave mound broken open by robbers (see discussions in Chapter 5). The account may not factually attest to the establishment of a Christian hermitage within the broken chamber of a prehistoric barrow; but it does provide a glimpse into the mind of an author creating a foundation myth, transposing biblical motifs and stories within more familiar local scenery. It is entirely possible that the narrative contains some element of truth. Guthlac may have specifically sought out a great burial mound as a setting for his personal battle. What is interesting is the account also discusses the burial of Guthlac in or next to his dwelling in the barrow and the development of an apparently royally sanctioned cult around the burial prior to the establishment of the monastery at some distance from the site of the holy man's cell.

Another foundation myth that includes reference to an ancient monument or ruin is the legend of St Frideswide dating to the twelfth century. This describes how she and her religious companions spent a period of solitary reflection in a lonely place called *Thornbiri*. OE *burh* was often used in relation to ancient earthwork enclosures (for example, Thornborough Henges, Yorkshire), and we might assume here that the writer was evoking the image of a disused fortification entangled in many trees and thorns (Blair 1988; 1994: 67–8). An even vaguer reference is Cedd's description of a monastery at Lastingham amid some steep and remote hills more suited to robbers and wild beasts (Miller 1891; see Chapter 5, pp. 153–5 for a full discussion).

As Katy Cubitt has argued, geography and topography were vital in the *Vita* (Cubitt 2000: 40–1). The motifs and snapshots used by writers were precise, and there is every reason to suspect they were rooted in real places and landscapes *and* real popular beliefs, in order to legitimize and corroborate the fantastic and to underpin the power of the foundation myth and the sanctity of the monastic foundation (Cubitt 2000). This selection suggests that certain types of place, ancient barrows, overgrown forts, ruins, and wild places were useful motifs to authors. They provided an anchor for the narrative in the real world and the local landscape, but, at the same time, their liminal ruinous qualities and associations with perhaps exile, despair, and terror rendered them ideal locales at which to stage a narrative of spiritual battle and triumph. In *De Abbatibus*, Æthelwulf's poem, holy Ecgberht instructs the first church to be built 'on a small hill with a bending downward path', overgrown by thorn bushes and the haunt of evil men' (*De Abbatibus*, lines 125–39; Campbell 1967: 12–13; see also Blair 1992: 227). The ideal topos is set out, one which other authors took and situated within their own particular landscape: the Anglian Fenlands, the Kentish Weald, the Wessex Chalk, and the Northumbrian Coast.

Christianity and monuments: a summary

This brief consideration of the wider evidence for Christian appropriation of Roman buildings and building material, together with a brief examination of several relevant written sources, reinforces several of the issues that emerged from the previous consideration of churches and prehistoric monuments. The appropriation of ancient monuments, whether Roman or prehistoric, by the Christian Church has no single explanation. There are strong regional distinctions and even individual motivations in *how* the Church turned ancient monumental landscapes to its purpose. This fits well with the current emphases on variety and regional differences in Christian practice *and* similar variances in the processes of conversion too presumably in broad terms reflecting the mix of Irish, British, and Roman Christian ideas that intermingled in the early years of Christianization in England (Carver 2001, 2011; Pluskowski and Patrick 2003; Gittos 2011; Morris 2011; Petts 2011: esp. 11–29). There are also indications of varying agendas in the data interrogated here, some communal and some individual. A significant number of incidences of appropriation seem to imply that monuments were already of some interest and used by elite and aristocratic groups for burial rites or settlement-related activity prior to the establishment of a minster or church at the site. In addition there are occasional intimations that prehistoric monuments may have had functions or roles that were particularly useful to the early Christian foundations—as sites of assembly and mustering or places of legend and fame.

A national approach to understanding the phenomenon of churches and prehistoric monuments, rather like that applied to the funerary use of prehistoric monuments, lacks the necessary subtlety needed if we are to understand the evidence set here. Small geographies are more significant. The antecedent landscape served to shape local identity and a sense of place and being, which in turn established a basis for the intellectual territory of the emerging elite powers. The Christian Church, whether Irish or Roman, had to negotiate and integrate with these local and regional influences and their antecedent origins, including presumably pockets of insular Christianity as well as non-Christian practice. It is noticeable in several of the examples discussed here that 'landscapes' of natural and monumental features may have been more significant than individual features, and that the prehistoric and Roman legacies may on occasion have together attracted Christian interest. This ties well to suggestions by Richard Morris that in some instances the Christian Church was involved in a complex reworking of extended landscapes of meaning and importance (Morris 2008, 2011). This might be at a reasonably large scale, as Sam Turner (2006: 131–69) suggests for the west of England, where churches and stone sculptures are argued as a material signature representing the selective reworking of elements of the landscape such as springs, rivers, enclosures, and old monuments. In a similar way, Martin Carver has made a case for the importance of prehistory to the pre-Christian beliefs of the Picts and its role therefore in shaping the new Christian sacred geography that emerged with the arrival and acceptance of Christianity (Carver 2008, 2011). At a lesser scale, recent exploration of the 'conversion' of the Witham Valley provides a useful example for a similar, more locally driven process (Stocker and Everson 2003; Everson and Stocker 2011). Everson and Stocker present evidence for the long-term ritual significance of the crossing points and causeways along the Witham. These were marked by prehistoric barrows and burials of the Bronze Age. These have been linked to long-term depositional rituals involving metal items, weaponry, and non-metallic objects. Everson and Stocker argue that the establishment of monastic foundations at each causeway, some pre- and some post-Conquest, represents the appropriation by the Christian Church of these significant places and perhaps even the rituals these crossing places and causeways had long demanded (see Figure 4.14). Along the Witham Valley, the natural and antecedent landscape as well as the long-term practices of local populations, all served to inform the intellectual agenda of the Church. The churches and monasteries on the Witham presumably benefited from the geographic location and the economic bounty created by being proximate to major thoroughfares and through-routes. These new monuments may also symbolically have mitigated the power of these crossing places, rendering safe passage across the dangerous fenland waters. Watery places are well acknowledged as locations synonymous with Christianity and spiritual battle (Gilchrist 1994, 1995; Gardiner and Rippon 2007; Wickham-Crowley 2006; Flatman 2010: 66–77). This case study is valuable in its indication that Christian negotiation took account of highly distinctive local agendas and local topography and that the Church could turn local landscapes to its advantage in a variety of ways. Just as the Roman legacy of the Tyne was distinctively harnessed to Christian elite agendas in the seventh and eighth centuries, the watery crossing places and ancient monuments of the Witham may have been used to reinforce ideas of conversion and spiritual battle. In other places, ancient barrows and prehistoric monuments may have been used in similar symbolic ways, perhaps to signal the triumph of Christianity over the old ways and ancestors or in some instances as a sign of an appropriated cult-site or founder grave.

Without significant archaeological intervention, the sites listed and discussed in this chapter will remain the subject of speculation. One suspects that, in a

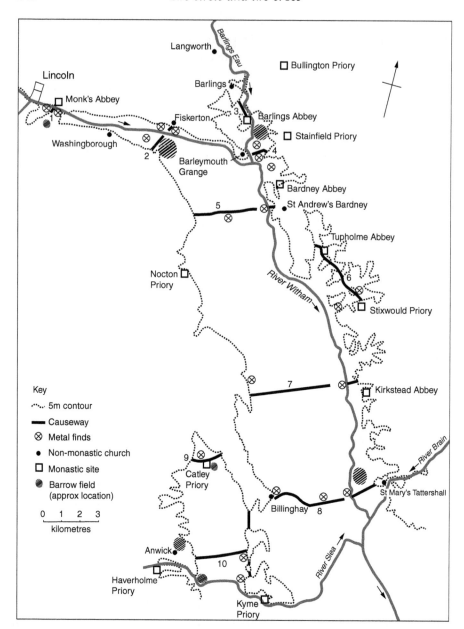

Fig. 4.13 Churches and causeways along the River Witham in Lincolnshire. After Stocker and Everson 2003: fig. 17.1. Reproduced by permission of David Stocker and Paul Everson.

number of cases, settlement and burial may have attracted the establishment of early church foundations. We can be certain from the full range of complimentary evidence, however, that these monuments and the landscape they were situated in shaped the identity of inhabitants in the uncertain centuries before the arrival of Christianity. A sense of place and system of local belief developed from the landscape in which people dwelled. Ancient sites have been shown in Chapters 2 and 3 to accrue value within the narratives of identity woven by communities. They may have shaped the 'intellectual territories' that were swiftly becoming a preserve and key tool of emergent Anglo-Saxon elite groups and families who needed to signal authority. Churches were founded at key places, royal and aristocratic palaces and residences, but also perhaps at potent places too: sites with important ancestral resonance or places intrinsically linked to the identity of the populations in the region. The examples discussed here point to the significance of graves of ancestral figures (Taplow), places of assembly and royal power (Yeavering), monuments associated with ancient events and heroes (Old Sarum), and powerful sites that symbolized spiritual battle or required special mediation (Crowland and Bampton).

The presence of churches in the shadow of prehistoric sites and monuments is rare, and few examples discussed here are without problem. They represent a highly diverse group and underline the multifarious meaning of ancient monuments in the conversion period. Some of those examples signal that ancient monuments retained their value to the newly established elite families of Anglo-Saxon England, and this served on occasion to make them of interest and value to the new Christian Church. They were harnessed to individual narratives of conversion and foundation myths, both in the fragmentary written record, but also physically in the appropriation of monuments and monument complexes by minsters and monasteries. In this way, the use of the prehistoric as places for the establishment of early Christian sites is not unlike the far more widespread, but regionally varied use of Roman structures and fabric in the creation of wide-scale and yet regionally distinctive, eastward-looking narratives of Christian identity. The use of prehistoric or early Anglo-Saxon monuments was driven, however, by the significance of ancient monuments to people and elites in the centuries prior to conversion as places of burial, as places of supernatural and ancestral power, and as visited and inhabited places with a rich symbolism and place in the local cosmology. These group and individual connections to prehistoric monuments were enduring, and after the arrival of Christianity may be reflected in the few examples where early Christian foundations appear to have referenced monuments with import and local potency. The main body of surviving literature, by contrast, however, valorizes the importance of the Roman past, in its accounts of the appropriation of Roman sites. This better documented tradition is also more frequently attested in material terms.

The prehistoric continued to draw the interest of the Church in the tenth and eleventh centuries and perhaps even later, as some examples discussed here imply; however, the ways in which ancient monuments were conceived in the Anglo-Saxon imagination and the physical uses to which they were put began to change. As the next chapters will reveal, the changing mentalities of Christian populations, mixed with the emerging royal administrative and judicial strategies and influenced perhaps by the increasingly strong Roman Christian Church, initiated new ways of using the ancient, although the potency of these old places and monuments sustained.

5

Changing meanings

Prehistoric monuments in literature and place-names
c. AD 700–1100

> *The dragon belongs in its barrow, canny and jealous of its jewels...*
> (*Maxims II*, Cotton Tiberius Bi, fo. 115a–b; trans.
> Bradley 1995: 513–14, lines 26–7)

The centuries after the conversion have left a wealth of documentary and literary sources: wills, laws, poetry, stories, charters, and annals. This translated excerpt from *Maxims II* is one of a number of literary references that attest to a late Anglo-Saxon imagination that included a landscape populated with heroes, mythical and supernatural beasts and potent and powerful places (see discussions in Semple 1998; Austin 2002; Hall 2006; 2007a: 54–74; 2007b: 299–317). Sources like these provide an opportunity to examine whether perceptions and beliefs surrounding ancient monuments are present within Anglo-Saxon literature. The surviving corpus of written documents represents the Christian, literate Anglo-Saxon world. They are products of writers working from a viewpoint, influenced by classical and late antique knowledge. However, these writers inevitably integrated vernacular traditions, legends, and tales into their own handlings of Christian literary traditions (Mitchell 1995: 194–5; and arguments centred on the *Lacnunga* by Jolly 1996; see also Lee 1998; Meaney 2001, 2005). The prose and poetry of this era survived bound into large compendia of whole and partial texts. These are considered to be the product of monastic scriptoria and, therefore, may reflect the highly educated and literate traditions of a Christian elite rather than popular folklore (but see arguments against the substantial recomposition of Old English poetry in scribal transmission; e.g. Fulk 2004: 16–25). The *Old English* bounds attached to Anglo-Saxon charters or land grants offer the possibility, however, of examining contemporary patterns of local vernacular belief connected to places in the landscape. Charters were issued from the late seventh century (Wormald 1986). The majority of boundary clauses refer to southern and western England (see Hill 1981: 24, fig. 35) and most survive as later copies. Although actual grants were liable to be forged, it is unlikely the boundary clauses—a list of landmarks denoting the real extent of the land or estate in question—were fabricated, as they set the limits of the land in question (see discussions by Hooke 1990: 2–3; Costen 1994: 97). Bounds were, however, updated on occasion in later copies to replace earlier and perhaps defunct place-names and lost landmarks with contemporary place-names (John Baker: pers. comm.). Ancient monuments—including barrows, hill forts, standing stones, stone cists, Roman buildings, Roman roads, and milestones—were frequently used as markers. These boundary descriptions provide an indication of how monuments were popularly named. Place-names that survive within the English landscape and in surviving documents offer another potential source of information on popular perception. References to possible prehistoric monuments are numerous in English place-names, but it is hard to distinguish indisputable references to upstanding prehistoric remains unless the name survives in firm association with a surviving monument.

This chapter brings together these literary and poetic sources with charter-bound terms and place-names. The density of information, greater and more compelling than the sum of its parts, points to the existence of a vivid popular perception of landscape and the ancient monuments within it. Schama (1995: 7) has argued that 'landscape is a work of the mind. Its scenery built up as much from strata of memory as layers of rock.' Place is argued by Carruthers as intrinsic to memory, and thus creativity, within the monastic community, with memorials and monuments as features that could provoke the sharing of experience and memories, spurring the creation of selective, collective identities (Carruthers 1998: 14, 30–40). As place-names attest, a sense of place can be developed and imposed by an individual and reflect his or her particular conception; or it can develop collectively, over time, between people and environment (Jones and Semple 2012: 2). This chapter proposes that ancient monuments played an important part in the creation of community and individual notions of place and identity and that these perceptions changed over time in response to the wider religious, political, and social changes of the first millennium.

The barrow and its inhabitants in Old English prose and poetry

Of all surviving sources, *Beowulf* is the most explicit in its description of a burial mound. The well-visited verses of the second part of this extraordinary literary survival recount how a dragon begins to stir from within the barrow in which he guards a hoard of treasure. The dwelling is described by a range of *OE* terminology, initially as a *stānbeorh* (stone-barrow) (Fulk et al. 2008: line 2213), and then in increasingly more poetic terms as an *ðām eorðsele* (earth hall) (lines 2232, 2410), and a *stāncleofu* (stone-cleft or crag) (lines 2545, 2718). The use of *beorge* (mound or barrow) (e.g. line 2546) is implicit in its identification of a burial mound, but the additional descriptive appellations are complex. *Boga*, 'stone-bows' or 'vaults', is unique to *Beowulf* and may allude to curved stone, perhaps more generally to something human-made and built (some have envisaged a stone-chambered barrow: Keiller and Piggott 1939; Leslie 1988: 55–6). Such a meaning fits well with the additional use of *enta ġeweorc* (pp. 179–80), Alaric Hall, in a deconstruction of the *Wife's Lament*, has drawn attention to the possible anti-meaning of *eorðsele*, 'earth hall', as a contrast to the motif of the peaceful, light, and warm Anglo-Saxon hall (Hall 2002: 8, acknowledging Wentersdorf 1981 and Hume 1974). He also suggests that the usage of such terms can allude to something human-altered and ancient. The burial mound was thus, on the one hand, a product of the ancient human past, but also represented a strange and ancient work as well *and* a place less welcoming and indeed contrary to the comforts and safety of the hall. The inhabitant, the dragon, variously referred to as *ūht-sceaða*, 'ravager of the night', and the *nacod nīðdraca*, 'smooth evil dragon' (Alexander 1987: 122, lines 2270–2; Fulk et al. 2008, lines 2270–4), is a hostile creature of darkness and revenge. Dragons are a well-recognized type of monstrous animal in both Anglo-Saxon art and literature, associated with the predatory beasts of pre-Christian artistic repertoires, and later with concepts of heathenism, evil and foreboding, and the devil. The *Anglo-Saxon Chronicle* famously depicts the first Viking raids on Northumbria with an entry describing fiery flying dragons (*ASC* (E) 793). Dragon-fighting saints occur in Anglo-Saxon homiletic, apocryphal, and hagiographic texts (Rauer 2001), and the combat of Michael and the dragon is occasionally depicted in eleventh-century stone carvings, including an example from Stinsford, Dorset (Cramp 2006: 113–14). An exceptional depiction of dragon fighting, influenced by the heroic tale of Sigurð, also features on a tenth-century grave marker from York Minster (see Figure 5.1) (Lang 1991: 71, no. 34, pl. 147). The dragon is consistently represented as evil and in opposition to Christianity in medieval sources (Vinycomb 1906: 70; Gravestock 1999: 126). This portrayal is argued to have developed from the influence of biblical texts and classical sources which render the dragon a beast symbolic of evil and monstrous adversity

Fig. 5.1 Sigurð killing Fáfnir. Tenth-century grave marker from York Minster. © Corpus of Anglo-Saxon Stone Sculpture. Reproduced by permission of Corpus of Anglo-Saxon Stone Sculpture.

(Rauer 2000: 52–3; see also the Book of Revelation 12: 7–9). Such perceptions may have been enhanced too by the significance of the dragon in pre-Christian societies, exemplified through its appearance in Norse mythology as an evil and dangerous creature (Ellis Davidson 1964: 159–62). The use of the dragon as a motif in decorative patterns, particularly as a predatory beast on elite martial gear such as the Sutton Hoo helmet (Carver 1998: fig. 18b–c), is suggested as part of a wider male aristocratic cosmology that embraced a range of wild and predatory animals (Pluskowski 2006a, 2006b, 2010). The association of this crafty, supernatural beast with an ancient and unwelcoming barrow provides a potent vignette of an ancient place, certainly frightenting, but also perhaps revered as a decaying place of ancient power and magificence. As the tale unfolds, the barrow is established as a site avoided by ordinary folk: a monument at which only the desperate—such as the tormented outcast and thief in *Beowulf*—would seek shelter (Alexander 1987: 121, lines 2223–9; Fulk et al. 2008).

The *Beowulf* manuscript (BL MS Cotton Vitellius A. XV) is dated by its script to the beginning of the eleventh century (Ker 1957: 13, 281), *c.* AD 975–1025 (Kiernan 1997: 10). The date of composition for the poem is, however, placed as early as the eighth century (for an overview of the variations in proposed dating for the composition of *Beowulf,* see Chase 1997; for eighth-century origins, see Bolton 1978 and Wormald 1978; for later origins, see Blake 1977 and Jacobs 1977; for recent arguments for an archaic origin, see Lapidge 2000 and Fulk, Bjork, and Niles 2008). The association between ancient barrow and evil serpent could thus originate in the eighth century, or even earlier if an oral origin for the tale is accepted. The tale implies that ancient barrows could be imagined as fearful places, housing other-worldly and evil creatures, and that they were best avoided. Corroboration is offered by *Maxims II*, as quoted at the opening of the chapter. This may have been influenced by the poem, but does suggest that association between dragon and barrow was a more widely held belief or superstition and not a device contained solely within the legend and text of *Beowulf*.

Wið Færstice

The burial mound is associated in other texts with a wider range of mythical beings. Elves are most notable perhaps, for their mention in *Wið færstice* 'a charm for a sudden stitch', alongside *ēse* and *hægtessan* (broadly translated respectively as 'pagan gods' and 'female shapers of fate, witches and violent dangerous *Furiae*': see Hall 2006; 2007a: 5 and 86, fig. 6). This charm survives within the *Lācnunga* or 'remedies' copied down within a compendium of other medicinal treatments and charms around AD 1000 (BL MS Harley 585). It opens with the words:

Hlude wæran hy, la, hlude, ða hy ofer þone hlæw ridan.
wæran anmode, ða hy ofer land ridan. (Cockayne 1864–5: 53)

This can be translated as: 'They were loud, yes, loud, when they rode over the (burial) mound; they were fierce when they rode across the land' (Hall 2007a: 2). The OE term *hlæw* can refer to natural hills, but is a common term for barrow and is translated as such by both Jolly (1996) and Hall (2007a, 2). It is not entirely clear who the riders are, but the charm is offering protection against them. Smiths are mentioned, *furies* or witches and the 'pagan gods' and elves—a myriad of 'Germanic spiritual agencies and mythological characters' (Jolly 1996: p. x; Hall 2007a: 1–3). It may be 'the powerful women' who are riding over the mound in the opening of the charm. These were other-worldly martial creatures, associated with witches and with violence, danger, shaping fate, and shape-shifting (see Hall 2007a: fig. 6, for an excellent diagrammatic rendition of *hægtessan* associations). They may also have represented a pairing to *ælfe* (Hall 2007a: 159). The *ælfe* could cause a variety of ailments, most prominently sharp internal pains, but they were also capable of inflicting altered states of mind (Hall 2007a: 115–56). Elves are at times—as here—associated with other monstrous beings, but Hall argues they were distinctly 'human-like' and part of the human in-group, distinct from the threatening monster-kind of the other world (Hall 2007a: 174). Jolly (1996), although urging caution, suggests *Wið Færstice* contains an abundance of 'untouched' folklore, reflecting the survival of 'magic' or 'pagan' elements in the late Anglo-Saxon *Lācnunga*. Hall, reflecting on the difference between this and later sources that appear to show the martial *hægtessan* replaced by a female *ælfe*, sees the text as evidence of the changing nature of supernatural beliefs (Hall 2007a: 88, 164, 174–5). These arguments suggest the association of burial mound and dangerous supernatural female may have its origins before the conversion, but that the process of Christianization could change popular beliefs.

The Wife's Lament

A less explicit and more enigmatic source is the poem known as *The Wife's Lament* (e.g. Niles 2003). *The Wife's Lament* is included in the Exeter Book and describes in a first-person narrative the exile of a woman after the death of her lord. The description seems to map out an imagined or mental landscape: 'its loneliness and desolation...a visible embodiment of the narrator's grief' (Lapidge 1997). A detailed deconstruction of the text has identified motifs of misery: inversions of the paradisiacal and images of the hellish (Hall 2002: 22). My original interest stemmed from the use of the words *eorðscræfe* and *eorðsele* in relation to the woman's abode: 'I was bidden to dwell among a thicket of trees under an oak tree in this earthen dugout [*eorðscræfe*]. Ancient is this earthen chamber [*eorðsele*]—I am quite consumed by longing—the dales are dark, the hills high, the bastioned towns grievously overgrown with briars, their habitations void of pleasures' (trans. based on Bradley 1995: 382–5).

> *heht mec mon wunian on wudu bearwe*
> *under actreo in þam eorðscræfe.*
> *eald is þes eorðsele, eal ic eom oflongad,*
> *sindon dena dimme, duna uphea*
> *bitre burgtunas, brerum beweaxne*
> *wic wynna leas*...(Mackie 1934: 152, lines 27–32)

These terms are applied to the burial mound in *Beowulf*. They physically describe the barrow but also represent the antithesis of all that represented safety and comfort (see p. 145).

The Wife's Lament has been connected several times to the image on the right-hand end of the Franks Casket (see Griffiths 1996: 34; Semple 1998; but also Gameson and Gameson 1996; Webster 1999; Hall 2002). The casket was manufactured in northern England in the eighth century (Webster 1999, 229), and the scene is thought to depict a Germanic legend (see Figure 5.2). Following Leslie Webster's interpretation: the setting is wilderness, forest, and marsh, a horse-like creature mourns over a barrow in which a figure can be made out, a female figure with a rod and goblet stands before the horse, and a bird flies

Fig. 5.2 The Franks Casket: scene from the right-hand end. © Trustees of the British Museum.

below; to the left, a half-human creature with wings sits on a mound, its muzzle bound by a serpent, and a helmeted warrior confronts or guards the creature; to the right, two cloaked figures appear to seize a third (Webster 1999: 243). The text is runic and partly encoded, but the translation is widely accepted as: 'Here Hos sits on the sorrow-mound; she suffers distress in that Ertae had decreed for her [had imposed it upon her], a wretched den [?wood] of sorrows and torments of mind' (Webster 1999: 243; but see also Page 1999: 177–9). The wording could infer Hos was sitting 'in' rather than 'on' sorrow-mound and the figure in the mound at the centre of the panel has been identified as Hos (Hall 2002: 2–3). The scene shares with *The Wife's Lament* an emphasis on the suffering and mental torment of the protagonists, a sense of confinement, enforced exile, and punishment. The frieze on the Franks Casket is thought to present a Germanic story, but it does so within the Christian context of the object. The right-hand end encapsulates concepts of capture and imprisonment, punishment, torture, and death, and perhaps of being outcast from God's mercy (Webster 1999: 241–4). The scene is used as a contrapuntal motif, contrasting with the image on the left-hand panel of Romulus and Remus nurtured by the she-wolf, which is thought to represent Rome and the Christian Church, salvation, and the nourishment of the faithful (Webster 1999: 239–41). Hall argues the uses of *eorðscræfe* and *eorðsele* in *The Wife's Lament* are intended to evoke a myriad of allusions: caves, barrows, ancient overgrown places, ancient human-built places, sacred altars, or groves. The use of the terms *eorðscræfe* and *eorðsele* are potent here in their reference and evocation of a place of dwelling laden with pre-Christian and hellish allusions. The relationship of *The Wife's Lament* with the scene on the right-hand end of the Franks Casket allows us to push these conceptual ideas back into the eighth century. Even at this early date, the barrow is being deployed as a motif in a design set in a contrapuntal and contrasting relationship to an image that evokes the salvation and nurture offered by the Christian Church.

The Life of St Guthlac

Leslie Webster has compared the scene of Hos on the sorrow-mound with Felix's account of St Guthlac's self-imposed exile in the fenlands. Composed in the early eighth century, the *Vita Sancti Guthlaci* is the primary source of knowledge on Guthlac. It embraces and uses several earlier accounts of saintly and ascetic lives (pp. 136–7). It is, however, peculiarly English in construction and detail (Colgrave 1956: 17–19; Stenton 1971: 178). The text deals with the saint's birth, childhood, and death, but concentrates mainly on his period of self-imposed exile, when the saint sought out an isolated location where he could live as a hermit. Guthlac seeks a desert, a solitary place and chooses the most dismal fen of immense size, which begins at the banks of the river Granta not far from the camp which is called Cambridge...

(*inmensae magnitudinis aterrima palus, quae, a Gronta fluminis ripis incipiens, haud procul a castello quem dīc unt nomine Gronte . . . (Vita Sancti Guthlaci XXIV)*

Tatwine, a local man, takes Guthlac to Crowland (*Crugland*), an island where no person had been able to dwell because of the phantoms and demons which haunted it (*Vita Sancti Guthlaci* XXV). Felix's narrative then proceeds to detail how on the island was

a mound built of clods of earth which greedy comers to the waste had dug open, in the hope of finding treasure there; in the side of this there seemed to be a sort of cistern, and in this Guthlac the man of blessed memory began to dwell, after building a hut over it.

(*insula tumulus agrestibus glaebis coacervatus, quem olim avari solitudinis frequenta-tores lucri ergo illic adquirendi defodientes scindebant, in cuius latere velut cisterna inesse videbatur; in qua vir beatae memoriae Guthlac desuper inposito tugurio habitare coepit. (Vita Sancti Guthlaci XXVIII).*

This description, using the term *tumulus*, a term for a grave and for a burial mound, mentions the feature as something broken open in a search for treasure. The description of a 'sort of cistern' in the side of the *tumulus* implies a partly excavated mound or a barrow with a chamber. As Colgrave noted, chambered barrows do not occur in the fenland region (1956: 1). Audrey Meaney has also emphasized this and argued that Felix was drawing here on the *Life of St Bartholomew* as an inspiration. Bartholomew is cited as Guthlac's spiritual mentor and saviour by Felix, and, according to other accounts, spent a period of time resident in a large and ancient ceramic urn (Meaney 2001, 2005; Roberts 2001). St Anthony too began his spiritual and ascetic career by taking up residence, not in an urn but in an old tomb, before moving on to a deserted fort (see the discussion of likely influential sources in Meaney 2002 and 2005). There are clearly influences here from other sources, but there is also an unquestionable use of naturalistic detail in the description of the setting of Guthlac's retreat in the fens (see discussions in Cubitt 2000). Just as the desert was re-created by Felix as the watery and impassable fenlands, so the tomb of Anthony and Bartholomew's urn is potentially transposed here into something more familiar in the mind of the writer: an old heathen barrow. It is perhaps irrelevant whether the cistern was imagined as the stone chamber of a long barrow or the shaft sunk into the mound by treasure seekers (see *Vita Sancti Guthlaci* XXVIII); what is important is that the writer chose a large old burial mound as the setting for Felix's exile and his subsequent tortures.[1]

---

[1] It is worth noting that aerial photographs are purported to show the remains of a chapel on Anchor Hill at Crowland, apparently superimposed upon a round barrow within an irregular ditched enclosure (Stocker 1993: 105).

Once ensconced, Guthlac was troubled first by despair (XXIX) and then by the Devil (XXX), after which numerous demons described as *maligni ergo* 'evil spirits' (XXXI), *in mundarum spiritum catervis* 'horrible troops of foul spirits' (XXXI), and *semen Cain* 'the seed of Cain' (XXXI) assailed him. Finally monsters confront him: *variorum monstrorum* (XXXVI). The text of the *Vita* is clear in its portrayal of the barrow as a place of trial, of exile, of supernatural assault and torment. One could argue that Felix chose to situate his main character (rather like Beowulf) within a theatre of adversities, evoked through the use of a topos that described the most remote, inaccessible, fearful, dreadful, and haunted place that he could conceive.

The 'Guthlac' Poems (A and B)

The use of the barrow as a motif takes on even more detailed allusions when *Guthlac A* and *B* are considered. These poems written about the saint's life survive in the *Exeter Book*, which is generally ascribed to the late tenth century. *Guthlac A* may be one of the earliest Old English poems composed during the lifetime of Guthlac's contemporaries (Hall 2007b: 209). While sections of Felix's *Vita* were used by the poet of *Guthlac B*, the author of *Guthlac A* seems to have created a work independent of the original *Vita* (Roberts 1979, 11). Both poems, but particularly *Guthlac A*, have seen extensive exploration, most recently by Alaric Hall. In line with the arguments presented here, Hall suggests this literary text offers additional and further insights into the Anglo-Saxon vernacular conceptions of sanctity and landscape (2007b).

Hall has identified that, in some contrast to the *Vita*, where the evil spirits come upon Guthlac after he had made his residence in the *tumulus*, in *Guthlac A* the saint sets out on a mission to confront and rid remote places of demons and build a home 'for pride he broke mounds/hills [*beorgas bræce*] in the waste where they, enduring, wretched adversaries, could previously spend time after torments, when they, accursed, came weary from wandering to rest...' (Hall 2007b: 215). The location of Guthlac's hermitage is also described as a *beorgseþel* (*Guthlac* A II, line 102) translated as 'a dwelling-place in the hills' (Roberts 1979: 21). Later in the text the hill is referred to as a *beorg* (A II, lines 140, 148; A IV, line 329) 'hill/barrow'; the *grene beorgas* (A III, line 232); and the *beorg on bearwe* (A II, line 148; VI, line 429) 'hill/barrow in the woods'. The poet of *Guthlac B*, who follows the *Vita* closely, uses *beorg* to denote the tumulus and *beorg* is commonly used for both small natural hills and barrows in literature and in the bounds attached to late Anglo-Saxon land grants (see pp. 160–4). The terminology used to describe the inhabitation of the barrow by Guthlac is, however, particularly informative and specific: *on westenne beorgas bræce* (III, lines 208–9). This is translated by Bradley as 'in the wilderness, he violated the hills...' (1995: lines 207–8), and later by Hall as 'he broke mounds/hills'. Indeed, a strong parallel can be found in the bounds attached to late Anglo-Saxon charters that relatively frequently refer to opened or robbed barrows as *þam brocene beorgas* ('broken or violated barrows') (see p. 161). For Hall, the poet of *Guthlac A* situates Guthlac as explicitly undertaking a campaign 'cleansing one mound after another of its demons in a divinely directed programme for extending Christian territory...' (2007b: 216), a task parallel to accounts of the driving of monsters from the land in the conversion of Scandinavia (DuBois 1999: 85–91). Indeed there are close parallels with heroic narratives in the sagas where a warrior would break into a barrow to confront a *draugr*, the undead incumbent (Hume 1980: 3–4; Hall 2007b: 218). The heroic nature of Guthlac's assault is likened by Hall to the saintly assaults on monsters, just as Rauer has suggested *Beowulf* encapsulates the model of hagiographical dragon fights (Hall 2007b: 221; Rauer 2000: 71). Further distinctions can be found in the ways in which the writer of *Guthlac A* describes Guthlac's supernatural attackers, referring to them as *scyldigra scolu* (III, lines 204–5), 'hordes of criminals'; *wræcmæcgas* (IV, lines 262–3), 'fugitives/mercenaries/exile-men'; *bonan* (VI, lines 429–30), 'murderous demons'; *myrðran* (VIII, line 650), 'murderers'; and *mánsceaþan* (VIII, line 650), 'criminal ravagers' (trans. from Roberts 1979 and Hall 2007b). The terminology is interesting in its portrayal of the demons in terms reminiscent of earthly sinners. In lines 203–14 the poet also implies that the inhabitants or demons had been allowed this lodging place after their punishments, again echoing the sentiments of *The Wife's Lament* and the Franks Casket that suggest the barrow as a place of hellish exile. Indeed, strong analogies can be drawn between *The Wife's Lament* (lines 27–42) and *Guthlac A* (lines 215–25):

They [the *ealdfeondes*, 'ancient foe/fiends/devils'] are not permitted to enjoy a habitation on the ground, nor does the air lull them into repose of their limbs; instead, shelterless, they lack homes and amid their sorrows they lament and wish for extinction and yearn for the Lord to concede, through the extinction of death, an end of their miseries.

> *ne motun hi on eorþan eardes brucan*
> *ne hy lyft swefeð in leoma ræstum*
> *ac hy hleolease hama þoliað*
> *in cearum cwiþað, cwealmes wiscað,*
> *willen þæt him dryhten þurh deaðes cwealm*
> *to hyra earfeða ende geryme.* (Roberts 1979: 89, III, 220–5)

In *Guthlac B*, the demons undergo a final and more evocative and monstrous transformation:

sometimes the damned faith-breakers would be transformed again into the shape of a dragon and the fire-crippled wretches would spew forth venom.

> *hwilum brugdon eft*
> *awyrgde wærlogan on wyrmes bleo,*
> *earme adloman, attre spiowdon.* (Roberts 1979: II, lines 908–12)

This motif may derive from the *Vita*, which records, among many other torments, how the evil spirits terrified Guthlac in the form of various beasts: including 'a serpent, too, rearing its scaly neck, disclosed the threat of its black poison' (*Vita Sancti Guthlaci* XXXVI; Colgrave 1956: 115). Colgrave notes that this is taken in part from Virgil's *Aeneid* (II, 218).

These three accounts, the *Vita* and poems *A* and *B* in combination, provide rich attestation of a conception of barrows as ancient places inhabited by supernatural creatures, monsters, and demons. The close analogies between Felix's work and *Guthlac A* and *The Wife's Lament* and the connections too with the right-hand panel of the Franks Casket provide strong testimony that the ancient barrow held a specific meaning for Christian Anglo-Saxon populations. This seems to have its roots in pre-Christian ideas but subsequently was absorbed and shaped by a new Christian ideology. Hall has pushed interpretations further, drawing on *The Wife's Lament* and *Guthlac A* to argue for 'an Anglo-Saxon poetic topos of banishment to a *beorg*' and the evocation of a 'pagan sacred place' within the topoi deployed in both poems, comprising recognizable allusions to ancient pagan ritual sites that comprised groves, trees, enclosures, and old barrows (Hall 2007b: 224–32). The barrow is thus not merely synonymous with misery and hellish exile, torment, and demons; its use was also specific in the evocation of remembered or imagined conceptions of 'heathen' places.

Fissures, clefts, hollows, and ruins in Old English prose and poetry

Barrows are not alone in late Anglo-Saxon literature as monuments associated with supernatural creatures and beasts. A range of other topographic phenomena played host to monsters and to devilish entities, not least of course watery places and meres. The lake or mere in *Beowulf* is a home to Grendel and his mother, and it is an interface the hero must cross to challenge the supernatural forces below, a conduit to another darker and dangerous world. Lakes as habitats for unpleasant and malign spirits features in *Maxims* as well, with the ominous warning: 'The monster must dwell in the fen, alone in his realm' (*Maxims II*, lines 42–3). Other types of feature that are more akin to barrows, and on occasion are referred to in the terminology that is also in sources in reference to burial mounds, are pits, clefts, or fissures. In the original eighth-century account of the establishment by Bede of a monastic community at Lastingham, North Yorkshire (*HE* III, 23), Cedd is said to have located his monastery 'amid some steep and remote hills which seemed better fitted for the haunts of robbers and the dens of wild beasts than for human habitation; so that, as Isaiah says, "In the habitations where once dragons lay, shall be grass with reeds and rushes"' (trans. Sherley-Price 1968: 181). Isaiah is recognized as a major source of inspiration for this account, in particular the chapter referred to by Bede that foretells the joyful flourishing of Christ's kingdom (*HE* I, 35, 7). The choice of an excerpt concerning dragons is interesting, given the symbolic significance of the dragon and the importance of Christian motifs of dragon-fighting and their influence on literature (see pp. 145–6, but also Rauer 2000). Of considerable interest, therefore, is the later rendition and translation of this account in the tenth-century *OE* version of the *Historia Ecclesiastica* (Miller 1891). The text closely follows Bede's description of Æthelwald's gift of land to Cedd, but the location of the monastery is now evoked as 'a retreat for robbers and a lair for beasts than habitation for man. There, according to the prophecy of Isaiah, sprang up a growth of reeds and rushes in the clefts, where formerly dragons dwelt: by which we should understand that the fruits of good works were produced, where formerly either beasts dwelt or men were wont to live like beasts' (Miller 1891, 231). The location chosen by Cedd, which Bede broadly placed on the moors, had become in this writer's mind a lair for robbers or beasts. The quotation from Isaiah follows, although it is no longer exact and *the habitations where dragons lay* is rendered as *the clefts, where formerly dragons dwelt*. *OE cleofum* is a particularly descriptive word indicating a cleft, hole, cave, or crack. The term *stāncleofu* occurs once in *Beowulf* in reference to the barrow (Fulk et al. 2008: line 2540) and has been interpreted by some as indications that the account describes a stone-built or stone-chambered barrow (Miller 1891, 231), but may be less literal, instead representing part of a composite allusion that can find a likeness in the 'Cliff of Death' topos, which uses stony cliffs, serpents, and darkness to evoke hell and hellish torment (Fry 1987: 215). It is interesting to note, however, that the Book of Isaiah contains reference to the banishment and exile of heathens and idols in the holes and caves in the earth, and clefts in the rock (Isaiah 2: 18–21). Such interweaving motifs, topoi, and allusions are hard to untangle, but it is argued here, and later in Chapter 6, that rocky clefts, hollows, and fissures, as well as barrows, were conceived of and imagined by late Anglo-Saxon populations as openings into the eternal torment and damnation of hell (Semple 2003b; see also pp. 204–7). This argument is strengthened by a range of additional references within the *Vita*. In *Andreas*, located in the Anglo-Saxon codex the *Vercelli Book* and dated on palaeographical grounds to the second half of the tenth century, Andreas, having suffered many torments and then been healed, calls up waters from the foundations of a great ruin or old work of giants, to drown the heathen city (XIV). Once he has humbled the people, he causes an awesome fissure to open in the earth and let in the flood. Within these waves, the worst of the crowd is swallowed, fourteen criminal enemies of the people hastening into perdition in the depths of the earth. These unfortunates are also referred to as 'warriors, sin-soiled and guilty of murder' (XIV). In this source, the significant term *eorðscræfe* is used to describe a fissure or chasm that opened and swallows evildoers and heathens (see earlier discussion on fissures and pits, pp. 71–2). It is worth noting that the prose homilies in the *Vercelli Book* have common themes of death, judgement, and punishment of worldly guilt. The swallowing of sinners in fissures or openings in the earth is not an isolated motif. The *Life of St Cuthman* survives in a post-Conquest text containing many archaic elements suggestive of an origin in the late, if not middle, Anglo-Saxon period (Blair 1997: 180). An old woman who curses Cuthman is picked up by the wind and blown across the downs and dropped to the ground and swallowed by the earth at a place subsequently known as Fippa's pit (Blair 1997: 176). A final source that ties in with the opening discussions of barrows as hellish places is the account of the foundation of Minster-in-Thanet in Kent. This relates how Domne Eafe claimed land from King Ecgberht by use of her pet hind. The story is examined in detail by Stephanie Hollis (1998), and the full version is found in three Latin Lives: the earliest recorded account is a *passio* of the murdered princes attributed to Byrhtferth dated to *c.*1000; Goscelin's *Vita St Mildrethae* (AD 1089x1099), and a *passio* of the murdered princes (mid-eleventh to early thirteenth century) (see Hollis 1998: 41). In this perhaps aetiological story, Ecgberht's councillor *Thunor*, seeking to protect the interests of the king, protests loudly against Domne Eafe, and the ground immediately opens and swallows him. The three Latin Lives then relate that the hind finished its circuit, and a huge mound was heaped over the site of the cataclysm, which 'to this day' is still known as *Thunoreshlæw*, 'Thunor's barrow'. Here, the evil councillor, working against the establishment of the holy foundation, perhaps not incidentally going by the name of a pagan deity, is swallowed by earth and the place later marked by a large barrow, a surviving local landmark that long after retained the appellation of the unfortunate Thunor.

As Chapter 6 will reveal, conceptions of barrows and mounds, and fissures, cracks, hollows, and pits, as openings to hellish underground places of torment and damnation, found a place in the realities of judicial punishment and in the illustrations of late Anglo-Saxon artists. These early medieval sources reveal such concepts were widespread and embedded within late Anglo-Saxon Christian literature and ideology.

Temporal changes in perception

Despite the difficulties in dating the creation of many of the stories discussed here, there is some intimation that changes in perception occurred between the eighth and eleventh centuries. The chronological pattern of the sources in part reflects the general survival of Anglo-Saxon texts. Many were preserved in large compendia, such as the late tenth-century *Exeter Book*, and likely derive from earlier eras. The early texts and sources under discussion here include *The Life of St Guthlac*, the scene from the right-hand end of the Franks Casket, and Bede's account of Cedd's foundation at Lastingham. All of these are accepted as eighth century in date. *Guthlac A*, *Beowulf*, and *Wið Færstice* potentially have their origins in the eighth century (see Lapidge 2000; Hall 2007a, 2007b). *Maxims II*, the tenth-century vernacular translation of the *Historia Ecclesiastica*, *Andreas*, *The Wife's Lament*, and perhaps *Guthlac B* are best placed at the late end of the Anglo-Saxon era, although the origins of some of these texts and stories, like *Beowulf*, could be considered to have evolved at a much earlier date. The versions we have, however, are those written down in the late tenth and early eleventh centuries and thus might provide evidence for the existence of a different, if related, perception of burial mounds and fissures, rocky openings and caves, from the earlier conversion period sources.

Identifiable differences are subtle and may point to evolving changes in perception, as Christian ideology permeated the fabric of vernacular life, absorbing, along the way, pre-existing ideas and practices. The eighth-century texts depict classic conversion motifs—confrontational scenes between good and evil—while the Franks Casket provides a scene of terror and horror as a directly contrapuntal motif to a scene symbolizing salvation. A useful addition here is the eighth-century account of Wilfrid's confrontation with the pagan magus on the mound in the kingdom of the South Saxons from the *Vita Wilfridi*, already discussed (see pp. 105–6). These accounts conform to the literary Christian traditions of conversion stories involving demon-fighting, cleansing, and the establishment of new Christian communities, and may reflect the realities of combating lingering heathenism or fresh memories of proactive conversion. Within these accounts (even with the stern warnings of Stanley in mind: see 1975 and 2000), it is possible to perceive traditional (originally pre-Christian) ideas of the sacred nature of the burial mound. Old barrows were connected with fearsome creatures, and might be used in the performance of spells and charms. From the viewpoint of the early Christian narrators, the ancient burial mound was being deployed as a motif of danger and hellish despair and sorrow—a place that existed in opposition to all that was Christian and good. Such topoi may even have been intended to reinforce proscription against the use of such places, by evoking the evil and terror of abandoned pre-Christian sanctuaries and provoking meditation on the folly and hellish consequence of 'pagan' beliefs. These sources, in sum, offer a powerful sense of Christian concerns in a century in which pagan practices still persisted. Christian churches and missionaries were working with people who followed beliefs and conducted activities that could not be absorbed or condoned. The spiritual theatre in which the triumphant Christian protagonists are depicted in these conversion period narratives is rich in its reference to the natural and antecedent landscape: Christianity was fighting heathen beliefs that embraced groves, trees, pools, ancient burial mounds, and enclosures, as well as fierce supernatural entities and otherworldly creatures and monsters. Burial mounds were portrayed very firmly as part of this heathen spiritual scene, as places of invocation and power, as dangerous places unfit for ordinary people, places where only Christian warriors might dare to go to. Such concepts are evident in *Beowulf*. The great barrow, symbolic of an ancient heathen past, the haunt of the evil serpent, and containing the cursed treasure unwanted by any but a thief, is present within this epic poem as a powerful visual and physical marker synonymous with the ancient heathen past and the passing of time: a theatre within which the hero meets his doom.

The sources definitively later in date offer a contrasting view. The realities of conversion are certainly implicit. The cunning dragon dwells in its barrow in *Maxims II*, but occupies the rocky clefts at Lastingham, and the sorrowful spirit of *The Wife's Lament* laments her exile and damnation confined to a hellish grove and barrow. In *Andreas* the *eorðscræfe* is a great fissure that swallows heathens described in judicial terms as criminals and murderers. Characters that oppose the mission of saints are gobbled down into the earth, presumably to hell. These sources imply that barrows may have shifted in the Anglo-Saxon psyche from places synonymous with pre-Christian spiritual potency to places of more mythical resonance. They retained associations with ancient heathenry but emerged by the late Anglo-Saxon period as the haunts of the marvellous, malevolent, and supernatural. The descriptions also increasingly make reference to late Anglo-Saxon conceptions of hell and the afterlife. The strong similarities between the way in which fissures, pits, and hollows were used as motifs for hell, damnation, and purgatory and the portrayal of barrows in similar ways suggest that both types of landscape feature held similar associations and fears in the late Anglo-Saxon imagination (see Chapter 6). This implies that the concepts of heathenism and monstrous associations present in the accounts of burial mounds in the eighth century may have resulted from the realities of the immediate impact of Christianity on the seventh- and eighth-century pre-Christian spiritual landscape. The absorption and effects of this encounter refracted throughout the intervening centuries. Burial mounds and their inhabitants consequently worked their way firmly into the fabric of popular belief. Through the process of Christianization, they became inseparably linked to late Anglo-Saxon traditions of damnation and hell.

Popular traditions and perceptions

These written sources may of course have been created only for a highly educated and literate elite. The Franks Casket, for example, is argued as an intellectual, visual centrepiece and talking point for a secular leader and his entourage (Webster 1999). The previous chapters have argued that prehistoric monuments in the centuries before Christianity took firm hold formed a major component within daily living and the shaping of local identity, and that their potency at a local level may in some instances have led to their retention as important places for assembly and for the establishment of ecclesiastical foci.

The sources of eighth-century date, point to a set of strong and insistent emerging beliefs that, in contrast, associate ancient monuments, specifically the burial mound, with very different qualities and with fearful associations. These ideas persisted into the very late Anglo-Saxon era. What is yet to be discerned is quite how widespread and popular such associations were and if such meditative topoi were meant only for a literate audience, or if such ideas, promoted perhaps by the conversion process, filtered throughout Anglo-Saxon society.

The bounds attached to Anglo-Saxon charters and English place-names offer a means of testing the popular take-up of these landscape associations. Both data sets have problems (see pp. 143–4), but the bounds attached to charters as somewhat more reliable and contemporary sources provide the main starting point here. Place-name data are introduced alongside discussion of the features used as boundary markers to argue for the wider popular uptake of certain landscape perceptions. A difficulty relevant to using both sources is the highly varied meanings of the *OE* terms applied to old monuments. *OE hlaw* and *beorg* and their variants can mean barrow, but also hill, mountain, hummock, and barrow-shaped knoll (see Kitson 1995, 2008). In a study of place-names, Margaret Gelling and Ann Cole considered that *hlaw*, in the south of England, denoted a man-made mound or one that looked built or 'made' (Gelling and Cole 2000). Barrows were of course elements of fifth- to eighth-century funerary ritual, and featured in Roman burial practices as well. Thus a *hlaw* or *beorg* might easily refer to an old monument or a barrow-like natural feature, but not necessarily a prehistoric burial mound. Leslie Grinsell suggested that *OE beorg* may have been used for prehistoric barrows and *OE hlaw* for Anglo-Saxon barrows (Grinsell 1991a). Della Hooke arrived at the same conclusions in a discussion of the West Midland charters (Hooke 1980–1). Although both papers are important contributions, the results are not entirely convincing. One only has to consider *Beowulf*, in which both terms are used to describe the ancient barrow inhabited by the dragon. *OE* terms like *dīc*, 'ditch', *burh*, 'fort', and *stān*, 'stone', could refer to contemporary as well as ancient features, and *stān* could denote natural boulders and glacial erratics.

There is no certain way of discerning without excavation the age of the features being referred to in charter-bounds and place-names. *Posses hlaew*, the location of the seventh-century female interment from Swallowcliffe (S468 [416]; see also Speake 1989), is a reused prehistoric tumulus. By the time these names were coined and inscribed, the Anglo-Saxons were no longer barrow builders. They were still monument builders, however, creating defensive and agricultural ditches, earthen defences, and forts. Barrows, by the tenth and eleventh centuries, must have seemed remote and *other*: the product of a past recent enough to be remembered but distant enough to represent something distinctively different in ideological terms. The heathen and pre-Christian connotations of these old places of burial may also have been reinforced by the reintroduction and revival of barrow burial, albeit rare, during the earliest phases of Viking settlement in the north of England. Here, in this section, which deals with sources for the south and south-east of England, both *beorg* and *hlaw* and their variants are considered, because by the ninth and tenth centuries all barrows in these regions, whether prehistoric, Roman, or early Anglo-Saxon, were old features in the landscape and may have come to hold the similar meanings despite their very different origins. All *burh, stān,* and *dīc* terms are also considered, to explore (even though prehistoric monuments are hard to identify) how such landscape features were named. This opening section deals with the evidence for how prehistoric monuments may have been described in general, drawing on numerous examples. The study is mainly confined to the charter-bounds of the south and south-west (Wiltshire, Hampshire, Sussex, and Berkshire) (Appendix 4 (ii–v)), simply to limit the extent of the discussion. Supernatural creatures mentioned in the charter-bounds are then discussed, drawing on the full national corpus of surviving *OE* bounds and it is here that place-names are introduced to explore the wider popularity of certain motifs (Appendix 4 (i)).

The naming of prehistoric monuments

A variety of basic terms were applied to monuments and monumental constructions. The *OE* terms *beorg* and *hlaw* 'barrow/mound/hill' were certainly used to name both prehistoric and Anglo-Saxon barrows. Both can be found on occasion in the same set of bounds. In West Ginge, Berkshire, for example, the perambulation begins *Ærest of lillanhlæwes crundele* 'at the chalk pit/quarry at Lilla's barrow' and later moves *middeweardan to loddere beorge* 'mid-ward to beggar hill or barrow' (S583/B918 [132]; Gelling 1976: 746). The terms here could apply to hills *or* barrows. The simultaneous usage of both terms may even have been intended as a means of distinguishing between hills and barrows in the bounds or perhaps even between very ancient barrows and those perceived by local communities to have been built in the more recent past. *Beorg* is sometimes used to refer to monuments that held a greater sense of age and antiquity, or perhaps in cruder terms to barrows and barrow-like features that were particularly large and old looking. A notable example is Dragon Hill, Uffington, Oxfordshire. A natural conical hill, with an artificially flattened summit, is referred to as *æceles beorg*. The first element is uncertain, perhaps 'church' or a personal name or even 'Achilles' (see Breeze 2000), and *beorg* rather than *hlaw* is used (S575 [51]). *Hlaw* could be applied to rich elite Anglo-Saxon barrow burials such as *posses hlæwe* at Swallowcliffe in Wiltshire (S468 [416]). It is impossible to distinguish any regional patterns of usage, or establish with certainty if one term applied particularly to more ancient burial monuments. It is possible, however, to conclude that both were used to refer to barrows and that their application would have been very specific, but related to very localized perceptions of these monuments and even the knowledge or beliefs of the individual that owned the estate or recorded the bounds.

OE burh is used alongside a range of other *OE* terms, including *fæsten* and *(ge)weorc*, to denote fortifications or strongholds (Baker 2008, 2012). All could be applied to old fortifications but were also used for contemporary Anglo-Saxon features. *OE dīc*, 'ditch', could refer to ancient or contemporary ditches too, as well as water courses and channels. In the majority of entries that record either a *burh* or *dīc*, however, the additional terminology is often very specific and can loosely imply the age of the feature. *Eald* 'old', for example, can be found frequently in combination with *burh* or *dīc*. *OE stān*, 'stone', was used for both naturally occurring stones and those comprising monuments raised in prehistory. As many of these markers are lost or impossible to locate with certainty, it is hard to be sure if these entries refer to prehistoric monuments unless the additional name terms indicate something specific about the monument or its age. Monuments are also mentioned and described in other ways. Occasionally hill forts are denoted by their entrances, for example: *of þam beorgæ in on þæt norþ geatt. Þo non on þæt suð geat*, 'from the barrow to the north gate, then to the south gate' (Uffington Hill fort, S575 [130]), or using the *OE* term *faestan*, 'stronghold', rather than *burh* (Froxfield, Hampshire S283 [251]). The *OE* term *han*, 'stone', occurs occasionally (S568 [407]), and, like *stan*, could have referred to a natural stone rather than a man-made monument.

Although not all of the entries collected from the south and south-west of England can be argued with certainty to refer to prehistoric monuments, they do offer some insight into how ancient monuments of the prehistoric, Roman, or early Anglo-Saxon past as well as contemporary constructions were distinguished in specific terminology relating to shape, form, age, colour, and sometimes also to legendary or superstitious associations. The data underpinning this study are presented in Appendix 4 (ii–v). All those cited in the discussion are cross-referenced numerically in square brackets to these appendices.

Beorg. 'Barrows/hills' are by far the most common type of monumental feature mentioned in bounds and on occasion are referred to by no more than the single term *beorg*, such as *on þonnæ beorg* in the bounds of East Woolstone (S575 [52]). One assumes such barrows were isolated and distinctive enough to have needed no further appellation or signpost, although at Milton the instructions were more precise with the entry *þanune on þone anlipan beorg*, 'to the solitary or only barrow', distinguishing what must have been an already obvious, isolated feature. A great majority were marked out and appreciated for their physical attributes: their texture or covering in the case of *ruwan*, 'rough' (S360 [170]); their shape, as in *wen*, 'boil' (presumably boil-shaped) (S312 [345]), *bradan*, 'broad' (S496 [66], and *lange*, 'long' (S513 [183]). The physical structure of the monument was a distinguishing feature as well: *stān* and *stanige*, 'stone' and 'stony', were frequent descriptive prefixes (see, e.g., S412 [203]), whereas *sond*, 'sand', was an isolated example (S348 [316]). The aesthetic qualities of the location or the monument itself were seldom commented on, although the *cealdan*, 'cold', barrow of a Wiltshire charter for 956 evokes a sense of its isolation and upland position (S585 [339]). Instances of *brocenan* or *borsenanbeorg*, 'burst', 'broken', or 'uneven' barrows were frequent (see S612 [352] and S448 [53]), and presumably in certain cases referred to barrows previously dug into, like *Þam beorgan þæs adolfen wæs*, 'the barrow that was dug into', in the bounds of Martyr Worthy (Hampshire) (S273 [196]). These monuments were also distinguished according to size: *miclan*, 'great' (S496 [73]) and *lytel* (S524 [63]); by their colour *grenan*, 'green', (S622 [46]); and by their foliate coverage, such as *fearn*, 'fern', *wad*, 'woad', and *sahl*, 'sallow tree' (S411 [47], S264 [317], S666 [346]). Most frequently they were picked out by reference to their position and distinction as landscape features. Numerical descriptions are common, ranging from the 'single/isolated' barrow, to occurrences of three, five, and seven barrows as markers (S465 [197], S800 [216], S784 [301]). *Twam beorgas* 'two barrows' were common choices for landmarks (e.g. S558 [75]). *Mearc/gemer* or 'boundary' barrows were mentioned (S1545 [50], S754 [199]), and barrows described as *midmestan*, 'mid-most' (S831 [351]), or *westmestan*, 'westernmost', (S598 [204]), or located in extremely precise terms, such as the barrow that *lið betweol twan langan beorg*, 'lies between the two long hills/barrows' (S374 [185]). Age was very occasionally distinguished, as in *þane to elden berwe*, 'to the old barrow', in the Ashbury bounds for 947 (S524/B828 [61]).

Barrows were also distinguished in the bounds by association with animals. Cats, foxes, eagles, wolves, geese, and other birds, particularly ravens, are mentioned (e.g. S639 [54], S496 [71], S619 [171], S444 [174], S425 [276], etc.). Margaret Gelling noted the occasional association of ancient hill forts with ravens, and recalled the connections made between the raven and the pre-Christian god Woden in Old Norse literature (1988: 144–5). Aleks Pluskowski has argued that the wolf was a malevolent and mythical creature in pre-Christian belief too, associated with the predatory repertoire of creatures that adorned the battle gear of male elites in the sixth and seventh centuries (2006a, 2010). Cats, foxes, geese, and lice (e.g. S574 [323]), however, seem relatively harmless and entirely plausible as animals that might inhabit or be seen around groups of barrows. To a modern audience, the association of animals with boundary features may seem transient, but animal sets and nesting places, if undisturbed, could have survived several decades, if not centuries. One has only to think, for example, of the long survival of large rookeries.

Barrows associated with personal names comprise a final category. This type of place-name was once thought to denote the name of a person buried within the barrow, but these are now interpreted as an indication of the name of the estate owner or owner of the portion of land adjacent to the barrow (Welch 1992: 96). In the *OE* bounds for Berkshire, Hampshire, Sussex, and Wiltshire, over thirty landmarks record the *OE* term *beorg* in association with a supposed personal name,[2] with only two repeated personal names, *colta* and *abban/abben*. Both of these were found in the Wiltshire bounds, and in the case of *Coltan beorg* (S449 [311]), recorded in the bounds of Kennett in 939, and *Colta beorg* (S784 [302]), mentioned in bounds for the adjoining Overton some thirty years later in 972, the feature referred to is clearly the same barrow. Some names are characters from the early stories of conquest, real kings, but kings whose actions were renowned and legendary. *Cerdic* is recorded as a founding father of the West Saxon kingdom: landing at *Cerdices ora*, 'Cerdic's Shore', in 495 (*ASC* (A) 495). *Cissa* is mentioned some thirty years previously, arriving with his father *Ælle* at *Cymenes ora*, 'Cymen's Shore', and driving the British into the Weald (*ASC* (A) 477). Both names appear in the surviving bounds for Hampshire (Grundy 1927a, 211 and 175). Although it is entirely possible that such personal names stayed current, it is also worth considering that barrows and other features of ancient interest may have acquired names associated with legendary and mythical characters as part of local folklore. Such names may have been coined as well to add a certain ancient legitimacy to bounds (see Baker in press). The meaning of the name Whittlebury, for example, which is interpreted as 'stronghold of a man called Witela' and which is presumed to refer to the local hill fort, has been postulated as a name that might refer to a legendary hero or character, along with Wandlebury in Cambridgeshire meaning 'Wændel's fort' (Mills 1998: 377; Forward 2008: 165).[3] The unique instance of a *kingberwes* or 'king barrow' might also fall into such a category, although the name may perhaps instead recognize the pre-eminent size or scale of the monument in question (S513 [182]).

A range of boundary barrows is also recorded in more unusual terms. In three cases, the *beorg* was recorded as a meeting place: *thaene gemot beorg*, 'moot barrow or meeting barrow', in Calbourne on the Isle of Wight (S274 [169]); a *gemot biorh* at Durrington in Sussex (S425 [279]), and the more well-known *swanabeorh* 'barrow of the freemen' (S568 [343]) in Manningford Abbots, Wiltshire, attested as a hundred meeting place at Domesday and still surviving today as the much denuded feature Swanborough Tump (see Figure 5.3 and Semple and Langlands 2001). It is difficult to say with certainty that all three moot barrows were active when recorded in the bounds (respectively AD 826; AD 934; AD 987), or whether these were reflections in some

---

[2] Listed as: Weard (could indicate a 'watchman', see Baker 2011), Ælfredes, Lorta, Imma, Enna, Babba, Hima, Mela, Cerdic, Cotel, Ceort, Æthelwold, Luca, Cissa, Wibba (could indicate a 'worm or beetle': John Baker: pers. comm.), Cylla, Beonna, Leodgeard, Woden, Colta, Abba, Winfel, Scufa, Ippa, Chetol, Oswald, Fuga, Luda, dolemannes (see Grundy 1919, 1920).

[3] I am grateful to Dr Richard Jones for drawing this to my attention.

Fig. 5.3 Swanborough Tump, Wiltshire: the meeting place of Swanborough Hundred. © Stuart Brookes. Reproduced by permission of Stuart Brookes.

instances of the past importance of the monuments. Swanborough Tump shows that at least in one instance the meeting mound was active at least from the late tenth to the late eleventh centuries. Other unusual terms include *loddere beorge*, 'beggar's barrow', in West Ginge, Berkshire (S583 [45]) and *æceles beorg*, 'church barrow', or perhaps even 'Achilles' barrow' (S575 [51]) at Uffington (see p. 159; Gelling 1978; Breeze 2000). *Tigga/el beorgæ*, 'tile barrow', in Exton, Hampshire, unsurprisingly refers to the ruins of a Roman villa, and is a good demonstration of how this term could be applied to barrow-shaped features or perceived, older monuments (S463 [210]). *Dinra beorg* in Compton Beauchamp, Berkshire (S564 [57]), seems to include *OE dinor* 'coin', and perhaps refers to a barrow where a large number of coins were found. Finally, the very unusual and intriguing *halignesse beorge* 'holiness barrow' in East Dean, Sussex, is unique, although this might imply similar associations to the Berkshire *æceles beorg* (S43 [274]).

Hlaw. The *OE* term *hlaw*, 'barrow/hill', was used considerably less frequently than *beorg* in the charters of the south and south-west. Whatever *hlaw* implied was distinct from *beorg*. There were less of them, or they were less frequently selected as boundary markers, or the word was less prevalent in these regional dialects. They also carried considerably more limited appellations. With the exception of a *hundeshlæwe*, 'hound's barrow', and *hafeces hlæwe*, 'hawk's barrow', both in Uffington, once in Berkshire and now in modern Oxfordshire

(S1208 [134 and 138]), there are no further animal associations. One barrow, again at Uffington, was described in terms of its composition: *uppan (or open) þa stanhlæwe*, 'up onto the stone barrow' (S1208 [139]; see too Electronic Sawyer 1208). In a handful of instances the barrows are described in terms of their topographic location. A *fontanhlewe*, 'barrow by the spring', is mentioned at Hardenhuish in Wiltshire (S308 [412]) and *broccæs hlæwe*, 'barrow at the brook', at Wootton St Lawrence, Hampshire (S874 [258]).[4]

All other instances of *hlaw* are prefixed by a personal name. It seems that a *hlaw* was far more likely to be associated with a personal name than the term *beorg*.[5] The associated personal names also include, in sharp contrast, a number of female names, and few, if any, seem to reflect names with mythical associations or early characters relating to the origin mythology of these southern regions and kingdoms. The exceptions would be *Lilla, Hild,* and *Hwittuc*. Grundy's association of the place-name *Hwittuc* with the characters from the legend of *Weland* the smith has been hotly disputed (see Grundy 1924: 69; Gelling 1976: 692–4). Lilla, the counsellor of Edwin (*HE* II, 9), and Hild, the aristocratic abbess of the monastery of Streanaeshalch (*HE* IV, 23), seem unlikely heroes for the local folklore of the south and west Saxons. It would appear more likely that these reflect the usage of Lilla and Hild as personal names.

It is difficult to interpret the striking differences in how the *hlaw* and *beorg* were described and distinguished in place-names, but it appears at least in this review that less imaginary and aesthetic licence existed when it came to the naming of a *hlaw*, and that these monuments were more likely to be associated with personal names including female names.

Dic. In contrast to the terms for barrows, *dic*, 'ditch', was predominately prefixed by the OE word *eald*, 'old'. Twenty-two instances of *eald dic*, 'old ditch', were identified in the south and south-west charter-bounds. A particularly evocative entry in the bounds of Blewbury, relevant to the discussions in Chapter 6, ran *þon hæþenum byrgelsum æt þære ealdun dic* 'from the heathen burials to the old ditch' (S496 [108]), whilst at Appleford in Berkshire *þæt on þa ealdan dic þæ lið betwux wigbaldincgtun and æppelforda* indicates the old ditch had to be distinguished as the feature that ran between the 'farm of Wigbald's people and the ford at the apple tree' (S355 [115]). Ditches were distinguished by reference to their physical appearance as well, with a *curspan* 'curly' ditch at Brightwalton in Berkshire (S448 [90]), a *gewrincloda* 'wrinkled' ditch (S962 [236]) at Kings Worthy, a *hocedan* 'hooked' ditch at Sutton Scotney (S374 [246]) (both in Hampshire), and a *wogan*

----

[4] This might also mean 'badger's barrow' or could include the personal name Brocc (John Baker: pers. comm.).

[5] Ceawa, Lilla, Hwittuc, Hild, Carda, Hod, Winter, Hilda, Heardulf, Lorta, Ceolbright, Hatheburh, Wada, Ashwold, Deneburh, Byrhtferthe, Eangyth, Wolfing, Poss.

'crooked' ditch at Wanborough in Wiltshire (S312 [370]). Length and shape were recognized as distinctive details: a possible ditch with a lip at Wootton (S590 [91]), a short ditch at East Woolstone, Oxfordshire (S575 [95]), and a wide ditch at South Damerham, Wiltshire, which can be identified as Bokerley Dyke (S513 [237]). Red and white ditches also feature, presumably referencing the colour of the local geology (e.g. S1546 [125], S360 [243], S962 [245]). Occasional mentions of *gemære dic*, 'boundary ditch'—in reference again presumably to a monument described by its function as an old monument used as a marker for the estate bounds—and an *easteran*, 'eastern', ditch show that these monuments were sometimes described according to their topographic position and their use as boundary markers and divisions (see S591 [92], S673 [124]), including *ða ealdan merc dic* in Bexhill, Sussex, a reference to an old boundary ditch as a marker for the estate bounds (see S108 [286]). Six ditches were associated with a personal name, including a female name, presumably indicating the personal ownership of the monument, adjacent land, or estate.[6] Some intriguing and less straightforward names include *Esnadiche,* translated as 'a serf's ditch' at Berwick St John (Wiltshire) (S582 [386], Grundy 1920, 33); *cyningesdic*, 'king's ditch', in Chilton, Berkshire (S354 [114]); a *witan dic*, interpreted as 'white ditch' but perhaps a 'wise man's ditch' (S861 [390], Grundy 1920: 97); and a *folces dic*, 'folk's ditch', or perhaps 'people's or army's ditch', mentioned in the bounds of Wanborough, Wiltshire (S312 [374]), and the adjoining bounds of Little Hinton (S312 [391]).

A final occurrence of note is several instances of camps or forts referred to in terms of their ditches rather than their ramparts or fortifications or their circular shape. Old Sarum, to the north of Salisbury, was described in 972 as *tha Ealdan Burhdic*, 'the old fortified ditch' (S789 [367]), and an entrance to Winklebury Camp at Berwick St John in Wiltshire was referred to in 956 as *miclen diches hes get*, 'the entrance/gate to the great ditch' (S630 [375]). Both descriptions tally with the early name for Avebury henge: the *Waledic*, which has been argued to derive from OE *wal + dic*, 'fortified or embanked ditch' (Kempson 1955), although others interpreted this lost name for the old henge as OE *weala-dic*, 'ditch/dyke of the Britons' (John Baker: pers. comm.). A now lost and unidentified *faestan dic*, 'fortified ditch or fort/stronghold ditch', at Crondall, Hampshire (S813 [249]), could be added to this list as another possible example of a fort referred to by its ditches rather than by its embanked enclosures or shape (see Baker 2012).

Burh, fæsten, and (ge)weorc. Many forts or camps are referred to using the term *eorðburh*, 'earthen stronghold/fortification', describing in very simple terms the composition of the monument (although see previous discussion of *eorþsele* and *eorðscræfe*, pp. 144–149). Seven examples exist in the Wiltshire

---

[6] Wulfstan, Bica, Bula, Ælfðryð, Ealcher, Sigewinne.

bounds (e.g. S524 [82], S463 [228], S368 [355], S366 [358], S688 [360], S366 [361] and [363], etc.), in contrast with a single reference to a *stānburg* 'stone fort' at Droxford in Hampshire (S276 [225]). A *michelan byrg* or 'great fort' at Berwick St John/Broad Chalke, Wiltshire (S582 [366]), represents the only reference to scale, but several forts are named in terms of their location, such as *cerenburh*, 'stronghold by the *Ceren* [name of stream] [84]; *heanbyrig*, 'high camp' (S840 [219]); *wuduburge*, 'burh by/in the wood', (S690 [222] and S582 [365]); and *meres byrig*, 'burh by the mere' (S487 [230]). Another frequent descriptive term in the bounds is *eald burh*, 'old fort/camp', a straightforward reference to the perceived age of the fort (see S558 [88], S699 [226], S695 [229]). Like barrows, several forts carry personal names: *friðela* (S663 [79]); *telles byrg* (S369 [86]); *widian byrig* (S840 [221]); *guthredesburg* (S379 [362]), and perhaps *hambres buruh* (S789 [357]); none of which appear to be names of mythical and historical note. Forts are also associated with ravens at *hremmesbyriges norðge-ate* (S1208 [80])and larks at *lauercebyrig* (S1208 [89]), both animal types found in association with *beorg*. Although ravens and larks may have been animal types encountered in the chalk upland, where such monuments frequently survived as abandoned earthworks, it is possible that ravens and larks as wild birds might allude here to the abandoned and ancient nature of these sites.

Again, some unusual references occur. Woolbury Ring on Stockbridge Down, Hampshire, even today a distinctive and surviving monument, is mentioned in 947 in quite unusual and specific terms: *thonne suth to thaere holan dic benithanwelnabyrig*, 'to the hollow ditch beneath the fort of riches' (S526 [223]). This may refer to the discovery of a hoard, but it could also imply a more romantic, poetic aesthetic in regards to naming these monuments or the existence of a local legend. An *Aboddes byrig*, 'abbot's burh', is recorded at Hunton, Hampshire (S381 [232]), and the rather unusual *Aethelware byrig*, possibly 'fort of the noble folk or royal line', is mentioned in 972 in the bounds of Stratford-sub-Castle in Wiltshire, perhaps referring to the camp at Old Sarum (S789 [359]). The same set of bounds begins at the great and ancient fort, however, describing it in more mundane terms: *Aerest of Afene on tha Ealdan Burhdic on thaene weg*, 'old fortified ditch' (S789 [367]). Sarum has a long and complex prehistory, and it was significant as a strategic Roman military fort controlling a major crossroads (Chapter 4, Figure 4.12). It is a sixth-century battle location too (see Chapter 3, p. 86), and is believed to have been a royal residence and *burh*.

Other terms exist that may refer to ancient earthwork fortifications, although these are rare occurrences in Old English bounds. A detailed review by John Baker has revealed six instances of *fæsten*, 'stronghold', recorded in charters. An *ealden fæsten*, 'old stronghold', now lost, is recorded by the River Meon in Hampshire in the ninth century (S283; Hooke 1994, 140; Baker 2012, table 19.1). *Fæsten* was also associated with words for colour, for stock including bucks and stallions, and interestingly, if place-names are taken into account, four to five instances indicate an association with holly, implying perhaps similar naming patterns to the association of abandoned forts and monuments with thorns, brush, and furze (see pp. 137–8 and Baker 2008, 2012). Another relevant term is *(ge)weorc* 'work or material construction'. Few instances survive within *OE* charter-bounds, although an *ealden ge[w]eorce*, 'old work/ construction', is recorded in an eleventh-century land grant at Culmstock, Devon (S386). The term is far more common within the English place-name corpus and is usually described as either *ald*, 'old', or *nīw*, 'new', (see Baker 2012: table 19.3). Although some names clearly refer to active places or contemporary constructions, most are argued by Baker (2012) to refer to strongholds of other periods, including Iron Age and Roman workings, and may in particular be associated with structures with an obvious build, such as masonry walls or foundations.

Stān. These names have their own distinctive range of associated descriptive terms. Like *hlaw*, *stān*-terms were overwhelmingly associated with male and female personal names, presumably indicative of the past and current ownership of adjacent land or the estate itself.[7] Stones were also described in terms of their colour: red, white, grey, and brown (see S496 [145], S559 [148], S448 [159], S631 [421], S449 [422], S459 [423]) and in one very specific instance by colour, position, and associated feature: *dunnan stanwith foan tham burg gete*, 'brown stone against the front of the fort' (S784 [448]). Size and shape were also important: with broad or wide, long and large stones mentioned (S448 [147], S713 [155], S317 [162]). Multiple stone settings occur, some of which may offer reference to lost prehistoric features. A *stanrǽwe*, 'stone row', is mentioned in the bounds of Hardwell, Berkshire (S369 [156]), and again at Chiseldon and Badbury, Wiltshire—bounds that also refer in addition to a setting of ten stones (S568 [437]). A setting of four stones is mentioned at Liddington, Wiltshire (S459 [436]). Finally, on one occasion a *gemerstan or* 'boundary stone' was mentioned (S368 [432]). Stones, it seems, were important monuments for marking boundaries and for claiming land and estates, as indicated by the numerous examples termed 'boundary stones' and the large number associated with personal names. It seems likely that stones may have been commonly resituated, raised, and set as new monumental markers, but that large and distinctive natural stones, and perhaps standing stones too, might be recycled as significant features for marking ownership of an estate. The naming patterns for stones demonstrate little variation and variety. There are few names that indicate the kind of curious, aesthetic, and superstitious interest that we can see for barrows and forts. This may relate to the fact that stones had a contemporary purpose and were used in the

---

[7] Ibban; ceobban; tættucan; cylman; cenelmes; Ceolbrihtes; bregeswithe; bode; Mann; Idhild; Beornulfes; wylberhtes; puntes; Aetheferthes; Sceobban; wullaf; beornwyne.

construction of land boundaries, estates, *burhs*, and monasteries. The few that carry names of interest include a possible 'hoard stone' at Ashbury in Berkshire (S524 [151]). In addition a *kinges stane* at Headbourne Worthy, Hampshire (S309 [262]), and a *cwuenstane*, 'queen's stone', at Selsey, Sussex (S1291 [293]), may indicate markers for royal estates, mustering points or places of proclamation and assembly, or some kind of legendary or superstitious association.

Naming trends

Barrows, ditches, camps, and stones were thus distinguished primarily in simple terms reflecting aesthetic considerations and distinguishing features: shape, size, texture, colour, and specific positioning in the landscape. Some monuments, however, evoked a much greater range of descriptive terms, and may thus have been more powerful features within the late Anglo-Saxon imagination. The way in which features termed *beorg* were described, for example, differed from those termed *hlaw*. The *beorg* was much more likely to be distinguished by association with wild animals, by vegetation and covering, and by terms indicative of the erosion and excavation of the monuments, and although both types of feature were associated with personal names, a *hlaw* by contrast was far more frequently described in association with a personal name than with any other type of descriptive appellation. Forts were also described in terms of their association with wild animals, their physical features such as ditches, entrances, their build and composition as earthwork constructions, and, interestingly, their age by means of the *OE* term *eald*. This is also true of ditches, which were described by age or by form, with a significant proportion distinguished as old or ancient by the prefix *eald*. Mentions of animal inhabitation, overgrowth, and the broken or ruinous state of the monument were all used to imply age as well. The *burh*, 'fort', and *dic*, 'ditch', were types of earth-built feature that were still being constructed by late Anglo-Saxon communities for military and non-military purposes. Such features may have been distinguished by their age, to differentiate them from recent features. *Beorg* and *hlaw* are not, however, distinguished by the term *eald* except in rare instances. This suggests these monuments were generally recognized as features of considerable age already, or that the name terms offered some form of age distinction. *Beorg*, like *burh*, is often described using references to overgrowth, wild animals, or the denuded or broken state of the monument, whereas *hlaw* is not. It is possible, therefore, that *beorg* was applied to a monument believed to be more ancient and more akin to an ancient *eald eorðburh* than a *hlaw*. A *hlaw*, despite being an old feature, may have been perceived as a monument, like a *stan*, which was raised within real or perceived memory. These could have been considered to represent burial mounds of the remembered Anglo-Saxon past rather than those from a more ancient, remote, and darker time. It is also possible that features termed *beorg* and *burh*, and also perhaps *eald dic*, were more evocative and potent in the Anglo-Saxon imagination as a result of their perceived antiquity and ancient history.

Hlaw and *stān* were described differently to other monument terms. Common associations with personal names and personal ownership as well as reference to their active role as boundary monuments, and a contrasting low occurrence of more functional descriptive terms associating these features with vegetation and wild animals, suggest they were perceived as types of monument that had more of an active role in late Anglo-Saxon society. Neither the *hlaw* nor *stān* is described in terms that imply these features were ancient, and very few examples exist of their association with special or unusual people, events or creatures, but the bounds indicate they were very important for establishing contemporary personal ownership of land and estates. Stones may well have been raised or relocated as boundary markers in the mid- and late Anglo-Saxon era, and might thus have been accepted as a common contemporary type of monument used for marking bounds and limits. A *hlaw* would have been old, by several hundred years or more, but perhaps in the late Anglo-Saxon mind a *hlaw* was old, but not 'other'; recognized as a monument of a fairly recent past, and like boundary stones, a feature likely raised by previous, remembered generations.

All these types of feature were, however, sometimes referred to by names indicative of local traditions and superstitions that linked these features to the supernatural world. *Hlaw* as well as *beorg* were associated with supernatural powers and entities. Supernatural associations are, as revealed by this study, present but very rare. They account for a very small proportion of the corpus of landmarks and monuments mentioned in *OE* bounds. This alone suggests that these markers were distinctive, singled out particularly as sites connected with stories, myths, or legends, perhaps because of their perceived age, but also perhaps because of certain local aesthetics, memories, or perceptions that are now lost to us, that distinguished these places as particularly evocative. *Beorg* and *burh* may have been considered more ancient and evocative, but examples of *hlaw*, *dic*, and *stān* can be found with supernatural and superstitious associations as well.

These land boundaries also indicate that monuments were used for purposes other than marking boundaries. The three incidences of monuments recorded as meeting places, as well as a number of weard-beorg and weard-hlaw place-names identified outside of this study (see Baker et al. 2013), suggest a continuing reworking and reuse of the prehistoric in the late Anglo-Saxon period for activities relating to administration and military concerns. Thus some monuments were active and not abandoned and forgotten, and this may have had a strong impact on which monuments and monument types emerged in the late Anglo-Saxon imagination as haunted sites associated with legends and myths.

Other folkloric trends can also be identified. At least some terms imply that monuments might have had legendary or mythical associations and had a place in local folklore. Reference to Anglo-Saxon legendary war leaders, mentions of kings and queens, and references to treasure are all possibilities. Names of kings or famous figures could, of course, imply the common usage of these personal names in late Saxon society; mentions of kings and queens could reflect no more than the royal ownership of an estate; mentions of treasure may reflect nothing other than the actual discovery of a hoard. Such naming patterns may, however, capture the vestiges of stories and legends that people and communities used as a means of situating themselves within their landscape. Traditions of treasure relate to particularly old and ancient sites. A *hordenestan* perhaps 'hoard stone' (S524 [151]) in Ashbury, Berkshire; Woolbury Ring, discussed on p. 166, described as *welnabyrig*, 'the fort of riches' (S526 [223]); and the *dinra beorg*, 'coin barrow', in Compton Beauchamp, Berkshire (S564 [57]), all fit this particular genre. To this we can add *hordwyllæs*, 'hoard well', in West Woolstone (S317 [168]) and *hord hlince*, 'hoard lynchet', at Welford (S552 [143]), both in Berkshire, and the *drakenhorde*, 'dragon's hoard', of the South Damerham bounds, Hampshire (S513 [29]). These landmarks were associated with the idea of treasure and wealth, perhaps because of discoveries of ancient metalwork and coins, but it is also possible such references, like those to historical characters and kings or queens, emerged and circulated as local legends and superstitions that developed around particular ancient features.

Supernatural names and unusual associations (Appendix 4i)

The vast majority of monuments in these bounds were described according to their size, physical form, colour, and topographic position, or associated with personal names. Occasionally, in these bounds, however, monuments were associated with mythical beings, supernatural creatures, and the heathen world. Three different *grimes dic* or 'Grim's Ditches' were referred to in Wiltshire at Burcombe (S631 [19]), Ditchampton (S1010 [20]), and Langford (S612 [21]). 'Grim', when found in reference to ancient earthworks such as ditches or occasionally mineshafts or forts, has been identified by Margaret Gelling as a reference to the supernatural character of Grim, the alter ego of the heathen god Woden (Gelling 1988). Woden too can be found in association with ditches in Wiltshire, at *wodnesdic* known today as Wansdyke (S647 [17]). The *flegerstane* recorded in the bounds of Chilton is interpreted as a 'giant's stone' by Gelling (1976: 767 (pp. 179–80)) and an *entan hlew* at Poolhampton Hampshire [34], suggests a barrow associated with a giant. This is without doubt corroboration for the types of mythical associations between ancient monuments and supernatural creatures identified here in the Anglo-Saxon poetic and prose literature. By extending the survey to all Old English bounds, a greater breadth of supernatural naming and terminology can be identified, although it is notable that such names are still very sporadic in the overall corpus (see Figure 5.4). By extending the search to the entire English place-name corpus, evidence

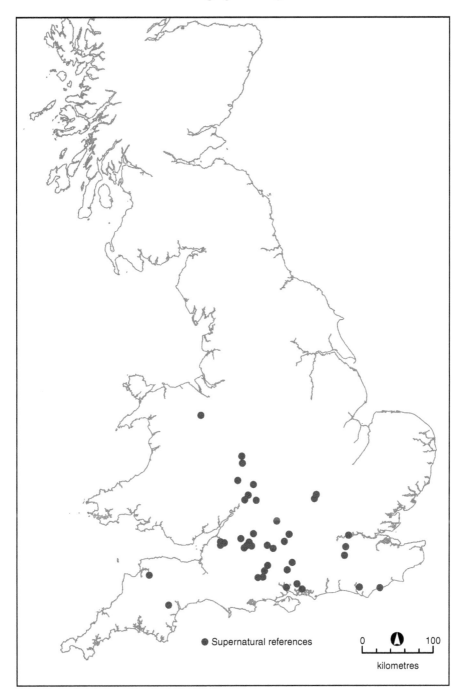

Fig. 5.4 The distribution of all supernatural references contained within the surviving corpus of Old English charter-bounds. Author's image.

emerges for the wider circulation of late Anglo-Saxon superstitions in which ancient monuments and other places in the landscape were associated with fearful and repugnant supernatural creatures.

Mythical characters and supernatural beasts (Appendix 4i)

Grendel. If tales like *Beowulf* circulated as oral traditions and stories, then the association of characters with prominent and suitable features in the landscape might be expected. In our modern landscape, associations between natural features and old monuments with characters such as Arthur and Robin Hood proliferate (for example, Robin Hood's Well, Skellow, Yorkshire; Adam's Grave, Wiltshire; or King Arthur's Hall, Bodmin Moor, Cornwall). The term *grendel* does indeed appear in charter-bounds, but not in place-names. Its meaning is disputed. In Ham in Wiltshire, the bounds lead *ðonne on grendels mere*, which is interpreted by Grundy as 'then to the Pond of the Green Quarry? (S416 [3]); Grundy 1919, 228 (31)). This interpretation suggests that the name derives from a combination of the *OE* terms *gren + delf\an*, referring to a 'green excavation/digging/quarry' and not a monster. Another possible interpretation might be 'gravelly place' found in Grindleton in West Yorkshire (Smith 1961d: 195–6). At Greendale, Clyst St Mary, in Devon, the place-name is similarly interpreted (Gover et al. 1932: 586). Jacobsson (1997: 417), however, considers the term *grendel* to refer to the fearsome supernatural beast of *Beowulf*, who dwelt in a deep pool and inhabited the wilderness. Several references within charter-bounds and place-names to *grendel* may therefore reflect local legends and tales linking the creature from the famous epic to local landmarks. Notable perhaps are *grendeles pytt*, 'pit', at Crediton in Devon (S255 [1]) and the *grendels mere*, 'lake/mere', at Old Swinford, Worcestershire (S579 [4]).

   Woden. Although seemingly one of the most frequently mentioned supernatural beings, the majority of references are to the same monument: S777 [5], S694 [6], S711 [7], and S735 [8] all refer to the West Wansdyke, an extensive linear earthwork of unknown date in Somerset, while S449 [14], S424 [15], S368 [16], and S647 [17] refer to what is considered the eastern portion of the same monument, the East Wansdyke in North Wiltshire. The name is recorded first in the early ninth century, and both portions of the monument retained their name throughout the ninth and tenth centuries. No further examples of *wodnesdic* were found in the place-name corpus, suggesting that this association of Woden with a great linear earthwork may be unique. Instead, in close spatial proximity to the Wansdyke at Alton Priors, North Wiltshire, Woden can be found in association with the probable Neolithic long barrow at Adam's Grave, referred to in 825 as *wodnesbeorge* (S272 [11]) and again in 900 as *wodnes beorge* (S1513 [10]). Woden is also connected to a neighbouring valley of *wodnes dene* (S449 [13]), AD 939. Some hundred years earlier a gap in the linear earthwork named *wodnesdic* is also referred to as *woddes geat* (S272 [12]). This has led to assertions by Margaret Gelling that this large area of landscape was ritually associated with the deity Woden (Gelling 1988). This is discussed briefly in Chapter 3, when the use of *wodnesbeorge* as a battle site in 592 and again in 715 (see *ASC* (A)) is linked with the finds of weaponry in the vicinity of the monumental prehistoric earthworks at the location (see pp. 83–6). Although the battle in 592 at *wodnesbeorg* could represent the first mention of Woden in relation to this portion of landscape, the earliest version of the chronicle was not copied before 891 (Swanton 1996, p. xxi). Thus Woden's association with this area of landscape cannot be placed earlier than the ninth century in documentary terms, although, archaeologically, military finds of sixth- and seventh-century date in the vicinity of *wodnesbeorg* do offer some corroboration for activity in and around the ancient barrow, and the causewayed camp at Knap Hill (see pp. 78, 83, 251). It is tempting to accept the long-term importance of the barrow and its associations with Woden as the reason why the long ditch and surrounding landscape acquired further associations with the pagan god (see Reynolds and Langlands 2006). *Wodnesdene* can be identified as a topographically distinctive narrow valley floor that leads from Lockeridge directly to *woddes geat*, a gap in the Wansdyke.

Several other places in the English landscape associated with the god Woden are equally as enigmatic. *Wodnesfeld* in Staffordshire (S1380 [9]) and again in Bedfordshire (see Gelling 1988: 161, fig. 11) represent the tendency for theophoric names to reference *natural spaces*: areas of wood pasture and open land for common pasture (Hines 1997: 385–6, table 12–1; see also Chapter 3, pp. 67–8). The place-names Wodneslawe in Bedfordshire (Gelling 1988: fig. 11) and Woodnesborough in Kent (see Ellis Davidson and Webster 1967) refer to barrows, using the terms *hlaw* and *beorg*. Wednesbury in Staffordshire, however, associates Woden with a fortification or camp (Gelling 1988: 161, fig. 11). Despite an overall paucity of place-names that reference Woden, and the concentration of references to Woden existing in a small portion of landscape between Lockeridge and Alton Priors, it appears that this particular theophoric name can be found in association with natural places and with ancient earthworks, in particular barrows and forts. In addition, the large earthwork of Wansdyke, considered to be eighth century in construction, demonstrates how theophoric names and associations between deities and landscape features might become iconic or popular enough to lend themselves to the later superstitious and legendary naming of more recent landscape features—in this instance leading to a reinforcement of the association of Woden with ancient earthworks and large ancient features and with this tract of landscape on the North Wiltshire downs.

Grim (see Figure 5.5(a)). Grim, the masked alter ego of Woden, is identified by Margaret Gelling as a figure particularly associated with linear earthworks (Gelling 1988: 148–50). At Langford (S612 [21]), Burcombe (S631 [19]), and

Ditchampton (S1010 [20]), three separate stretches of dyke, all in Wiltshire, were connected with Grim. Natural places too were linked with this entity: for example, *grimes hylle* in Hawling, Gloucestershire (S179 [18]). Unfortunately these associations cannot be taken entirely at face value. It is clear from the charters that Grim was a personal name in use in late Anglo-Saxon England. In charter S1497 a reference to *Grim and his wif and Eadgiðe and Eadflæde* can be found, while *Grim and his broðor* are mentioned in a Peterborough charter (Robertson 1939, no. 40). Thus *grim gelege*, 'Grim's clearing/wood pasture (S354; B565/3), or *grimes hyll*, 'Grim's hill', could denote personal ownership. Margaret Gelling distinguished references to Grim in association with ancient earthworks as a collective of names that probably referred to supernatural associations with the mythical character rather than to personal ownership of the monuments or the land associated with them (Gelling 1988: 148–50). It is interesting to note that the *grimes dic* referred to at Langford in 956 (S612 [21]) is described some ten to fifteen years earlier both as *maerdic*, 'boundary ditch' (S469), and as simply *dic*, 'ditch' (S1811, AD 963 for 943). This highlights just how specific such naming could be, reflecting the viewpoints and beliefs of individuals in a single generation. It might also point to the association of Grim with linear earthworks and ditches as a particularly

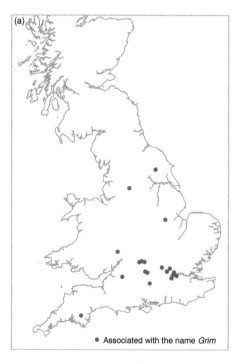

Fig. 5.5(a) Place-names and toponyms associated with the name *Grim*. Author's image.

late development in Anglo-Saxon nomenclature for landscape features—a fashion or belief that emerged long after the arrival and widespread acceptance of Christianity. It certainly suggests that these associations may have had more to do with late Anglo-Saxon stories, perhaps elite narratives or folk beliefs, than the realities of pre-Christian beliefs.

References to Grim's Ditches in English place-names are in fact widespread (see Table 5.1 and Figure 5.5(a)). All are recorded no earlier than the twelfth century, but their existence does corroborate the suggestion that this supernatural character was particularly associated with linear entrenchments and ancient ditches. Such names attest to a long-held popular fashion for associating earthwork features, especially ditches, with Grim, that may have lasted beyond the Conquest. Grim is also associated in English place-names with a range of other topographic features, including furlongs, scars, and headlands (see Table 5.2). Given the problems of discerning references to the supernatural entity Grim from the personal name, it is difficult to suggest that any of these are with certainty references to similar superstitious or popular perceptions. Grim, however, is also mentioned in various place-names in connection with mounds, holes, mines or pits, and ancient earthwork enclosures (Table 5.2). One known association between Grim and a mound at Grimshoe Hundred, Norfolk (Anderson 1934–9: i. 75), refers to a meeting and assembly mound. Three associations with earthen fortifications can be identified: Grimsbury Castle, Hampstead Norris (undated), Grimespound, Manaton (1797), both in Devon, and *Grimberie* (1086), Banbury, Oxfordshire. Grimespound refers to a Bronze Age earthwork enclosure. Grimesholes, recorded in the thirteenth century in Reading, Berkshire, and the better-known prehistoric flint mines, comprising mine shafts and spoil heaps at Grimes Graves in Norfolk, offer two further associations with holes, pits, or chasms. Thus, despite the difficulties of discerning whether *Grim* or *ON Grimr* names provide, in charter-bounds or place-names, references to the supernatural character Grim, it is clear that a distinct

Table 5.1 Grim's ditch place-names

Place-name	Parish	County	Date	Reference
Grymesdych	Bray	BRK	1316	Gelling 1973: 51
Grim's Ditch	Blewbury	BRK	Undated/modern	Gelling 1973: 152
Grim's Ditch	East Hendred	BRK	Post-medieval/modern	Gelling 1974: 483
Grimsditch	Aldworth	BRK	Undated/modern	Gelling 1974: 496
Gryme's Dyke	Colchester	ESX		Reaney 1960: 119
Grimesdich	Linkenholt	HMP	1272	Reaney 1960: 119
Grymesdich	Berkhampstead	HRT	1295	Ekwall 1960: 205
Grimesdich	Edgeware	MDX	?	Ekwall 1960: 205
Grimesdich	By Wallingford?	OXF	c.1216 and 1300	Gelling 1953: 5

Table 5.2 Place-names containing the element *Grim/Grimr-*

Place-name	Feature	Parish	County	Date	Reference
Grimeshole	Hole	Reading	BRK	C13th	Gelling 1973: 183
Grimesforlong	Furlong	Kennington	BRK	Undated	Gelling 1974: 455
Grimsbury Castle	Fort	Hampstead Norris	BRK	Undated	Gelling 1988: 149
Grimespound	Enclosure	Manaton	DEV	1797	Gover et al. 1932: 482
Grimshoe	Mound	Hundred	NFK	1086	Anderson 1934–39: i. 75
Grimes Graves	Mines	Weeting	NFK	Undated	Gelling 1988: 149
Grimesheuedesden	Headland	Witney	OXF	1300	Gelling 1954: 334
Grimberie	Fort	Banbury	OXF	1086	Gelling 1954: 413
Grimanlea	*Leah*	Grimley	OXF	851	Ekwall 1960: 205
Grimscar	Scar	Halifax	YOW	1771	Smith 1961c: 36
Grimestorp	*Thorp*	Grimsthorpe	YOW	1297	Ekwall 1960: 205
Grimeston	*Ton*	Kirkby Underdale	YOE	1086	Smith 1937: 130

group of names exists, outside of areas settled by incoming Scandinavian groups, where Grim can be found associated with large earthworks, especially linear entrenchments, and also with forts, barrows, and fissures or holes in the ground. The large number of post-Conquest place-names that make reference to Grim in association with such features, some as early as the twelfth century and several that are post-medieval and later, may point to such associations and naming fashions surviving well into the antiquarian and Romantic eras.

Thunor and Tiw (see Figure 5.5(b)). Thunor/Thor, the Germanic pagan god or deity, is consistently associated with groves and open spaces in written sources and place-names (see Table 5.3). Like most theophoric names, the majority refer to associations with natural spaces—the *leāh* and the *feld*—areas of wood pasture and open land for common pasture (see Hines 1997: 385–6, table 12–1). Although the unidentified *Thunresfelda*, 'field of Thunor', in Wiltshire and *Tislea*, 'clearing of Tiw', in Hampshire may have been natural places devoted in the pre-Christian era to activities venerating these deities, these place-names may also represent later mythic and superstitious coining, reflecting a late Anglo-Saxon curiosity and popular interest in the supernatural and the legendary. The small corpus of names that mention these deities do not entirely refer to the natural environment and references to monuments do exist. Thunderlow or *Thunor's hlaw*, Essex, *Thunreslau*, Suffolk, and the lost *thunoreshlæw*, mentioned in the foundation myth for Minster-in-Thanet, Kent (see Hollis 1998), all link Thunor or Thor with hills or barrows; remarkably they do so with *hlaw* rather

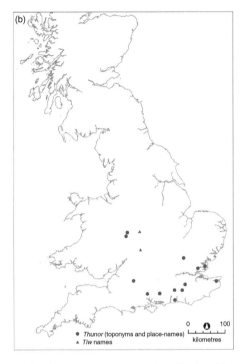

Fig. 5.5(b) Toponyms and place-names associated with the deities: *Tiw* and *Thunor*. Author's image.

Table 5.3 Place-names containing the *OE* element *Thunres/Thunor*

Place-name	Feature	Parish	County	Date	Reference
Tondreleia	*Leah*	Thunderley Hall	ESX	1143 BM	Ekwall 1960: 471
Thunreslea	*Leah*	Thundersley	ESX	1086 DB	Ekwall 1960: 471
Thoresle	*Leah*	Thursley	SUR	1286 BM	Ekwall 1960: 472
Þunresfleld	*Feld*	Thunderfield	SUR	*c.*880	Ekwall 1960: 471
Tonrinch	Ridge	Thundridge	HRT	1086 DB	Ekwall 1960: 471
Thur(e)stapel(l)	Post	Hundred Name	ESX	1086 DB	Pewsey and Brooks 1993: 80
Thunders barrow	Barrow	Shoreham	SSX	Undated	
Thunoreslowe	Barrow	Minster-in-Thanet	KNT	*c.*1000	Hollis 1998: 49
Thunreslau	Barrow	lost	ESX	Undated	Gelling 1988, 161: fig. 11

than *beorg*. None of these is definitely a prehistoric monument, but the Minster-in-Thanet story mentions a barrow that could be pointed out in the landscape when the legend was set down in around AD 1000 (see p. 155). It is also interesting that, like the Cuthman legend (see p. 155), the doomed councillor Thunor was swallowed into the earth at a spot marked by a barrow known as *thunoreshlæw*. Although no charter-bound markers or place-names offer us a Thunor's Pytt or Thor's Hole, the barrow in this tale marks the location of a gobbling pit or fissure.

Tiw, by contrast, is mentioned very sporadically indeed, occurring once in the charter-bounds in reference to a lake or pool (S1272 [28]). The lost place-names Tislea (Hampshire) and Tuesley (Surrey) connect the god to woodland clearings, and at Tysoe (Warwickshire) with a spur of land (Reaney 1960: 118; Gelling 1988: fig. 11). No mentions exist in written sources or in place-names connecting *Tiw* to monuments of ancient or early medieval date.

Dragons. The dragon was a beast of particular importance to Anglo-Saxon communities. Its predatory nature, cunning, and ruthlessness have already been outlined. Both *Beowulf* and *Maxims II* leave no doubt regarding the association between dragons and ancient burial mounds and ancient treasure, and it is no surprise to see such perceptions reflected more widely in charter-bounds and place-names, suggesting such ideas held popular currency. However, dragon place-names do need to be treated with some caution. It is possible that Old English contained a term *draca* used to refer to a male duck (Alaric Hall: pers. comm.). The term is securely attested in Middle English (Hough 1996: 613–15). There is no phonological distinction between these etyma, and so the associations listed in Table 5.4 may of course indicate places frequented by male ducks rather than dragons. The types of place are, however, compelling: pits, mounds, and holes dominate the list rather than lakes, pools, or meres, and the connection to hoards is also a strong indication that these names reflect perceptions of places and features associated with dragons rather than ducks.

The *drakenhorde* 'dragon hoard' in South Damerham, Hampshire (S513 [29]), may refer to a place where a hoard or ancient treasure was found. It might also be a poetic allusion to a barrow as well. In Garsington, Oxfordshire, the field-name Drakehord furlong (*drakenhord c.*1230) occurs in proximity to the field-name *brocenebereue*, 'broken barrow' *c.*1250, suggesting perhaps that the *dragon hoard* field-name was a reference to both a barrow and perhaps a barrow where treasure had been located. There is certainly one reference of 942 to a *dracan hlāwen*, 'dragon barrow', which survives as the modern place-name Drakelow in Derbyshire (S484). The remaining place-names are all post-Conquest in date, and it is possible such names were coined subsequently in the medieval and even post-medieval periods, reflecting the continuity of folk legends and superstitions regarding dragon-inhabited caves, fissures, and crags and perhaps barrows too. Many are firmly twelfth to fourteenth century in date and of these at least five refer to barrows or mounds and two to holes

Table 5.4 Place-names referring to dragons

Place-name	Feature	Parish	County	Date	Reference
Dracan hlāwen	Mound	Drakelow	DRB	942	S484
Dragley	*leah*		LNC		Reaney 1960: 224
Drachou	Mound	Draker	NTB	Medieval	Reaney 1960: 224
Drakeholes	Holes		NTB		Reaney 1960: 224
Drakenhull	Hill	Artington	SUR	1318	Reaney 1960: 224
Drakebergh	Mound	Dragberry	SUR	1384	Reaney 1960: 224
Drakenes, -eck/h	Edge	Hemlingford	WAR	1183	Gover et al. 1936: 17
Drakelowe	Mound	Wolverley	WOR	1240	Mawer and Stenton 1927: 285
Drakehead Lane	Edge?	Conisbrough	YOW	Undated	Smith 1961a: 127
Drakehou	Mound	Kirksmeaton	YOW	*c.* 1220	Smith 1961b: 52
Drakylgate	Road/gap	Snydale	YOW	1328	Smith 1961c: 123
Drake Pit	Pit	Birstall	YOW	Undated	Smith 1961c: 33
Drakeholt	Wood	Kirkburton	YOW	1551	Smith 1961b: 240

or pits. The rest indicate dragons that might be associated in the medieval imagination with edges or spurs, hills, and woodland and wooded clearings.

Giants. These creatures, although frequent within late Anglo-Saxon literature and poetry, are rare in the late Anglo-Saxon landscape. An *enta hlewe* or 'Giant's barrow' exists in the bounds of Poolhampton, Hampshire (see S970 [33] and S465 [34]), and an *enta dic*, 'Giant's ditch', is recorded at Kings Worthy also in Hampshire (S962 [32]). In Hagbourne, Berkshire, a *flecgesgara* has been interpreted by Gelling as 'Giant's triangular piece of land' (*ON fleggr* 'giant') (S354[31]) and again at Chilton, she suggests *flege stane* as 'Giant's stone' (S934[30]).

In *Andreas*, a late-tenth-century account of the ministry of St Andrew (see discussions on pp. 154–5), the saint is dragged across stone-paved roads described as *enta ærgeweorc*, 'ancient or former works of giants' (line 1232), and later instructs a river to spring from: *stapulas standan, storme bedrifene, eald enta geweorc*, 'some great pillars standing, weather-beaten columns, the old work of giants' (line 1492). *The Ruin*, contained in *The Exeter Book*, fo. 123b–124b, and dated to the second half of the tenth century, describes a decaying city and opens with the line: *Wrætlic is þes welælstan, wyrde gebræ-can; burgstede burston, brosnað enta geweorc*, 'Wondrously ornate is the stone of this wall, shattered by fate; the precincts of the city have crumbled and the work of giants is rotting away' (translation from Bradley 1995). Just as the barrow is considered synonymous with the dragon, and the fen with the monster or *þyrs* (see pp. 184–5), so in *Maxims II* the giant is associated with worked or built things (perhaps Roman structures and ruins). *Ceastra*, 'cities', are described as *enta geweorc*, 'the works of giants' (London, BL Cotton Tiberius Bi, fo. 115a–115b, *Maxims II*, lines 1–3).

Although these poetic and prose sources associate the *ent* or giant with ruined cities and buildings, the term occurs three times in *Beowulf* with a different application. The ancient sword retrieved by the hero from Grendel's abode, and used to kill Grendel's mother, is described as *enta-ærgeweorc* (Fulk et al. 2008: line 1679), and the stone-chambered barrow is twice described as an *enta ġeweorc* (line 2717) and an *eald enta ġeweorc* (line 2774). There is clearly a strong association between *enta* and *worked* things, particularly ancient stone ruins. The barrow and ditch associated with giants in the Hampshire charters could perhaps refer to 'worked' features; perhaps stone-built or constructed monuments. As only two imaginative references using the term *ent* or *enta* come from the mundane world of estate-bounds, it seems that this motif may have been the preserve of poets and literary scholars. It is notable, however, that both references can be found in bounds attached to charters dated to the first half of the eleventh century, although the *enta hlew* is mentioned in an earlier charter for Poolhampton in 940 (see [34]). This suggests that popular perceptions of *enta geweorc* were circulating at the same time that literate accounts were being produced by ecclesiastical scholars of stories that connected such creatures with ruins and ancient works.

Puca and scucca (see Figure 5.5(c)). The *OE* word *puca* is usually translated as 'goblin' (Gelling 1988, 150), whilst *scucca* seems to have had more sinister connotations, occurring in texts with reference to demons and even to the Devil. Ælfric refers several times to *scucca* in his *Homilies*, and it seems to be a term for demons, but in *Catholic Homilies* I, 11, 172.22, *Crist cwæð þa to ðam deofle, ga ðu underbæc scucca*, Christ appears to address the Devil by the term *scucca*. Two related terms are *pucel*, 'small goblin', a diminutive form of *puca*, and *ON skratti*, 'demon', a term which seems very similar if not identical in meaning to *OE scucca*. In the charter-bounds, *puca* is associated with springs whilst the *scucca* is connected with a barrow (for *puca* see S508 [36] and S108 [39]). In Horwood, Berkshire, a *scuccan hlāw*, 'demon or goblin barrow', is recorded in a charter of AD 795 (S138 [35]).[8] Place-names in Oxfordshire, Warwickshire, and Yorkshire connect demons or goblins with barrows, and both the terms *hlāw* and *beorg* are referred to. Three camps or forts are referred to as well: one in Staffordshire and two in Yorkshire. In fact, the *OE scucca* and *ON skratti* are overwhelmingly connected with barrows or mounds and forts (see Table 5.5).

---

[8] Hall also notes the unusual *pucelancyrce* (S553), apparently 'little goblin's church' (Hall 2006: 78).

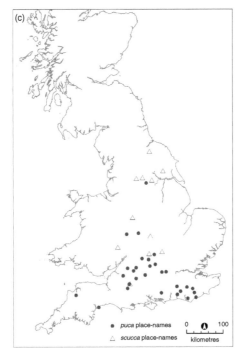

Fig. 5.5(c) Place-names and toponyms associated with *puca*, *skratti*, and *scucca*: goblins or demons. Author image.

Table 5.5 Place-names containing the *OE scucca* and *ON skratti*, 'goblin'

Place-name	Feature	Parish	County	Date	Reference
Shokenhulle	*Scucca* hill	Shucknall	HER	1377	Ekwall 1960: 421
Socheslowe	*Scucca* mound/barrow	Steeple Barton	OXF	1233	Gelling 1954: 250
Shugborough	*Scucca* fort/camp	Shugborough	STF		Gelling 1988: 150
Socheberge	*Scucca* mound/barrow	Shuckburgh	WAR	1086	Gover et al. 1936: 143
Scratchburie	*Scucca* fort/camp	Norton Bavant	WLT	1609	Gover et al. 1939: 154
Scrathowe	*Skratti* mound/barrow	Osmotherley	YON	1388	Smith 1928: 215
Scrathou	*Skratti* mound/barrow	Hayton	YOE	C13th	Smith 1937: 233
Scrathaigh	*Skratti* enclosure	Kexborough	YOW	1841	Smith 1961a: 319
Scratch Lane	*Skratti* lane	Cridling Stubbs	YOW	1847	Smith 1961b: 62
Shokeforth-bro(o)k(e)	*Scucca* brook	Morley	YOW	1412	Smith 1961c: 71
Shugden Hall	*Scucca* dene/valley	Halifax	YOW	1488	Smith 1961c: 87

In contrast, *puca* and *pucel* are associated with farms, hills, ridges, narrow valleys, woods, nooks, and cattle sheds, and frequently connected with water (wells, bridges, streams, springs, and pools) and with pits or holes. Neither the *puca* nor *pucel* is mentioned in the bounds attached to charters. All examples (see Table 5.6) listed come from the English place-name record and all are post-Conquest, with many recorded no earlier than the fifteenth century. A significant problem with these name terms is the potential derivation from *OE pohha/pocca* rather than *puca* or *pucel*: a word that could mean 'bag or baggy' and could plausibly act as a qualifier for a pit or hole but sits relatively uneasily with the watery associations. This term has also seen recent reinterpretation as 'fallow deer' (Hough 2001). The association of fallow deer with woods, clearings, pools, and streams is entirely plausible and consequently one might be tempted to dismiss the list of names incorporating *puca* or *pucel* as no more than references to watery places associated with the regular presence of these creatures. However, Carole Hough's reinterpretation has been questioned by Naomi Sykes and Ruth Carden, who point to the complete absence of zooarchaeological evidence for this species in England before the eleventh century (Sykes and Carden 2011). Fallow deer were introduced into England during the eleventh and twelfth centuries not as quarry for the hunt but as exotica, kept for their 'visual' and 'symbolic' qualities (Sykes and Carden 2011: 156). It seems fallow deer are questionable for pre-Conquest place-names, but the large number of post-Conquest place-names considered to encompass or derive from these terms could of course refer to a species introduced at the Conquest. It is of course also possible that some other type of animal is being referred to, but the attestations in S108, S508, S553 at least suggest that *puca* should not be entirely dismissed either. The place-names have been retained here, in the hope of promoting some further consideration of the potential associations of goblins (small or large) with these types of associated feature. Before dismissing them outright, one cannot avoid a brief mention of Robin Goodfellow: 'Those that "hobgoblin" call you, and "sweet puck", You do their work, and they shall have good luck' (*A Midsummer Night's Dream*, Act II, Scene i. lines 32–42). Shakespeare borrowed Puck from contemporary, late medieval folklore and literature. He was a well-known character within the late-sixteenth-century writings on witchcraft and lore (see, for example, Reginald Scot's *Discovery of Witchcraft* 1586). These watery sites may thus have acquired associations with hobgoblins long after the Conquest.

Although names associated with *puca* or *pucel* are open to some dispute, those names that refer to the *ON skratti* or *OE scucca* through their early appearance in charter-bounds and the consistency of their association with ancient earthworks, as well as their occasional guest appearances in literature and prose, can be taken as evidence of yet another supernatural creature. This creature was malevolent and even demonic or devilish, believed or perceived to haunt and inhabit mounds, barrows, and other ancient earthworks.

Table 5.6 Place-names containing the *OE* elements *puca* and *pucel*

Place-name	Feature	Parish	County	Date	Reference
Puckmere	Pool	Bray	BRK	1283	Gelling 1973: 46
Gt Puckwell	Well	Twyford	BRK	Undated	Gelling 1973: 135
Pokelande	Land	Shaw-Down	BRK	Undated	Gelling 1973: 265
Powcrofte	Croft	Hungerford	BRK	Undated	Gelling 1974: 301
Pokesden	Dene	Steventon	BRK	1439–40	Gelling 1974: 420
Puchelahole	Hole	Putshole	DEV	1301	Gover et al. 1931: 75
Pocheella	Hill	W Budleigh	DEV	1086	Gover et al. 1931: 415
Pukkespytte	Pit	Newington	OXF	*c.*1470	Gelling 1953: 133
Poukwelle	Well	Bicester	OXF	1432–8	Gelling 1953: 200–01
Poukebridge	Bridge	Eynsham	OXF	1470	Gelling 1954: 263
Poukputte	Pit	Burford	OXF	1435–6	Gelling 1954: 312
Poukeput	Pit	Harting	SSX	1350	Mawer and Stenton 1929–30: i. 37
Pokerle	Lea	Henfield	SSX	1327	Mawer and Stenton 1929–30: i. 218
Poukhill	Hill	Rusper	SSX	1614	Mawer and Stenton 1929–30: i. 233
Puckeride	Stream	Cuckfield	SSX	1570	Mawer and Stenton 1929–30: ii. 265
Puckstie	Path	Hartfield	SSX	1287	Mawer and Stenton 1929–30: ii. 358
Pook Pit	Pit	Wadhurst	SSX	Undated	Mawer and Stenton 1929–30: ii. 387
Poukerhale	Nook	Alciston	SSX	1350	Mawer and Stenton 1929–30: ii. 415
Pokeleserse	Small goblin	Brightling	SSX	1176	Mawer and Stenton 1929–30: ii. 472
Poghgrove	Wood	Bexhill	SSX	*c.*1375	Mawer and Stenton 1929–30: ii. 493
Puckgrove	Wood	Solihull	WAR	1638	Gover et al. 1936: 71
Pokkput	Pit	Purton	WLT	1398	Gover et al. 1939: 40
Puckwell	Wellspring	West Knoyle	WLT	Undated	Gover et al. 1939: 177
Pukshepene	Cattleshed	Beechingstoke	WLT	1303	Gover et al. 1939: 319
Poukeryche	Ridge	Sherston	WLT	1300	Gover et al. 1939: 472
Pukpole	Pool	Bishopstrow	WLT	1232	Gover et al. 1939: 480
Pocklechurch	Church	Lyneham	WLT	1570	Gover et al. 1939: 495
Pokeleston	Farm	Kidderminster	WOR	1240	Mawer and Stenton 1927: 252
Puckenhale	Nook	Sandal Magna	YOW	1310	Smith 1961b: 108

Pyrs (see Figure 5.5(d)). The term *þyrs* is usually interpreted as 'giant'. In *Maxims II*, line 42, *þyrs sceal on fenne gewunian ana innan lande*, 'the monster shall dwell in the fen, alone in his realm' (see *Maxims II*, London, BL Cotton Tiberius Bi, fo. 115a–115b), the *þyrs* is similar to Grendel: the demonic fen-dwelling monster in *Beowulf*. In a single instance from Cleeve Prior in Worcestershire, dating to the ninth or tenth centuries, the boundary clause runs: *Ondlang þaes sices innon þone þyrs pytt*, 'to the demon/monster's pit' (S222 [38]). Place-names reveal additional mentions of this creature. It was associated with pits (see Thyrspit at Ussleby in Lincolnshire, for example, recorded no earlier than 1372); with barrows (see Thirshowe, Barmston, East Yorkshire); and ditches and pools (see Table 5.7). Thirst House in Derbyshire, a cave in Deep Dale, also seems to retain a name connecting a *þyrs* with an opening and fissure into the underworld. There are further instances in Northumberland, Northamptonshire, and Derbyshire mentioned in previous published researches, but these proved untraceable during this study (see Reaney 1960). A distinctive distribution covering the east and north-east of England is apparent. It is possible that, just as *scucca/skratti* showed a sharp concentration in Yorkshire, so the *þyrs* was a creature particularly feared by the inhabitants and communities of the fenlands and regions north of the Humber.

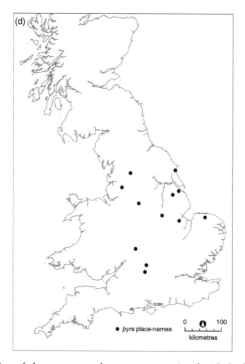

Fig. 5.5(d) Distribution of place-names and toponyms associated with the *þyrs*. Author's images.

Table 5.7 Place-names containing *OE Pyrs*

Place-name	Feature	Parish	County	Date	Reference
Thorsdiche	Ditch	Sparsholt	BRK	1321	Gelling 1974: 491
Thirlspot	Pot/pool		CMB	Modern	Gelling 1988: 150
Thirst House	Cave	Deep Dale	DRB	Modern	Reaney 1960: 224
Thurspits	Pit	Bottesford		1679	Cameron 2001: 27
Thyrspit	Pit	Usselby	LIN	1372	Cameron 1992: 171
Thirspittes	Pit	Waltham	LIN	1601	Cameron 1996: 192
Thirsdall	*Deill*, 'share of land'	Wykeham	LIN	1577	Cameron 1991: 244–5
Turesford	Ford	Thursford	NFK	1086	Ekwall 1960: 472
Toresmere	Mere/pool	Hardwick	OXF	1086	Gelling 1953: 216
Thirshowe	Mound/barrow	Barmston	YOE	1292	Smith 1937: 84
Thursemyer	*Pyrs*, mere/pool	Broughton	YOW	1553	Smith 1961d: 44

Wicce, biccan, hæþenan. In contrast to the other terms discussed here, which may be rare in charter-bounds but are found more widely in English place-names, these terms are highly unusual and are not evident outside of the *OE* bounds attached to late Anglo-Saxon charters. *Wicce*, 'witch', may occur once. A marker along the bounds of Heighton, Sussex, reads: *on Echilde hlæwe a þa smye wicce* (S648 [41]). The form of *wicce* is incorrect, however, and so any association with a witch or witches is dubious (Alaric Hall: pers comm.). *Hæþenan* or 'heathen' is a term discussed by Andrew Reynolds in relation to the frequent mention in bounds of *OE hæþenanbyrigels* 'heathen burials', thought to refer to places of burial for criminals and outcasts (Reynolds 2002, 2009a). Two examples of 'heathen barrows' have been identified: a *hæþenan beorge* in the bounds of Drayton, Hampshire (S956 [40]), and a *hæðebe beorge* in the bounds of Bengeworth, Worcestershire (S1590 [42]). These 'heathen barrows' may refer to execution sites but they may also reference an added perception that a *beorge* was not simply an ancient burial place, but a heathen place too. Similarly, the reference to Echild's barrow implies the mound on the boundary might be a place of execution and interment of a witch. As Chapter 6 will show, this mode of disposal for those considered to have committed crimes that forfeited their right to normal burial is well attested from the eighth century onwards. These references, however, while they may have their root in common judicial practices of the late Anglo-Saxon period, also reinforce how the location of such practices might acquire names associated with the activities that had happened there, and served to commemorate the heathenism, and evil of such places.

A final association worth mentioning, although deeply obscure, is references to a *biccan hlew*, 'bitches barrow' (S635 [411]), and *bicenditch*, 'bitches ditch' (S459 [393]), both in Wiltshire; although the location of the barrow is no longer known, the ditch lay somewhere in the parish of Liddington. These may be derogatory namings perhaps referencing local folk stories, or they may refer to an association with a female wild dog or canine animal, or include a form of the personal name *Bica*, found in S564 [100].

Ælf and mære. These creatures have not been subject to intensive study here owing to an absence of association with monuments or indeed with place-names in general; however, a review of the types of supernatural creatures that inhabited the Anglo-Saxon landscape would be incomplete without some mention of elves. No *ælf* place-name can be identified within the English landscape with confidence, and Alaric Hall (2006, 61–80), in an attempt to 'locate' the *ælfe* in the Anglo-Saxon landscape, has identified only two convincing place-names containing the noun *ælfe*: *ælfrucge* in Kent and *ylfing dene* in Berkshire. These and a handful of other possible names are used by Hall to make an argument for an association between *ælfen* and hills and valleys. The correspondence with other mythical and theophoric names is noted such as Tysoe, Warwickshire, and *Wodnesdene*, Wiltshire, and by contrast and using post-Conquest sources Hall argues for the association of the *ælfen* with woods, meadows, and high hills—wild places in the English landscape.

The *mære* is even more elusive. This entity, related to the *ælfe*, is considered by Hall and others to compound the concept of dreams and visitation with a corporeal form. There are hints that this creature was associated with the kinds of martial dangerous supernatural females described earlier in this chapter (Hall 2007a, 124–6). It had similar topographical associations to the *ælfe*. The place-name *mareshilsike* (1492), Halifax, Warley, West Yorkshire, for example, might encompass the term *OE mare* or *mære* and if so attests to a hill associated with this night-visitor. It is interesting too that *wudumære*, 'wood-*mære*', is used as a gloss for the name of the nymph Echo, who after rejection by Narcissus was doomed restlessly and unrequitedly to haunt the woods and woodland pools and diminish until she remained just a voice amid the trees (Hall 2007a, 85). Another nymph-like spirit that can be associated with wild and natural features is the *OE nicor*, 'water spirit/demon/monster', referred to in Nikerpool, Mildenhall, Wiltshire. These beings are not found in association with old or ancient monuments or ruins, but they do have specific 'haunts' and connections to certain types of natural place. Such names attest to additional layers of numinosity and meaning in the natural landscape, with wild and remote places, woods, and pools, identified as places where these kinds of supernatural creatures might be encountered.

Where the wild things are . . .

Despite the rare mentions of supernatural creatures in late Anglo-Saxon charter-bounds and their infrequent survival in the place-name record, the evidence remains evocative and tantalizing. A late Anglo-Saxon vernacular perception of landscape is hinted at that included demon-inhabited pools, pits, and mounds occupied by corporeal monstrous beings, constructions of lost and mighty civilizations, and places sacred to ancient gods. This contrasts with the extraordinary range of mundane descriptive qualifiers used to denote monuments in the Anglo-Saxon landscape. Two observations can be made on this small corpus. The full range of creatures is associated with varied topographic locations, including pits and fissures, old workings, stones, pools and wet places, hills, and notably ancient monuments. Old barrows are consistently found within this corpus. These features seem to have been a natural harbour in the Anglo-Saxon imagination for the malevolent ghosts and demons that haunted the landscape. Entities not associated with barrows include the *puca* and *pucel*, which instead show a consistent association with watery places and pits. This may be a result of a misinterpretation of the term and the place-names, or the influence of late medieval folklore on naming patterns, *or* an indication that, like the *ælfen*, the natural home of these creatures was the wilderness rather than places associated with human activity, even if long abandoned. If these place-names are discounted, over half of the corpus of supernatural names associate entities or beings with ancient earthworkings of some kind. Nearly two-thirds of the names that refer to Grim can be argued to reference an ancient earthwork, most often a linear ditch. A third of *Thunor* place-names refer to barrows. Over a third of the collected dragon place-names associate these beasts with barrows, fissures, caves, or pits. Over half of *scucca/skratti* place-names refer to ancient prehistoric remains, most often barrows. Nearly half of the names that include the element *Pyrs* refer to ancient monuments or fissures. In short, the locational evidence points to popular beliefs that encompassed a landscape within which all kinds of supernatural creatures dwelled. They lived in particular places and habitats and most were especially drawn to ancient ruins and monuments.

The preponderance of haunted nooks, hollows, fissures, pits, and watery places is compelling. All such places could have carried potency as imagined interfaces or access points with other supernatural worlds. The consistent appearance of ancient earthworks and particularly barrows alongside these other appellations serves to reconfirm earlier assertions that ancient burial mounds may have been perceived, like pits and fissures, as entrances to a hellish underworld and places fit for monsters or damned and restless souls. The range of potent places in the landscape within the late Anglo-Saxon psyche also bears an uncanny resemblance to the types of natural and human-altered places argued in Chapter 3 as resonant and spiritually charged within pre-Christian beliefs. Another minor detail, and yet one that brings such conceptual ideas more vividly into human focus, is the relationship between these monsters and the nighttime. In *Beowulf* the supernatural characters are particularly associated with the night. Only at twilight, when the visible boundaries of the real and physical world began to dissolve, would such creatures stir and venture from their fissures, barrows, and pools, released to walk the landscape or haunt their place of habitation.

Summary

A wide array of literary and poetic sources, charms, place-names, and boundary markers provide a rich, if partial narrative that describes a landscape charged with the supernatural, inhabited by a fearsome array of liminal creatures. The second part of this chapter, by exploring the Old English bounds attached to land grants, has revealed that the stories and mythology encountered in the prose and poetic courses of the Christian era had a place in popular vernacular culture as well. The motifs identified in late Anglo-Saxon prose and poetic sources were mirrored by a set of widely held folk superstitions.

The literary and poetic accounts, despite being set down in writing within a Christian time frame by scribes almost certainly working within monastic environments, attest to a rich imaginative folklore that described many natural and ancient elements of the landscape in terms of supernatural agency and other-worldly inhabitation. There are subtle changes to be discerned within these sources, in terms of how confrontations between monuments, monsters, and people were enacted. It is suggested here that some of the sources of probable eighth-century date encapsulate the confrontational nature of conversion, as a process by which landscape might be cleansed of the evils of heathenism, and Christian sanctity ascribed where previously evil had dwelled. Based upon Hall's arguments, there are also several subtle indications of belief and practice that may stem from before the reintroduction of Christianity: the *hægtessan*, martial, and dangerous and supernatural females; the associations of beasts, spirits, and creatures with the burial mound; and the potency of the ancient burial mound for invocations, curses, and charms. The late Anglo-Saxon charter-bounds and later literary sources provide evidence for the settling and embedding of such beliefs and the associated entities within the fabric of the late Anglo-Saxon 'imagined' landscape. These types of creature were frequently associated with ancient monuments, particularly ancient barrows, as well as other types of place that might be considered potential 'interfaces' with other worlds: springs, lakes and pools, caves, fissures, and pits.

Not all ancient remains attracted such associations, however; the place names and boundary marks represent just a small fraction of the total corpus. Many monuments were described in other ways: by hue, by shape and form, by size and location. Ancient monuments are also, on occasion, described in terms of their contemporary or recent function, or recent activity in their environs, such as assembly mounds, or broken and robbed barrows. Unusual ascriptions occur, including the church barrow or hill at Uffington, now in modern Oxfordshire; the fortification of the noble folk at Salisbury, Wiltshire; and the hollow ditch beneath the fort of riches at Stockbridge Down, Hampshire. These naming patterns are a testimony to the importance of local context in the shaping of perceptions of relict features. Old and earthen are also common qualifiers, attesting to local perceptions of the ancient and the past, and if poetic allusion can be taken into account, acknowledgement too of the inhospitable nature of such ancient and long abandoned places. Personal names and animals feature frequently, and the sample here seems to reveal that legendary or mythical figures *might* be found in association with *beorg* more often than *hlāw*, although there are clearly exceptions such as *Thunor's hlāw*, Thunderlow in Essex, *Thunreslau* in Suffolk, and the lost *thunoreshlæw* at Minster-in-Thanet, Kent. Personal names connected with monuments may attest to local legends or memories relating to contemporary land ownership at the time the charter-bounds were set down, or local tales or stories associating characters and events with places. It still remains a possibility that personal names connected with burial mounds might imply knowledge, memory, or mythical belief surrounding the dead incumbent of the barrow. Animals as qualifiers could represent the inhabitation of abandoned places by a range of ordinary creatures, but one also senses here a kind of vernacular Romanticism, with animal inhabitations, and of course descriptions of vegetal coverings, used as common allusions to the empty and discarded nature of the recorded ruins. In summary, late Anglo-Saxon populations recognized ancient features and accepted many as old and ancient places. They bothered to describe and distinguish them and sometimes used them for a variety of purposes. Some monuments acquired additional meaning and potency, leading to their association in popular folklore with supernatural entities. The prose and poetic sources of the era reinforce this, using ancient monuments, especially barrows, as theatrical settings for encounters with the supernatural and demonic.

It seems that, by the late Anglo-Saxon era, perceptions of the ancient in the English landscape had changed. The allusions to pre-Christian sanctuaries or pagan places within *Guthlac A* and *The Wife's Lament,* alongside associations between ancient burial mounds and the supernatural in *Wið Færstice,* and indications of magical rituals involving the power of burial mounds in the *Vita Wilfridi*, may suggest that the changing perceptions captured in the prose, poetry, and place-names represent an increasingly Christianized response to a legacy of memories and perhaps even persistent beliefs and practices centred on the pre-Christian potency of ancient places, especially burial mounds. The issue of ancestors and the power of ancestral places has been explored in previous chapters, and it remains possible that ancient monuments, and barrows in particular, were representative of the ancestral past and the power of the supernatural in pre-Christian cosmologies. The creators of the late Anglo-Saxon prose and poetic sources were Christian and well schooled within Christian literature and lore but were also clearly familiar with vernacular traditions and folk belief too. It is possible, within eighth-century sources such as the Franks Casket, that intentional usage of such motifs was at play. Depicting traditional places of burial and ancestral importance in evil terms may have been a beneficial mode of dissuading communities from traditional burial methods and from the veneration of ancestors and ancestral places. It is also possible that the dangers of angry, neglected pagan ancestors may have also occupied a place in the Anglo-Saxon imagination in the eighth century, enhancing traditions of haunted monuments. There are indications that these kinds of supernatural association developed and embraced all the types of numinous place discussed in Chapter 3. Such associations may have swiftly grown from the conversion process, emerging within the changing consciousness of the populace in Anglo-Saxon England as an indirect result of their acceptance of Christian teachings on death and the afterlife and their rejection of ancestral places and sites of pagan importance. It is possible that this process was also encouraged by the kinds of Christian texts and writings discussed in the opening of this chapter.

Another complication in this changing scene is the archaeological evidence for the use of ancient monuments, again particularly barrows (prehistoric and Anglo-Saxon), as places of late Anglo-Saxon execution and deviant burial. The next chapter will take up this theme and explore the evidence further, but it can be no coincidence that, in the same era such monuments were becoming synonymous with monsters and hellish connotations, they were put to a new purpose as *cwealmstow* or 'killing places' for the execution of felons, the display of their remains, and the interment of their bodies. Such novel practices no doubt helped to transform these locations in local belief and superstition. A complex process of transmission is apparent, with the great legends and tales such as *Beowulf* filtering into common and popular folk myths surrounding features in the landscape; and the leaching of folk perceptions into the high literature of the era, perhaps through the familiarity of the writers, scribes, and translators who put down these tales for posterity.

It is impossible to say with absolute certainty that the kinds of practices evinced within the archaeological record in the pre-Christian era—burial, votive rights, cultic associations, the erection of shrines and posts—prompted the antipathy of the Christian Church, and as a consequence, by Christian teaching, these places were reworked within the popular Anglo-Saxon consciousness. It is certain, however, that some types of place were potent enough to attract the foundation of churches and monasteries, and that some of these places, as discussed in Chapter 4, were marked by barrows and have indications of pre-Christian burial and also suggestions of cultic associations. The appropriation of Roman sites and Roman building fabric were equally popular, if not more so, and it remains a possibility that, just as the Christian Church may have used stories and teachings to disassociate people from the pre-Christian spiritual landscape, so too an emphasis was placed on recycling and restoring Roman places, buildings, and monuments for Christian purposes, thus re-evoking emphasis upon Roman ancestral origins and connections. The confrontational motifs of the eighth century also beg comparison with the evidence for the foundation of early minsters within the shadow of barrows and other ancient monuments. Perhaps these case studies in particular represent the same early Christian battle, with persistence of belief at a local level wedded to potent features within the landscape.

Attempts to absorb and Christianize specific locations and wider landscapes were not ubiquitous. The emergence of new ways of thinking about and responding to the prehistoric and the ancient must have emerged simultaneously, leading to the othering or alienation of some locations at the same time that some were successfully brought into the ambit of Christian practice. It is possible that memory and myth were distinguishing factors within these processes. Monuments raised within living memory, or by oral tradition associated with Anglo-Saxon rites and activities, may have been more reluctantly surrendered by local populations and perhaps more readily absorbed by the Church. Monuments and barrows perceived as truly 'ancient' or even mythical, created in a time before the migration stories and before the recognizable Roman past took shape, may have already held a conspicuous place in the pre-Christian Anglo-Saxon psyche as fearsome and dangerous places, connected with the unknown, the other world, and the supernatural. Such 'local world views' have been suggested by Roymans, who has argued for the natural and antecedent features as shaping forces within the mentalities and world views of late Iron Age and medieval communities (1995; Roymans and Kortland 1999). Such sites may, within a Christianized world, have proved extremely problematic and difficult to assimilate. It is impossible to say with any certainty how such changing perceptions came about, but the strong message of previous chapters is an emphasis on the local values ascribed to ancient features, and the existence of a multiplicity of local world views that both shaped pre-Christian belief and praxis and may have moulded localized receptions of Christianity, creating the development of distinctively local and regional Christian landscapes.

The alienation of ancient monuments within the prose and poetic discourses and Christian narratives also attests to the emergence or even creation of supra-regional frameworks of belief, which embraced local traditional values but sought to establish a broader conformity in terms of Christian ideas. In discussions on pp. 155–9 it was suggested, albeit tentatively, that changing perceptions could be discerned within the Christian sources themselves, with a slow development from discourses that valorized the confrontational notions of conversion to tales that implied a more ready acceptance of a mythical and supernaturally inhabited and charged landscape, reorientated along with its monsters to fit more securely with Christian allegory and biblical motifs. In short, by the late Anglo-Saxon era, barrows and burial mounds and their monstrous inhabitants were still present within an Anglo-Saxon psyche but were no longer dramatically reminiscent of lost pre-Christian ways. Instead they may have represented a testimony to the fate of those who insisted on pursuing heathenry.

In the next chapter evidence for the physical appropriation of such places for the purpose of punishing the 'heathen' is discussed, as well as an apparent elite interest in utilizing the ancient in the landscape for the purpose of framing power and enacting authority. It is possible that the early stages of such processes can be seen here in the changing literary narratives of the eighth to tenth centuries. In the seventh and eighth centuries, elites were increasingly interested in harnessing the ancient to their own specific purposes—from barrows and Roman remains to mythical characters in genealogies. New Christian perceptions of pre-Christian barrows and cemeteries and ancient prehistoric and Roman remains may have opened up the use of such features in the creation of new narratives of authority, whereby elite dynastic claims to larger territorial areas could be signalled and vindicated: the ancient used to situate extensive networks of power. Within this new, forward-looking scene, aspirant elites could root their new power in narratives of conquest, cleansing, and Christian sanctity and yet still use the ancient in the landscape as theatrical settings for the disposal of felons and for the purposes of legitimating royal kingship and authority. For less ambitious families and communities, the pre-Christian and ancient remained potent elements. Their environment may have acquired new resonances and places of sanctity as well as new monumental foci as a consequence of Christianity, but as the Christian charms and remedies suggest, spiritual potency was still multifarious and connected to seasonal patterns of activity and agricultural regimes. The landscape retained residual wells of tradition that the Church was unable entirely to eradicate or to absorb (see Lees and Overing 2006: 15; Wickham-Crowley 2006). Human activity too made certain that some places and practices remained insistent in the Christian landscape for gatherings and exchange or places of ritual and blessing. It is also clear that these populations lived in a landscape that contained places they may have feared and been afraid of. Within vernacular culture, some ancient monuments and other types of place were connected with the monstrous and heathen and considered as haunted and inhabited places where the unsuspecting might well encounter creatures of malevolent intention.

6

Royal and religious theatre

Monuments and power in mid to late Saxon England

> [I]n the seventh week after Easter he [Alfred] rode to Egbert's Stone to
> the east of Selwood, and there came to join him all Somerset and
> Wiltshire and that part of Hampshire that was on this side of the sea—
> and were glad of him. And one day later he went from those camps to
> Island Wood, and one [day] later to Edlington, and there fought
> against the whole raiding-army, and put it to flight . . .
>
> (ASC (E) 878; Swanton 1996: 76)

This account of a major muster in the ninth century describes the location of a
major political event at a well-known landmark. The stone, which may have
survived at Kingston Deverill (Peddie 1999), carried the name of a previous king
of Wessex: a successful ruler renowned for his military victories. There is
perhaps little coincidence in the choice of this landmark for a gathering that
was to lead to a major victory for Alfred and the subjugation of Guthrum, king of
the Danes. This account, which could, of course, draw on the imaginative skills
of the chronicler as much as the real details of the occasion, is one of several that
suggests an emerging interest in late Anglo-Saxon society, in situating major
spectacles and events at settings that had historical and cultural resonance.
Temporary gatherings for the purpose of military muster, battles, political
debate, fairs, and religious festivals are well documented in past and present
societies. In early medieval Europe differing forms of assembly are recorded
from one territory to the next, for example, the Scandinavian *thing*, the *mallus* in
Frisia, and the *Óenach* in Ireland. Ritualized demonstrations of power are now
accepted as an important part in the enactment of medieval royal power (e.g.
Leyser 1994; Barrow 2001; Althoff 2003). The proclamation of law in medieval
society is argued by some, for example, as an oral performance—planned and
executed as a dramatic series of symbolic acts (Goldberg 2006: 212–15). In a
recent compelling account of the public rituals associated with the issue of
diplomas in tenth- and eleventh-century England, Levi Roach has argued the
need for historians to recognize evidence for patterns of 'ritual and symbolic'
communication by kings and elites (Roach 2011: 183, citing Barrow 2001). The

documentary accounts of early medieval political life across Christian Europe provide evidence for systems of regularized meetings within structures and in the open air, formalized processes for feud resolution, evidence of courtly culture, diplomacy and decision-making on the part of kings, aristocrats, and the ecclesiastical establishment (e.g. Cubitt 1995, 2003; Leyser 1994; Geary 1999; Stocking 2000; Althoff 2003). The Anglo-Saxons and their early medieval contemporaries across the Irish and North Seas enjoyed, it seems, a good theatrical spectacle, and emergent powers, both religious and secular, were willing to engage in public theatre, set within visually demonstrative settings, as a means of establishing and consolidating authority.

In previous chapters intimations of these processes have already emerged. The burgeoning elite interest in ancient barrows, other large prominent monuments and monument complexes in the seventh century, and their use for situating particularly prestigious burials, major battles, and meetings or assemblies, is explored in Chapter 3. Arguments were presented for the pre-Christian importance of such features as physical and symbolic markers in the formation and signalling of local identity, and for their potency within the spiritual pre-Christian canvas. The apparent adoption or absorption of some of these monuments by the early Christian foundations has also been suggested to relate to their local importance (as much symbolic as spiritual), leading to the selective reworking of particular places, monuments, and in some instances whole landscapes by the early Church. In the previous chapter, however, the potential pre-Christian potency of ancient monuments, most particularly barrows, was emphasized, but arguments were presented as well for the existence of changing perceptions during the conversion. Such features were relocated in the Anglo-Saxon mind to a more liminal place, associated with supernatural creatures and the evils of the heathen past.

The archaeological record for mid to late Anglo-Saxon England offers extraordinary corroboration for these post-conversion attitudes. Ancient features continued in use as places for burial, but for the execution and disposal of felons rather than for community cemeteries or individual elite graves. These *cwealmstow* or 'killing-places' emerged sporadically in the late seventh and eighth centuries, just as attitudes to ancient places were changing and as Christian belief and thinking were taking root within Anglo-Saxon society. By the eighth and ninth centuries in the south and south-east of England, places of execution at older monuments and cemeteries were established more widely as part of emerging displays of supra-regional authority. By the tenth and eleventh centuries, they formed an integral part of an Anglo-Saxon landscape that had been manipulated and shaped to create an architecture of power by successive kings and dynasties. These palimpsests, redolent with memory and legend, now lent themselves to the staging of political and ritual theatre designed to unite old divisions and establish the supremacy of individual rulers and families.

This chapter concludes the arguments presented here by examining the role of ancient monuments and places in the establishment of new systems of authority and power in middle to late Anglo-Saxon England. The use of ancient monuments, especially barrows, for political and judicial events is established, and the rationale explored. This chapter also questions whether distinctly 'elite', large-scale ritual and resonant 'landscapes' were forged in England over time, and whether these served the theatricalities of how and when late Anglo-Saxon rulers were revealed to their subjects by means of itineraries, councils and assemblies, and religious festivals. It is suggested here that this conscious manipulation of the landscape and prehistoric, Roman, and pre-Christian 'antiquity' was not merely a means of establishing authority over extensive kingdoms. It also served to create a grammar of power, symbolic of legitimate and ancient authority, shared and understood by pagan and Christian rulers across north-west Europe in the latter part of the first millennium.

Places of execution in late Anglo-Saxon England

From the conversion to the eleventh century, the time when the legends, stories, and myths discussed in Chapter 5 were being committed to writing, some ancient monuments were being selected for use in the staging of major councils and coronations. Other surviving prehistoric features were providing arenas for the killing, display, and burial of those who contravened elite and royal rule. The emergence of separate places for the execution and burial of felons occurred sporadically during the seventh and eighth centuries, but by the late Anglo-Saxon era they formed components in a regularized system of punishment within the kingdoms of the south and south-east of England. The archaeology of this judicial system, in particular the emergence of late Anglo-Saxon execution sites, has been extensively explored by Andrew Reynolds (2009a). Even at the earliest examples of execution sites, created when such practices lacked the systematic organization apparent in later centuries, prehistoric monuments were a preferred feature for this activity. Hill forts, linear ditches, barrows, and even Stonehenge were utilized as locations for judicial killing, alongside rivers, crossroads, and major territorial boundaries.

The discovery and dating of a decapitate buried close to a low mound situated by the circle of monoliths at Stonehenge on Salisbury Plain, has been considered by several authors in the context of the royal palace at Amesbury (see Semple 2009) (see also Colour Plate 5). Amesbury hundred is argued as an archaic royal unit or small territory with a royal palace and place of council and assembly at its heart (Brookes in press). Stonehenge lies on the boundary of this hundred and seems to have been used as a formal place of execution in the eighth century (Pitts et al. 2002; Hamilton et al. 2007). Bran Ditch in Cambridgeshire appears to be another early example. The post-Roman linear earthwork lying on a valley floor, and later marking the division of Thriplow and Armingford Hundred, was used for the disposal of a large number of individuals, many showing signs of decapitation (Lethbridge and Palmer 1929). Walkington Wold, in North Yorkshire, is a rare northern example with an early date of inception (see Figure 6.1). Two large prehistoric barrows, one used as a temple or religious site in the Roman era as indicated by the numerous scatter of Roman coins across the mounds were used as an execution place and cemetery, with strong indications that killing was largely by decap-itation (Bartlett and Mackey 1973; Buckberry and Hadley 2007). Activity began in the seventh century at Walkington and continued into the eleventh, offering evidence for a sporadically used, but enduring location for killing—a pattern that can be found at many other later sites.

These types of early execution sites held commanding views over territory, Roman routes, and river communications. On occasion they marked crossroads between land and river routes (Reynolds 2008). A close relationship with old Roman centres is also possible, and an emerging connection as well to royal Anglo-Saxon centres (for example, Sutton Hoo and Rendlesham, Suffolk) (Reynolds 2008). These early places of judicial authority and power were also perhaps intentionally being set at the limits of major developing political entities; indeed their creation may well be symptomatic of the territorial expan-sion in this era by major kings who brought authority and control to areas well beyond their royal heartlands and kingdoms (Reynolds 2008: 47). This posited royal 'authorship' is significant in any argument for the reworking of the pre-Christian landscape and its antecedent features within a new rhetoric of royal power. These sites have unique attributes too that may point to the influence of regionally distinctive traditions or perceptions involving ancient sites. The prehistoric barrow at Walkington Wold was an important Roman ritual focus (Bartlett and Mackey 1973); at Sutton Hoo the execution site was situated at a pre-Christian royal dynastic cemetery (Carver 2005). Staines and Cambridge exploit positions on major Roman thoroughfares (see Reynolds 2008: 27, 31) and may relate to newly formed, eighth-century Mercian *burhs* and fortified power centres (Stuart Brookes: pers. comm.; see Jones 2010: 43, for Staines; Haslam 1987 for Cambridge). Each site is connected with some element of the prehistoric, Roman, or pre-Christian past. The use of ancient features was not yet uniformly explicit in the design of these places, but it can be argued that legitimacy and authority were being uniquely forged at each place by means of the careful selection of the situation, locale, *and* the ancient monument.

Planned landscapes of justice and punishment

A more regularized system emerged during the eighth to tenth centuries. These sites became commonplace in the south and east of England, situated with explicit reference to the hundredal geography (Reynolds 2009a: 152–3, 233). It is during this secondary phase that earlier monuments and earthworks became integral to the architecture of these sites. Of 27 known execution sites, 13 are associated with mounds or barrows of varied date, 8 with linear earthworks, and 3 with hill forts (see Tables 6.1–6.3). Only three do not refer to any old or contemporary land mark.

Mounds and barrows (see Figure 6.1). These were frequently chosen for execution (see also Table 6.1). Only four can be identified with certainty as prehistoric features. Large and prominent barrows were preferred, and all were situated on administrative divisions close to major thoroughfares and routes. All four prehistoric tumuli were components in larger barrow groupings— something that must have enhanced their visual status in the landscape.

Four execution sites were situated in relation to Anglo-Saxon barrows and early Anglo-Saxon funerary activity. At Ashtead (Surrey) no mound or upstanding physical feature can be identified, but the execution site was located at an early Anglo-Saxon cemetery (Hayman 1991–2). Such places may have been brought into use owing to their 'heathen' associations and perceived role as pre-Christian burial grounds. Though mounds were important, prehistoric barrows were not singled out for this purpose. Several of the barrows used for execution and the burial of felons are not dated. These are suggested as purpose-built monuments created by the late Anglo-Saxons as necessary embellishment for late execution sites (Reynolds 2009a: 143–4). At all sites, with the exception of Stockbridge Down, however, the grave-cuts for deviant burials truncate and therefore presumably post-date the mound construction. At South Acre burials cut the upper fills of the ring-ditch (Whymer 1996, 88; Reynolds 2009a: 125–6). At Burpham the burials are described as secondary features cut into a long mound with indications that some were laid head to foot, perhaps orientated along the ditches of a long mound (Lovett 1893–6; Collyer 1895–6). The only exception is Stockbridge Down, where the undated and non-sepulchral mound is particularly small at around 5 to 6 metres in diameter and lacks a ring-ditch (Hill 1937: pl. 3; Reynolds 2009a: 120–2). None of the execution burials at Stockbridge is focused upon, or orientated around, or cuts, the mound. The burials cluster instead around the pairing of postholes—postulated as the setting for a gallows (Reynolds 2009a: 122).

Ditches. Ditches and dykes—old and new—were used by early medieval societies to mark agricultural, defensive, and political boundaries. Not all the linear earthworks chosen as places for execution therefore were prehistoric or Roman; some may have been near contemporary constructions. The use of Wandsdyke, now thought to be eighth century, for a tenth-century gallows is one such example (Reynolds and Langlands 2006; Reynolds 2009a: 279, no. 100). Bokerley Dyke, Wallingford, Bran Ditch, and Malling Hill, however, all represent large and prominent linear earthworks that were old by the time the execution sites were established (see Table 6.2).

The primary significance of these features may have been their role as physical and visual divisions. They offered an ideologically suitable place for

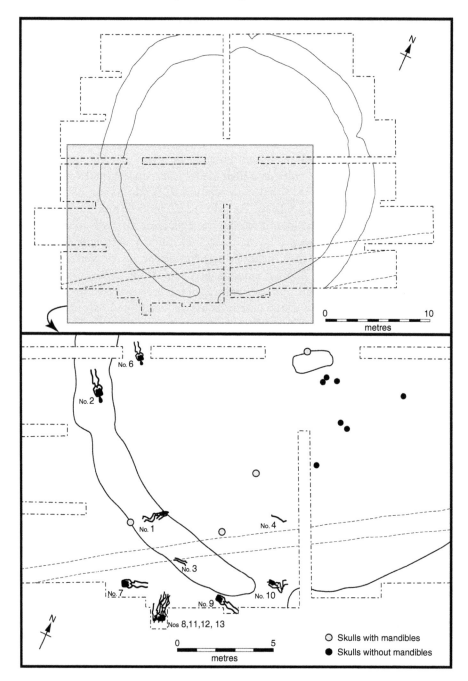

Fig. 6.1 The seventh-century execution site at Walkington Wold, Yorkshire. After Buckberry and Hadley 2007: fig. 2. Reproduced by permission of Dawn Hadley.

Table 6.1 Mounds, barrows, and execution cemeteries

Site	County	Monument*	Date of burials	Reference
Dunstable	BDF	BA round barrow/round barrow cemetery	Undated, broadly C8th–C11th	Dunning and Wheeler 1931; Dingwall and Young 1933
Galley Hill	BDF	BA barrow/robbed central grave/two additional BA barrows and two later mounds	Undated, broadly C8th–C11th	Dyer 1974
Wor Barrow	DOR	Neolithic long barrow/two round barrows now lost and boundary ditch	Undated, broadly C8th–C11th	Pitt Rivers 1898: 58–79
Stockbridge Down	HMP	Purpose-built mound	C10th–C11th	Hill 1937
South Acre	NFK	Undated, large ploughed-out barrow and ring-ditch	Single dated C9th burial but broadly C8th–C11th	Whymer 1996
Crosshill	NTT	Undated barrow 50 m from Fosse Way/post-Roman, with signs of robbing	Undated	Kinsley 1993
Sutton Hoo	SFK	Pre-Christian Anglo-Saxon barrow cemetery	Radiocarbon dates suggest C8th–C12th	Carver 1998, 2005
Gally Hills	SUR	Anglo-Saxon round barrow with C7th interment	Undated but post-C7th	Barfoot and Price-Williams 1976
Guildown	SUR	C6th Anglo-Saxon cemetery, perhaps with barrows	C10th and later	Lowther 1931
Burpham	SSX	Undated long mound	Undated, broadly C8th–C11th	Lovett 1893–6; Collyer 1895–6
Old Sarum	WLT	Undated barrow	Undated, broadly C8th–C11th	Blackmore 1984
Roche Court Down	WLT	Linear earthwork and barrow-like knoll	Undated, broadly C8th–C11th	Stone 1932
Walkington Wold	YOE	Pair of BA round barrows	C7th–C11th	Bartlett and Mackey 1972; Buckberry and Hadley 2007

* BA = Bronze Age.

Table 6.2 Linear ditches, earthworks, and execution cemeteries

Site	County	Monument	Date of burials	Reference
Bran Ditch	CAM	Post-Roman linear earthwork	C7th–11th	Fox and Palmer 1926; Lethbridge and Palmer 1929; Palmer et al. 1931
Chesterton Lane	CAM	Earlier linear feature/Roman town limits	C8th–10th	Mortimer and Regan 2001; Cessford et al. 2007
Old Dairy Cottage	HMP	Roman and Iron Age ditches and gullies/Roman road side/ boundary some 2 km from the centre of Winchester	C8th–11th	Nenk et al. 1995: 199, no. 142
Staines	MDX	Sited along Roman road/ Roman period boundary ditches/river crossing	C8th–12th	Hayman and Reynolds 2005
Wallingford	OXF	Grim's Ditch, Iron Age linear earthwork	Undated	Hinchcliffe 1975
Malling Hill	SSX	Pre-existing substantial lynchet	C10th–12th	Reynolds 2009a: 144–5
Bokerley Dyke	WLT	Long linear earthwork pre-Roman	C8th–11th	Pitt Rivers 1892
Roche Court Down	WLT	Linear earthwork and barrow-like knoll/feature	Undated/ broadly C8th–11th	Stone 1932

execution, representing the archetypal *liminal* place, a physical no-man's-land on the boundary of administrative districts. The liminality of such features may have been reinforced in the Anglo-Saxon imagination by their association in popular folklore with supernatural entities and pre-Christian deities—indeed at least one of the sites is associated with a monument named Grim's Ditch (see pp. 173–6; see also Hinchcliffe 1975). Though liminal within the mental maps of local inhabitants, the selection of such spots as locations for late Anglo-Saxon execution may also provide evidence that execution places could be situated to reinforce the symbolic value of old divisions within a new geography. They were positioned frequently at crossing points and gaps along the earthworks, visible from nearby routes. Movement can be identified as a driving factor in the manipulation and reworking of the landscape to suit the theatricalities of royal power. Royal itineraries, for example, record the seasonal movements of kings from place to place in late Anglo-Saxon England (see Hill 1981: 82–4; see also discussion on pp. 213–16). Such journeys must have been undertaken using major land routes and thoroughfares that passed by places of execution and displays of executed victims, visually reinforcing the consignment of these unfortunates to limbo and damnation.

Table 6.3 Hill forts and execution cemeteries

Site	County	Monument	Date of burials	Reference
Castle Hill	BRK	Foot of the rampart/ Iron Age hill fort	Undated/broadly C8th– C11th	Chambers 1986
Wandlebury	CAM	Iron Age hill fort/ south of outer rampart and internal	Undated/documented as site of two major assemblies in the C10th–C11th	Taylor and Denton 1977
Meon Hill	HMP	Iron Age enclosed settlement	Late Anglo-Saxon	Liddle 1933

Hill forts. Only a small number of execution sites are located at old forts. All three examples, however, occupy prominent and interesting locations within the late Anglo-Saxon royal and administrative geography in the south and east of England (see Table 6.3).

Wandlebury hill fort was, in the tenth to twelfth centuries, a location of decision-making in relation to the legal jurisdiction of lands in 'nine hundreds' (Hart 1966: nos 54 and 73), and is twice recorded as a meeting site for the late Anglo-Saxon *witan* (see Figure 6.2). The hill fort sits adjacent to the meeting point of three hundred units: Flendish, Chilford, and Thriplow. Flendish, which takes its name from Fleam Ditch or Dyke, the 'ditch of the fugitives', is named from the broken stretch of linear earthwork some 4 kilometres north-east of Wandlebury. The hundred meeting place of Flendish is Mutlow or the 'moot barrow'. This Bronze Age barrow lies at a break in the dyke and was used as a 'temple' or ritual focus in the Roman era. This meeting mound in fact may have served all three neighbouring hundreds of Flendish, Radfield, and Staine, and may thus lie at the heart of a larger and earlier territorial grouping (Brookes forthcoming).

This complex 'layering' of old features, later administrative units, and late places of royal assembly and hundred meeting sites offers evidence for the choice of large and distinctive monuments as places of major royal assembly, despite the close proximity of suitable local hundredal meeting sites. Just as Athelstan chose the palace at Grateley and its hill fort as a location for a specific royal event (see p. 211), Wandlebury hill fort too seems to have lent itself on occasion to the enactment of royal power at the highest of levels. The presence of execution burials at this meeting place is unusual (Reynolds 1999; Pantos 2002: 90–4), but may reflect a supra-local purpose and a royal audience. Wandlebury, as a place of decision-making for the people of four or more hundreds, may have served meetings that sometimes involved decision-making and judgement by the highest officials and even the king; execution may therefore have taken place as part of this royal theatre (Pantos 2002: 93).

Stockbridge Down lies very close to Woolbury hill fort, a monument that marks the meeting of three parish boundaries. The site was active in the early to mid-eleventh century and perhaps before (Dolley 1957; Blackburn and Pagan 1986: no. 251). It is one of the few sites that does not correspond to a hundred

Fig. 6.2 Wandlebury hill fort, Cambridgeshire. © Cambridge University.

boundary, but instead references the boundary of a royal estate (Reynolds 2009a, 155). Meon Hill, listed here as an execution site associated directly with a late prehistoric enclosed settlement (Liddle 1933), lies on the same estate boundary. Both are located within the northern part of the hundred of Somborne. The execution site at Meon Hill seems to have been active in the same time frame as Stockbridge Down (Liddle 1933; Reynolds 2009a: 116). The large royal estate is listed at Domesday. It comprised several manors, including the royal manor belonging to Edward the Confessor, which held jurisdiction over the two hundreds. One cannot escape the unusual nature of two active execution sites on the bounds of a large late Saxon royal estate, both of which have a rather theatrical setting and relationship with ancient hill forts. Perhaps these execution sites were particularly devoted to displays of power and authority by the late Anglo-Saxon royal house. They were certainly both situated in places with high visibility over the immediate thoroughfare: a major Roman road linking London to Old Sarum and Exeter.

Castle Hill in Berkshire immediately overlooks a bend and bridging point on the Thames at Dorchester-on-Thames and thus the original Domesday boundary separating the counties of Berkshire and Oxfordshire (see Figure 6.3). Dorchester-on-Thames, already mentioned in relation to the early Wessex heartland,

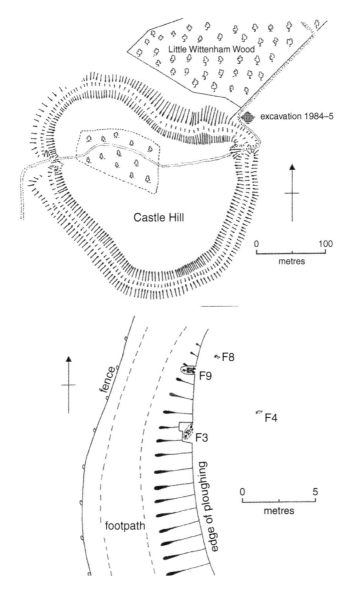

Fig. 6.3 Castle Hill, Berkshire, showing the location of the excavations (above) and the area excavated (below). Redrawn from Reynolds 2009: fig. 15. Reproduced by permission of Andrew Reynolds.

was a Roman town, a place of importance in Anglo-Saxon times, attested by cemetery evidence in its hinterlands (Atkinson et al. 1951: 5–18; see also Meaney 1964: 208). The place was granted to Birinus in the early seventh century as an episcopal see (*HE* III, 7). The execution burials were recovered at the foot of the rampart on the side of the hill fort. A surviving charter of *c*.862 includes the bounds of an estate at Wittenham (BCS 565), and these are suggested to cut between the two peaks of the Sinodun Hills some 400 metres south-east of Castle Hill. The bounds for Brightwell and Sotwell from 945 and Brightwell again in 947 (see S517 and S523; Gelling 1976: 761–3) also run close to the monument, and both record 'heathen burials' (see Reynolds 2009a: appendix 4, nos 44 and 45). The site thus lies on a later county division, the edge of several ninth- and tenth-century estates, and the meeting point of the hundredal divisions of Blewbury, Stottisford, and Sutton. By the nature of its place on county and hundred boundaries, Castle Hill immediately presents itself as an execution site that may have been operating well above hundredal level.

These sites may all have been used as places of royal assembly and council. The reuse of these late prehistoric monuments as locales for execution may therefore represent a greater role as places suitable for the settlement of disputes and feuds, within the presence of royal authorities. It is possible that certain hill forts retained a supra-regional value as symbolic markers of early territories or territorial identity, resulting in their adoption and use in late Anglo-Saxon England for a variety of purposes but especially activities relating to royal presence and status (such as royal assembly, execution, monastic activity). This is rather speculative, but further micro-level mapping may reveal similar patterns of places of supra-regional theatre consciously interleaved with the late Anglo-Saxon hundredal geography. What can be asserted with more confidence is that the reuse of hill forts seems to have had little to do with a perception of heathen origin for these monuments. These seem more indicative of a royal interest in creating theatrical settings for justice that reinforced a sense of supra-local power and authority. It is interesting to note, however, that even though locations may have served as arenas for the display of royal power; the disposal of the dead still took place within the ramparts and ditches of each hill fort, reinforcing the liminality and exile of the executed victims.

Power and alienation: the ideology of execution sites

The evidence for an increasingly formalized use of old monuments as places of execution and as burial sites for executed felons chimes with the literary and documentary evidence discussed in Chapter 5. These suggested a reworking of the meaning or place of the barrow in the Anglo-Saxon psyche after the conversion to Christianity. The association of ancient monuments with the heathen past, and with monstrous and mythical creatures, had developed by the late Anglo-Saxon era into a full-blown association between burial mound and hellish torment and damnation. The use of barrows and other features for the persecution of those who contravened royal and Christian law can only have served to reinforce these ideas in the late Anglo-Saxon popular imagination. Indeed, at the turn of the millennium, an artist illustrating a copy of a great ninth-century Carolingian manuscript on loan to Winchester chose to create a series of illustrations that drew upon his personal knowledge and contemporary experience of this late landscape of justice and power. The innovative illustrations of Artist F contained in London, British Library MS Harley 603, are unusual and inventive, containing references to royal, political, and monastic life (Temple 1976: 81–3, no. 64; Duffey 1977; Semple 2003b). A particularly Anglo-Saxon vision of hell and damnation is outlined in the drawings of Artist F. This comprised a living-dead existence, trapped within the earth, often within a hollow beneath a hill or mound, tormented by demons. The images of suffering contain one or two figures whose punishment is depicted in explicit detail (see Colour Plates 6 and 7). The portrayal of single figures or small groups in torment provides a highly personalized form of torment, something ostensibly much closer and of much greater impact to a reader or viewer of the manuscript than the massive, indistinguishable hordes of the damned found in the compositions of the Utrecht exemplar. The hell pits were set within a landscape full of vents and smoking fissures, depicting multiple access points to the underworld: a topographical rendition that also conveyed a sense that hell was much closer to the Anglo-Saxon than he might suspect. This idea is rather similar to the tales and motifs discussed in Chapter 5 that portrayed sinners being gobbled down and swallowed into the earth for challenging the words of saints or saintly monastic founders (see pp. 153–5). The landscape within which Artist F set his tormented souls, and the punishments inflicted on them, closely reflect contemporary Anglo-Saxon judicial practice. By depicting hell as holes, pits, or clefts beneath mounds, F seems to have been developing the motifs found in the Utrecht Psalter representing hell and hell's mouth, and creating illustrations that conveyed the contemporary practice of interring criminals, suicides, unbaptized, and other sinners in old and heathen barrows. The bodies of sinners at the mouth of hell or in torment within hell are rendered as mutilated amputees, decapitated and naked, abandoned corpses, with their severed heads lying close-by (e.g. fo. 72r and fo. 67r). In fo. 67r (Colour Plate), the relationship to judicial practices is most vivid. The composition depicts a mound or hill motif without a rocky fissure or opening and four decapitated bodies, two prostrate, one bent forwards and one bent backwards. The heads are bleeding and separate from the bodies. The illustration follows the words of Psalm 129: 4–5: 'The Lord who is just will cut the necks of sinners: let them be confounded and turned back that hate Sion.'

Late Anglo-Saxon conceptions of the afterlife of the sinner have been shown to focus on awareness of death, burial, and bodily corruption (Thompson 2003: 234–8; 2004). There are very clear parameters for what might be considered a *good* death and a *bad* death; indeed there was no moment of death: the process was perceived as a long transition from the deathbed to the afterlife. A good death might be characterized as quick and quiet, whereas a bad death could be portrayed as a continued existence in the grave, aware of the bodily corruption, and suffering harrowing mental torment and horror at the confinement within the grave (Thompson 2002: 234–8; 2004). A final illustration worth consideration can be found in London, British Library MS Cotton Tiberius B.V, in a section known as 'Marvels of the East' (see Temple 1976: 104–5, no. 87). This full-page composition, fo. 87v see Colour Plate 8, is a powerful image with no direct Continental parallel, and it contains many of the motifs employed by Artist F in Harley 603. The picture shows Mambres and Jannes, the magicians of the Pharaoh, who confront Moses (Ex. 7: 11–8: 19). They are not named in the Old Testament but are identified in 2 Timothy 3:8 (Biggs and Hall 1996: 69). Biggs and Hall have argued that the tradition of Mambres and Jannes may have had some currency in late Anglo-Saxon ecclesiastical circles and the excerpt could have been composed in England. The text describes the raising of Jannes from hell by his brother Mambres by means of necromancy. Hell is described as living among the dead, confined to the narrow space of the grave (Biggs and Hall 1996: 71, n. 5; after Förster 1902). There are congruencies here with the vision of hell portrayed in the illustrations by Artist F in the Harley Psalter and the Anglo-Saxon perceptions of hellish torment found in late Anglo-Saxon literature and explored in Chapter 5. In the accompanying illustration (fo. 87v) Colour Plate 8, a large mound or hill with an internal opening or chamber represents hell. Inside are serpents and the bodies of the damned, and emerging is Jannes, resplendently monstrous, green, and hairy. In 'Marvels of the East', by contrast to the illustrations in the Harley Psalter, there is no reference to late Anglo-Saxon judicial processes, but the portrayal of a monster inhabiting an underground chamber or cavern, perhaps in a barrow, is strongly reminiscent of the contemporaneous Anglo-Saxon popular beliefs regarding landscape discussed in Chapter 5.

The Christian writings of the eighth century may have initiated the metamorphosis of the heathen dead in their earthen barrows into the monsters, elves, dragons, and ghosts of the late prose and literary sources, but these illustrations imply that changing perceptions were likely reinforced by the physical appropriation of these monuments as locations of execution for criminals. It was difficult to distinguish in the texts discussed in Chapter 5 whether the writers were referring to prehistoric or Anglo-Saxon burial mounds. The archaeological evidence discussed here helps solve this perplexing issue. By the late Anglo-Saxon period at least, the prehistoric and Anglo-Saxon barrows used as deviant burial grounds and killing places were not being distinguished as products of different eras; they were viewed as common symbols of a pre-Christian *heathen* past. Just as the late Anglo-Saxon writers imagined such landscape features to be haunted by ghosts and demons, the physical appropriation of these monuments and old cemeteries as locations of execution and deviant burial attests to their role as suitably evil and desolate places, synonymous with past heathenism and pagan potency, where sinners could be condemned to eternal torment. Whether hill forts and linear earthworks were placed within the same category in popular superstition is more difficult to answer. They could certainly be associated with supernatural and pagan entities, but liminality may have led to the choice of linear entrenchments, and execution at hill forts could reflect the use of such places for royal assembly.

Palaces, monuments, and assembly

The seventh and eighth centuries are acknowledged as a time during which the elite of Anglo-Saxon society, like their north European contemporaries, began to experiment with material ways of establishing power, lineage, and authority. As outlined in earlier chapters, there is good emerging evidence for the role played by prehistoric monuments and pre-Christian Anglo-Saxon cemeteries and burials in the definition of small localities and power structures in the fifth to seventh centuries (see Chapter 3). Prehistoric monuments and monument complexes were used not only for burial but sometimes as locations for settlement as well (pp. 94–5). These relationships can be traced in early Anglo-Saxon England, but by the seventh and eighth centuries sites such as Yeavering point to the development of the structured use of monuments and space in the creation of elite sites of power and authority.

By this era more formalized settlement sites can be recognized, which operated at an elite and supra-local level (Hamerow 2002: 96–9; see pp. 97, 101, 104, 108, 120–1). The arrangement of buildings on these sites was more organized, with planned layouts, sharing strong similarities (Hamerow 2002: 97–8; 2004; Reynolds 2003; Hamerow 2011b: 128–95). A changing style of hall also suggests an increased investment in elaborate, large buildings, and the introduction of restricted and bounded areas with fenced enclosures that, although not confined to these sites, served to demarcate and shape space perhaps even regulating access and movement (Hamerow 2002: 96–9; Walker 2010). This increasing emphasis on the design of the larger buildings and in the layout of these sites implies that more formalized hierarchies were emerging (Reynolds 2003; Hamerow 2011a; 2011b; Ulmschneider 2011). Several of these 'palace' sites lie in proximity to ancient monuments (see Crewe 2012: 207–9). At Hatton Rock, the arrangement of large halls dating to the sixth and seventh centuries seems to acknowledge the presence of a large ring-ditch (Rahtz 1970). At Yeavering, already explored in Chapter 3, the settlement took advantage of an impressive backdrop of ancient monuments (see Hope-Taylor 1977; Bradley 1987a; Frodsham and O'Brien 2005). The hill fort, barrow, and stone circle were important in the initial layout of the sixth-century settlement, and they remained important in the planning and creation of the grand seventh-century layout. In these phases, some structures such as Structure E were retained and large aligned elaborate halls were added, a fenced open area created, and new foci for burials developed. Whether built initially for preaching, conversion or secular debate, E was certainly designed to house an audience (see Hope-Taylor 1977; Barnwell 2005). The older monuments on the complex continued to structure the development of new phases of building and presumably activities at the site. Sutton Courtney provides a useful example for more detailed exploration. It is the place of a royal palace in the ninth century and of a royal council in the eleventh (*c.*1042). Early Anglo-Saxon settlement activity was recognized here by Leeds (1923, 1927, 1947). The site has seen considerable investigation since revealing an extensive complex with areas of settlement activity (Hamerow et al. 2007). A scatter of structures of Anglo-Saxon date stretches some 750 metres from north to south. The survey and excavations undertaken most recently suggest the clustering of buildings to the north, recognized and excavated by E. T. Leeds, indicating activity during the fifth to seventh centuries (Hamerow et al. 2007: 115; Leeds 1923, 1927, 1947). To the south, an L-shaped complex of halls, exceptionally large and prestigious, fits the definition of palace or high-status settlement on the basis of its size and layout (see Figure 6.4). Finds suggest this hall-complex was active in the sixth and seventh centuries, and the size of the halls supports a seventh-century phase of development (Hamerow et al. 2007: 168–9). The complex seems to have been established in an intentional,

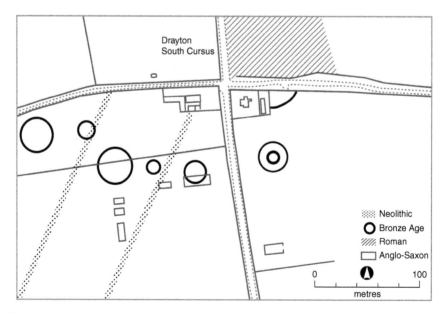

Fig. 6.4 Anglo-Saxon settlement at Sutton Courtney, Berkshire. Redrawn from Crewe 2010: fig. 6.11. Reproduced by permission of Vicky Crewe.

structured relationship with a large prehistoric barrow and its smaller companions (see discussion by Crewe 2012: 145–51). It also overlay several earlier sunken-featured buildings, suggesting the early settlement too may have developed in relation to an underlying palimpsest. At Sutton Courtney, as at Yeavering, the subtle relationship between the early settlement and the older barrows in the vicinity was, however, superseded by a complex with a more overt relationship to older monuments. The activity at Sutton Courtney does not end in the seventh century, although there are suggestions that the hall-complex did not last much beyond this. Finds from the field containing the hall furthest to the south-east include brooches, mounts, and buckles of sixth- and seventh-century date and fourteen sceattas *c.* AD 700–30. The coins imply eighth-century activity in this area, perhaps related to assembly or marketing activities (Hamerow et al. 2007: 183–5). Over a century later, by AD 868 Sutton Courtney is attested as a royal centre, joining a number of other West Saxon royal places of continuing long-term importance (S338a (= S539); Blair 2005, 325).

John Blair has distinguished between major, stable centres such as Canterbury, London, Tamworth, and the more common *villa regia* of the seventh to ninth centuries that he considers to be less permanent places, unstable and short-lived, facilitating the enactment of power but not representing fixed and permanent places of centralized authority (Blair 2005: 279). The relatively short lifespan of such complexes, like Sutton Courtney and Yeavering, may reflect the instability of the age and the impermanence, signalled even in the language used to describe the sites of royal assembly and the vills used for such events (Blair 2005; see also Ulmschneider 2011: 161–2). It is striking, however, that at these and other sites the landscape setting and the investment in elaborate and formal architecture seem geared to conveying a sense of 'ancestry' and heritage and thus perhaps permanence, implying that elite families were aspiring to permanent power, even if it would be some time before this was fully realized.

The increasing investment in organized arrangements, including the provision of large halls, is also likely to relate to a need for spaces in which gatherings and ceremonial activities could take place (see Walker 2010). The emergence of a greater formality in the setting and layout of these types of elite settlement may thus equate not just to the development of social hierarchies, but also to a need for spaces in which power could be enacted and communicated. The seventh and eighth centuries witnessed a period of extensive territorial expansion by a small group of kings and their families (Arnold 1988; Bassett 1989). Acquiring and managing greater territories had a profound effect on kingship. No longer responsible for a war band, followers, and kin, kings were now responsible for the subjects dwelling in increasingly large territories (Yorke 1990: 16–24). The maintenance of large tracts of landscape involved several innovations. Laws governing all people were drawn up with an emphasis on controlling the movement of people and goods, and of dealing with those under royal protection such as travellers, merchants, and missionaries (Yorke 1990; see also laws listed in Attenborough 1922). Kings both campaigned to acquire territory and travelled to maintain control of conquered lands. Power was therefore peripatetic, enacted periodically at designated sites like Yeavering and Sutton Courtney. The royal itineraries of the earliest documented kings list their seasonal sojourns around their territories, staying at royal centres or vills, wīcs, and monasteries, and occasionally at places that seem, at least to our modern eyes, rather un-diagnostic, places apparently without a known settlement of secular or religious import (Sawyer 1978; Hill 1981: 82–4). A *villa regia*—royal vill, estate centre, or palace—was thus not merely a temporary residence in middle Anglo-Saxon England but a place that, when it housed a king and his entourage, became a nodal point for a large surrounding territory (see discussion in Yorke 1990: 16–17). Not only did this territory and its inhabitants provide food and rents to the visiting royal entourage; they might also experience the authority and justice of the king too. These temporary royal residences were used for assemblies and councils, events where a king might proclaim their authority, sign documents, make law, and enact justice (Yorke 1990: 157–77; Blair 2005; Lavelle 2005). One suspects that the emergence of this kind of formalized royal theatre may inevitably have led to the development of more formal settings for royal ritual.

Ancient monuments and palimpsests on occasion structured funerary activity over relatively large areas (see Chapters 2 and 3). Although far more work is required to elucidate similar large-scale patterns within the settlement record, it is worth noting that the setting of the seventh-century complex at Sutton Courtney is not an isolated incidence within the immediate locality. It lies comparatively close to the earlier settlement complex set amid a prehistoric palimpsest at Barrow Hills, Radley (see Chapter 3). It also lies close to Dorchester-on-Thames, a Roman town that emerged as a focus of Anglo-Saxon activity in the fifth to seventh centuries (Cook and Rowley 1985) and in the seventh century was granted to Birinus, the Roman bishop sent to convert the West Saxons (*HE* III, 7). These sites, with their remarkable and complex relationships with prehistoric and Roman palimpsests, ruins, and burials, may represent the forging of a heartland of power, the rich prehistoric, Roman, and even early Anglo-Saxon activity serving to shape the strategies and 'material narratives' of elite power in the seventh century. Just as Vicky Crewe has argued in relation to the archaeological evidence of the east Midlands, here too perhaps the early Anglo-Saxon past and its traditions were being drawn upon alongside the 'heritage' of surviving ancient prehistoric and Roman monuments, to situate and signal new and ambitious royal power (Crewe 2010; 2012).

Although these seventh- and eighth-century 'palace' complexes did not often survive, there are indications that the harnessing of ancient monuments to new elite strategies saw a continuum of growth. Despite the changing geographies of power and the changes and innovations in settlement type and pattern in the eighth and ninth centuries (Ulmschneider 2011: 161–2), visually 'situating' power seems to have remained a concern. It is difficult to identify the 'apex' of the settlement hierarchy in the middle Anglo-Saxon era: planning was more commonplace, hall structures were not radically changed or embellished in any additional grandiose ways, enclosure and planning were increasingly common to differing types of settlement: secular elite residences, monastic sites, and sites of 'urban' appearance (Ulmschneider 2011: 160–5). One has only to consider the large number of early church and monastic sites situated with reference to Roman buildings or built from the remains of Roman structures, or indeed placed with reference to late prehistoric enclosures (see Chapter 4), to realize that ancient places and features retained a hold over elite practices. Royal palaces continued to be situated, or survived at important seminal locations. One such place is Grateley in Hampshire. Ryan Lavelle has made a strong argument for the intentional setting of a major *witangemot* or royal council at this presumed royal palace as a result of its prominent setting and visual aesthetics (2005). Lavelle's argument centres on context of the promulgation of Athelstan's 'first "national" law code' in *c.*AD 925x930. This was a momentous event with a fitting location. The royal palace was situated in the shadow of the large hill fort of Quarley Hill. The approach road was a Roman street—the Portway—the original paving of which still survived in the seventeenth century (Lavelle 2005: 161). The hill fort, which provides an uninterrupted and clear view of the landscape, dominated the view from the road and may also have been marked with the ruinous remains of a large Roman villa. The convenient location of Grately, matched with the ability of the estate to support a visit by a large entourage, and the likely attraction of immediate hunting grounds, were all likely factors in its use for a royal meeting. The visual dominance of the ancient hill fort and symbolism of the Roman road facilitating access to the council may, however, also have influenced the choice of this location for a council that witnessed the first royal, 'national' code of law (Lavelle 2005: 161–3).

By the late Anglo-Saxon period, investment in new forms of monumentality related to the structure and layout of elite settlements is in evidence. Planning and structured layouts and large enclosures with elaborate gateways are features present at Cheddar, Goltho, Steyning, and Little Paxton (see Gardiner 2011: 199–207; Ulmschneider 2011: 165–7). The visual approach to such structures is suggested to have been an important factor in their design: the entrances and enclosures used as a means of framing the buildings 'in a manner which was no less formal than the designed landscapes found around castles from the twelfth century onwards' (Gardiner 2011: 203). Travel to and arrival at these locations with their impressive and formal settings and entrances fit well with our understanding of increasingly well-defined ritualized itineraries and more formalized royal activities of the tenth and eleventh centuries (see, for example, the itineraries of Edgar, Edward, and Ethelred in Hill 1981: 90–1). Amesbury is certainly a royal site. It is situated at a nodal junction between a great river bend and a junction of early routes (Haslam 1984). The settlement lies in the shadow of Vespasian's Camp or *amesbyrig*, 'ambres burh', a large hill fort that gave its name to the settlement. Excavations within the hill fort have produced significant evidence of early prehistoric ritual activity, and the monument lay within the ritual compass of the Stonehenge Neolithic landscape (Semple 2009). Amesbury has strong royal connections: the presence of the king and meetings of the *witan* are recorded at Amesbury in 858 (Ass), 932 (S418–19), and 995 (*ASC* (E) 995). Alfred bequeathed Amesbury to his younger son and Eadred gave it to his mother. She is purported to have founded a nunnery at Amesbury c.979, but this may have replaced an earlier minster associated with the royal vill (Macmahon 2001). The minster lands of Amesbury are suggested to be more or less co-extant with the hundred of the same name (Pitt 1999). An earlier administrative unit or royal estate is suggested, which would concur with the attestations of royal councils at Amesbury in the ninth and tenth centuries. Early Anglo-Saxon activity is known in the areas with stray finds and inhumations east of the modern town that date to the fifth and sixth centuries (Macmahon 2001). This is a place argued by Stuart Brookes and John Baker as a seminal site—a place so bound up with ancient history and the history of the kings of Wessex that it achieved a primary importance as a place for assembly and royal ritual (Baker and Brookes 2015). The palace and assembly place of Amesbury lies within a landscape full of prehistoric monuments and remains. Not only was the site overlooked by the large hill fort, but the roads and routes into the settlement were flanked by ancient prehistoric barrows and monuments. As the royal entourage and assembly arrived at Amesbury in the ninth and tenth centuries, they would have approached a royal palace set at the great bend of a river, framed by the natural chalk lands and overshadowed by the ancient hill fort. Along the routes into Amesbury they would have passed the long and round barrows still visible today, and if approaching from the west across the chalk downs, they would have passed the remarkable monuments and remains of the Stonehenge environs. Within the proceedings of the royal court, felons would have been tried and sentenced and may even have been taken for execution at Stonehenge. The use of this extensive landscape of ancient monuments as a frame and setting for a royal activity—a residence, royal assemblies, and judicial executions—may be indicative of a type of widescale reworking of the landscape for the purpose of elite power. There are implications here of a far-reaching vision in which the ancient, whether prehistoric or Roman, and perhaps the physical remnants and memories of the pre-Christian past, were being drawn upon in a variety of ways to create a network of theatres and arenas in which power and authority were enacted.

It is thus fitting to end with Edgar, a master of spectacle and theatricality. The *Anglo-Saxon Chronicle* records that in 973 (*ASC* (A)) Edgar, ruler of the English, was consecrated 'as king in a great assembly' at Bath. Immediately after, according to version E of the chronicle, 'he led his whole raiding ship-army to Chester, and their six kings came to meet him, and all pledged that they would be allies on sea and on land'. Further details are provided by a later chronicler who detailed that eight under-kings,

that is: Kenneth king of the Scots, Malcolm king of the Cumbrians, Maccus king of many islands, and five others, Dufnal, Siferth, Hywel, Jacob, Juchil, met him as he commanded, and swore that they would be faithful to him and be his allies by land and sea. On a certain day he went on board a boat with them, and, with them at the oars, he took the helm himself and steered it skilfully on the course of the River Dee, proceeding from the palace to the monastery of St John the Baptist, attended by all the company of ealdormen and nobles also by boat. Having prayed there, he returned to the palace with the same pomp. (Swanton 1996: 119)

The selection of two great Roman towns as the setting for these symbolic rituals can be no accident. It is worth underlining that St John the Baptist's Church sits immediately adjacent to the Roman amphitheatre at Chester: not only the largest stone-built amphitheatre constructed in Roman Britain with unique stone-built stairwells, but a feature that survived as a ruin and a used open space, long enough to influence medieval activity and town planning (Ward 2008). Julia Barrow has skilfully argued that the Dee-rowing ceremony was in fact a type of ritual favoured by the Carolingians and Ottonians, with classical antecedents (Barrow 2001: 84). Rather than signalling overlordship over the subject kings, Barrow has shown that, in Continental contexts, this type of ceremony, conducted especially at borders, was designed to signal peaceful accord between kings—to 'agree mutual status' (Barrow 2001: 84–8). Edgar is noted by Barrow as a king who took a keen interest in the activities and ceremonies of his Continental neighbours, but he also had a sharp eye for harnessing important ancient sites to his own brand of symbolic ritual. It is interesting that Edgar, known for his peacemaking rather than military successes, seems to have been a master of political theatre, able to create ritualized and symbolic displays of power that used the physical remains of the Roman past to lend credibility to the political process, enhancing his lordship and rule but also more effectively staging his peacemaking strategies. It is also important and relevant that Edgar and his predecessors and successors were staging rituals at a wide variety of places and indicating that the reworking of places of power was taking place at the largest of geographic scales.

Prehistoric monuments and law in the localities

Local assembly has already seen some discussion in Chapter 3, in which pre-Christian burial sites, ancient monuments, and natural features were argued to have significant local importance to people's sense of place and the definition of their local world view. The highly organized system of hundred units and assemblies in place by the tenth century represents, however, an era of replanning. This reorganization is also intimately related to the burgeoning development of execution sites. Almost all known examples of the latter relate to the hundredal geography of central and southern England (Reynolds 1998: 78–84; 2009a). The

Fig. 6.5 A meeting at the Wroth Stone, Knightlow, in Warwickshire in 1899. © Victoria and Albert Museum, London.

emergence of this planned administrative regime developed after the conversion and in its full-blown form was operational largely in the ninth to eleventh centuries. The arguments for open air meeting places as survivals from 'archaic' kin-based frameworks of local organization and places of cult and assembly do not therefore describe the entire picture (see Meaney 1995, 1997; and Chapter 3). Persistent local traditions may have survived the major social, political, and religious upheaval and change across the seventh to ninth centuries, leading to the survival of some 'seminal' or 'cultic' location hundred meeting places, but many must also have been eroded, lost, and replaced with new choices.

This is a note of caution, however, rather than a dismissal. There are many extraordinary instances of shire and hundred assembly places that have survived as places of gathering long into the medieval period and beyond. Meetings continue to be held even today at dawn each year on 11 November at the Wroth Stone at Knightlow, Ryton-on-Dunsmore, Warwickshire (see Figure 6.5). The stone is an old cross base (Anderson 1934–9: i. 134, no. 1; Nelson 1951: 87–8), but it sits upon a large barrow, presumed to be the *hlāw* of the *cnichtas*, 'the knights or lads'. Knightlow at Domesday comprised three hundreds: 'Bomelau', 'Stanlei', and 'Meretone', and these were combined during the twelfth century into the larger unit of Knightlow (Salzman 1951, 1–2). Knightlow Hill, Ryton-on-Dunsmore, was the meeting place of the shipsoke (Anderson 1934–9: i. 133–4; Gover et al. 1936: 95–6,

98–9; Pantos 2002: 442–3). The meeting at the Wroth Stone seems to date from at least this era when dues were paid by surrounding parishes and holdings to the Duke of Buccleuch. The shire meeting place of *Cwicchelmes hlæwe [Cwichelmeshlæwe]* at Hendred in Berkshire, discussed in the opening to this book (*ASC* (E) 1006; S1454), still operated as a place of barter and trade in the seventeenth century (Peake 1935: 102–7).[1] The *thing* or assembly at Tynwald Hill on the Isle of Man was still active as a meeting place in the thirteenth century and continues to today (Darvill 2004: 218). The place-name deriving from *þingvöllr* 'parliament field' suggests an even earlier incarnation as a Viking Age *thing*, and the stepped mound has been discovered through excavation to have 'pre-Norse roots' dating back to the first millennium BC (Darvill 2004). Meeting place networks could be fissile and changing, and yet in some instances the places themselves have proved highly persistent as locations of gathering over many centuries.

Prehistoric monuments were, without question, chosen as places of outdoor assembly. A comprehensive assessment is beyond the scope of this book, but the highly detailed work by Aliki Pantos (2002) and the ongoing work of the *Landscapes of Governance Project* at UCL and *The Assembly Project* (HERA) render any additional comprehensive study unnecessary. It would be an omission, however, not to use the last part of this chapter to make a short acknowledgement of the use of prehistoric features as foci or landmarks for outdoor meetings in the planned administrative system evident in late Anglo-Saxon England.

Meaney's exceptionally detailed and informative study of the Cambridge region, already discussed in Chapter 3, identified over thirty meeting places at natural places such as fords, the occasional hill, stone, and tree, *and* three or four prehistoric barrows and one Roman site (Meaney 1997: 234–9). If one moves west to Dorset, of the thirty-three hundreds, eleven seem to have met at barrows, seven on hills, hill forts, or in earthworks, six on lakes, in a coombe, or by a tree, and nine were named after minster churches or royal vills (Harte 1986). Sussex contains the largest number of hundreds of all the counties surveyed by Anderson. Of the thirty-seven hundreds considered to exist at Domesday, the vast majority of hundred names seem to refer to natural features or places, to woodlands and woodland clearings, and the feld or 'open land' (Anderson 1934–9: ii. 66–108). There are five potential barrows, an old fort, a Roman road, and two enclosures, all of which may refer to ancient features or landmarks (Anderson 1934–9: ii. 66–108). Hundred and shire assembly sites and wapentakes were located at a wide variety of locations. Often the name of the unit is the main evidence that the meeting place may have been an ancient

---

[1] In 1620 a licence was acquired to hold a market at East Ilsley, prohibiting marketing and bartering from taking place at *Cutchinloe* (Peake 1935: 102–7).

monument, but instances where we can actually identify the site and the monument are far more elusive.

The comprehensive research of Aliki Pantos covers fifteen English counties (2002). This important contribution to our understanding of local administrative frameworks and assembly places before the Conquest has identified a myriad of sites where the place-name at least implies a late Anglo-Saxon assembly was held at or within an older feature or monument. Her survey lists over a hundred assembly places that may potentially reference an old monument of some kind, including stones, forts, barrows, or enclosures (see Pantos 2002: ii. 175–461). This accounts for less than a fifth of her corpus. Of course many meeting places are lost, and a proportion located in past scholarship are shown by Pantos to rest on speculative assumption rather than good corroborating documentary and archaeological evidence. Of the 114 sites that have potential connections to the prehistoric, however, it is interesting that nearly two-thirds (80 instances) are associated with one or more round or long barrows. There are seventeen cases where stones are mentioned or known as an assembly marker, only eight forts and five smaller enclosures, three sites where a combination of monuments may have provided a focus, one Roman road, and one Roman fort.

Mounds or barrows were identified by Aliki Pantos as the most common 'physical feature' referred to in the names of meeting places. *OE hlāw, beorg,* and *ON haugr* are all terms that potentially refer to barrows or burial mounds (Pantos 2002: 69–70). Mound terms occur in frequent relationship to personal names or descriptors and a significant number were identified as having a term denoting speech or assembly, in particular *OE gemōt*. Pantos associated a number of assembly places with barrows, even when the associated hundred name failed to mention this type of feature. At Longtree Hundred, Gloucestershire, a barrow located at the meeting point produced evidence for early medieval burials (Anon. 1843–9), and at Narresford the meeting place at the ford lay next to a prehistoric barrow cemetery (Meaney 1993: 82; Pantos 2002: ii. 380). In many instances, however, the mound or monument that featured in the name of the unit is now lost, or having been recorded in the seventeenth and eighteenth centuries, has since been levelled. In nineteen instances a mound has survived, or survived long enough to be described and excavated in the past.[2] Of these, only two are likely prehistoric constructions. *Cwicchelmes hlæwe* [*Cwichelmeshlæwe*] has been discussed already (see pp. 1–2). The pre-Conquest meeting place of the Domesday hundred of Roeburg ('rough barrow') in

---

[2] Roeberg, *Cwicchelmes hlæwe* [*Cwichelmeshlæwe*], Scutchmer's Knob (Berkshire); Dusteberg, Siglai (Buckinghamshire); Awre, Brictwoldesburg (Gloucestershire); Loveden (Lincolnshire); Bernedeslawe, Togartone (Northamptonshire); Chadlington, Ploughley (Oxfordshire); Alfnodestou (Rutland); Offelau, Tatemaneslau (Staffordshire); Knightlow, Patelau, Stanleie, Tremelau (Staffordshire); and Ildeberga (Warwickshire).

Berkshire is argued by Pantos, on the basis of limited but sound corroborating evidence, to lie in the vicinity of Rowbury Farm at Boxford, where a ditchless barrow was destroyed in the nineteenth century, producing finds of charcoal. Another unexcavated barrow lies in the vicinity (Grinsell 1935–6: 52; Pantos 2002: 202–3). The remaining examples are largely unexcavated and undated mounds. Some are quite confident associations, such as the mound or barrow associated with the Domesday hundred of Brictwoldesberg, 'Beorhtweald's beorg'. A meeting of the hundred was recorded in 1400 at *la berge* at Hatherop. This survives as a substantial round barrow with evidence of a silted ring-ditch, although undated despite excavation (O'Neill and Grinsell 1960: 117). Some of the associations are more tenuous (Pantos 2002: 286). At Dusteberge, for example, the meeting place is identified as Desborough Castle, a prehistoric hill fort reworked as a fortification again in the late eleventh or early twelfth century. This feature is considered to be the monument from which the Domesday hundred takes its name. The second element of the name *OE beorg*, 'hill or barrow', is in later documents confused with *burh*, 'fortification'. Pantos suggests the meeting place may have originally been associated specifically with the large mound on the western side of the castle as well as the hill fort (Collard 1988: 15–41; Pantos 2002: 214–15).

Five of these meeting mounds seem to be associated with Anglo-Saxon burials. Loveden Hill is a well-known example where the meeting mound, although natural, lies at the heart of an extensive cremation cemetery (see Williams 2004). Shipton Barrow is substantial in size and placed in a situation with extensive views. With a diameter of 52 metres, the scale of the monument suggests a prehistoric date. Straight earthworks enclose the barrow on its north, west, and south sides. Excavations at the site produced two skeletons, one with a late Anglo-Saxon buckle, which, given their location and unusual positioning (one above the other, both pinned down with stone), might indicate these are victims of execution (Chambers 1978; Pantos 2002: 215). The likely prehistoric date, combined with what might be evidence of modification and perhaps late Anglo-Saxon execution, make this an intriguing and compelling case. Iverishaghe, *ON*, *Ívarr + hagi*, 'Ivarr's enclosure', identified as the meeting place of Togartone Wapentake, Mount Alstoe, in Burley and the possible meeting mound of Tremelau at Moothill, Lighthorne, are also all sites with good evidence for early Anglo-Saxon burial evidence in the immediate vicinity (Pantos 2002: 403–4, 426, 450–1).

Though some of the most familiar instances of meeting places at ancient monuments represent hill fort sites, examples are in fact rare by comparison to meeting mounds.[3] Of the eight identified in the corpus created by Pantos,

---

[3] Blewbury (Berkshire); Desborough Castle and Lamua (Buckinghamshire); Mobberley (Cheshire); Salmonsbury (Gloucestershire); Yarborough Camp (Lincolnshire); Gisleburg and Borough Hill (Northamptonshire).

two represent lost and untestable associations (Lamua and Mobberley). Blew-bury and Salmondsbury are well-known examples where the fort or *burh* referred to in the hundred name survives and is a late prehistoric fort (Pantos 2002: i. 70). At Blewbury, however, there is no firm evidence that the hundred met at the monument, but it certainly gave its name to the early hundred (Pantos 2002: 192–4). At Salmonsbury the hundred court met at the site in 1293, and meetings of the court leet were still being held at a gap in the northern ramparts as late as the eighteenth century (for overview of original sources, see Pantos 2002: 306). The name of the hill fort is recorded in an eighth-century charter (S114; Grundy 1935–6: 52), and its centrality to the eleventh-century hundred might imply the unit is considerably more ancient (Pantos 2002: 307). A number of burials associated with Roman and early Anglo-Saxon finds has been located in the compass of the hill fort, and unaccompanied skeletons too (Meaney 1964: 93). There are, of course, other examples too: Badbury or Wandlebury could be added to the list. Nevertheless, hill forts associated with assemblies represent a tiny proportion of hundred, wapentake, or shire meeting places.

Stones are a final category worth brief consideration. Meeting places associated with stones are more common in the record than assemblies associated with hill forts, but identifying such features in the modern landscape is extremely difficult. It is impossible, therefore, to state very often whether the stone referred to was a natural boulder, a prehistoric monument, a Roman stone, or indeed an Anglo-Saxon stone sculpture. Of those listed by Pantos, only seven can be located with any certainty.[4] The stones identified in the names of the remaining eleven hundreds and wapentakes are lost. The *OE stān* element in Hammenstan is suggested to refer to a natural boulder—which, as the name suggests (*OE hamen*, 'scarred or mutilated'), is marked and scarred (see Pantos 2002: pl. 19). At Gutlacistan, the meeting place is associated with a bridge, but 'Guðlac's stone' is lost (Pantos 2002: 326–8), and similarly at Cudulvestan, 'Cūþwulf's stone' is lost, but the location of the meeting place is argued to lie at or by Cuttlestone Bridge in Penkridge (Duignan 1902: 48; Pantos 2002: 432). In the four remaining examples, the stone or stones can be identified, but they are not prehistoric. The *teoboldestan* or 'Þeobald's stone' of Tetboldestane hundred is named in a pre-Conquest charter (S1554). The Tib-blestone lies at an important crossroads on a significant tenth-century route. It is not decorated, but has a heavily marked surface and a roughly cylindrical shape some 1.5 metres high (Pantos 2002: pl. 25). The Elloe Stone is a late tenth- or

---

[4] A complete list of meeting stones is not given here. This list includes only examples discussed within the text: Atiscros (Cheshire); Hammenstan (Derbyshire); Tetboldestane Hundred and Kiftsgate Stone (Gloucestershire); Gutlacistan (Leicestershire); Elloe Stone (Lincolnshire); Court of the Four Shires at Ildeberg, Bengeworth, by Evesham (Oxfordshire); Cudulvestan (Staffordshire); Walescross Wapentake (Lindsey); Walecros Wapentake (Derbyshire).

early eleventh-century cross-head (Everson and Stocker 1999: 162–4, pls 171, 172). Again its precise original position is uncertain, but local tradition picked up by early antiquarian research carries evidence of its original positioning back as far as the fifteenth century. The stone is first mentioned in 1491 (Cameron 1988: 41). Evidence of repair and weathering are argued to indicate that the stone has long stood in its current position. The hundred name of Elloe, *OE Ella* (pn.) + *hōh*, 'Ella's spur', suggests, however, that the original meeting site may have been elsewhere. The stone itself is a grave marker (Cameron 1988: 164) and may thus have been reused from some other original setting. As Everson and Stocker note, it is not the only stone sculpture to have provided a marker for an assembly. For example, Atiscros in Cheshire contains the *ON* element *kross*, and a cross-shaft was noted by Pennant in the eighteenth century but had vanished by the nineteenth century (Pennant 1773: 52). The name of Walescross Wapentake recorded at Domesday contains *ON* element *kross* (Cameron 1992: 1; Pantos 2002: 364), as does Walecros Wapentake (Pantos 2002: 272). Another enigmatic example is the Kiftsgate Stone. Kiftsgate hundred was formed by 1220 from three earlier hundreds: Witelai (*OE with* + lēah, 'clearing in the bend'; Smith 1964–5: 230), Cheftesihat (*OE cýft* + *geat*, 'meeting or conference gate or gap'; Smith 1964–5: 261–2), and Celfledetorn (*OE Cēolflæd* + þorn, 'Cēolflæd's thorn'; Smith 1964–5: 229). Cheftesihat 'meeting or conference gate or gap' thus survives in the name of the later, larger hundred. Meetings or courts are recorded for this unit at *Kyftesgate* in the fourteenth and sixteenth centuries, and this is presumed to refer to the site of the stone on Western-sub-Edge (Smith 1964–5: 231, 250, 261). It bears no marks other than a perforation around its mid-point, but is shaped and broken, and survives to roughly 1 metre in height (Pantos 2002: 189–90, pl. 24).

Some of these markers are clearly natural but unusually marked or shaped. Some are worked roughly and some are fragments of larger worked sculptures. No example can be said to be definitively prehistoric or Roman. Several are worked stones of early medieval date and may be original markers for meeting sites or have been recycled from other places. There is little about such features that implies antiquity or indeed veneration of the ancient. Despite their relatively small size and portable qualities, however, these stones have retained an amazingly potent local presence as markers for assemblies, courts, and judgements over many centuries, underlining the enduring value connected by communities to places of importance for local decision-making. It is worth finishing by underlining the very plausible assertion by Pantos that assembly places were multifocal and occupied large areas marked with several features (2002: 70–85). In numerous instances, multiple features seem to be relevant to assembly sites and practices. At several sites, the ancient monument or marker is not the sole feature of the site. At Salmonsbury hill fort, for example, other barrows and monuments are recorded within the camp. At Desborough

Castle too, the large mound that flanks the hill fort rather than the hill fort itself is argued as the meeting location.

This topic is currently receiving much wider and more comprehensive attention, as it deserves. The short review here places emphasis on the sheer variety of types of ancient, natural, and contemporary marker used for meetings and the persistence of some of those places as sites for courts and decision-making in the medieval and sometimes post-medieval periods. The widescale use of natural places, as well as fords, bridges, crossing points, and the limited evidence for any congruence with pre-Christian places of worship, suggest that, rather than seeking an early 'sacred' origin for every assembly place, the likely importance of many may have stemmed from their enduring and prominent role as important local features (see Chapter 3, pp. 89–94). Indeed, in the rolling-out of new systems of administrative organization in the ninth and tenth centuries, it seems likely that features of local value may well have been selected as new meeting places, alongside monuments and locations that held an enduring place in the consciousness of local communities. Open land and grazed woodland may have provided important areas outside of the cultivated and settled zones, which were not only as Pantos has suggested a 'no-man's-land', but were shared resources, key to the success, comfort, and survival of several communities. Water could be added here too (spring, fords, rivers, confluences) as a category of place that represented a vital resource, that may even have been shared, and like crossing places, roads, and bridges required joint responsibility for its maintenance.

How then do ancient monuments fit in? These too are markers of local import—landmarks and well-known features. There are certainly places of potentially sacred or ideological importance included in the corpus. Wenslei hundred in Bedfordshire, for example, indicates a meeting place at a mound dedicated to the deity Woden, now sadly lost (Morris 1962: 75; Pantos 2002: 188). Such associations are, however, rare. The corpus instead presents a collection of sites that read like important local landmarks—places largely of significance to the contemporary population as notable features in the local landscape, some perhaps with longer histories and associated legends, but others perhaps merely visual curiosities or important local resources. It takes a potent, local collective memory, however, to curate knowledge of and perpetuate meetings at a local natural monument for literally 600 or 700 years (for example, Salmonsbury in Gloucestershire or Knightlow in Warwickshire). The lifespan of some of these meeting places is astonishing. There may be evidence here therefore of revival and reinvention as well as local memory. The eighteenth-century convening of the court leet at a gap in the north rampart at Salmonsbury, for example, was commemorated it seems with the placement of a stone marked with the date 1794 and the initials of the parish officers (O'Neill 1977: 18–19). One suspects that, just as the Abbot of Fécamp sought a special kind of local legitimacy for his justice by seeking permission from Henry III to hold his hundred court at this hill fort, the later parish officers also saw a form of legitimacy in their use of the same hill fort as a place of meeting for the court leet.

The sheer variety of types of place chosen as hundred meeting sites can be argued to reflect the kind of diverse, localized sense of identity discussed in earlier chapters in relation to the pre-Christian scene. This diversity of places reinforces the idea that, at the most local level, populations remained strongly interconnected with landscape not only by dwelling in it, and using its re-sources, but also through memory and local legend. Monuments certainly acted as facilitators in the creation of an enduring local sense of place, but the potency and value of the natural world were equally important in the shaping of enduring local identity. What is an unlooked for outcome is the scale of usage of mounds or barrows. Compared with stones, forts, or enclosures, barrows, mounds, and things that looked like barrows were by far preferred as places for late Anglo-Saxon local assembly. It is frustrating that, as a result of the extensive destruction of such features in the past, and limited exploration in the present, we still know little about how many of these were prehistoric, how many were reused for early Anglo-Saxon burial, and how many were non-sepulchral. At least some early cemeteries and individual burials asserted a hold on the memory, imagination, and identity of late Anglo-Saxon communities long after the con-version to Christianity. Such evidence again points to the long-lasting nature of popular perceptions and beliefs. The Church may have successfully discouraged the use of established community burial grounds and traditions of barrow burial, and even helped reshape perceptions of the pre-Christian past, but it could not, it seems, wholly eradicate the popular traditions associated with local landmarks that may have shaped some of the administrative geography of the late Anglo-Saxon era.

Summary

The patterns of local assembly in the localities of late Anglo-Saxon England point to an enduring sense of landscape, situation, and place, on the part of local communities. By contrast, the introduction of a systemized network of places for the punishment and disposal of criminals in late Anglo-Saxon England implies that other forces were at work too in the localities, reshaping elements of local geography into nodal points within larger, elite systems of power. The ancient monuments in these landscapes remained integral to local identity, alongside natural features, places and resources, but some were revived as places for theatrical displays of elite power aimed at reinforcing the emerging mechanisms of state. Types of settlement that emerged within and were active during the sixth, seventh, and eighth centuries, which are termed estate centres or palaces, took advantage of situations in the landscape marked by clusters of prehistoric monuments and Roman settlement remains, and also monuments. Indeed elites and kings can be argued to have developed a marked eye for this type of aesthetic. The royal house of Wessex developed its early power base in a heartland rich in ancient monuments. By contrast, in the north, Edwin and his successors shaped their new power over the northern territories by means of places of gathering and centres of ceremony shaped by ancient and more recent standing features and enhanced with new monumental additions too. Some fifty years later, Ecgfrith, asserting again the Christian authority and overlordship of the Deiran dynasty in the north, established his rule along the Tyne, drawing upon the ruinous but prominent Roman material legacy along this major inland communication to situate his power, palaces, and a new array of Christian monuments signalling his consolidation of a Northumbrian royal heartland (Rollason 2003: 45–52; Wood 2006).

In the succeeding centuries, some of these places became enduring settings, returned to repeatedly by royals and kings, and chosen for the staging of momentous events and assemblies. The accrued history of such places must have made them ideal situations for the performance of royal rhetoric and ceremony. Their setting within familiar landscapes, resonant with memory, marked by ancient remains and newer monumental forms, provided a resounding signal too of the ancient legitimacy of the power of these elites and their dynastic lines.

Such sites formed components in what could be envisaged as an ambitious vision of landscape and territory, prompted by the conquest and overlordship of increasingly larger territories. Places of power became crucial in the management of people and resource, and the staging of royal ritual became essential at long-established and new sites. It is within this framework that kings experimented with the prehistoric as a theatrical medium for staging power. Major councils were held at ancient monuments, and battles too continued to be situated on occasion at ancient markers in the landscape. It is also worth reflecting on the discussion in Chapter 4 of minsters, monastic houses, and even standing stone crosses established in relation to prehistoric palimpsests and monuments, and considering if these too were components in a royal and elite reworking of place and 'history' to serve their new ambitions. Yet what is exceptional within these processes is the emergence of some monuments as fearful, haunted places and the harnessing of ancient barrows and monuments to the purpose of judicial killing. The use of ancient barrows and other monuments as places where wrongdoers were taken, often tied, sometimes mutilated, and always killed, and then displayed and cursorily buried, reinforces the evidence discussed in Chapter 5 for the growing association of old barrows with ancient heathenism, evil, and latterly hell and damnation. This evidence speaks in many ways of the true reach of late Anglo-Saxon royal power: kings had not merely the ability to judge crimes and commit men to eternal damnation and exile from grace, but power over the ancient landscape too. They were able to harness associations with the pre-Christian and heathen past to their new vision and order to enforce authority and at the same time use the ancient past to enhance their legitimacy. Situating execution sites at ancient heathen places of burial surely signalled their triumph over the old order and their new Christian affiliation and power, but may also have implied too that they retained an ability to draw upon the supernatural and the ancestral at will and unleash it if needed in the punishment of those who contravened their law. Differing scales of perception existed, however, shaped by the differing groups and levels within society. Monuments certainly held a significant place in the vision of the late Anglo-Saxon royal and ecclesiastical elite, but they continued to perform a role in the most local of narratives as well, remaining important in the definition and curation of local identity.

7

Visions of the past

The Anglo-Saxons and the ancient landscape

And they buried torques in the barrow, and jewels
and a trove of such things as trespassing men
had once dared to drag from the hoard.
They let the ground keep that ancestral treasure
gold under gravel, gone to earth,
as useless to men now as it ever was.

(*Beowulf*, trans. Heaney 1999, 99, lines 3163–8)

These poignant lines are a reminder that the crucible in which Anglo-Saxon identity was forged was the great era of warriors, gold, and largesse, attested in archaeological record for the sixth and seventh centuries. The literature that remembers and evokes this 'heroic age' was put into writing some several hundred years after. Memory is intrinsic to many of the arguments put forward in this volume. The rich potential of material culture as a creative 'medium of remembrance' has been extensively explored (e.g. Connerton 1989: 36–40; Baudrillard 1996: 73–82; Effros 2001). Monuments and tombs in particular are argued to be central to the early medieval perception and construction of the past, facilitating a sophisticated understanding and signalling of identity through commemorative topography and mortuary activity (see Effros 2001; Williams 2006a: 215–21). What has been underestimated until now is the sheer scale, in temporal and selective terms, at which the ancient past was recognized and harnessed to the purpose of tradition-making by communities and elite families and individuals in Anglo-Saxon England.

This book does not claim to be comprehensive. It has taken an aspect of early medieval practice—the recognition and use of ancient prehistoric features—and has explored it from the earliest activities of the fifth century, through the changes of the long eighth, to the perceptions and beliefs of the populations of late Anglo-Saxon England. The ancient monuments that marked the landscape were meaningful features to populations through-out the era. Much of the 'meaning' ascribed to them relied on their early

significance as prominent features in the immediate and local landscape. Populations and families in the fifth, sixth, and seventh centuries sought out ancient
prehistoric monuments as places at which to bury their dead, creating new connections to place and landscape, and shaping their territory and terrain by means
of mortuary events and practices. Monuments had other roles too, as physical
landmarks, as places for battles, assemblies, and musters. Not all monuments were
important or significant, but some accrued importance, serving as places of
repeated activity, acquiring a seminal status that seems to have led to their continued reuse at key moments across the early medieval period. It is suggested here
that the ancient, human-altered features of the landscape were intrinsic elements,
alongside the natural, in the shaping of the local world view of populations,
irrespective in these early centuries of any sense of ethnic affiliation or descent.
The early medieval communities in England were developing a sense of being and
place that was intimate to their immediate world (see Jones and Semple 2012).

By the seventh century, changes are discernible in how such features were
used. Elite groups and families developed a particular interest in these monuments and were intentionally appropriating and using them within their own
particular ambit: developing their role in funerary ceremony, assembly, battle
ritual, and royal theatre, etc. Other ancient sites, some once used for burial,
were forgotten, as the new aspirations of elite families controlling larger territories created a need for new rituals and theatre and thus engendered a selective
reworking of the landscape in order more effectively to situate and extend their
power (Chapters 3 and 6). The ancient monuments of the English landscape
became mnemonic markers that assisted the new elite of the Anglo-Saxon
Kingdoms in the curation and management of memory and legends that valorized tales of the Anglo-Saxon genesis. They marked places where the ancient
dead and ancestors lay; they signalled sites where Anglo-Saxon victories were
achieved; where the British were defeated and where great military and political
moments had once been enacted.

This study of the ancient prehistoric monuments in the English landscape
between *c*.400 and *c*.1100 thus provides an insight into the changing complexities of Anglo-Saxon society. The ancient in the landscape was pivotal to the
shaping of early identities, the forging of new intellectual narratives, and the
emergence of a materiality linked to an aspirant elite that used the ancient to
mould its power in the present. It also provides an insight into how the arrival of
Christianity and the emergence of supra-regional power structures served to
change how people conceived of time and place. The scales of existence also
changed. Local scenes were subsumed into larger geographies: regions, kingdoms, and eventually the Anglo-Saxon state. Ancient monuments and seminal
locations were nodal, however, in interlocking ordinary and elite experience,
providing theatres where memory and activity linked populations with their
perceived Anglo-Saxon identity and the myths of the Anglo-Saxon nation,
and where people could encounter kings. The Church may have endeavoured
successfully to stop the types of funerary tradition that embraced ancient places

and monuments and that placed emphasis on pre-Christian ancestry; but the power of ancient monuments and places remained accessible to and pivotal within royal and elite ritual. Roman and prehistoric were embraced in theatrical displays of power aimed at evoking new traditions and intellectual narratives of identity and power. Kings traversed their territories on Roman roads, used symbolic meetings and rituals at seminal monuments and natural places, and meted out their power in landscapes of justice and authority that used the memories of heathenism to delimit and reinforce the new Christian order.

Regional and local identity

The relationship between early medieval communities and their immediate landscape is shown here to be complex. Although fifth- to seventh-century populations across England made clear reference to the prehistoric and Roman features around them by means of funerary rites (as originally profiled by Williams in 1997), I have argued in this book that preferences and choices may have varied from region to region. These 'local' signatures are suggested to relate to the availability of differing types of monument from region to region, and the underlying shape of the geography itself. In West Sussex, the river valleys attracted settlement, created cohesion between communities, and served to shape the 'mental' space of these early populations, leading to the burial of the dead in the fifth to seventh centuries around the upper slopes of the valleys, with a marked preference for selecting old monuments of varied date as places for cemeteries and for the burial of individuals. Choices and preferences could also be connected to movement through a landscape, as the evidence from East Yorkshire suggests. Here the terrain, the wooded Wolds, and the shifting political geography of the sixth to early eighth centuries seem to have promoted the rite of burial using pre-existing older monuments, and that rite may have been increasingly restricted in terms of access, only to certain sectors of the population. By contrast, in North Wiltshire, the wealth of surviving prehistoric remains on the chalk seems to have promoted and encouraged their use for secondary burial, but competition and conflict in the seventh century may have resulted in a proliferation of elite graves situated in isolation, in reference to large and visible prehistoric barrows along the borderlands or frontiers between Wessex and Mercia.

There are inevitable problems in using data that include the results of anti-quarian excavations and in focusing on areas that witnessed extensive explor-ation in the eighteenth to late nineteenth centuries. The prolific barrow digging in all three regions will have created a bias in the data, and potentially an enhanced view of monument reuse, specifically the use of barrows for early medieval burial. This does not negate, however, the differences apparent in *how* ancient monuments were used in each region and the variations in terms of *when* they were being used. These stand as indications of the existence of more subtle, locally or regionally varied approaches to the ancient before the conversion. This chimes with the discussions in Chapters 2 and 3 of distinctive connections to place, forged at a very local and eventually regional level, and as a result the development of local cosmologies and world views shaped by the immediate environs—the natural world, natural resources, and the ancestral and ancient resources in the surrounding landscape.

Such approaches are suggested here, to relate to the need for populations in the fifth and sixth centuries to forge 'a sense of place': an identity tied to landscape and resource (see Chapters 2 and 3). Monuments provided a means of signalling affiliation with the land and perceived ancestral places. Burying the dead in and around older monuments and features represented a physical process of creating connections to place, and a process of myth-making, in terms of forging origin narratives and stories about ancestral claims and ownership. Such practices need not have been the preserve of any specific group; indeed the close association with the existing geography, topography, and routes of communications, and the variety of practice, support instead evidence for the creation of diverse narratives that must have embraced and interwoven, as well as alienated, existing and new claims to place.

Pre-Christian religions, beliefs, and ritual

Burial rites were not the only activity, however, situated at ancient monuments. A host of other events and practices may have occurred within the shadow of upstanding prehistoric remains, including the erection of standing posts and structures, the establishment of settlement sites, meetings, musters, and battles too. A small group of weapons, found without associated funerary activity, may also provide evidence for votive rites connected to ancient barrows and other old monuments.

The archaeological and documentary evidence underpinning this chapter is recognized as scarce and contentious, and open to reinterpretation. The aim, however, to balance the previously heavy focus on funerary reuse is successful. The evidence presented in Chapter 3 matches the highly varied funerary evidence, implying a diversity of secondary uses of ancient monuments that is both interesting and compelling, underlining the idea that pre-Christian practices and perceptions and indeed uses of the ancient were not homogenous but localized and multi-scalar. A single monument may repeatedly attract activity of varying kinds, or a landscape or palimpsest containing the physical remnants of a variety of structures and monuments might serve to shape a variety of practices. The numinous and sacred natural world and landscape were intrinsic to the beliefs of people before the conversion, but an argument can be made too for the potency of ancient monuments in this spiritual canvas.

In combination, the funerary evidence and that for other types of activity in relation to antecedent monuments strongly suggests that the communities and families of the fifth to seventh centuries were negotiating their own contemporary narratives in relation to the landscape and its physical features. Although prehistoric monuments, especially barrows, were frequently a part of this, how they were reused was multifarious. Ancestors and ancestral concerns cannot be dismissed, but neither were they the sole progenitor for such activities. The power of the past, the ancient, the mythical, and the remembered was being both curated and manipulated. Although this book focuses on the prehistoric, Roman remains are certainly a part of these processes. Portable material, both Roman and prehistoric, was also relevant (e.g. Eckardt and Williams 2003: 141–70). There are intimations here that the seventh-century population and later were influenced by the memories, material, and monumental remains of their more recent 'ancestors'. Thäte has made this point in relation to the recycling of older monuments for funerary activity in Scandinavia (2007), and Crewe has made a compelling case too for the influence of early Anglo-Saxon Saxon material and monumental legacies on middle and later Anglo-Saxon communities (Crewe 2012: 217–8). We now have a strong sense of how the prehistoric and the Roman influenced the practices and perceptions of fifth- to seventh-century populations, but as yet have only limited understanding of how early settlement remains, grave-fields, and timber- or earth-built monuments shaped the practices and activities of successive generations in England. Although this book has captured changing attitudes and Christianized conceptions of the pre-Christian landscape, and has reinforced the idea that the ancient and more recent 'past' became increasingly important to elites by the seventh century, the valorization, recycling, revival, and recirculation of material legacies of the pre-Christian Anglo-Saxon past by later generations would benefit from greater exploration.

The repeated use of certain places and their long 'biographies' lasting well into the conversion period as places of meetings, royal power, or places associated with ancient events, legends, and mythical figures attests to the intrinsic value and potency of place and monuments to the psyche of the Anglo-Saxons over the long term. The landscape and the monuments, indeed the ancient whether 'real' or 'imagined', were a cultural resource, harnessed and used for a variety of purposes, but increasingly drawn upon by a diminishing number of powerful people and families (see Driscoll 1998 and 2004 for similar arguments relating to the Picts). By the seventh century, prehistoric monuments seem to have increasingly come within the ambit of elite groups or families at precisely the times when Anglo-Saxon identity became a culturally dominant force. Of particular note here is the emerging evidence for the formalization of relationships between activity and monument. The laying-out of prestige settlements with large halls and aligned complexes of buildings in reference to prehistoric monuments—with what appear to be increasingly stricter architectural relationships with preceding monuments—appear at some sites in the seventh century and later (see Crewe 2012: 207–18). At the same time burial practices involving ancient monuments seem to have become the preserve of fewer, wealthier people, and, as John Blair has noted, structures or shrines and posts placed in relation to prehistoric monuments points perhaps to the revival and the development of novel modes of monumentalizing important locales and ancestral sites (Blair 2005, 2009). None of these activities can be said to have been widespread, but it seems they were, at least in the funerary sphere, increasingly limited to certain groups. Not only does this fit with the ideas of experimentation and ostentation asserted for seventh-century elites (Geake 1997; Carver 2002); it also implies that a localized and even individual interest in making 'ancestral' connections with older monuments was being superseded by the creation of new strategies by a select sector of society. These drew upon the prehistoric and Roman past, but took inspiration too from a well pool of pre-Christian activity. Such changes fit with a broader interpretations of the seventh century as a time when small elite groups were securing greater supra-local and regional power and were investing in the creation of dynastic traditions signalled through the forging of new links between the living and dead and old and contemporary places. The increasing number of ancient monuments used for elite burial also underlines, perhaps, the increasing management of the old and ancestral as a source of power. Perhaps monuments were more than a means of legitimation; they may have been perceived as a resource by a forward-looking and ambitious Anglo-Saxon elite that wished to manage, curate, and of course, use the ancestral and supernatural in the protection of their kingdoms to facilitate greater reach and control over the populations under their sway.

It is important to stress, however, that not all monument types were special and not all types of activity were funerary. There is evidence that they were considered potent and powerful places, arguably associated with perceived ancestry, but certainly points of reference for communities seeking to establish a sense of place, authority over land and resource, and an identity in the post-Roman landscape. The evidence also suggests an intensely localized response to individual monuments and complexes in the fifth and sixth centuries, but the increasing exploitation of such features for elite purposes after this.

Landscape, prehistoric monuments, and the material rhetoric of elite power

By the early seventh century, the use of prehistoric monuments as burial sites was widespread, while the various 'special' sites and sacred landscapes discussed in

Chapter 3 were at their most developed. In this century, a preoccupation emerged with situating single, high-status burial in prehistoric barrows and new relationships were forged at some settlement sites, between large hall complexes and upstanding prehistoric remains. The arrival of Christianity also led to an increasing diversity of use, with Roman sites monuments and *spolia* brought into the reworking of place and landscape by the new Christian Church and its royal patrons. Some Christian sites seem to have been established or situated in relation to prehistoric monuments as well.

Similar tactics involving Roman sites, ruins, and *spolia* can be identified in Merovingia, Hispania, and North Africa (see Chapter 4, pp. 132–3). In Anglo-Saxon England the placement of elite settlements and burials within the shadow of prehistoric monuments or complexes were not novel actions; they represented a continuum of tradition from fifth- and sixth-century activity where such sites, places, and ancient potency had a role to play within the shaping of identity and belief (Crewe 2012: 212–18). A knowledgeable elite sector in England and in other European societies were beginning purposefully to exploit local and popular traditions of spirituality, ancestry, and place, re-creating them as new traditions that were the preserve of a select group within society—drawing familiar symbols into specific and new narratives of authority.

These practices did not occur in a vacuum. The harnessing of the ancient for elite secular and ecclesiastical purposes was relevant within many societies inhabiting the North and Irish Sea basins in the first millennium AD. Charlemagne is accepted as an intelligent architect of power who used place, art, and architecture to revive the spirit of Rome within a renaissance that signalled his aspirant ambitions for his Carolingian empire (see Airlie 2000; Christie 2005). Indeed, in the seventh and eighth centuries, Chris Loveluck has argued for the development of a new kind of elite settlement in Carolingia. These utilized in some instances late Roman towns and fortifications as well as new architectural forms and stone building materials, evoking the power of late antique buildings, cities, and monuments, suggesting these palace complexes provided a new means of status and display as 'theatres of kingship' (Loveluck 2005: 237–43).

Such processes were not confined to the courts of powerful elites in Christian mainland Europe. In Ireland too, the ancient past was being used to map and shape new territories and to legitimate and underwrite the claims of early medieval Christian kings and dynasties (Aitchison 1994; Newman 1997). Prehistoric, multiperiod palimpsests in the Irish landscape are identified in medieval written accounts as ancient regional centres of pre-Christian kingship that functioned as theatrical settings for royal ritual and activity in the late Iron Age (Aitchison 1987, 1994; Newman 1997; Breathnach 2001; Warner 2004; FitzPatrick 2004a, 2004b, etc.). The ancient burial mound was an especially significant element of these valorized landscapes, facilitating access to a parallel and supernatural world called the *síd* (Sims-Williams 1990; Warner 2004: 32–3). By the time medieval scribes committed these legends to writing, the sites of Tara (Meath) and Navan (Ulster) and their prehistoric enclosures and mounds were synonymous with accounts of the rituals and royal symbology of a pre-Christian age. So powerful was the concept of signalling legitimate authority at these ancient prehistoric seats of power that they remained places for symbolic statements well into the second millennium, such as the visits made by Brian Boru and his descendant Muircheartach, both High Kings of Ireland, to the ancient seat of Navan at crucial political moments in their kingships.

The recent publication of extensive excavations at the late Iron Age 'central place' at Lejre in Denmark brings into clear focus evidence of concerns in non-Christian early medieval societies (see Niles 2007 for a complete overview). Lejre is situated in the middle of Zealand. The site is marked by mounds and ship settings, and known for finds of treasure before the twentieth century. It is also recorded by medieval chroniclers as the royal manor of the Sjoldung kings (Niles 2007: 27, 29–31). The location and wider setting of the settlement are suggested to be an important ritual centre from the late Stone Age. The landscape is marked by surviving Neolithic and Bronze Age burial mounds (Niles 2007: 180–1). By *c.* AD 500–1000 a substantial settlement had developed: an Iron Age hall-complex accompanied by a substantial seventh-century burial mound, succeeded by a Viking hall-complex and Viking cemetery with ship-shaped stone settings. The positioning of the earliest hall seems to have been dictated by the presence of a Bronze Age barrow situated on a prominent hill (Niles 2007: 189 and map 2). Its position made spatial reference to other Bronze Age monuments at a greater distance, leading to the assertion by Niles that the sixth-century hall at Lejre was located in a place 'saturated with ancient associations' (Niles 2007: 189). The creation of the large cremation mound 'Grydehøv' in the mid-seventh century, some distance from the hall, seems to have signalled a change; the first halls were dismantled at broadly the same time (Niles 2007: 193). A new location was identified and a new hall built close to the approach roads and in a situation that would have made it highly prominent to those travelling in the region and to the site. Standing at the entrance to this new complex, one would have looked out at the 'Grydehøv' mound (Niles 2007: 193–7). A second hall was constructed nearly a kilometre away in the late seventh century. This building—identical in scale and size— was positioned close to a sacrificial mound and seems to have survived and served as structure for 300 years. A cemetery was also established next to 'Grydehøv' and seven ship-settings were erected. The second hall was dismantled at the turn of the first millennium, perhaps relating to the arrival of Christian ideas and traditions (for discussion of second hall and cemetery, see Niles 2007: 195–7).

The creative use and harnessing of ancient and more recent antecedent land-scapes are thus a feature emergent in a wide range of early medieval societies in north-west Europe. The legacy of Rome exerted a strong influence on the emergence and setting of power in regions of Europe that had once been part of the Roman Empire, but the use of the prehistoric to situate and frame the enactment of early medieval authority and law is strongly evident too and is not, as previously suggested, a solely Celtic phenomenon (*contra* Aitchson 1994: 310; Driscoll 1998: 144–5), or restricted to non-Christian societies.

A final site for discussion moves the debate away from residential or palatial complexes, but continues to emphasize the role of ancient monuments in the enaction and display of power. The monumental site of Anundshög, Västman-land, in Sweden is well attested in the written sources as a Viking *thing*-site active in the tenth and eleventh centuries. It has been subject to recent survey and excavations that have discovered an extensive array of hitherto unknown monumental features on the site (see Sanmark and Semple 2011). The location of the *thing*-site is partly bounded by a water course and marsh. It is highly accessible, located on a junction between a major land route, lake and navigable water course. The location represents a multiperiod palimpsest, with activity dating as early as the Bronze and Iron Ages. Excavations have produced evidence of Bronze Age activity, including a worked area or wooden platform to the south-east of the monument complex, and numerous hearths or cooking-pits and dumps of hearth material have been revealed in and around the main complex dating largely to AD 100–250. The large burial mound post-dates one of these cooking areas and is likely therefore to have been constructed in the Migration period. The ship-settings post-date this, and were probably added in the Viking Age. The recent field investigation at Anundshög revealed in addition a row of very large postholes for monumental timber settings, which stretched nearly 200 metres across the site from the fording place. This seems to have provided a formal boundary, both dividing the site from the route way and flanking *Eriksgata*, a route identified as a ceremonial way that linked assembly sites, and was used for ritualized royal itinerary by medieval kings (Bratt 1999; Sanmark 2009). There is more field investigation to be done, but the similarities are immediately evident. A naturally distinctive and accessible site attracted activity in prehistory. By the Migration period major funerary monuments were being constructed. There is considerable evidence from hearth material and cooking-pits for the use of the site repeatedly and periodically for assemblies and communal events of some kind. Funerary activity and additional monu-ments (such as ship-settings) were added throughout the Viking Age. The location of late Viking Age *thing*-sites, on major communications, at bridges and crossing places has been acknowledged by Alexandra Sanmark, who has pointed to the probable connection between this type of positioning and the need for kings to unify territory, for local magnates to participate in royal levels of administration, and for elites to signal royal authority and power to a subject population (Sanmark 2009). This ancient site, perhaps already a place of gathering periodically in the Migration period and after, was formalized as a *thing*-site by the addition of a range of new stone, timber, and earthen monuments that bounded the site, and perhaps even directed access and movement to, and at, the *thing*. This prestigious place of assembly, accessible via the royal route *Eriksgata*, reached its climax in terms of ceremonial architecture in a time when kingdom or state formation processes were at play in southern Sweden (Sanmark 2009; Sanmark and Semple 2011). The great inauguration sites of Ireland and the royal sites of Scotland demonstrate the purposeful selection of seminal, ancient places and landscapes for the setting of new aspirant statements of power in the historical moment when kings began to aspire to rule larger territories. Anundshög and other late Viking Age assembly sites came into operation under similar circumstances, as formal and ceremonial places of assembly—using ancient settings and marked with new monumental structures—linked into emerging royal itineraries. These ritualized routes circumnavigated territory and allowed kings to meet people at the assembly and to solicit support and enact power (Sanmark 2009; Sanmark and Semple 2011). Alex Sanmark has noted that this process of 'assembly site' formation might lie particularly in the tenth and eleventh centuries, within the period in which Christianity came to be adopted as the main religion in medieval Sweden and other parts of Scandinavia (Sanmark 2009). This provides an interesting potential framework for understanding the increasing monumentality connected with the setting of royal ritual. Christian influences might well have introduced concepts of formalized assembly and council and the correct choreography and setting for such practices. The evocation of the past, even if prehistoric, may potentially have been stimulated by contact with Christian societies and the Christian Church, within which linear time and the Roman Imperial past were highly significant in the framing of early medieval Christian power. It remains clear, however, that, in the sixth to tenth centuries, the political shift from local power structures to supra-regional systems of governance, and the emergence of families with 'nation-building' aspirations in societies within and without the Christianized world, resulted in an increasing adoption of ancient and antecedent monuments and places for the purpose of staging and enacting power.

Monuments and power in late Anglo-Saxon England

The evidence from Anglo-Saxon England points to a variety of intentional elite strategies that harnessed the ancient to royal and aristocratic activities including elite settlement, the choreography of conflict and the establishment of ecclesiastical foci, the funeral, assembly and public decision-making, and acts of punishment and damnation. Places of execution, also used for the burial of executed victims, were initiated sporadically in the seventh century, but became both more common and more regularized in and after the eighth century. In 1998, I argued that the seventh and eighth centuries saw dramatic change in how communities perceived and used prehistoric monuments. Locations initially sought out for individual burials or community burial grounds were emerging as locations for the execution of felons and the interment of the executed. Although the more detailed reworking of the evidence here largely supports this, it is also evident that this change in perception was not wholesale nor perhaps as dramatic as first envisaged. The evidence of persistent funerary rites involving prehistoric monuments in the eighth and even perhaps the ninth and tenth centuries (Chapter 2) suggests the widespread rites and practices of the fifth to seventh centuries were not relinquished suddenly or even willingly. In isolated cases, communities clung onto traditions involving the use of barrows and other types of monument for burial. However, as Chapters 4, 5, and 6 have argued, the changing use of barrows and other prehistoric monuments and the emergence of popular superstitions and beliefs around such features occurred simultaneously alongside the varied use of such features for a variety of elite spectacles. The harnessing of the prehistoric, in an increasingly rigid and formalized manner, to the purpose of judgement and execution, ties in with the less dramatic but nevertheless compelling evidence of the use of hill forts, Roman towns, and barrows as places for assemblies, councils and even inauguration rituals. The increasingly regularized adoption and use of old barrows and cemetery sites for the purpose of execution fits with evidence for a growing elite reach in terms of managing movement, activity, and the enactment of authority within their realms. To take this a step further, it also underlines the power of elite families and kings, who, it seems, could host an assembly at a major ancient landmark, use it as a theatrical frame to enhance the gravitas of an event, and consign an unfortunate felon to execution and burial to an eternal limbo and damnation beyond the sanctity of Christian burial. Royal individuals, despite the conversion, may have retained a power over the ancestral, and were able to use and bend it to their will and purpose.

By the eighth century, as Chapter 5 has explored, barrows (notably prehistoric ones) were featuring in literature in which they were portrayed as evil and haunted places associated with monsters and hellish creatures. The emergence of such perceptions in literature, in what broadly be considered the end of the conversion period, implies the introduction and acceptance of Christianity may have caused these changes in perception. In Chapter 5, the possibility of an intentional ecclesiastical emphasis on discouraging traditions and beliefs associated with old burial mounds is raised. Such stories may have encouraged people to turn away from important localized and popular ancestral places and the traditions connected with them. In the seventh and eighth centuries kings formalized legislation against criminal activities, the movement of goods and people in the landscape, and the rendering of tribute and the payment of wergild. The advent of deviant cemeteries certainly represents a simultaneous move to formalize the judicial powers of the king and the way in which justice was enacted. In light of the discussions of councils set in monumentalized places and within ancient hill forts, the situation of battles, and musters at historic and monumentalized sites, one begins to suspect that the choice of ancient places as locations for the punishment of criminals and the display of their bodies was a choice by kings too.

It is impossible to unpick the motivations, but the prose and poetic sources or indeed illustrative sources echo a clear archaeological signature and together they attest to the emergence of some types of ancient monument, notably barrows, as places synonymous with fear, with damnation, with monstrous inhabitants, and with hell by the late Anglo-Saxon period. In the same era that councils were held in monumental settings, and criminals were being executed at ancient barrows, churches were being built, refurbished, and embellished at sites hosting prominent and visible old earthworks including prehistoric and pre-Christian monuments. Individual monuments as well as 'landscapes' of remains were attracting the attention of the Church. The evidence presented in Chapter 4 certainly has its limitations, but it does at least signal a far greater variety of Church-driven activity in the shadow of prehistoric sites and monuments. This goes some way to countering the imbalance of attention given to the use of Roman sites and monuments and Roman building material by the Christian Church (see earlier discussions and Stocker with Everson 1990; Eaton 2000; Bell 2005). There is sufficient evidence to make a case for parallel traditions of situating churches and ecclesiastical sites in relation to prehistoric monuments and remains. The evidence is in itself diverse, however: encompassing minsters set in hill fort enclosures, early churches situated next to barrows of early Anglo-Saxon or pre-Christian as well as prehistoric date, and the occasional church set within multiperiod palimpsests. Royal and ecclesiastical interests can be discerned as well as potentially strong local influences exerted over church placement, resulting from popular preference, local tradition, and nodal places of political or spiritual pre-Christian significance. The siting of churches next to barrows emerged in Chapter 4 as something especially distinctive—leading to its use even as a motif or vignette in the *Vita Sancti Guthlaci*. It is possible that a barrow and its burial, irrelevant of actual date, could have emerged as an important pre-Christian cult-site, and the appropriation of such a place might represent a more large-scale assimilation of potent local places into the new geography of the Christian Church. Alternatively, the process could reflect a need to Christianize the burial place of a non-Christian family member, and thus redeem him or her from damnation—and might thus be allied to our increasing bundle of seventh- and eighth-century elite strategies. The act in some instances might even encompass an attempt to translate an ancestor into a Christian cult figure or saint (Stocker, Went, and Farley 1995).

At the very least, the consideration given here to churches situated in proximity to old pre-Christian and prehistoric remains suggests that the continental material narratives that attest to the aristocratic assertion of a new sanctity and status, achieved through the recycling and use of old Roman structures and *spolia*, may have been present too in England, but this was only of the material repertoires harnessed to elite, spiritual ends. Ancestral places, graves, enclosures, and on occasion large palimpsests, already seminal and resonant within the locality and region. They became a resource that secular elites increasingly sought out for use, and it would appear, a resource that the early Church was keen to manage as well (see also Stocker and Everson 2003; Everson and Stocker 2011).

Popular perceptions and landscape

By the ninth and tenth centuries, the use of prehistoric remains as locations for execution and deviant burial had become an accepted part of judicial practice, whereas the interment of individuals at prehistoric monuments for positive reasons had virtually, if not wholly, ceased. The choice of ancient monuments as execution sites was one component of a highly defined judicial process that sought to alienate the wrongdoer as far as possible from all conventional aspects of late Anglo-Saxon society. Prehistoric monuments which lay on administrative boundaries were favoured, the liminality of the location enhancing the separation of the wrongdoer from society. The use of a prehistoric monument (most often a barrow) also condemned the victims to a type of location increasingly portrayed in written and illustrative sources in terms that likened it to a hell-mouth or entry point to damnation and eternal torture. The use of several early Anglo-Saxon cemeteries as execution sites is extremely important. It emphasizes that by the tenth century the use of prehistoric barrows was almost certainly driven by a conception that these were burial places of the distant Anglo-Saxon heathen past.

The portrayal of barrows (by now all deemed ancient) and other types of prehistoric monument as haunted and evil locations also featured in prose and poetic sources, ecclesiastical literature, and place-names too. These perceptions, it seems, arose in the eighth century, perhaps initially as a product of changing landscape perception, encouraged by an ecclesiastical wish to distance people from traditional methods of funerary display. By the tenth century, such popular beliefs were more widely held, place-names attesting to the local perception of ancient monuments as haunted or monster-inhabited locations. This view was almost certainly encouraged by the increased use of such sites as places of execution and locations of burial for the executed (the damned), while popular perception in turn no doubt influenced the common use of such places as execution sites. What is especially clear from all the source material is that these locations were feared because they were viewed as places where the dead were still living or where the other world (hell) was close and tangible (see Hall

2002, 2007b). In late Anglo-Saxon literature, strong analogies are made between the grave and the torment and torture one would experience in hell. It is clear too that, in popular tradition, the living lived in fear of the dead, attested by evidence of a variety of unusual practices surrounding the corpse and the place of burial, such as stoning, the use of wooden planks and stakes, post-mortem beheading, and other forms of interference with the bodily or skeletal remains (Blair 2009). In the source material, which refers to barrows, by this late point there is a tendency to portray the monument as a fissure or opening to hell—indeed a hell-mouth. It is interesting that, in the place-name corpus, all the types of locations associated with supernatural creatures are places where one could imagine finding entry to the supernatural world: pits, holes, pools, wells, and, of course, burial mounds. The types of places that had perhaps once been perceived as conduits to the other world, re-emerged as access points to the heathen afterlife in a Christian hell. These perceptions are apparent in several remarkable late Anglo-Saxon manuscript illuminations in which hell, or the mouth of hell, is represented by mounds in which the damned are depicted with injuries concurrent with contemporary judicial punishments (see Chapter 6 and Semple 2003b).

The march of literacy and knowledge seems to have diminished the fears and associations apparent in the first literary accounts of the eighth century. The use of these sites for aristocratic, military, and judicial purposes must certainly have served to break down even further the widespread reverence and mythic invest-ment in ancient monuments that we can discern immediately before and after the conversion. Their role as ancestral sites and places synonymous with ancestry and identity changed. These monuments became more symbolic of the heathen past after the conversion and as time moved on they were bound into tales and stories with folkloric and legendary qualities. After the ending of Anglo-Saxon England, evidence for associations between the supernatural and prehistoric monuments are few and far between. Belief in treasure-guarding dragons can be tracked well into post-medieval folklore, but the dragon rarely, if ever, occupied a barrow after the Norman Conquest, inhabiting instead hills, caves, or rocky fissures (Simpson 1978). The court assizes for Cutteslowe in Oxfordshire in 1199, however, record the inhabitation by thieves of the *hoga* or 'barrow' at Cutteslowe, implying that although the superstitious and imaginative associations of the late Anglo-Saxon world may have evaporated, barrows still survived in the English landscape as the haunts of robbers and were still perhaps considered liminal and undesirable places to visit or reside (Cam and Crawford 1935).

Final thoughts and future paths

There is much that remains to be explored within the broad perimeters of this topic. The use and circulation of prehistoric material, for example, is not inter-rogated here. The special selection of prehistoric artefacts and their curation and usage by early and later medieval societies are a rich area for exploration. The recent discovery at Street House in North Yorkshire of a polished and set glass bead of Iron Age date, matching the discovery of a similar jewel at the elite female burial at Cow Lowe, is just one indication that it was not just the material remains of the Roman past that were being circulated and recycled by Anglo-Saxons (Sherlock and Simmonds 2008). Likewise the long-term curation of specific items such as bronze spear-heads and stone axes, as well as their use in apotropaic rituals, suggest such objects on occasion retained a potent agency for later generations (Carelli 1997; Gerrard 2007).

The association between settlements and monuments could also be taken further. The indications in a recent paper by Mark Gardiner (2011) of formalized approaches and settings for late Anglo-Saxon elite residences provides a starting point for an investigation of the environmental and historic setting of such seats of power. The wider European scene is also beginning to produce far more evidence of the situation of large hall-complexes and places of ceremony and assembly with reference to ancient remains, and this too remains uncharted as a comparative study, and one that should be undertaken alongside a consideration of the valorization of the Roman material legacy by Christian elites on the Continent.

The interrogation of this strand of Anglo-Saxon practice has thus turned up a surprising array of evidence. It is no longer possible to dismiss 'reuse' as something blandly homogenous, found only within the funerary arena or indeed relevant only to discussions of pre-Christian Anglo-Saxon society. Instead, it has assisted in seeing the 'longitudinal' view. Such practices may have changed but served to influence the choices and preferences of successive generations. The elite strategies that lie at the heart of this debate can be seen to stem and develop from the localized traditions and practices of the fifth and sixth centuries. New emerging royal families were able to draw selectively upon popular local traditions, sites and places and the mythology that had developed around people, and their place in the land. The Anglo-Saxons can now be considered as a society with a strong awareness of the prehistoric as well as the Roman past. The evidence here suggests that, before conversion and literacy, a sense of past was already present and connected to the early medieval population's sense of place, and the physical landscape was a means of describing that. The influences of Christianity are perhaps most profound in the introduction of ideas that stimulated elites to have a longer and more far-reaching vision of the past and the future. This can be argued to have prompted a multiplicity of strategies for articulating power, identity, and lineage that involved the harnessing of the ancient to physical forms of spectacle and display. By the late Anglo-Saxon era, evidence suggests that kings were using ritualized activity at selected places in the landscape to create authority intentionally situated with reference to the past. It can be argued that this, in itself, was the creation of a grammar of power, built upon the inherited intellectual territory of past centuries. This existed, however, alongside a vibrant popular perception of landscape that was influenced by the Church and state, but also had a profoundly local flavour. Anglo-Saxon populations retained memories of the past, embedded within and around ancient features in the landscape, but also creatively worked the landscape into their folklore and stories. These legends, by their development and transmission, served to connect people to place and were powerful enough to render certain places and monuments important for almost six centuries, allowing them to exert a profound influence on the shape of elite secular and ecclesiastical activity as late as the eleventh century.

Appendices

Abbreviations

B	barrow
BA	Bronze Age
C	crouched
D	diameter
E	east
Ex	extended
F	fixed
N	north
P	prone
R–D	ring-ditch
S	South
W	West

Appendix 1

Burials of fifth- to eighth-century date in the East Yorkshire study area

Birdsall, SE8240 6290

B108 (Aldro group) excavated by Mortimer in 1868. D: 24.6 m with R-D. Central circular hollow contained a clean, burnt deposit of unurned, calcined bone. Finds included portions of burnt and fused bronze weapons, portions of two or three daggers 'cast in a mould', and many other pieces 'twisted by fire'. A circular fragment of bronze, *c*.1.25 cm, set with a circular piece of polished rock crystal or glass and a second piece containing a similar glass setting were also present. Indications that the mound had been disturbed above this cremation deposit. Lucy suggests C5th/6th (Mortimer 1905: 56–7, figs 107–8; Lucy 1999: 24).

Bishop Wilton, Beacon Hill, Garrowby Wold, SE8123 5635

B69 excavated in 1866 by Mortimer. D: 13.4 m. A skull, parts of an arm bone, a spear-head, and portions of two blades from a pair of iron shears were located near the centre. A circular hole containing the calcined bones of an adult and portions of burnt wood were located in the barrow, indicating a prehistoric date for the monument. Lucy suggests C5th/6th, but Williams suggests C7th on the basis of shears (Mortimer 1905, 144–5; Baldwin Brown 1915: iv. 805; Meaney 1964: 288–9; Eagles 1979: 423; Williams 1996; Lucy 1999: 24).

Huggate, SE8580 5596

Cremation urn discovered in a chalk bank at Cross-Dykes pre-1984. The linear earthwork may be late BA in origin (Dent 1984: 33; Lucy 1999: 26).

Kilham, TA0792 6598

Several urns and other finds located in a chalk pit, *c*.2 miles from Kilham in C19th. Further finds include a C5th square-headed brooch, a radiate brooch with geometric decoration, a developed cruciform brooch of the C6th, five pairs of wrist-clasps, three pairs of flat annular brooches and two odd ones, a bronze ring, strap ends, two buckles and weapons including spear-heads, and a shield-boss (all at York Museum). Excavations in 1824 by Thomas Cape of Bridlington located in addition a skeleton in a sandpit 'where we had formerly been successful', head to the NW with the legs crossed. Buckle, brooches, wrist-clasps, and beads found near the lower part of the body. Lucy suggests C5th/6th (Mortimer 1905: 344; Smith 1912b: 87–8; Baldwin Brown 1915: iv. 806–8; Elgee and Elgee 1933: 180–1; Meaney 1964: 292; Eagles 1979: 211; Lucy 1999: 26).

Kilham, TA0570 6460

Child burial with two annular brooches and a bronze pin. Lucy suggests C5th/6th (Eagles 1979: 438; Lucy 1999: 26).

Kilham, TA0740 6450

Six inhumation burials in coffins found in a water-main trench, pre-1979. Suggested C8th (Eagles 1979: 438; Faull 1979: 306; Lucy 1999: 40).

Painsthorpe Wold, Kirkby Underdale [B4], SE8221 593 [Meaney 8230 5820]

B4 of the Painsthorpe Wold group, prehistoric in date. Numerous interments likely to be prehistoric in date, but later secondary inhumations also present. One with fragments of Anglo-Saxon pottery and one occupying a central position at a rough depth of 50 cm, comprising a C female burial, head WSW, on right side, accompanied by an annular brooch, knife, beads, a bronze workbox, and the remains of a chatelaine, suggesting a C7th date. Other undated inhumations in secondary positions may also represent burials of C5th–7th date (Mortimer 1905: 114; Smith 1912b: 92; Baldwin Brown 1915: iv. 805; Meaney 1964: 295–6; Eagles 1979: 439; Williams 1996; Lucy 1999: 36).

Painsthorpe Wold, Kirkby Underdale [B102], SE8246 5826

B102 on the western margin of the chalk hills, D: *c*.9 m. A secondary burial (C) was found slightly below the base of the mound on its left side with an iron knife at the pelvis with impressions of woven cloth. C5th–7th (Mortimer 1905: 123; Eagles 1979: 209; Lucy 1999: 27).

Painsthorpe Wold, Kirkby Underdale [B200], SE8270 5850

B200 had suffered late disturbance but was established as a prehistoric barrow, and a thin bronze cup or dish and an iron spike belonging to the shaft of an Anglo-Saxon spear were found in a central position, implying a centrally placed, secondary burial had been disturbed. Possibly C7th (Mortimer 1905: 120; Meaney 1964: 296; Eagles 1979: 439; Lucy 1999: 27).

Uncleby, Kirkby Underdale, BX, SE8219 5941

D: 29 m, contained seventy-six individuals located in seventy-two graves. The bodies were laid on the surface of the mound and then covered in earth, increasing the dimensions of the mound. Those beyond the limit of the monument were in conventional grave-cuts. Most burials F. Orientation also varied. Burials showed a tendency to cluster towards the southern half of the barrow, with the highest concentration to the SE. A group of female burials were clustered in the SW sector of the barrow. Twenty had no grave goods and seven had knives only. Weapons were few. Grave goods included disc pendants, workboxes, a tripod ring bowl, and annular brooches with Style II animal heads. Placed in the C7th (Greenwell and Rolleston 1877: 135–6; Mortimer 1905: 118; Smith 1912a; 1912b: 89–92; Baldwin Brown

1915: iv. 805–6; Sheppard 1919: 311–12; Elgee and Elgee 1933: 184; Meaney 1964: 302–3; Eagles 1979: 439; Williams 1996; Geake 1997: 159; Lucy 1999: 36).

Londesborough, SE8715 4625

Cemetery located adjacent to a Roman road. Chalk quarrying between 1870 and 1895 produced many inhumations with glass and amber beads, bronze brooches, bronze and iron buckles, iron knives, and food vessels. Additional discoveries with beads, buckles, and 'iron blades' suggest additional early Anglo-Saxon graves. C5th–6th (Mortimer 1905: 353; Smith 1912b: 77–8; Baldwin Brown 1915: iv. 804; Meaney 1964: 294; Sheppard 1919: 314–15; Swanton 1974; Eagles 1979: 441; Cramp and Miket 1982: 6–8, fig. 5; Lucy 1999: 27–8).

Market Weighton, SE870 410

Two burials S of modern settlement. A female burial (P) was located in a rock-cut grave with an amber and glass necklace, a pair of massive developed cruciform brooches, a single cruciform brooch, a possible belt plate, two pairs of wrist-clasps, a horn ring, a pair of girdle hangers, and pots, indicating a C6th date. The adjoining grave was that of a male of C7th date. A knife, buckle, spear-head, and part of a seax accompanied the male burial. No associated monumental structure (Sheppard 1906a, 1906b; 1907: 77; Sheppard 1909: 67, fig. 30–1; Smith 1912b: 74–5, 87; Sheppard 1919: 319; Meaney 1964: 295; Geake 1997: 158; Lucy 1999: 28, 36).

Nunburnholme, SE8640 4887

Three skeletons located in a chalk pit near a possible early route. All C, with heads to the E. Associated goods included silver earrings, silver finger rings, three brooches, two wrist-clasps, toilet implements, an urn, iron objects, a bronze buckle, and a bead necklace. Lucy suggests C5th/6th (Eagles 1979: 444; Faull 1979: 96; Lucy 1999: 28).

Rudston, TA097 677

A pair of C5th brooches found pre-1912 in the immediate proximity of the churchyard (Smith 1912b: 89; Baldwin Brown 1915: iv. 806–7; Meaney 1964: 297; Lucy 1999: 29).

Rudston, TA1132 6721

Inhumations were discovered in a sandpit. An inhumation burial with a knife is recorded and a biconical urn and iron spear ferrule with the remains of an additional inhumation burial. Eagles notes that these burials were made in or near a linear dyke, an association verified by the Royal Commission survey. A strap-end was also found at the same location, and in 1970 a coin of Eanred (810–41). Lucy places these burials in the C5th/6th. Records of the discovery of 'small plain handmade sherds, a fragment with incised line and another with a hollow boss' suggest fragments of Anglo-Saxon pottery and the possibility of cremation burials or perhaps settlement activity in the vicinity (Eagles 1979: 445; Faull 1979: 307; Lucy 1999: 29).

Rudston, TA1121 6746

Urns, swords, and spears, probably of early Anglo-Saxon date, were found during landscaping at Thorpe Hall. C5th–6th (Sheahan and Whellan 1856: 489; Eagles 1979: 445; Lucy 1999: 29).

Rudston, TA1073 6657

Excavations of a large barrow D: 30.5 m provided extensive evidence of prehistoric burials. Five burials were identified as secondary Anglian burials: three, E and S, had 'hands placed on hips', another with head to the SW and C, and close-by another heavily disturbed secondary burial. The body positions of the three male burials found in close proximity suggest these are secondary burials, but of an indeterminable date (Meaney 1964: 296–7; Williams 1996).

Sledmere-Fimber Station, SE9076 6131/9104 6144

Undated human remains discovered during quarrying 'at a point where the entrench-ments are cut by the road to Sledmere' some 366 m eastwards from the crossroads near Fimber Station. Human bones and 'an iron sword' were noted 'where the road to Malton cuts the same entrenchments', about 274 m N of Fimber Station. Lucy suggests C5th/6th. Given the presence of a sword, a C6th or C7th date is also plausible. An entrenchment recognized by Mortimer is shown on the 1st edition OS and is recorded in the name of the field: 'Old Dike Plot'. The two groups of burials are both related to this linear entrenchment and are located only c.300 m apart (Mortimer 1905: 192–3; Eagles 1979: 448; Lucy 1999: 29).

Garton Slack I, Garton-on-the-Wolds, Sledmere, SE9566 6181

Numbers of skeletons discovered in C19th. Mortimer recorded forty-two graves in the earthwork known as the Double Dyke, all W–E and supine, twenty-nine Ex, one contracted and nine C. Fragments of Anglo-Saxon pottery and one or two knives, a spear-head, arrowhead, and a bone comb were found. The finds appeared to be residual, apart from the bone comb. In 1959, c.91 m to the E and beyond the cross-roads, seven W–E burials were located, Burial five with an iron knife and Burial two with a group of eight series G, J, K, and R sceattas contained in a purse under the left side of the pelvis, indicating a date of deposition after c.720–5. A large communal cemetery of mixed sex is suggested, associated with an older linear earthwork. The cemetery was in existence in the C8th. Survey by the Royal Commission indicates the presence of a curvilinear enclosure complex immediately S of the site that may be early medieval in date by comparison to sites like West Heslerton, Rudston, and Boynton. The pottery and animal bone may therefore be residual and derive from disturbed domestic contexts. The cemetery and settlement may not be contemporary. Garton Slack I and II can be identified, however, as groups of burials placed in a spatial relationship with this undated settlement complex (Mortimer 1905: 264–70; Smith 1912b: 82; Sheppard 1919: 313; Meaney 1964: 289–90; Grierson and Blackburn 1986: table 13; Geake 1997: 158; Lucy 1999: 40).

Garton Slack II, Sledmere, SE9500 6100

In 1868 Mortimer excavated a barrow D: *c*.21 m positioned on a natural rise. Four secondary burials were located in the silted barrow ditch and comprised a juvenile burial (C), located next to some burned juvenile bones; an adult, head to the SE, with legs bent back from the knees; an adult positioned on right side, head to W, knees bent up, hands in front of the breast, with traces of the bones of an infant NNW of the skull. No objects were found in association. An even shallower burial, head to the N and knees bent, was associated with two corroded pieces of iron, a knife, and a long iron point, found in the belt area. In 1872 a further burial (C) and accompanied by pig bones was located on the extreme northern edge of the prehistoric mound. This burial group suggested by Mortimer to lie some 200 yards (*c*.182 m) S of Garton Slack I. The position has remained unknown, but the Royal Commission survey shows a curvilinear settlement complex within this area (see pp. 34–5 and Fig. 2.8). Two ring-ditches are apparent as part of these crop marks and one is located *c*.182 m S of the linear earthwork (Mortimer 1905: 245–6; Smith 1912b: 80–1; Meaney 1964: 290).

Warter, SE8990 5310

A complex of five prehistoric barrows (D: *c*.18–24 m), E of Blanch Farm, produced an inhumation burial with a sword and pot. Precisely which barrow contained this inhumation is unknown (Mortimer 1905: 322; Eagles 1979: 451; Williams 1996; Lucy 1999: 30).

Wharram, SE8360 6272

Two skeletons were located in the up-cast of a ditch cutting a prehistoric round barrow (D: *c*.14 m): a male inhumation, supine, and parts of disturbed skeleton. No accompanying objects were located. The burials were disturbed by a later linear ditch, perhaps demarking the parish boundary which bisected the barrow and ran the length of the entrenchment. An upright post had been erected on the barrow at some point (Mortimer 1905: 50–2; Meaney 1964: 303; Eagles 1979: 422; Williams 1996; Lucy 1999: 30.)

Fimber, SE8940 6060

'Church Hill' barrow stood on a natural prominence in the centre of the village of Fimber. In 1869 the old church was removed and foundations for the new structure were excavated. Traces of an earlier and larger church structure were evident with signs of burning. It had stood upon an oval mound constructed of horizontal beds of clay, interspersed with patches of loose flint. At the W end of the church, beneath the position of the old tower, *c*.1.5 m below the present surface and 0.9 m below the debris of the original church, were some animal bones, carbonized wood, a flint axe, and several small urns. To the SE there were indications of a trench *c*.2 m deep extending due S, and many ox teeth and animal bones were noted in the fill. Within the new church foundations, at a depth of *c*.30 cm, an adult skeleton was discovered, with the burnt bones of a juvenile below. Struck flints were discovered and an oval grave containing an adult skeleton, head NW (C), accompanied by struck flint and a food vessel. A further burial near the E-end of the porch was found with a pennanular brooch close-by. Another burial near the eastern end was unaccompanied, but a curious article of bronze and copper lay close-by. Later in the C19th some 73 m SE of the church, the remains of six or more bodies (C) were recovered accompanied by fragments of iron and pottery. The skeletons were female and juvenile. These burials were made close to the York Street Roman road (Mortimer 1905: 190–2; Smith 1912b: 79; Meaney 1964: 288; Eagles 1979: 431; Faull 1979: 319; Williams 1996; Geake 1997: 158; Lucy 1999: 35).

Kemp Howe, Cowlam, Cottam, SE9616 6628

B209, excavated by Mortimer in 1878, proved to be a prehistoric long barrow modified into a round barrow. D of combined monuments: 26–30 m. Six unfurnished adult interments on the SE side were in narrow graves, knees F, heads to the NW, and no goods. Five of the burials were dug into the mound and one was positioned in the ditch. Subsequently, in 1969, twelve burials in ten graves were located during re-excavation of the site by Brewster. Brewster's graves A and B, from the mound, are suggested to be Mortimer's graves four and three respectively. Geake suggests that the burials were arranged W–E to S–W and N–E with heads towards the centre of the mound. Although Lucy suggests seven burials were in coffins and Williams cites five with coffins with corner straps of iron, citing Wilson and Hurst (1969), Geake argues that one was buried in a coffin with a hook fastening and the layout of two others suggested the presence of coffins. Calibrated radiocarbon dates from two burials are centred between AD 725 and 745. Two sunken-featured buildings and a further possible post-built structure were identified. Activity continued after the Conquest: a stone-lined pit was located in the forecourt of the long barrow, containing Staxton ware and C13th–14th pottery (Mortimer 1905: 336–7; Meaney 1964: 292; Wilson and Hurst 1969: 241, 285; Eagles 1979: 427; Faull 1979: 303; Williams 1996; Lucy 1999: 40).

Thwing, TA032 708

During the 1970s and 1980s a settlement of Anglo-Saxon date was discovered and excavated within a prehistoric circular earthwork. A cemetery was positioned centrally in the enclosure containing at least 132 individuals. It may have been associated with a mortuary chapel. Twenty-six graves had coffins or chest fittings, and wooden markers were found with a similar number. Two anomalous decapitated burials were found. Amber and glass beads and a knife were located in one grave, radiocarbon-dated to AD 789–992. Other dates centred on the C7th–8th. Further calibrated dates obtained from bones are 410–670, 434–643, 642–758, 650–860, 673–852, 724–961, and 781–991. The cemetery is associated with the settlement. The use of coffins and grave markers, as well as the presence of a possible chapel, suggest a Christian community, but the mix of male, female, and juvenile graves argues against a monastic establishment (Geake 1997: 159; Lucy 1999: 40; Terry Manby: pers. comm.).

Appendix 2

Weaponry discovered in possible non-funerary contexts at prehistoric monuments

Cherbury Camp, Berkshire, SU373 963

Type E1 spear-head, C6th or earlier. Surface find at Cherbury Camp, a multivallate hill fort (Swanton 1973: 77–81; 1974: 40).

Devil's Dyke/Ditch, Cambridgeshire, TL6100 6100/TL621 613

Two axes, spur and stirrup, and lance head all of iron (spur and stirrup lost), discovered during the levelling of part of Devil's Dyke on Newmarket Heath. No human remains reported. (Fox 1923: 263, 292, pl. 35; Lethbridge 1938: 309; Meaney 1964: 64).

Badbury Rings, Dorset, ST964 030

Single type E1 spear-head, C6th or earlier. Badbury Rings, multivallate hill fort (Swanton 1973: 77–81; 1974: 30).

Hardown Hill (Whitchurch Canonicorum Parish), Dorset, SY405 944

Ten spear-heads of broadly C5th–7th date, 'an iron axe like a Roman wood cutter's axe', a knife, a shield-boss, and a broken square-headed small-long brooch. No recorded human remains. Recovered from one of a group of barrows on Hardown Hill. There are indications that this was a robbed barrow, and the soils are likely acidic (Wingrave 1931; Meaney 1964: 81; Swanton 1973: 49–55, 103–7; 1974: 55).

Spettisbury Rings, Dorset, ST915 020

Four spear-heads broadly C5th–7th. Surface finds in the univallate hill fort (Swanton 1973: 37–9, 49–51, 77–83; 1974: 83).

Wendens Ambo, Essex, TL518 363

A pot and three or four spear-heads and a conical shield-boss found in the N side of Mutlow Hill. Other old pieces of iron are mentioned, a pot showing signs of burning, and a spear-head. No human remains were found. Broadly C5th–7th. Mutlow Hill is a natural knoll of sand and clay, and thus bone is unlikely to survive. A late Anglo-Saxon assembly site. (Fox 1923: 265; Meaney 1964: 89).

Preston Candover, Hampshire, SU604 403

Anglo-Saxon spear-head and a seax suggesting a C7th–8th date discovered in Long Barrow Field on the S of Preston Candover on chalk geology. The spear-head was located in the barrow and the seax at the edge (Shore 1893: 285–6; Hawkes 1940a: 278, n. 5; 1940b; Meaney 1964: 99; Gale 1989: 71; Geake 1997: 72–4).

Whitchurch, Hampshire, SU477 518

Sword, described as Anglo-Saxon, no date or illustration, found when a long barrow on Twinley Farm was ploughed out, round barrow also recorded. Chalk downland (Crawford 1933: 296; Meaney 1964: 101).

Ditton, Kent, TQ713 588

Type H3 spear-head, C5th–6th from a natural knoll or barrow (Kelly 1962; Swanton 1973: 111–14; 1974, 43).

Langham, Norfolk, TG020 411

Iron spear-head with fragments of the haft and a shield-boss. No human remains. Likely C5th–7th, located in BA barrow at the bend in the bank of the parish boundary. On chalk (Clarke 1938–40: 238–9; Meaney 1964: 177).

Poningland, Norfolk, TG271 020

Five iron spear-heads, and a sixth large spear-head. C5th–7th. Found in a barrow on Poningland Heath, now lost. No human remains recognized, but the geology may be acidic (Meaney 1964: 180; Clarke 1938–40: 248).

Barrasford, Northumberland, NY919 736

Shield-boss 'of extraordinary dimensions', six silver discs from a shield, a broad two-edged sword and knife, C6th–7th. BA cairn on escarpment above Barrasford Burn. On limestone, thus survival of bone is unlikely. No illustration (Rome Hall 1876: 14–15; Meaney 1964: 198; Miket 1980: 290).

Chinnor, Oxfordshire, SP765 002

Shortly before 1899, workmen came across two spear-heads, a javelin head, and a U-shaped scabbard chape. Undated. One of a pair of barrows on Hempton Plain, 366 m (400 yds) SW of Bledlow Cross; geology unlikely to preserve human bone well (Thurlow Leeds 1939: 348; Meaney 1964: 206).

Lyneham, Oxfordshire, SP297 210

A shield-boss, seax, and two spear-heads, all unassociated with human remains. The seax suggests a date in the C7th/8th. Shield-boss located at the NE end of the long barrow, while the spear-heads were located on the NE edge of the camp known as the 'Roundabout'. Skeletal evidence survived in the mound, but these items were not found in association. Five or six barrows in the vicinity. Evidence of a cemetery, barrow burials, and an undated secondary burial in the long barrow. A 'sword' found in isolation is thought to be an ingot bar (Conder 1893–5: 404–10; Thurlow Leeds 1939: 358; Meaney 1964: 210; Gale 1989; Geake 1997: 72–4).

Wredon/Readon Hill, Ramshorn, Staffordshire, SK085 467

Iron spear-head with shaft remaining and narrow iron knife *c.*20.3 cm long, no association with human remains; found in a large barrow on Readon Hill. Two skeletons also found, separate to spear-head, central in the mound and secondary (Bateman 1861: 122–3; Smith 1908: 209; Meaney 1964: 221).

Coombes, Sussex, TQ182 084

Knife and spear-head found *c.*270 m from a BA barrow above Combes. The spear-head seems close to Swanton's type E2, which is likened to an C11th Scandinavian type. Chalk downs (Dixon 1849: 269; Grinsell 1934: 236; Meaney 1964: 248; Swanton 1973: 81–3).

Barbury Castle, Ogbourne St Andrew, Wiltshire, SU150 763

Iron seax, fragments of others, smaller single-edged knives, and two iron spear-heads. Spear-heads are suggested as type E2, thus C6th–7th, but seaxes suggest a C7th–8th date range. Found inside Barbury Castle hill fort, the spear-head separate from the group of iron objects. No evidence of burials, although a series of undated burials were located in the ramparts. There is some confusion as to whether these finds are Iron Age or Anglo-Saxon, and whether they were found together with a group of Iron Age iron tools (Cunnington 1933–4: 174; Grinsell 1957: 94; Meaney 1964: 265; Swanton 1973: 81–3; Cunliffe 1978: 418, fig. 34).

Swallowcliffe Down, Wiltshire, ST967 255

Spear-head, Swanton type, C2, C5th–7th. Found in the top of the barrow beneath the surface on the southern side. The BA barrow was reused in the C7th for an extravagant female bed-burial. Type C2 spear-heads are found in early contexts but are also common in the C7th. The spear-head was not associated with the burial, but was an isolated find in the mound make-up. The barrow stood on the chalk downland. Perhaps an intentional deposition or the remnant of a ploughed-out male secondary burial, or a disturbed find from the female grave (Swanton 1973: 52–3; Speake 1989: 8).

Knap Hill, Wiltshire, SU121 637

Iron sword considered C6th in date found during excavations of the Iron Age/Romano-British enclosure adjacent to the Neolithic causewayed enclosure on Knap Hill. Located in surface accumulation on the northern fringe of a long mound within the plateau enclosure. The long mound is in fact a midden of Roman date. The find was not in association with human remains and the site is on the chalk downland (Cunnington 1911–12; Robinson 2002).

Fimber, East Yorkshire, SE894 606

See discussion in Appendix 1 for full context. Spear-head, undated, located during work on the village pond situated beneath the spur on which the church now sits (Mortimer 1905: 192; Smith 1912b: 79; Meaney 1964: 288).

Severus's Hills, Yorkshire, SE574 512

Ornamented spear-socket with boss of mixed metal of Ringerike style, C10th. A chance find from one of three glacial mounds, one of which is named Howe Hill 2 miles W of York city walls. The acidic soils are likely to have consumed traces of human bone, but the late date of the object remains interesting (Wardell 1849: 401–2; Lang 1981: 159–60).

Four Crosses, Llandysilio, Wales, SJ272 185

Iron spear-head and javelin in a position that suggests they had been thrust into the ground. The spear-head is thought to be C5th/6th, the javelin C5th–7th. Neither is thought to be of Anglo-Saxon workmanship, although both linked to Germanic areas N of the Rhine. Discovered during excavation of a prehistoric ring-ditch near the Welsh border in immediate proximity of Offa's Dyke. The opposing side of the monument was used for early medieval secondary burials (Barford et al. 1986).

Appendix 3

Medieval churches situated with reference to prehistoric monuments

Aylesbury, Buckinghamshire, SP815 135. St Mary the Virgin. C13th fabric and a *c.*1160 font; earliest documentary reference at DB indicates mother-church status; C12th life of St Osyth says the saint was brought up in the minster at Aylesbury in the C7th. Minster church and town lay within an Iron Age hill fort. The ramparts were re-fortified in the C7th (Allen and Dalwood 1983; Yeoman 1986; Blair 1994: 27).

Cholesbury, Buckinghamshire, SP929 071. St Lawrence. C14th fabric and a C13th font. Church sits within a prehistoric subcircular earthwork, enclosing *c.*10 acres (Clinch 1908: 22–3; Jennings 1908: 334–5).

Edlesborough, Buckinghamshire, SP 969 190. St Mary the Virgin. C13th. Positioned on an undated, stepped mound/earthwork (Allcroft 1927–30: ii, pl. III, no. 2; Jennings 1925; Lipscomb 1831–47: iii. 349).

Great Kimble, Buckinghamshire, SP824 058. St Nicholas. Mid-C13th fabric and a late C12th font. Entrenchments and a mound described to the N of the church, close to the churchyard boundary (Jamison 1908a).

Stone, Buckinghamshire, SP785 125. St John the Baptist. C12th. The font dates to *c.*1140. Described as situated on an artificial mount/barrow, near the intersection of two ancient tracks (Lipscomb 1831–47: iv. 463; Jamison 1908b; Pevsner and Williamson 1994: 658–9).

Taplow, Buckinghamshire, SU906 821. Unknown dedication. Geophysical survey identified the plan of what may be a post-Conquest church. Positioned next to a large, flat-topped mound. Excavations in 1883 recovered a late C6th–7th rich elite male burial. The 1883 excavations of the mound noted several flint tools. Excavation of the hilltop has revealed a large Iron Age hill fort. Barrow was exterior to the entrance (Stevens 1884; Meaney 1964: 59; Stocker et al. 1995; Elias Kupfermann: pers. comm.).

West Wycombe, Buckinghamshire, SU827 949. St Lawrence. Formerly the parish church; C18th alterations have virtually obscured all evidence of the historical development, but C13th–14th fabric is visible. Nearly circular earthwork, destroyed to the SE by the construction of the Dashwood mausoleum. Undated (Jenkinson 1925).

Chapel House Farm, Wervin, Cheshire, SJ419 719. Unknown dedication. Ruined chapel, described as a C13th chapel of ease. Chapel stands on an artificial mound, which geophysical survey indicated may be a long barrow (Nenk et al. 1995).

Carn Brea, Cornwall, SW685 407. Unknown dedication. Chapel destroyed in the C18th. Hilltop was intensively occupied in prehistory. Neolithic huts have been excavated. Enclosed by Iron Age fortifications. Inside, traces of Roman occupation are known and evidence for a medieval cliff castle and a chapel (Allcroft 1927–30: i. 145–6; Pevsner 1951: 41).

St Buryan, Cornwall, SW409 257. St Berian. Ecclesiastical community mentioned in 1086, but perhaps as early as the C10th. Iron Age/Romano-British round earth-built ringwork, reoccupied in the Christian period (Youngs et al. 1986).

Awliscombe, Devon, ST134 018. St Michael. Post-Conquest, with much C16th remodelling. Large stone at the threshold of the W door (Cherry and Pevsner 1999: 141–2).

Knowlton, Dorset, SU023 102. Dedication unknown. A ruined church with a C12th nave and chancel. Church sits on a low, oval mound, within a subrectangular enclosure defined by a low bank, at the centre of a large oval earthwork enclosure of Neolithic date. The Neolithic henge is one of four enclosures of probable prehistoric date (Anon. 1975: 111–15; Morris 1989: 72–3, fig. 18).

Alphamstone, Essex, TL878 354. St Barnabas. Saxon or Norman nave with Roman brick quoins. Stands on a raised area above the surrounding fields. Rodwell and Rodwell note the thickness of the nave walls, suggesting they may be pre-Conquest. BA and Iron Age pottery found within the churchyard. Many sarsens are present on the site, and one large example projects from under the SW corner of the nave. The Sites and Monuments Record mentions a BA cremation (Rodwell and Rodwell 1977: 94).

Wickham St Paul, Essex, TL826 371. All Saints. C13th screen and a C16th tower. A mound is a central feature in the churchyard (Rodwell 1981: 132; Pevsner 1996: 425).

Beckford, Worcestershire, SO976 358. St John the Baptist. Norman. Large oval barrow, 50 m due E of the church plus evidence of activity of the C2nd BC in the locality (John Blair: pers. comm.; Pevsner 1968: 76–7).

Aston, Herefordshire, SO461 718. St Giles. Norman. Mound, 120 yards NE, likely to be a motte. Second smaller mound lies half a mile NNE of the church (Gould 1908a: 224; Pevsner 1963: 67).

Thruxton, Herefordshire, SO436 346. St Bartholomew. Early Perpendicular E window, but mostly decorated. 'A possible BA barrow, 126' in diameter lies 100 yards W of the church surrounded by a ditch with a slight outer bank on the NW.' Pevsner records that a C19th excavation revealed a rough-hewn chamber of stones within the mound. No record of these excavations can be traced. Recorded as a motte (Gould 1908a: 229, 231; Pevsner 1963: 300).

St Weonards, Treago, Herefordshire, SO496 243. St Weonard. C13th. Large flat-topped mound 70 yards SSW of the church. Traces of a surrounding ditch on E side of the mound. Evidence of two prehistoric cremations beneath the mound, one within a stone cist. No evidence for multiple phases could be discerned in the report (Wright 1855; Pevsner 1963: 284–6).

Bramshaw, Hampshire, SU270 160. St Peter. Some fabric of C12th date survives in the N transept. Positioned upon the summit of a raised oval/subrectangular hill with appearance of an artificially altered knoll, perhaps the site of a small enclosure/fortification or large barrow (Allcroft 1927–30: ii. 335–6).

Brockenhurst, Hampshire, SU305 017. St Nicholas. Norman. Church positioned on a natural hill; height of the churchyard, the drop to the new cemetery to the N, and the mounded appearance of the immediate area around the building suggest positioning over some kind of earlier earthwork (Allcroft 1927–30: ii. 252–3; Pevsner and Lloyd 1967: 146).

Burton/Buriton, Hampshire, SU740 200. St Mary. C12th date. Supposedly constructed on a mound (Shore 1892: 32; Allcroft 1927–30: ii. 252; Pevsner and Lloyd 1967: 154–5).

Cheriton, Hampshire, SU581 285. St Michael. C13th fabric and font. *Chiriton* 1162 is suggested as *OE Ciricetun*, 'church farm', which would imply that a church was present before the Conquest. Church is positioned on an extraordinarily large mound, which has all the appearance of an artificial or artificially altered feature (Laughton and Locke 1908; Pevsner and Lloyd 1967: 164; Coates 1989: 52).

Corhampton, Hampshire, SU612 202. Dedication unknown. Early C11th. Described as 'standing on a little mound on the right-hand bank of the stream, the churchyard lying to the S and containing a Yew tree 26' in circumference'. On a striking, oblong/oval rise, perhaps a natural spur, although earthworks are clearly visible within churchyard describing some form of subrectangular enclosure or platform. A supposed Roman sarcophagus lies in the churchyard (Brough 1908: 246; Taylor and Taylor 1965: i. 176–8; Pevsner and Lloyd 1967: 182).

Hinton Ampner, Hampshire, SU597 275. All Saints. Late Anglo-Saxon church *c*.950–1100. Barrow lies a short distance WNW of the church (Taylor and Taylor 1965: i. 316–17; Pevsner and Lloyd 1967: 294).

St Catherine's Hill, Winchester, Hampshire, SU483 276. St Catherine. C12th. Iron Age hill fort.

Kings Capel, Hereford, SU559 288. St John the Baptist. Late C13th. Adjacent to large barrow (see 1st edn 25 inch Ordnance Survey map). Capel Tump, is S of the churchyard, the church is aligned SW–NE (Pevsner 1963: 204).

Tetbury, Gloucestershire, ST890 930. Dedication unknown. A minster mentioned in 681. A substantial earthwork enclosure on the S side (Leech 1981: 86–9; Pevsner 1999: 684–5).

Willersey, Gloucestershire, SP118 387. Dedication unknown. 'Cada's minster' is a landmark mentioned in the bounds attached to a late C10th charter restoring an estate to the abbey of Pershore (S786; B1282). Church would have been located somewhere near the NW corner of Willersey Iron Age hill fort (Hooke 1987).

Coldred, Kent, TR274 475. St Pancras. Saxo-Norman. Church stands within the lines of 'an ancient fortress, a fosse with a ballast thrown inwards'. VCH mentions relics of the Roman age from within the enclosure. A large mound is evident in the SE corner. *A fortified* enclosure with a motte? The mound appears to overlie the entrenchment (Gould 1908b: 394; Newman 1983: 277–8).

Kennardington, Kent, TQ974 321. St Mary. Fabric in the perpendicular style, and a fragment of C13th cross-shaft, incorporated in a wall. Vestiges of an irregular enclosure, undated (Gould 1908b: 397; Newman 1980: 351).

Woodnesborough, Kent, TR308 567. St Mary the Virgin. Tower, aisles, and nave just precede 1200. High conical mound once existed near the church, from which a glass vessel, fibula, and spear-head were found. A collection of thirty glass vessels were also located at the mound, and Akerman illustrates a single survivor: a glass claw-beaker (Akerman 1855: 34–6; Meaney 1964: 141; Ellis Davidson and Webster 1967: 7–8; Newman 1983: 502–3).

Melling, Lancashire, SD598 711. St Wilfrid. *c.*1300. Mound due E of the church, possibly a motte, but has the appearance of a barrow (John Blair: pers. comm.; Gardner 1908: 529–31; Pevsner 1991: 176–7).

Breedon-on-the-Hill, Leicestershire, SK405 233. St Mary and St Hardulf, also perhaps St Peter. Base of the church tower is Norman, the rest medieval and later. Monastery founded here in the late C7th. Early Christian cemetery has been excavated on the site. The sculptural fragments indicate rebuilding or extensive additions in the C8th. The early monastery and current church are within an Iron Age hill fort (Dornier 1977; Jewell 1986; Morris 1989: 456).

Edenham, Lincolnshire, TF062 218. St Michael and All Angels. Pre-Conquest fabric *in situ*, inside the church, in the S aisle. Three-foot section of cross-shaft: C9th. The church is on a platform, bounded by earthworks (Taylor and Taylor 1965: i. 227, figs 459–60).

Crowland, Lincolnshire, TF250 104. Crowland Abbey. According to the *Vita Sancti Guthlaci* a monastery was established in AD 716 by Æthelbald, King of Mercia. See Chapter 5 for discussion of the *c.*730–40 written source that describes St Guthlac inhabiting an ancient barrow. Examination of the island has identified a place about 500 m N of the church at Anchor Hill. Stukeley identified a chapel here, the last remains of which were destroyed in 1870. Air photographs suggest the building may have overlain a round barrow and sat within an irregular ditched enclosure (Canham 1890; Lane 1988; Stocker 1993).

Bessingham, Norfolk, TG166 370. St Mary. Saxo-Norman, *c.*1100. Church placed on high land which appears to form part of an earthwork (Taylor and Taylor 1965: i. 62, fig. 385).

Cranwich, Norfolk, TL782 949. St Mary the Virgin. Pre-conquest (950–1100). Church is positioned on distinctive circular mound or rise (Allcroft 1927–30: ii, pl. II, no. 1, 253; Taylor and Taylor 1965: i. 181–2).

Winwick, Daventry, Northamptonshire, SP625 738. St Michael. C13th. Positioned on a large circular mound (Allcroft 1927–30: i. 12, fig. 3; Pevsner 1973: 463–4).

Yeavering, Northumberland, NT 925 305. Unknown dedication. C6th–7th royal residence, with a hall-like structure surrounded by a cemetery, interpreted as a church. Bede describes how Paulinus travelled to Ad Gefrin in 626 and conducted a mass baptism. From its earliest phases the complex incorporated prehistoric remains including a round barrow and ring-ditch (Hope-Taylor 1977).

Bampton, Oxfordshire, SP312 033. St John the Baptist. Norman or possibly Late Anglo-Saxon core. The Deanery, to the W, contains a Norman two-storey chapel. The early Norman two-storey chapel overlies a BA ring-ditch, and may have replaced some form of pre-Conquest religious focus. The church, with a possible Late Anglo-Saxon core, now known to overlie a smaller ring-ditch, while a third, undated barrow is suggested on the S side of the church, within the churchyard. Three fragmentary *in situ* burials overlay the inner lip of the smaller ring-ditch, and the earliest is radiocarbon-dated to AD 680–890, showing it could be as early as *c*.700. Burial was thus taking place, in relation to the barrows/ring-ditches, before the first documented reference to the Christian religious community in the 950s (Blair 1994, 1998, 1999, 2005).

Eynesham, Oxfordshire, SP433 091. Eynesham Abbey. C7th–10th monastic activity, pre-dating the 1005 abbey buildings. BA enclosure formed a focus for several C6th–7th buildings. The ground-level timber structures of C7th–10th date overlay this (Blair 1994: 63).

Ludlow, Shropshire, SO511 747. St Laurence. Church enlarged in 1199. Barrow partly removed during the enlargement of the church. Three interments were found identified by the clergy as the bones of Irish saints, and were interred in the church. The place-name (*Ludelawe* 1138, 'barrow by the torrent'), is considered to refer to the barrow demolished in 1199 (Hearne 1774: iii. 407; Wright 1841: 13–14; Gelling and Foxall 1990: 186).

Stapleton, Shropshire, SJ470 045. St John the Baptist. Unusual C12th two-storied parish church, in odd alignment SW–NE. Originally a domestic chamber block? A large artificial mound on the SE edge of the churchyard (John Blair: pers. comm.; Pevsner 1958a: 293).

Cadbury Castle, Somerset, ST62 25. Dedication unknown. Cruciform structure (E1) assigned to the late Anglo-Saxon period. Iron Age fortification used as a mint-town (occupation and re-fortification are also apparent in the C5th–6th). Numismatic evidence indicates the life of the *burh* was particularly short, *c*. AD 1010 to 1020 (Hill 1978: 223; Alcock 1995).

Stanton Drew, Somerset, ST598 631. St Mary. Church remodelled in 1889, but chancel may date from C13th. Three stone circles, a 'cove', and a single standing stone, all dating to the second millennium BC (Grinsell undated; Pevsner 1958b: 262–3).

Croxall, Staffordshire, SK197 136. St John the Baptist. Chancel *c*.1200. Large mound on the S side of the church contained bones; a tumulus is marked on the 1st edn. 25 inch Ordnance Survey map, immediately E of the church (Pevsner 1974: 110–11).

Wednesbury, Staffordshire, SO986 953. St Bartholomew. *c*.1200. Church built on a hill, on which are remains of an Iron Age hill fort (Ekwall 1960: 503; Ellis Davidson and Webster 1967: 8; Pevsner 1974: 298–9; Palliser 1976: 42; Gelling 1988: 161).

Alfriston, Sussex, TQ521 030. St Andrew. C14th. Church positioned on a large low mound. An Anglo-Saxon cemetery of C5th–7th date overlooks the settlement (Nairn and Pevsner 1965: ii. 396–7, pl. IV, no. 1; Welch 1983: ii. 345–7).

Apuldram, Sussex, SU841 033. St Mary. C13th. C19th drawing shows the church positioned on a large, low mound. The church, in a low-lying area of land, is positioned on a low circular mound (Allcroft 1927–30: ii. 313, fig. 2; Crook 1953a; Nairn and Pevsner 1965: 84–5).

Berwick, Sussex, TQ518 049. Unknown dedication. Nave, chancel, and other details late C13th–15th. An obvious barrow, of oval plan within the churchyard (Nairn and Pevsner 1965: 414–15; John Blair: pers. comm.).

Chithurst, Sussex, SU842 231. St Mary. Intact C11th church with probable pre-Conquest date. Situated on large subrectangular/oval platform with artificial appearance

(Manwaring 1912; Allcroft 1927–30: ii. 312–13, fig. 1; Nairn and Pevsner 1965: 186–7; Taylor and Taylor 1965: 157–8).

Ditchling, Sussex, TQ325 152. St Margaret. C13th. Church sits on a natural rise/spur, surmounted by a distinct mound or platform (Nairn and Pevsner 1965: 481–2).

Ford, Sussex, TQ002 037. St Andrew. Saxo-Norman. Fragment of Anglo-Saxon sculpture decorated with interlace is visible above the doorway in the vestry. A radial arrangement of six burials, placed in a circle with the heads inwards discovered in churchyard 5 feet below the ground surface. Area is flat and low-lying and the church sits on an oval rise. A much larger square platform lies adjacent to the churchyard (Manwaring 1900: 106; Nairn and Pevsner 1965: 225–6).

Lewes, Sussex, TQ414 104. St John sub Castro. A late Anglo-Saxon doorway attached to the E of the church derives from old church, which stood a little to the N. Two barrows lie within the churchyard, one of BA date. These are part of a series of tumuli considered by Bleach to be Roman (Nairn and Pevsner 1965: 552; Bleach 1997).

Pagham, Sussex, SZ883 974. St Thomas the Martyr. The structure dates from the C13th, although a fragment of C11th herringbone work survives. Cremations, possibly of Anglo-Saxon date were found within the churchyard, while more recently BA cremations were recovered. Church positioned on distinctive spur (Crook 1953b; Nairn and Pevsner 1965: 289–90).

Brinklow, Warwickshire, SP436 796. St John the Baptist. Earliest fabric: Late Perpendicular. A mound called Brinklow Mount, believed to be a barrow, stands near to the E of Brinklow churchyard. Identified as a motte in the VCH, but the name Brinklow might indicate that it started life as a barrow (Gardner 1904: 360–2; Pevsner and Wedgwood 2000: 218).

Stoneleigh, Warwickshire, SP330 726. St Mary. Norman. An artificial mound lies 300 yards SSW of the church: Motslow Hill (*OE* gemot + stow), a medieval moot site (Gover et al. 1936: 184; Pevsner and Wedgewood 2000: 405).

Avebury, Wiltshire, SU099 699. St James. A church of *c.*1000 survives fossilized within the current structure. Three cross-shaft fragments of C10th date attest to an earlier ecclesiastical focus. Church is positioned exterior to the western entrance to the Neolithic henge and stone circle (Semple 1994).

Chisbury, Wiltshire, SU280 659. St Martin. The small chapel within the eastern entrance to a late Iron Age hill fort, built mainly in flint, appears to be of C12th date. Identified with small *burh* of Chisbury mentioned in the Burghal Hidage, which disappeared from the record during the reign of Athelstan (Cunliffe 1973: 431; Hill 1978: 219).

Malmesbury, Wiltshire, ST 930 873. Malmesbury Abbey. Mid-C7th. Malmesbury was a major centre for defence and trade by the mid-C10th. Haslam considers that the Christian foundation was established within or by an Iron Age hill fort. An Iron Age ditch and Iron Age and Anglo-Saxon ramparts were revealed with associated ceramics, adjacent to *The Nun's Walk*. A series of radiocarbon dates suggest a range of *c.*800–110 BC for the development of the hill fort (Watkin 1956; Hill 1978: 219; Luce 1979: 1–15; Haslam 1984: 111–17; Anon. 2000: 249).

Ogbourne St Andrew, Wiltshire, SU1888 723. St Andrew's. Fabric mid-C12th. Large round barrow in churchyard immediately E of the chancel. Excavated in 1885 revealing BA sequence of deposits and a secondary Anglo-Saxon burial. Male buried in coffin with elaborate metal clamps and fittings. Fittings could be placed broadly in the C8th–11th, but perhaps more likely to be of C9th–10th date (Cunnington 1885; Goddard 1913–14: 300, no. 11; Baldwin Brown 1915: iii. 150, pl. XVIII, no. 2; Cunnington 1933–4: 165; Cunnington and Goddard 1934: 60; Grinsell 1957: 93–4; Meaney 1964: 272; Freeman 1983: 138–9; SMR no. SU17 SE609; summary of discovery, context, and dating of fittings and burial in Semple 2003a; comparable fittings from York Minster: Kjølbye-Biddle 1995: 515, 518 and fig. 187; from St Oswald's Priory, Gloucester: Webber 1999: 210–13, 215, fig. 5.24 (E); from Paderborn Cathedral: Stiegemann and Wemhoff 1999: 339).

Old Sarum, Wiltshire, SU136 327. St Mary. Large circular Iron Age hill fort. C6th as a British stronghold attested by battle in 552 (documented in the C9th). Hill fort re-fortified in time of Alfred, and coins of Athelstan (925–40) and Edgar (959–75) found within the enclosure. It was an emergency *burh* in the C11th and a mint. By the end of the Anglo-Saxon period a chapel or church with this dedication is suggested. The cathedral was constructed at Old Sarum in the last quarter of the C11th. Another church, placed at the east gate, was dedicated to the Holy Cross and was observed by Leland in 1540. This may be no earlier than the C13th (Hill 1962; Hill 1978: 223; Anon. 1980: 1–46; Haslam 1984: 124–5).

Overton, Wiltshire, SU133 68. St Michael and All Angels. Overton church rebuilt in C19th. Earlier structure had a C14th chancel arch and C15th fabric. A BA barrow identified by Fowler immediately E of the church (Stevenson 1980; Fowler 2000: pl. XLVII, fig. 8.2).

Hanbury, Worcestershire, SO954 644. St Mary. The C18th church stands on the site of the Anglo-Saxon minster, established in the C8th. Associated prehistoric remains: Iron Age hill fort (Pevsner 1968: 183–4; Blair 1988: pl. V).

Kempsey, Worcestershire, SO848 490. St Mary. Minster first mentioned in 799. Stands within an early earthwork on the gravel terrace (Pevsner 1968: 183–4; Sims-Williams 1990: 375–6).

Cropton, Yorkshire, SE756 892. St Gregory. Earliest fabric: 1844. Large mound in churchyard with artificial appearance (John Blair: pers. comm.; Pevsner 1966: 133).

Fimber, Yorkshire, SE894 606. Dedication unknown. Present church C19th. See full discussion in Appendix 1 (Mortimer 1905: 189–93).

Goodmanham, Yorkshire, SE889 432. All Hallows. Earliest phase C12th. C19th images show church perched on large mound or knoll. A contour survey has not provided conclusive support. Churchyard heavily eroded by the encompassing roads, particularly on the E and S (Blair 1995: 22–4).

Rudston, Yorkshire, TA097 677. All Saints. Norman tower represents the earliest phase, but a Christian focus is likely in the late Anglo-Saxon period, given the place-name. OE *rod* + *stan*, 'rood/cross stone'. Large artificial monolith in churchyard, probably of Neolithic date (Stoertz 1997: 25–7).

Stanwick, Yorkshire. St John the Baptist. C13th, but C12th fabric and pre-Conquest sculpture suggest an earlier foundation. Stands within and close to areas enclosed by substantial fortifications of the C1st BC to the mid-C1st AD. Church situated in circular, embanked enclosure. Stanwick hoard discovered in small copse to N. One possible Roman or Anglo-Saxon burial known in vicinity of the prehistoric earthworks. These large broken-ditched enclosures are a class of monuments now associated with gathering, assembly, and perhaps seasonal trade and craft production in the late Iron Age (Wheeler 1954; Morris 1989: 454–5; Haselgrove et al. 1990: 37–90).

Thwing, Yorkshire, TA02 70. No dedication. Small, rectangular structure associated with cemetery and C7th–10th settlement. See full discussion in Appendix 1 (Manby 1985, 1987; Terry Manby: pers. comm.).

Ripon, Yorkshire, SE313 713. Cathedral of St Peter and St Wilfrid. Earliest phase: C7th. Mound *c.*200 m E of Cathedral—a natural knoll. Ailcy Hill derives from the *OE* term *elf*, 'elf' + *ON haugr*, 'mound/barrow' (Hall and Whyman 1996).

Appendix 4

Monuments and the supernatural in Anglo-Saxon charter-bounds

(B: Birch 1885–93 Cat. No.; G: Gelling 1976; K: Kemble 1839–48 Cat. No.; S: Sawyer 1968 Cat. No.)

The terms listed and translated here were initially collected using the Old English Microfiche Concordance (Di Paulo and Venezky 1980) and later cross-referenced using the Electronic Sawyer (http://www.esawyer.org.uk/). References to supernatural creatures or entities are listed first (4(i)). These are drawn from the entire corpus of surviving charter-bounds. Excerpts from the bounds of Berkshire (4(ii)), Hampshire (4(iii)), Sussex (4(iv)) and Wiltshire (4(v)) follow. Counties are those that preceded the reorganization of 1974. All known mentions of the following terms: *beorg* (hill/barrow), *burh* (stronghold), *dic* (ditch), *hlaw* (barrow), and *stan* (stone). For expediency, only key relevant words are translated here. The interpretation of the Old English terms relies largely on published translations and those offered by the Electronic Sawyer. The entire list has also been checked and some translations revised by Dr John Baker of Nottingham University. The date of the charter is given and the modern place-name and a reference to Sawyer's 1968 handlist as well as references to the handlists published by Birch and Kemble when relevant.

4(i) SUPERNATURAL CREATURES AND ENTITIES

Grendel

1. of doddan hrycge on grendeles pyt/of grendeles pytte on ifigbero, 'grendel's pit'. AD 739. Crediton (DEV) S255 (B1331).
2. 7 and lang hagan to grendeles gatan æfter kincges mearce innan brægentan; of brægentan æfter merce innan tatan, 'grendel's gate'. AD 951. Blecceanham/Hampstead (MDX). S1450 (B1290).
3. ðonne on grendles mere ðonon on dyrnan geat, 'grendel's mere'. AD 931. Ham (WLT). S416 (K353/B677/B679). Grundy 1919: 224–8; Jacobsson 1997: 147.
4. and long dices in grendels mere; of grendels mere in stancofan, 'grendel's mere'. AD 951x955. Old Swinford (WOR). S579 (B1023). Hooke 1990: 165.

Woden

5. Þonne suð rihte on wodnes dic, 'woden's ditch'. AD 970. Clifton near Bath (SOM). S777 (B1257/7). Grundy 1935: 211–13.

6. Ærest westan norþ and hyt mæraþ wodnes dic, 'woden's ditch'. AD 961. South Stoke (SOM). S694 (B1073/1/6). Grundy 1935: 206–8.

7. Þonne forð a be wyrit truman þæt on wodnes dic, 'woden's ditch'. AD 963. Stanton Prior (SOM). S711 (B1099/3/4). Grundy 1935: 190–2.

8. of ðære leage be wyrt walan oð wodnes dic, 'woden's ditch'. AD 965. Stanton Prior (SOM). S735 (B1164/3). Grundy 1935: 193–5.

9. This beoþ ðe mere to Bilsetnetun, & to Wodnesfeld & erest of Hindebroce in ðeo dic bitwonem Ettingeshale & Bilsetnetun, 'woden's field/open ground'. AD 996. Upper Arley, Eswich, Bilston, Willenhall, Wednesfield, Pelsall, Ogley, Hilton near Wall, Hatherton, Kinvaston, Hilton near Wolverhampton and Featherstone (STF). S1380.

10. upp to þam ealdan herepaðe be westan wodnes beorge, 'woden's hill/barrow'. AD 900. Alton Priors (WLT). S1513 (B1513/Rob 17/14). Grundy 1919: 159–64.

11. upp to þam ealdan herepaðe be westan wodnes beorge, 'woden's hill/barrow'. AD 825. Alton Prior's (WLT). S272 (B390/2.1). Grundy 1919: 159–64.

12. on woddes geat, 'woden's gap/gate'. AD 825. Alton Prior's (WLT). S272. Grundy 1919: 159–64.

13. Þonne On wodnes dene, 'woden's valley'. AD 939. East Overton (WLT). S449 (B734/2). Grundy 1919: 240–7.

14. Þonne on hyrs leage up to wodnes dic on titferþes geat, 'woden's ditch'. AD 939. East Overton (WLT). S449 (B734/3). Grundy 1919: 240–7.

15. And swa to wodnes dic, 'woden's ditch'. AD 933. North Newton and Oare in Wilcot (WLT). S424 (B699/10). Grundy 1919: 187–91.

16. Ðonne ofer wodnes dic, 'woden's ditch'. AD 903. Stanton St Bernard (WLT). S368 (B600/6). Grundy 1919: 210–15.

17. Þonon on þa wearh roda on wodnes dic, 'woden's ditch'. AD 957. Stanton St Bernard (WLT). S647 (B998/10). Grundy 1919: 210–15.

Grim

18. of grimes hylle þæt hit cymþ to sponwælle, 'grim's hill'. AD 816. Hawling (GLO). S179 (B356/19).

19. Þonne up to grimes dic, 'grim's ditch'. AD 956. Burcombe (WLT). S631 (B985/4). Grundy 1919: 237.

20. Of ðam paðe on ðane greatan þorn ðe stynt wið Grimes dic, 'grim's ditch'. AD 1045. Ditchampton (WLT). S1010 (K778/5). Grundy 1919: 191.

21. þonon andlang grimes dic to hunan wege to þam stane, 'grim's ditch'. AD 956. Langford (WLT). S612 (B934/4). Grundy 1919: 283.

Thunor and Tiw

22. on þonæ greatan beam of þam beamæ on þunres lea middæ, 'Thunor's wood pasture/clearing'. AD 939. Droxford (HMP). S446 (B742/15).

23. Þonne on thunres lea middæ weardæ swa gæ, 'Thunor's wood pasture/clearing'. AD 826. Droxford (HMP). S276 (B393/16). Grundy 1924: 77.

24. and lang mearce on þunres lea norþeweardne þonon andlang mearce on holan weg, 'Thunor's wood pasture/clearing'. AD 956. Millbrook (HMP). S636 (B926/2). Grundy 1926: 242.

25. And swa east andlang mearce on þunres lea norðeweardne, 'Thunor's wood pasture/clearing'. AD 1045. Millbrook (HMP). S1008 (K781/6). Grundy 1926: 242.

26. Pedan hrycg & æt læce þæt forræþe on þunres feld norþan an hid, 'Thunor's field/open land'. AD 956. Merstham (SUR). S528 (B820/12).

27. Ðone to ðunres felda, 'Thunor's field/open land'. AD 854. Hardenhuish (WLT). S308 (B469/4). Grundy 1919: 171.

28. In tyes mere, 'Tiw's pool'. AD 849. Crofton Hackett, Rednal, Wast Hills (WOR). S1272 (B455). Hooke 1990: 135–40; Jacobsson 1997: 158.

Dragons

29. and anne to þes drakenhorde in on þar siderer, 'dragon's hoard'. AD 994x996. South Damerham, Martin, Allenford and Toyd (HMP). S513 (B817/11). Grundy 1924: 69.

Giants

30. to flegestane, 'Giant's stone'. AD 1015. Chilton (BRK) S934 (K1310). Gelling 1976: 767.

31. ðonon flecges garan suðe wardan, 'Giant's triangular piece of land'?. AD 895. Hagbourne/Didcot/Upton (BRK). S354 (B565/K1069/GIII(b). Gelling 1976: 756–7.

32. thonne to Aenta dic, 'Giant's ditch'. AD 1026. Kings Worthy (Hampshire). S962 (Kemble 743). Grundy 1926: 168.

33. Ðonne on enta hlewe on fecces wudu, 'Giant's barrow'. AD 1033. Poolhampton in Overton (Hampshire). S970 (K752/6). Grundy 1927a: 180–1.

34. Þonon on entan hlew, 'Giant's barrow'. AD 940. Poolhampton (HMP). S465 (B763/7). Grundy 1927a: 178.

Puca and Scucca

35. Scuccan hlaw, 'demon/goblin's barrow'. AD 795. Warren Farm, Horwood (BUC). S138 (B264/B849).

36. Of lytlan wylle into pucan wylle, 'goblin's well'. AD 946. Weston (SOM). S508 (B814/22).

37. Of þam cumbe up on hone lytland hæþfeld on pucan wylle, 'goblin's well'. AD 772. Bexhill (SSX). S108 (B208/3.2).

Þyrs

38. Ondlang þæs sices innon þone þyrs pytt, 'giant's pit'. AD 883x911. Marlcliff, Cleeve Prior (WOR). S222 (B537/6). Hooke 1990: 157.

Other supernatural and heathen references.

39. be eastan welandes smiððan, 'wayland's smithy'. AD 955. Compton Beauchamp (BRK). S564 (B908). Gelling 1976: 692–4.

40. Of Leofwynne mearce to þam hæþenan beorge. And of þam hæþenan beorg eft in to Drægtune, 'heathen hill/barrow'. AD 1019. Drayton (HMP). S956 (Edwards/4). Stenton 1955: 82–3; Whitelock 1955: 553; Finberg 1964: no. 153.

41. of hafokes beorhge on þonne wyte wege on þæt sclæde of þam sclæde on Echilde hlæwe a þa smye wicce, of Echilde hlæwe on hengestes earæs, 'to Echild's barrow to the——? witch'. AD 957. Heighton (SSX). S648 (B1000/1).

42. Of ðam homme on hæðene beorge, 'heathen hill/barrow'. Date unknown. Bengeworth (WOR). S1590 (K1358/3). Grundy 1927b: 107–12, 146.

4(ii) MONUMENTAL MARKERS IN BERKSHIRE CHARTER-BOUNDS

43. þanune on þone anlipan beorh, 'only/solitary barrow/hill'. AD 956. Milton. S594 (B935). G714.

44. on grenan beorh, 'green hill/barrow'. AD 949. Welford. G663, 5.

45. middeweardan to loddere beorge, 'beggar hill/barrow'. AD 956. West Ginge. S583 (B981). G746–7.

46. of þam hamma on grenan beorh, 'green hill/barrow'. AD 956. Welford. S622 (B963). G665–7.

47. Ærest of fearnbeorhge, 'fern hill/barrow'. AD 935. Farnborough. S411 (B682), G671–2.

48. wið eastan brocenan beorg, 'broken or uneven hill/barrow'. AD 935. Farnborough. S411 (B682), G671–2.

49. þanen to þan stanberwe, 'stone hill/barrow'. AD 947. Ashbury. S524 (B828), G694–6.

50. and ðanon on gemærbeorg, 'boundary hill/barrow'. AD 868. Lockinge. S1545 (B523). G742.

51. þonon on æceles beorg, 'eceles or church hill/barrow' or 'Achilles' hill/barrow' (Dragon Hill, an artificially flattened natural mound). AD 958. East Woolstone. S575 (B902). G682–4; see Breeze 2000: 142–4 for discussion of Achilles.

52. on þonnæ beorg, 'hill/barrow'. AD 958. East Woolstone. S575 (B902). G682–4.

53. of hæsel lea west rihte to borsenan beorge, 'burst (uncertain) hill/barrow'. AD 939. Brightwalton. S448 (B743). G660–1.

54. to laurocan beorghe, 'lark's hill/barrow'. AD 957. Buckland. S639 (B1005). G715–16.

55. þonon on wæardæs bæorh, 'Weard's or possibly watchman's hill/barrow'. AD 856. West Woolstone. S317 (B491). G680–2.

56. andlang ge maæres on ælfredes beorh, 'Ælfred's barrow'. AD 977. Kingston. S828 (K1276). G708–9.

57. of mæres crundelle on dinra beorh, 'barrow/hill of coins'. AD 955. Compton Beauchamp. S564 (B908). G692–4.

58. andlang furh on þone stan beorh. 'stone hill/barrow'. AD 931.Watchfield. S413 (B675). G697–8.

59. on mærbeorh, 'boundary hill/barrow'. AD 931. Watchfield. S413 (B675). G697–8.
60. so up endlangfurtz to mereberwe, 'boundary hill/barrow'. AD 947. Ashbury. S524 (B828). G694–6.
61. þane to elden berwe, 'old hill/barrow'. AD 947. Ashbury. S524 (B828). G694–6.
62. þanen on lortanberwe, 'Lorta's hill/barrow'. AD 947. Ashbury. S524 (B828). G694–6.
63. þare þanen to þe litel berwe, 'little hill/barrow'. AD 947. Ashbury. S524 (B828). G694–6.
64. andlang herpaþes to imman beorge, 'Imma's hill/barrow'. AD 944. Brimpton. S500 (B802). G643–4.
65. on þonæ beorh, 'hill/barrow'. AD 958. East Woolstone. S575 (B902). G682–4.
66. to þon bradan beorge, 'broad hill/barrow'. Blewbury, Aston Upthorpe and Tirrold. S496 (B801). G758–61.
67. On weasthealf ðrym beorgas, 'three hills/barrows'. AD 964. Hendred. S724 (B1142). G747.
68. to totan cumbe æt þam beorge, 'hill/barrow'. AD 944. Blewbury, Aston Upthorpe and Tirrold. S496 (B801). G758–9.
69. oþ foran on gean þone beorh, 'barrow/hill'. AD 956. Wootton and Sunningwell. S590 (B932), G726–9.
70. Ðonne þis synd þa gemæro þæe mæde æt ennanbeorgu, 'Enna's hills/barrows'. AD 956. Wootton and Sunningwell. S590 (B932), G726–9.
71. to foxes beorge, 'Fox's hill/barrow'. AD 944. Blewbury, Aston Upthorpe and Tirrold. S496 (B801). G758–61.
72. of braccan heale on ruwanbeorh, 'rough barrow'. AD 942. Winkfield. S482 (B778), G646–7.
73. þæt up to þam miclan beorge, 'big barrow'. AD 944. Blewbury, Aston Upthorpe and Tirrold. S496 (B801). G758–61.
74. þon on cat beorh, 'cat hill/barrow'. AD 948. Stanmore. S542 (B866). G651.
75. þonne þær west ofer þa twegen beorgas, 'two barrows'. AD 951. West Chieveley. S558 (B892). G652–5.
76. þonon andlang gemæres on þone lytlan beorh, 'little barrow'. AD 951. West Chieveley. S558 (B892). G652–5.
77. Ærest on heafd beorh, 'head barrow'. AD 944. Brimpton. S500 (B802). G643–4.
78. þonon suð andlang heafda on babban byorh, 'Babba's hill/barrow'. AD 964. S724 (B1142). G747–8.
79. þæt on friðelabyrig, 'Friðela's stronghold'. AD 955x957. Wytham and North and South Hinksey. S663 (B1002). G729–31.
80. in to hremmesbyriges norðgeate, 'the north gate/gap of the Raven's stronghold'. Date unknown. Uffington. S1208 (B687). G686–9.
81. of lange dic in to æscæsbyriges suðgeate, 'the south gate/gap of Æsc's stronghold'. Date unknown. Uffington. S1208 (B687). G686–9.
82. on þare crundel bi est þa Ertheburgh, 'earthwork/earth built stronghold'. AD 947. Ashbury. S524 (B828). G694–6.
83. to Rammesbury, 'Raven's stronghold'. AD 947. Ashbury. S524 (B828). G694–6.
84. east andlang þære lace þæ scyt wið cerenburhg westan, 'stronghold by the Ceren [name of stream]'. Date unknown. Charney Bassett. G704–5.

85. þonon ofer bleo byrig dune, 'variegated stronghold' (Blewbury Hillfort on Blew-burton Hill). AD 964. Aston Upthorpe. S725 (B1143). G766–7.

86. þæm wudu wege be eastan telles byrg, 'Tell's stronghold' (Hardwell Camp). AD 903. Hardwell. S369 (B601). G684–6.

87. in to paddebyrig, 'toad stronghold'. Date unknown. Uffington. S1208 (B687). G686–9.

88. be westan þære ealdan byrig, 'old stronghold' (Bussock Camp). AD 951. West Chieveley and Beedon. S558 (B892). G652–5.

89. uppan lauercebyrig, 'lark stronghold'. Date unknown. Uffington. S1208 (B687). G686–9.

90. Ærst of curspandic, 'curly ditch'. AD 939. Brightwalton. S448 (B743). G660–1.

91. þon' on lippan dic, uncertain—perhaps 'Lippa's ditch or ditch with a lip'. AD 956. Wootton and Sunningwell. S590 (B932). G726–9.

92. on þa mærdic, 'boundary ditch'. AD 956. Benham. S591 (B942). G668–9.

93. þon on wufstanes dic, 'Wulfstan's ditch'. AD 956. Wootton and Sunningwell. S590 (B932). G726–9.

94. þær utt andlang dic, 'ditch'. AD 958. East Woolstone. S575 (B902). G682–4.

95. on scortan dic, 'short ditch'. AD 958. East Woolstone. S575 (B902). G682–4.

96. þæt on ða dic, 'ditch'. AD 956. Hawkridge Wood. S607 (B919). G645.

97. of þam stanæ on þa æaldan dic, 'old ditch'. AD 856. West Woolstone. S317 (B491). G680–2.

98. to þære dic, 'ditch'. AD 968. Cumnor. S757 (B1222). G731–2.

99. Of þam steorte. In to bulen dic, 'Bula's ditch'. Date unknown. Uffington. S1208 (B687). G686–9.

100. of bicandice, 'Bica's ditch'. AD 955. Compton Beauchamp. S564 (B908). G692–4.

101. of þan þorne on þa readan dic, 'red ditch'. AD 955. Compton Beauchamp. S564 (B908). G692–4.

102. ðet on þa ealdan dic, 'old ditch'. AD 968. Cumnor. S757 (B1222). G731–2.

103. into sceorten dic, 'short ditch'. Date unknown. Uffington. S1208 (B687). G686–9.

104. be eastan welandes smidðan, 'Wayland's Smithy' (Wayland's Smithy—chambered long barrow). AD 955. Compton Beauchamp. S564 (B908). G692–4.

105. of hudes lade to þære scortandic, 'short ditch'. AD 956. Fyfield. S603 (B977). G709.

106. andlang weges on ða dic æt, 'ditch'. AD 956. Wootton and Sunningwell. S590 (B932). G726–9.

107. on ða ealdan dic, 'old ditch'. AD 956. Kennington. S614 (B971). G725–6.

108. to þon hæþenum byrgelsum æt þære ealdan dic, 'to the heathen burials at the old ditch'. Blewbury, Aston Upthorpe and Tirrold. AD 944. S496 (B801). G758–61.

109. andlang weges to hæsel dic, 'hazel ditch'. AD 956. Wootton and Sunningwell. S590 (B932). G726–9.

110. andlang mores ðonon on ðone ealdan dic, 'old ditch'. AD 895. Cholsey and Moulsford. S354 (B565). G757.

111. Ærest on ða ealdan dic, 'old ditch'. AD 968. East Hanney. S759 (B1224). G742–3.

112. on ða dic, 'ditch'. AD 942. Appleton with Eaton. S480 (B777). G723–4.

113. and so endlangdiches, 'ditch'. AD 947. Ashbury. S524 (B828). G694–6.

114. of wittan mære on cyninges dic, 'king's ditch'. AD 895. Hagbourne, Didcot, Upton and Chilton. S354 (B565). G756–7.

115. þæt on þa ealdan dic þæ lið betwux wigbaldincgtune and æppelforda, 'old ditch'. AD 895. Appleford. S355 (B581). G754–5.
116. of þam more on ða ealdan dic, 'old ditch'. AD 968. Fyfield. S758 (B1221), G710.
117. of ðam pyttan east be gemere on byttaman dic—meaning uncertain. AD 1032. West Hanney. S964 (K746). G748–9.
118. on ælfðryþe dic, 'Ælfðryð's ditch'. AD 956. Fyfield. S603 (B977). G709.
119. Ærest of hacce broce on rugan dic, 'rough ditch'. AD 964. Aston Upthorpe. S725 (B1143). G766–7.
120. of þane stane andlang dice, 'ditch'. AD 977. Kingston. S828 (K1276). G708–9.
121. east andlang þære ealdan dic, 'old ditch'. AD 1032. West Hanney. S964 (K746). G748–9.
122. þonne on þa mærdic, 'boundary ditch'. AD 959. Longworth. S673 (B1047). G707–8.
123. on þa ealdan dic, 'old ditch'. AD 959. Longworth. S673 (B1047). G707.
124. Ærest on þa mærdic, 'boundary ditch'. AD 959. Goosey. S673 (B1047). G745.
125. þæt hit sticað up on þa readan dic, 'red ditch'. AD 931. Shellingford. S1546 (B684). G696–7.
126. þanon to holan dic, 'hollow ditch'. AD 956. West Ginge. S583 (B981). G746–7.
127. Ærest of stirigan pole to þære dic, 'ditch'. AD 968. Cumnor. S757 (B1222). G731–2.
128. of wadleahe ðet on þa ealdan dic, 'old ditch'. AD 968. Cumnor. S757 (B1222). G731–2.
129. on ða dic, 'ditch'. AD 947. Denchworth. S529 (B833), G744–5.
130. of þam beorgæ in on þæt norþ geatt. þo non on þæt suð geat, 'north and south gate/gap' (Uffington hill fort). AD 958. East Woolstone. S575 (B902). G682–4.
131. to ceawan hlewe, 'Ceawa's barrow'. AD 947. Denchworth. S529 (B833), G744–5.
132. Ærest of lillanhlæwes crundele, 'quarry of (by) Lilla's barrow'. AD 956. West Ginge. S583 (B981). G746–7.
133. of þam wylle on rupelmes hlau, 'rupelmes [personal name?] barrow'. AD 964. Hendred. S724 (B1142). G747–8.
134. in to hafeces hlæwe 'hawk's barrow'. Date unknown. Uffington. S1208 (B687). G686–9.
135. of ræde on hwittuces hlæwe, 'Hwittuc's barrow'. AD 955. Compton. S564 (B908). G692–4.
136. on hildes hlæw, 'Hild's barrow'. AD 955. Compton. S564 (B908). G692–4.
137. on þam hamme on cardan hlawe, 'Carda's barrow'. AD 949. Welford. S552 (B877). G663–5.
138. in to hundeshlæwe, 'hound's barrow'. Date unknown. Uffington. S1208 (B687). G686–9.
139. uppan þa stanhlæwe, 'stone barrow'. Date unknown. Uffington. S1208 (B687). G686–9.
140. uppen hodes hlæwe, 'Hod's barrow'. Date unknown. Uffington. S1208 (B687). G686–9.
141. þonon on wintres hlewe, 'Winter's barrow'. AD 940. Garford. S471 (B761). G711.
142. be westan yttinges hlawe, uncertain first element, perhaps 'Yting's Barrow'. AD 942. Appleton with Eaton. S480 (B777). G723–4.
143. þonon to hord hlince, 'treasure lynchet'. AD 949. Welford. S552 (B877). G663–5.
144. to ibban stane, 'Ibba's stone'. AD 951. West Chieveley and Beedon. S558 (B892). G652–5.

145. andlang weges oþ þa readan hane, 'red stone'. AD 944. Blewbury, Aston Upthorpe and Tirrold. S496 (B801). G758–61.
146. swa of lodder þorne to flegestane, 'giant's stone'. AD 1015. S934 (K1310). G767–8.
147. to þan brandan stane, 'broad? stone'. AD 939. Brightwalton. S448 (B743). G660–1.
148. to hwitan stan, 'white stone'. AD 952. Barkham. S559 (B895). G642–3.
149. of ruhan leahe on þone haran stan, 'grey or hoary stone'. AD 968. Cumnor. S757 (B1222). G731–2.
150. on ceobban stan, 'Ceobba's stone'. AD 956. Wootton and Sunningwell. S590 (B932). G726–9.
151. and so north on rigt to Hordenestone, first element unknown 'stone'. AD 947. Ashbury. S524 (B828). G694–6.
152. to þan stan, 'stone'. AD 947. Ashbury. S524 (B828). G694–5.
153. of þan gate to þan stan, 'stone'. AD 947. Ashbury. S524 (B828). G694–6.
154. eft to þam stane, 'stone'. AD 931. Watchfield. S413 (B675). G697–8.
155. þonon on gerihte on ða bradan stanas, 'broad stones'. AD 963. Kingstone Lisle. S713 (B1121). G691–2.
156. on ane stanræwe, 'stone row'. AD 903. Hardwell. S369 (B601). G684–6.
157. þonnæ þæt on tættucan stan, 'Ta/ettuca's stone'. AD 856. West Woolstone. S317 (B491). G680–2.
158. ufewearde to þam haran stane, 'boundary stone'. AD 959. Bessels Leigh. S673 (B1047). G724–5.
159. of ðam beorge west riht on þone haranstan, 'grey/hoary stone'. AD 939. Brightwalton. S448 (B743). G660–1.
160. of ruhan leahe on þone haran stan, 'grey/hoary stone'. AD 968. Cumnor. S757 (B1222). G731–2.
161. north to þan Whytestone, 'white stone'. AD 947. Ashbury. S524 (B828). G694–6.
162. Ðonnæ and lang wægæs oð þonnæ mægen stan, 'great stone'. AD 856. West Woolstone. S317 (B491). G680–2.
163. west on þone weg to þam stan, 'stone'. AD 935. Farnborough. S411 (B682). G671–3.
164. on cylman stane, 'Cylma's stone'. AD 956. Welford. S622 (B963). G665–7.
165. swa forþ on cenelmes stan, 'Cyn(e)helm's stone'. AD 949. Welford. S552 (B877). G663–5.
166. on gerihte to þam stane on hrig weg, 'stone'. AD 903. Hardwell. S369 (B601). G684–6.
167. to þan stone whytoute þar Irwelond, 'stone outside the ploughed land'. AD 947. Ashbury. S524 (B828). G694–6.
168. þanon on hordwyllæ on þonæ ealdan hord wyllæs wæg, 'from the treasure spring, to the old Hardwell way'. AD 856. West Woolstone. S317 (B491). G680–2.

4(iii) MONUMENTAL MARKERS IN HAMPSHIRE CHARTER-BOUNDS

169. thanon on thaene gemot beorh, 'moot hill/barrow'. AD 826. Calbourn. S274 (B392; K807). Grundy 1921: 137.
170. on ruwan beorh, 'rough hill/barrow'. AD 900–1. Cranbourne. S360 (B596/25; K332). Grundy 1927a: 307.

171. Aerest of Citwara Beca on hremnes beorh, 'raven's hill/barrow'. AD 956. Meon. S619 (B982/3). Grundy 1926: 205.

172. and lang stræt on himan beorgas, 'Hima's hills/barrows'. AD 932. West Meon. S417 (B689/19; K1107). Grundy 1926: 229.

173. Aerest of Mearc beorge, 'boundary hill/barrow'. AD 932. West Meon. S417 (B689/19; K1107). Grundy 1926: 224.

174. of earnes beorg, 'eagle's hill/barrow'. AD 938. Tichborne and Beauworth. S444 (B731/4; K1118). Grundy 1921: 158.

175. Of mælan beorge on hig leage, 'Mela's hill/barrow'. AD 938. Tichborne and Beauworth. S444 (B731/4; K1118). Grundy 1921: 157.

176. to abrocenan beorge, 'broken hill/barrow'. AD 979. Long Sutton. S835 (Kem 622/3). Grundy 1927a: 255.

177. thonne andlang weges on thone beorg aet waecces treowe, 'hill/barrow at Waecc's tree'. AD 900. St Mary. S359 (B594; K1077). Grundy 1927a: 213.

178. on þone litlan beorh, 'little hill/barrow'. AD 959/963. Meon. S811 (B1319/3). Grundy 1926: 197.

179. thonne andlang weges on Ceardices Beorg, 'Cerdic's hill/barrow'. AD 900. St Mary. S359 (B594; K1077). Grundy 1927a: 211.

180. on undernbeorh, 'lower hill/barrow'. AD 961. Ringwood. S690 (B1066/2). Grundy 1927a: 195.

181. and thanne so to Cotelesburgh, 'Cotel's hill/barrow'. AD 944/946. South Damerham. S513 (B817). Grundy 1924: 68.

182. and so endelang ther wite lak up on kingberwes, 'king hill/barrow'. AD 944/946. South Damerham. S513 (B817). Grundy 1924: 66.

183. and ende langweyes to than langeberghe, 'long hill/barrow' (Knap Barrow). AD 944x946. South Damerham. S513 (B817). Grundy 1924: 69.

184. 'thone to brocaenan beorge, 'broken or uneven hill/barrow'. AD 973/974. Crondall. S820 (B1307; K594). Grundy 1924: 55.

185. þone beorh þat lið betweox þan twan langan beorgan, 'hill/barrow that lies between the two long hills/barrows'. AD 904. Sutton Scotney. S374 (B604/1; K337). Grundy 1927a: 308; Forsberg 1950: 202–3.

186. Þonon on þone beorh, 'hill/barrow'. AD 956. Polhampton. S613 (B974/3). Grundy 1927a: 179.

187. andlang weges to aeses beorge, 'hill/barrow of the ashtree'. AD 900. St Mary. S359 (B594; K1077). Grundy 1927a: 210.

188. to þam hæþenan beorge, 'heathen hill/barrow'. AD 1019. Dreyton. S956 (K730). Whitelock 1955, 599.

189. on ruwan beorh, 'rough hill/barrow'. AD 961. Crux Easton (Hurstbourne Tarrant). S689 (B1080/5; K1235). Grundy 1926, 153–4.

190. of tham stan beorge, 'stone hill/barrow'. AD 931. Eccinswell. S412 (B674/19). Grundy 1924: 98.

191. to ceortes beorge, 'Ceort's hill/barrow'. AD 900. Micheldever. S360 (B596/8; K332). Grundy 1926: 234.

192. swua forð to Aðelwoldes beorge, 'Æthelwold's hill/barrow'. AD 939. Worthy. S351 (B740/4; K1121). Grundy 1926: 188–9.

193. þone þweores ofer þone beorg, 'hill/barrow'. AD 956. Polhampton, Overton. S613 (B974/3). Grundy 1927a: 179.

194. up wið reofnes beorges, first element uncertain 'raven's (?) hill/barrow'. AD 924. River Meon. S283 (B377/18; K1031). Grundy 1926: 215.

195. Ærest of þrim beorgum to ruwan beorge, 'rough hill/barrow'. AD 940. Poolhampton. S465 (B763/4; K1136). Grundy 1927a: 177.

196. Ðonan feorðe healf grið be westan þam beorgan þæ adolfen wæs, 'west of the hill/barrow that was dug open'. AD 825. Martyr Worthy. S273 (B389/7; K1033). Grundy 1926: 184.

197. Aerest of thrim Beorgum, 'three hills/barrows'. AD 940. Poolhampton. S465 (B763/9; K1136). Grundy 1927a: 177.

198. Thonne andlang streames to brocenan beorge, 'broken barrow'. AD 900. Micheldever. S360 (B596/8; K332). Grundy 1926: 235.

199. on mearc beorh, 'boundary hill/barrow' (the same as 'little barrow' in B1319). AD 967. Meon and Farnfield in Privett. S754 (B1200/12). Grundy 1926: 219.

200. on lucan beorh, 'Luca's hill/barrow'. AD 961. Ringwood. S690 (B1066/2). Grundy 1927a: 194.

201. Þæt on cissan beorg middan weardne, 'then to the middle of Cissa's hill/barrow'. AD 909. Overton. S377 (B625/3; K1094). Grundy 1927a: 175.

202. on norþ hand þæræ beorga, 'to the north side of the hill/barrow'. AD 940. Exton. S463 (B758/2.61; K1131). Grundy 1924: 114.

203. Of tham stan beorge, 'stone hill/barrow'. AD 931. Ecchinswell. S412 (B674/38; K1103). Grundy 1924: 98.

204. andlang dene to þam westmestan beorgan, 'westernmost hills/barrows'. Date unknown. Chidden. S598 (B976/3; K1192). Grundy 1926: 108.

205. on thone rugan beorh, 'rough hill/barrow'. AD 1045. Hinton. S1007 (Kem780/6). Grundy 1926: 141.

206. on ðone middemestan beorh, 'midmost hill/barrow'. AD 1045. Hinton. S1007 (Kem780/6). Grundy 1926: 140.

207. on ræling beorgas, '? hills/barrows'. AD 1045. Hinton. S1007 (Kem780/6). Grundy 1926: 142.

208. utt with feld beorga, 'hill/barrow on open ground'. AD 900. St Mary. S359 (B594; K1077). Grundy 1927a: 212.

209. on north hand thaerae beorga, 'hill/barrow'. AD 940. Exton. S463 (B758). Grundy 1924: 114.

210. Þonnæ suþ and lang lea to tiggæl beorgæ, 'tile hill/barrow'. Exton. S463 (B758). Grundy 1924: 114.

211. Of þam rugan beorge, 'rough hill/barrow'. AD 934. Enford. S427 (B705/2.10). Grundy 1919: 231.

212. to thon lytlan stan beorge, 'little stone hill/barrow'. AD 931. Eccinswell. S412 (B674). Grundy 1924: 98.

213. of stodfaldun to wibbanbeorge, 'Wibba's hill/barrow'. AD 959. Bighton. S660 (B1045). Grundy 1921: 108.

214. æt þæne mearc beorh, 'boundary hill/barrow'. AD 935. Havant. S430 (B707/6; K111). Grundy 1926: 120.

215. to ruwan beorge, 'rough hill/barrow'. AD 900. Brown. S360 (B596; K332). Grundy 1921: 141.

216. to fif beorgan. 'five hills/barrows'. AD 975. Fyfield. S800 (B1316/5; K592). Grundy 1926: 101.

217. andllang dene to than westmestan beorgan, 'westernmost hill/barrow'. AD 956. Hambledon. S598 (B976; K1192). Grundy 1926: 108.

218. of risc mere on stan beorg, 'stone hill/barrow'. AD 955/959. Godshill. S1663 (B1025; K475). Grundy 1926: 103.

219. swa hit gaeth to heanbyrig, 'high stronghold'. AD 982. Longstock. S840 (K633). Grundy 1926: 178.

220. and swa forth to thaere byrig, 'stronghold'. AD 854. Headbourne Worthy. S309 (B473; K1055). Grundy 1926: 130.

221. hit gaeth to widian byrig, 'Widia's stronghold'. AD 840. Longstock. S840 (K633). Grundy 1926: 178.

222. up on wudeburge hlinc, 'the linchet by/at/near the wood stronghold'. AD 961. Ringwood. S690 (B1066). Grundy 1927a: 194.

223. to thaere holan dic benithan welnabyrig, 'to the hollow ditch beneath the stronghold of riches' (Woolbury Ring). AD 947. Leckford Abbas. S526 (B824). Grundy 1926: 173.

224. to naesan byrig, 'stronghold by the ness'. AD 900. Micheldever. S360 (B596; K332). Grundy 1926: 234.

225. thonne on stan burg, 'stone stronghold'. AD 826. Droxford. S276 (B393; K1038). Grundy 1924: 74.

226. Aerest on tha ealdan byrig, 'old stronghold'. AD 961. Avington. S699 (B1068; K1229). Grundy 1921: 95.

227. to thaere byrig, 'stronghold'. AD 931. Eccinswell. S412 (B674; K1102). Grundy 1924: 100.

228. thonan waest on eorth burge, 'west of the gate to the earthern stronghold'. AD 940. Exton. S463 (B758). Grundy 1924: 114.

229. of eadmundes were on tha ealdan byrig, 'old stronghold'. AD 961. Easton. S695 (B1076; K1230). Grundy 1924: 88–9.

230. thaet swa to meres byrig westan on tha dic, 'stronghold by the mere' (enclosure next to dew pond on Ladle Hill). AD 943. Burghclere. S487 (B787; K1145). Grundy 1921: 131.

231. thonne be slade to thaere byrig, 'stronghold'. Edward. Hunton. S381 (B629; K1096). Grundy 1926: 148.

232. forth be ea oth hit cymth to thaes Abbodes byrig, 'Abbot's stronghold'. Edward. Hunton. S381 (B629; K1096). Grundy 1926: 149.

233. thonne and lang streates oth ceapmanna del, 'peddler's pit' (a circular embanked earthwork). AD 961. Crux Easton. S689 (B1080; K1235). Grundy 1924: 59.

234. andlang there ealdan dic to Ceotan stapole, 'old ditch'. AD 931. Eccinswell. S412 (B674; K1102). Grundy 1924: 94.

235. ende land thare dich to than frimde dich, 'frimde? Ditch'. AD 944/946. South Damerham. S513 (B817). Grundy 1924: 69.

236. on tha gewrincloda dic, 'wrinkled ditch'. AD 1026. Kings Worthy. S962 (K743). Grundy 1926: 167.

237. ant than riht in the wide dich, 'wide ditch' (Bokerley Dyke). AD 944/946. South Damerham. S513 (B817). Grundy 1924: 69.

238. and swa endelang ther strete dich to wilton weie, 'street ditch'. AD 944/946. South Damerham. S513 (B817). Grundy 1924: 68.

239. on tha miclan dic, 'big ditch'. AD 900. Brown. S360 (B596; K332). Grundy 1921: 141.

240. Aerest on Efer fearn on tha readan dic, 'red ditch'. AD 961. Crux Easton. S689 (B1080; K1235). Grundy 1924: 58.

241. andlang andheafda on tha witan dic, 'white ditch'. Egbert. Alresford, New and Old. S284 (B398; K1039). Grundy 1921: 70.

242. thonne to Aenta dic, 'giants' ditch'. AD 1026. Kings Worthy. S962 (K743). Grundy 1926: 168.

243. of eadulfes hamme on tha readan dic, 'red ditch'. AD 956. Farley Chamberlayne. S360 (B596; K332). Grundy 1924: 120.

244. of thaere hwitan dic, 'white ditch'. AD 1023. Hannington. S960 (K739). Grundy 1926: 115.

245. thanon to witan dic, 'white ditch'. AD 1026. Kings Worthy. S962 (K743). Grundy 1926: 168.

246. on tha hocedan dic, 'hooked ditch'. AD 904. Sutton Scotney. S374 (B604; K337). Grundy 1927a: 309.

247. to thaere Easteran dic, 'easterly ditch'. AD 931. Eccinswell. S412 (B674; K1102). Grundy 1924: 96.

248. thonne on thone weg the scyt ofer tha dic, 'ditch' (Devil's Ditch). AD 900. St Mary. S359 (B594; K1077). Grundy 1927a: 211.

249. thonne west on tha faesten dic, 'stronghold ditch'. AD 970x975. Crondall. S813 (B1307; K595). Grundy 1924: 52.

250. and thane to thes drakenhorde in on thar siderer, 'dragon hoard'. AD 944x946. South Damerham. S513 (B817). Grundy 1924: 69.

251. Thanan east up suae thet Ealden Faestan scathe, 'old stronghold'. AD 909. Froxfield, East Meon. S283 (B377; K1031). Grundy 1926: 212.

252. thonon up on tha dune to thaer dic on tha hlew, 'to the barrow'. AD 901. Abbot's Ann. S365 (B597). Grundy 1921: 65.

253. A/erest of Hilda hlaewe, 'Hilda's barrow'. AD 953. Clere. S258 (B179/1). Grundy 1926: 133.

254. up to Heardulfes hlæwe, 'Heardulfes barrow'. AD 947. Leckford. S526 (B824/3). Grundy 1926: 173.

255. andlange weges on suþhealfe gætes hlæwe þæt cymþ to feower treowum, 'to the south side of the barrow of the gate'. AD 932. North. S418 (B692/2). Grundy 1927a: 243.

256. þonon on entan hlew, 'giants' barrow'. AD 940. Poolhampton. S465 (B763/7). Grundy 1927a, 178.

257. Aerest on Hilda hlaewe, 'hilda's barrow'. AD 953. Highclere. S565 (B905/10). Grundy 1926: 133.

258. on broccæs hlæw, 'barrow at the brook'. AD 990. Wootton St Lawrence. S874 (Kem 673/5). Grundy 1927a: 315.

259. Ðonne on enta hlewe, 'giant's barrow'. AD 1033. Poolhampton in Overton. S970 (Kem 752/6). Grundy 1927a, 180–2.

260. and lang hærpadæs in to lortan hlæwe, 'Lorta's barrow'. AD 934. Enford. S427 (B705/2.2; K1110). Grundy 1919: 228.

261. thonne west to Ceolbrihtes stane, 'Ceolbriht's or Ceolbeorht's stone'. AD 973/974. Crondall. S820 (B1307; K595). Grundy 1924: 52.

262. up to kinges stane, 'king's stone'. AD 854. Headbourne Worthy. S309 (B473; K1055). Grundy 1926: 128.

263. and lang weges on bregeswithe stan, 'Bregeswith's stone'. AD 953. Highclere. S565 (B905; K1170). Grundy 1926: 134.

264. andlang mearce on thaene hwitan stan, 'white stone'. AD 1045. North. S1012 (K776). Grundy 1927a: 249.

265. andlang dic on thone stan, 'stone'. AD 955x959. Godshall. S1663 (B1025; K475). Grundy 1926: 103.

266. to beofan stane, 'beofan? Stone'. AD 900. Brown. S360 (B596; K332). Grundy 1921: 141.

267. thaet and lang hunig wiellaes weges to braeges withae stanae, 'Breguswith's stone'. AD 909. Ashmansworth. S378 (B624; K1091). Grundy 1921: 93.

268. to bodestan, possibly 'Boda's stone' or 'messenger stone'. Edgar. Romsey. S812 (B1187). Grundy 1927a: 202.

269. up to holan stan, 'hollow stone'. AD 854. Headbourne Worthy. S309 (B473; K1055). Grundy 1926: 128.

4(iv) MONUMENTAL MARKERS IN SUSSEX CHARTER-BOUNDS

270. of here grafe to twam beorgum, 'two hills/barrows'. AD 947. Washington. S525 (B834; K1159). Barker 1949: 65, 67.

271. Ærest æt thrim beorgam, 'three hills/barrows'. AD 930. Medmerry. S403 (B669; K350). Barker 1948: 140.

272. and swa suð to cyllan beorge, 'Cylla's hill/barrow'. AD 772. Bexhill. S108 (B208). Barker 1947: 92. 94.

273. of wigan campe to bennan beorg, 'Beonna's hill/barrow'. AD 947. Washington. S525 (B834; K1159). Barker 1949: 65, 67.

274. of þam hlince to halignesse beorge, 'holiness or sanctuary hill/barrow'. AD 775. East Dean. S43 (B144). Barker 1947: 66–7.

275. swa west be sæ oð Þri beorgas, 'three hills/barrows'. AD 957. Selsey. S1291 (B997; K464). Barker 1949: 83.

276. ðonan on wulfa biorh, 'hill/barrow of the wolves'. AD 934. Durrington. S425 (B702; K634). Barker 1948: 150.

277. of deneburge hleawe to stan beorg, 'stone hill/barrow'. AD 947. Washington. S525 (B834; K1159). Barker 1949: 65, 67.

278. of readdan wille to lydgeardes broge. Of lidgeardes beorge, 'Leodgeard's hill/barrow'. S525 (B834; K1159). Barker 1949: 65, 67.

279. ðonne on gemot biorh, 'moot hill/barrow'. AD 934. Durrington. S425 (B702; K364). Barker 1948: 150.

280. ðonne on lytlan biorh, 'little hill/barrow'. AD 934. Durrington. S425 (B702; K364). Barker 1948: 150.

281. ðonon on mearc biorh, 'boundary hill/barrow'. AD 934. Durrington. S425 (B702; K364). Barker 1948: 150.

282. ðonne betweonnan twæm biorgum, 'between the two hills/barrows'. AD 934. Durrington. S425 (B702; K364). Barker 1948: 150.

283. ruwan biorg, 'rough hill/barrow'. AD 934. Durrington. S425 (B702; K364). Barker 1948: 150.

284. of þæm byrgelsan to billingabyrig, first element uncertain 'stronghold of the people of Billa (?)'. AD 775. East Dean. S43 (B144). Barker 1947: 66–7.

285. andlang diceson ðeodweg, 'ditch'. AD 775. East Dean. S43 (B144). Barker 1947: 66–7.

286. 7 swa up on þa ealden merc dic, 'old ditch'. AD 772. Bexhill. S108 (B208). Barker 1947: 90, 92.

287. of stan beorwe to haþeburge hlæwe, 'hatheburh's barrow'. AD 947. Washington. S525 (B834; K1159). Barker 1949: 65, 67.

288. prentsan hlaw, '?barrow'. AD 934. Durrington. S425 (B702; K364). Barker 1948: 150.

289. hinc in uuadan hlæu, 'Wada's barrow'. AD 680. Pagham. S230 (B50; K18). Barker 1947: 51, 53.

290. Ærast on æscwoldes hlaw, 'Ashwold's barrow'. AD 934. Durrington. S425 (B702; K364). Barker 1948: 150.

291. of tatmonnes apoldre to deneburge hleawe, 'Deneburg's barrow'. AD 947. Washington. S525 (B834; K1159). Barker 1949: 65, 67.

292. of þam ealdan feld on manning stan, 'Mann's stone'. AD 963. Ambersham. S718 (B1114). Barker 1949: 89, 90.

293. forð be stronde to cwuenstane, 'queen's stone'. AD 957. Selsey. S1291 (B997; K464). Barker 1949: 83, 85.

294. thonne æt langan stona, 'long stone'. AD 930. Medmerry. S403 (B669; K350). Barker 1948: 140, 143.

295. of þære denu on id hilde stan, 'Idhild's stone'. Ambersham. S718 (B1114). Barker 1949: 89, 91.

4(v) MONUMENTAL MARKERS IN WILTSHIRE CHARTER-BOUNDS

296. upp to tham Ealdan Herepathe be westan Wodnesborge, 'woden's hill/barrow'. AD 825. Alton Priors. S272/1403 (B390). Grundy 1919: 160.

297. thanen on brochenenberge, 'broken hill/barrow'. AD 860. Teffont. S326 (B500; K284). Grundy 1919: 181.

298. thonan on lytlan beorg. 'little hill/barrow'. AD 955. Stanton St Bernard. S368 (B600; K335). Grundy 1919: 214.

299. thonen on lusa beorg, 'hill/barrow of the lice'. AD 892. Newton. S348 (B567; K320). Grundy 1919: 190.

300. and langan thes smalan pathes on rugan beorh, 'rough hill/barrow'. AD 947. Ebbesbourne. S522 (B832). Grundy 1919: 297.

301. on seofon beorgas, 'seven hills/barrows'. AD 972. Overton. S784 (B1285). Grundy 1919: 245.
302. innan Colta beorg, 'Colta's hill/barrow'. AD 972. Overton. S784 (B1285). Grundy 1919: 245.
303. thonon on thone stanigan beurh, 'stony hills/barrow'. AD 957. Stanton St Bernard. S647 (B998; K467). Grundy 1919: 213.
304. thanon on bradanbeorg, 'broad hill/barrow'. AD 921. Collingbourne. S379 (B635). Grundy 1919: 217.
305. andlang dic on finbeorh, 'heap hill/barrow'. AD 957. Upton Lovell. S642 (B992; K469). Grundy 1920: 61.
306. thanen on brochenenberge, 'broken or uneven hill/barrow'. AD 860. Teffont. S326 (B500; K284). Grundy 1919: 181.
307. 7 thanon an lang faccan cumbes on rugan beorh, 'rough hill/barrow'. AD 863. Buttermere. S336 (B508). Grundy 1919: 185.
308. on thone beorh to than rigwege, 'hill/barrow'. Cenwalh. Downton. S229 (B27; K985). Grundy 1919: 148.
309. ruh beorh, 'rough hill/barrow'. AD 826. Bishopstone and Stratford Tony. S275 (B391). Grundy 1919: 149.
310. Beorch, 'hill/barrow'. AD 956. Untraceable. S635 (B962). Grundy 1920: 56.
311. thonne on Coltan beorh, 'Colta's hill/barrow'. AD 939. Kennett. S449 (B734). Grundy 1919: 242.
312. on tha thri beorgas, 'three hills/barrows'. AD 947. Ebbesbourne. S522 (B832). Grundy 1919: 297.
313. thanen to Abbanberghe, 'Abba's hill/barrow'. AD 944. Nettleton. S504 (B800; K398). Grundy 1919: 296.
314. on beorh dic, 'hill/barrow ditch'. AD 892. Newton. S348 (B567; K320). Grundy 1919: 190.
315. on thone stanigan beorh, 'stony hill/barrow'. AD 956. Wilton. S586 (B1030). Grundy 1919: 294.
316. to sond beorge, 'sand hill/barrow'. AD 892. Newton. S348 (B567; K320). Grundy 1919: 189.
317. in longum gemaerweges to wadbeorg, 'woad hill/barrow'. AD 778. Little Bedwyn. S264 (B225; K133). Grundy 1919: 154.
318. on winfles beorg, 'Winfel's hill/barrow'. AD 854. Little Hinton. S312 (B477/8/9; K1053). Grundy 1919: 174.
319. thannen on Leon berg, first element uncertain perhaps 'Lion's hill/barrow'. AD 860. Teffont. S326 (B500; K284). Grundy 1919: 182.
320. scufan borwe, 'Scufa's hill/barrow'. AD 850. Dauntsey. S301/1580 (B457/8). Grundy 1919: 166.
321. and lang furh on thone rugan beorg, 'rough barrow'. AD 934. Enford. S427 (B705). Grundy 1919: 231.
322. to twig beorgas, 'two hills/barrows'. AD 949. Pewsey. S547 (B875). Grundy 1919: 249.
323. on Luseborg, 'hill/barrow of the lice'. AD 949. Pewsey. S547 (B875). Grundy 1919: 249.

324. thannen on abbenberog, 'Abba's hill/barrow'. AD 860. Teffont. S326 (B500; K284). Grundy 1919: 182.

325. andlang herpothes in on beorg, 'hill/barrow'. AD 937. Burcombe. S438 (B714). Grundy 1919: 236.

326. be westan than greatan beorhge, 'great or big hill/barrow'. AD 1045. Ditchampton. S1010 (K778). Grundy 1919: 291.

327. endlangweies biweste brokenanberwe, 'broken hill/barrow'. AD 955. Chiseldon inc. Badbury. S568 (B904; K434). Grundy 1919: 209.

328. on rugeburwe, 'rough hill/barrow'. AD 968. Edington, East Coulston. S765 (B1215). Grundy 1920: 83.

329. thanen nath fur bodelusburgge, uncertain but perhaps 'hill/barrow'. AD 968. Edington, East Coulston. S765 (B1215). Grundy 1920: 82.

330. on gemer beorgas, 'boundary hills/barrows'. AD 955. Stanton St Bernard. S368 (B600; K335). Grundy 1919: 213.

331. thonne to ippan beorge, 'Ippa's hill/barrow'. AD 955. Berwick St John. S582 (B917). Grundy 1920: 34.

332. up betweox tha twegan beorgas, 'up between the two hills/barrows'. AD 939. Kennett. S449 (B734). Grundy 1919: 242.

333. ruwan beorch, 'rough hill/barrow'. AD 956. Untraceable. S635 (B962). Grundy 1920: 56.

334. bryd beorh, 'bird or woman/bride hill/barrow'. AD 956. Untraceable. S635 (B962). Grundy 1920: 56.

335. oth that hit cymth to Chetoles beorg, 'Chetol's hill/barrow'. AD 955. Berwick St John and Broadchalke. S582 (B917; K436). Grundy 1920: 28.

336. up andlang dene up to Gosa beorge, 'hill/barrow of the geese'. AD 955x957. West Knoyle. S666 (B956; K462). Grundy 1920: 22.

337. Lusebeorh, 'hill/barrow of the lice'. AD 987. Manningford Abbots. Liber Hida. Grundy 1920: 108.

338. thonon to Oswaldes berghe, 'Oswald's hill/barrow'. AD 931. Norton. S416 (B677; K353). Grundy 1919: 225.

339. cealdan beorge, 'cold hill/barrow'. AD 956. Wroughton, Lydiard Millicent, Lydiard. S585 (B948). Grundy 1920: 55.

340. on stanbeorch, 'stone hill/barrow'. AD 986. Stratford. S861 (K655). Grundy 1920: 97.

341. up on than Enlippanberwe, 'only or single hill/barrow'. AD 955. Chiseldon inc. Badbury. S568 (B904; K434). Grundy 1919: 209.

342. on there tweie iberges, 'two hills/barrows'. AD 940. Liddington. S459 (B754; K386). Grundy 1920: 14.

343. Swanabeorh, 'barrow of the herdsmen or freemen'. AD 987. Manningford Abbots. S568 (B904; K434). Grundy 1920: 106.

344. endlangstrete on the berghes, 'hills/barrows'. AD 955. Chiseldon inc. Badbury. S568 (B904; K434). Grundy 1919: 206.

345. on wen beorge, 'boil hill/barrow'. AD 854. Little Hinton. S312 (B477/8/9; K1053). Grundy 1919: 176.

346. thanon to sahl beorge, 'hill/barrow of the sallow tree'. AD 955x957. West Knoyle. S666 (B956; K462). Grundy 1920: 21–2.

347. on fugan biorge, 'Fuga's hill/barrow'. AD 901. Chiseldon. S366 (B598). Grundy 1919: 204.

348. on ludan beorh, 'Luda's hill/barrow'. AD 947. Ebbesbourne. S522 (B832). Grundy 1919: 298.

349. on grenan byorh, 'green hill/barrow'. AD 901. Chiselden. S366 (B598). Grundy 1919: 203.

350. on dolemannes beorh, 'Doleman's hill/barrow'. AD 986. Stratford. S861 (K655). Grundy 1920: 96.

351. ofer Bican dune on thone midemestan beorh, 'mid-most barrow'. AD 977. Wiley. S831 (K611). Grundy 1919: 265.

352. to brocenan beorh, 'broken hill/barrow'. AD 956. Langford. S612 (B934; K446). Grundy 1919: 283.

353. Aerest of thare Anlipigan Aec to Maetelmesburg, 'Maeþelhelm's stronghold'. AD 949. Pewsey. S547 (B875). Grundy 1919: 248.

354. up ofer tha eorth burg, 'earth stronghold'. AD 940. Wiley. S469 (B757; K379). Grundy 1919: 262.

355. thaet to thare eorthbyrig, 'earth stronghold'. AD 955. Stanton St Bernard. S368 (B600; K335). Grundy 1919: 214.

356. thonne bi eastan cester slaed byrg, 'stronghold at the valley by the Roman fort' (Chiselbury Camp). AD 901. Fovant. S364 (B588; K331). Grundy 1919: 194.

357. fram hambres buruh, 'Ambri's or buntings stronghold' (Amesbury). AD 972. Stratford-sub-castle. S789 (B1286). Grundy 1920: 87.

358. Aerest of Eorthebyrg to Symbroce, 'earth stronghold'. AD 901. Chiselden. S366 (B598). Grundy 1919: 201.

359. to Aethelware byrig, 'stronghold of the noble folk or Æthelwaru's stronghold'. AD 972. Stratford-sub-Castle. S789 (B1286). Grundy 1920: 87.

360. thonne on tha eorth burg, 'earth stronghold'. AD 961. Burbage. S688 (B1067; K1236). Grundy 1920: 62.

361. thaet eft on eorthebyrig, 'earth stronghold. AD 901. Chiselden. S366 (B598). Grundy 1919: 204.

362. thanon on guthredesburg, 'Guthredes stronghold'. AD 921. Collingbourne. S379 (B635). Grundy 1919: 218.

363. on eorthebyrg, 'earth stronghold'. AD 901. Chiselden. S366 (B598). Grundy 1919: 204.

364. thonne with thaere eorth byrig, 'earth stronghold' (Guthredesburg, no. 369). AD 968. Great Bedwyn. S756 (B1213; K1266). Grundy 1920: 77.

365. thara land gewyrtha oth wuduburh, 'wood stronghold' (Winklebury hill fort). AD 955. Berwick St John and Broad Chalke. S582 (B917; K436). Grundy 1920: 27.

366. thanne to michelan byrg, 'big/great stronghold'. AD 955. Berwick St John and Broad Chalke. S582 (B917; K436). Grundy 1920: 28.

367. Aerest of Afene on tha Ealdan Burhdic on thaene weg, 'old stronghold ditch' (Old Sarum). AD 972. Stratford-sub-Castle. S789 (B1286). Grundy 1920: 87.

368. on rugan dic, 'rough ditch'. AD 892. Newton. S348 (B567; K320). Grundy 1919: 190.

369. Aerest on ealdan dic, 'old ditch'. AD 948. West Knoyle. S531 (B870; K422). Grundy 1920: 19.

370. swa innan tha wogan dice, 'crooked ditch'. AD 854. Wanborough. S312 (B477/8/9; K1053). Grundy 1919: 177.

371. to thaere scortan dic, 'short ditch'. AD 931. Norton. S416 (B677; K353). Grundy 1919: 227.

372. on grimes dic, 'Grim's ditch'. AD 968. Sherrington. Wilton Cartulary II. Grundy 1920: 111.

373. ealdan dic, 'old ditch'. AD 987. Manningfored Abbots. Liber Hida. Grundy 1920: 107.

374. innan folces dic, 'folk's ditch'. AD 854. Wanborough. S312 (B477/8/9; K1053). Grundy 1919: 180.

375. thanen on miclen diches get, 'gate/gap of the great ditch' (Winklebury Camp). AD 956. Berwick St John. S630 (B970). Grundy 1920: 35.

376. thanon on scortan dyc, 'short ditch'. AD 921. Collingbourne. S379 (B635). Grundy 1919: 217.

377. thonne up to grimes dic, 'Grim's ditch'. AD 956. Burcombe. S631 (B985; K456). Grundy 1919: 237.

378. up to thare dic, 'ditch'. AD 956. Burcombe. S631 (B985; K456). Grundy 1919: 236.

379. and lang ealdre dic, 'long old ditch'. AD 955. Berwick St John and Broadchalke. S582 (B917; K436). Grundy 1920: 26.

380. on rugan dic, 'rough ditch'. AD 901. Fovant. S364 (B588; K331). Grundy 1919: 195.

381. on thone dic, 'ditch'. AD 825. Alton Priors. S272/1403 (B390). Grinsell 1919: 163.

382. on the olde dich, 'old ditch' (also 'bitches ditch'). AD 955. Chiseldon inc. Badbury. S568 (B904; K434). Grundy 1919: 209.

383. on the dich, 'ditch'. AD 955. Chiseldon inc. Badbury. S568 (B904; K434). Grundy 1919: 207.

384. greatan dic, 'great ditch' (Grim's Ditch). AD 956. Untraceable. S635 (B962). Grundy 1920: 56.

385. oth tha greatan dic, 'great ditch' (Grim's Ditch). AD 961. Coombe. S696 (B1071; K1232). Grundy 1920: 67.

386. Thonan to Esnadiche geate, 'gate of the serf's ditch'. AD 955. Berwick St John. S582 (B917). Grundy 1920: 33.

387. on tha ealdan dic, 'old ditch'. AD 968. Bemerton. S767 (B1216). Grundy 1920: 85.

388. thanen est be wirtrume oth bridinghe dich, 'the ditch of or associated with Bryda'. AD 956. Donhead St Andrew. S630 (B970; K477). Grundy 1920: 58.

389. on tha greatan dic, 'great ditch'. AD 986. Stratford. S861 (K655). Grundy 1920: 97.

390. on tha witan dic, 'white ditch'. AD 986. Stratford. S861 (K655). Grundy 1920: 97.

391. on folces dic, 'folk's ditch'. AD 854. Little Hinton. S312 (B477/8/9; K1053). Grundy 1919: 176.

392. on ealcheres dic, 'Ealchere's ditch'. AD 854. Little Hinton. S312 (B477/8/9; K1053). Grundy 1919: 176.

393. of thane pitte on bicendich, 'bitch's or Bica's ditch' (old ditch, no. 389). AD 940. Liddington. S459 (B754; K386). Grundy 1920: 15.

394. erest of elde dich, 'old ditch'. AD 940. Grittleton. S472 (B750; K381). Grundy 1919: 252.

395. that on tha ealden ditch, 'old ditch'. AD 860. Teffont. S326 (B500; K284). Grundy 1919: 182.

396. on tha dic, 'ditch'. AD 854. Little Hinton. S312 (B477/8/9; K1053). Grundy 1919: 175.

397. Thonne ofer Randune to thaere Ealdan Dic, 'old ditch'. AD 825. Alton Priors. S272/1403 (B390). Grundy 1919: 161.

398. holde diche, uncertain perhaps 'dependable ditch' or 'ditch of the bodies'. AD 850. Dauntsey. S301/1580 (B457–8). Grundy 1919: 166.

399. thanon on readan dic, 'red ditch'. AD 863. Buttermere. S336 (B508). Grundy 1919: 186.

400. thonan to Brydinga dic, 'the ditch of/or associated with Bryda'. AD 955. Berwick St John. S582 (B917). Grundy 1920: 37.

401. on thane Greatan thorn the stynt with Grimes dic, 'Grim's ditch'. AD 1045. Ditchampton. S1010 (K778). Grundy 1919: 291.

402. and swa to wodnes dic, 'Woden's ditch'. AD 892. Newton. S348 (B567; K320). Grundy 1919: 190.

403. thonon andlang Grimes dic, 'Grim's ditch'. AD 956. Langford. S612 (B934; K446). Grundy 1919: 283.

404. Thonne on sigewunne dic, 'Sigewinne's ditch'. AD 901. Fovant. S364 (B588; K331). Grundy 1919: 193.

405. andlang thaere ealdan dic, 'old ditch'. AD 934. Enford. S427 (B705). Grundy 1919: 234.

406. and from it to the ditch which runs as far as Wolf Pond, 'ditch'. AD 796. Purton. S149 (B279/a; K174). Grundy 1919: 158.

407. up on the hane, 'stone'. AD 955. Chiseldon inc. Badbury. S568 (B904; K434). Grundy 1919: 209.

408. that hit cymth to Beaces hlawe, very uncertain 'beacon(?) barrow'. AD 955. Berwick St John & Broad Chalke. Grundy 1920: 30.

409. on thaet hlaew, 'barrow'. AD 986. Stratford. S861 (K655). Grundy 1920: 97.

410. in to Lortan hlaewe, 'Lorta's barrow'. AD 934. Enford. S427 (B705). Grundy 1919: 229.

411. biccan hlew, 'bitch's barrow'. AD 956. Untraceable. S635 (B962). Grundy 1920: 56.

412. thonne on fontanhlewe, 'barrow by the spring'. AD 854. Hardenhuish. S308 (B469; K270). Grundy 1919: 171.

413. byrhtferthes hlaewe, 'Byrhtferth's barrow'. AD 949. Laverstock. S543 (B879; K428). Grundy 1920: 22.

414. on eangythe hlew, 'Eangyth's barrow'. AD 957. Ebbesbourne. S640 (B1004; K1209). Grundy 1919: 299.

415. Wolfingesleww, 'Wolfing's barrow'. AD 956. Brokenborough. S629/1577 (B921/2). Grundy 1920: 46.

416. to posses hlaewe, 'Poss's barrow' (Swallowciffe Down). AD 940. Swallowcliffe. S468 (B756; K387). Grundy 1919: 259.

417. on thane scearpan stan, 'sharp stone'. AD 955. Stanton St Bernard. S368 (B600; K335). Grundy 1919: 212.

418. of than beorge on thonne Holan stan, 'hollow stone'. AD 854. Little Hinton. S312 (B477/8/9; K1053). Grundy 1919: 174.

419. tha twegen dunne stanas, 'two brown stones'. AD 972. Overton. S784 (B1285). Grundy 1919: 246.
420. Thonne on aenne stan on Woncumb, 'to the single or first stone'. AD 825. Alton Priors. S272/1403 (B390). Grundy 1919: 161.
421. thonne ta tham graegan stane, 'grey stone'. AD 956. Burcombe. S631 (B985; K456). Grundy 1919: 237.
422. on thone Dunnan stan, 'dark/dull/brown stone'. AD 939. Kennett. S449 (B734). Grundy 1919: 243.
423. on thane red stan, 'red stone'. AD 940. Liddington. S459 (B754; K386). Grundy 1920: 13.
424. andlang thare dic on Beornulfes stan, 'Beornwulf's stone'. AD 956 for 959. Wilton. Grundy 1919: 293.
425. Stane, 'stone'. AD 956. Wroughton, Lydiard Millicent, Lydiard. S585 (B948). Grundy 1920: 55.
426. thanon on wylberhtes stan, 'Wylberht's stone'. AD 921. Collingbourne. S379 (B635). Grundy 1919: 218.
427. to puntes stan, 'Punt's stone'. AD 956. Langford. S612 (B934; K446). Grundy 1919: 283.
428. On thon Stan, 'to the stone'. Cenwalh. Bishopstone and Stratford Tony. S229 (B27; K985). Grundy 1919: 147.
429. andlang herpathes on tha dic with suthan Aetheferthes Stane, 'ditch to the south of Aethelferth's stone'. AD 939. Kennett. S449 (B734). Grundy 1919: 243.
430. on Sceobban stan (Cobban Stan), 'Sceobba's stone' (Cobba's Stone). AD 955. Stanton St Bernard. S368 (B600/998; K335). Grundy 1919: 212.
431. Thonne on aenne Stan aet Ceorlacumbes heafde, 'to the single or first stone at the head of Churl's combe'. AD 825. Alton Priors. S272/1403 (B390). Grundy 1919: 161.
432. thonne on gemerstan, 'boundary stone'. AD 955. Stanton St Bernard. S368 (B600/998; K335). Grundy 1919: 212.
433. Thonon on anne Micelne Stan aer thaer Hlinca, 'to the first great stone'. AD 825. Alton Priors. S272/1403 (B390). Grundy 1919: 162.
434. Thanen on the stourewe (stanraewe), 'stone row'. AD 955. Chiseldon inc. Badbury. S568 (B904; K434). Grundy 1919: 210.
435. on hordestan, 'hoard or treasure stone'. AD 901. Chiselden. S366 (B598). Grundy 1919: 204.
436. on foer stanes, 'four stones'. AD 940. Liddington. S459 (B754; K386). Grundy 1920: 14.
437. thanene endlangweyes on tha ten stanes, 'ten stones'. AD 955. Chiseldon inc. Badbury. S568 (B904; K434). Grundy 1919: 207.
438. Thonon on otherne Micelne stan, 'to the other great stone'. AD 825. Alton Priors. S272/1403 (B390). Grundy 1919: 162.
439. to wullafes stane, 'Wullaf's stone'. AD 854. Wanborough. S312 (B477/8/9; K1053). Grundy 1919: 177.
440. to anan stan, 'one stone'. AD 955. Stanton St Bernard. S368 (B600; K335). Grundy 1919: 213.

441. on thone stan, 'stone'. AD 854. Little Hinton. S312 (B477/8/9; K1053). Grundy 1919: 175.

442. on thone haran stan, 'hoary stone'. AD 854. Little Hinton. S312 (B477/8/9; K1053). Grundy 1919: 174.

443. on thone stan, 'stone'. AD 949. Pewsey. S547 (B875). Grundy 1919: 250.

444. and swa west on butan on bradanstan, 'broad stone'. AD 892. Newton. S348 (B567; K320). Grundy 1919: 190.

445. thonne to draeg stan, uncertain 'portage(?) stone'. AD 892. Newton. S348 (B567; K320). Grundy 1919: 190.

446. Of smitan on thone stan, 'stone'. AD 854. Little Hinton. S312 (B477/8/9; K1053). Grundy 1919: 172.

447. beornwyne stane, 'Beornwin's stone'. AD 949. Laverstock. S543 (B879; K428). Grundy 1920: 22–3.

448. innan thone dunnan stanwith foran tham burg gete, 'brown stone by the camp/fort entrance'. AD 972. Overton. S784 (B1285). Grundy 1919: 246.

449. innan tha twegen stanes, 'two stones'. AD 854. Wanborough. S312 (B477/8/9; K1053). Grundy 1919: 179.

Bibliography

Adkins, R. A. and Petchey, M. R. (1984). 'Secklow Hundred Mound and Other Meeting-Place Mounds in England', *Archaeological Journal* 141: 243–51.

Airlie, S. (2000). 'The Palace of Memory: The Carolingian Court as Political Centre', in S. Rees Jones, R. Marks, and A. J. Minnis (eds), *Courts and Regions in Medieval Europe* (York: York Medieval Press), 1–20.

Aitchson, N. B. (1987). 'The Ulster Cycle: Heroic Image and Historical Reality', *Journal of Medieval History* 13(2): 87–116.

—— (1994). *Armagh and the Royal Centres in Early Medieval Ireland: Monuments, Cosmology and the Past* (Woodbridge: Boydell and Brewer for Cruithne Press).

Akerman, J. Y. (1855). *Remains of Pagan Saxondom* (London: J. R. Smith).

Alcock, L. (1988). 'The Activities of Potentates in Celtic Britain, AD 500–800', in S. Driscoll and M. R. Nieke (eds), *Power and Politics in Early Medieval Britain and Ireland* (Edinburgh: Edinburgh University Press), 22–46.

—— (1995). *Cadbury Castle, Somerset: The Early Medieval Archaeology* (Cardiff: University of Wales Press).

Aldrich, M. and Wallis, R. J. (eds) (2009). *Antiquaries and Archaists, the Past in the Past, the Past in the Present* (Reading: Spire Books Ltd).

Alexander, M. (trans.) (1987). *Beowulf: A Verse Translation* (Harmondsworth: Penguin Books).

Allcroft, A. H. (1927–30). *The Circle and the Cross: A Study in Continuity.* 2 vols (London: Macmillan).

Allen, D. and Dalwood, C. H. (1983). 'Iron Age Occupation in Aylesbury, 1981', *Records of Buckinghamshire* 25: 1–60.

Allison, K. J. (1974). *The Victoria History of the Counties of England: A History of the County of York, East Riding,* ii (London: Oxford University Press).

Althoff, G. (2003). *Die Macht der Rituale: Symbolik und Herrschaft im Mittelalter* (Darmstadt: Primus).

Amesbury (2009). <http://www.open.ac.uk/Arts/classical-studies/amesbury/2009>.

Amory, P. (1994). 'Names, Ethnic Identity, and Community in Fifth and Sixth Century Burgundy', *Viator* 25: 1–30.

Anderson, O. S. (1934–39). *The English Hundred Names,* i–iii (Lund: Lunds Universitets Arsskrift).

Annable, K. and Eagles, B. (2010). *The Anglo-Saxon Cemetery at Blacknall Field, Pewsey, Wiltshire,* Wiltshire Archaeological and Natural History Society Monograph, 4 (Devizes: Wiltshire Archaeological and Natural History Society).

Anon. (1843–9). 'Proceedings for Thursday, February tenth, 1848', *Proceedings of the Society of Antiquaries,* 1st ser. 1: 241–2.

—— (1932–4). 'Report on the Field Archaeology 1931–2', *Proceedings of the Hampshire Field Club* 12: 208–9.

——(1975). *An Inventory of Historical Monuments in the County of Dorset, Vol. 5, East Dorset* (London: HMSO).

——(1980). *Ancient and Historical Monuments in the City of Salisbury*, i, Royal Commission on Historical Monuments (England) (London: HMSO).

——(2000). 'Malmesbury, Excavation and Fieldwork in Wiltshire, 1999', *Wiltshire Archaeological and Natural History Magazine* 94: 249.

——(2007). *Excavations at Lanton Quarry, Northumberland*, Archaeological Research Services Ltd Report, no. 2007/14.

——(2009). *Lanton Quarry, Northumberland: Report on an Archaeological Excavation*, Archaeological Research Services Ltd. Report, no. 2009/27.

Arce, J. (1997). '*Otium et negotium*: The Great Estates', in L. Webster and M. Brown (eds), *The Transformation of the Roman World 400–900* (London: British Museum Press), 19–32.

Arnold, C. (1980). 'Wealth and Social Structure: A Matter of Life and Death', in P. Rahtz, T. Dickinson, and L. Watts (eds), *Anglo-Saxon Cemeteries 1979: The Fourth Anglo-Saxon Symposium at Oxford*. BAR British Series, 133 (Oxford: BAR), 81–142.

——(1982). *The Anglo-Saxon Cemeteries of the Isle of Wight* (London: British Museums Publications Ltd).

——(1988). *An Archaeology of the Early Anglo-Saxon Kingdoms* (London: Routledge).

Atkinson, R. J. C., Piggott, C. M., and Sandars, N. K. (1951). *Excavations at Dorchester, Oxon* (Oxford: Printed for the visitors of the Ashmolean Museum).

Attenborough, F. L. (ed. and trans.) (1922). *The Laws of the Earliest English Kings* (Cambridge: Cambridge University Press).

Austin, G. (2002). 'Marvelous Peoples or Marvelous Races? Race and the Anglo-Saxon *Wonders of the East*', in T. S. Jones and D. A. Sprunger (eds), *Marvels, Monsters and Miracles: Studies in the Early Medieval and Early Modern Imaginations*, Studies in Medieval Culture 42 (Kalamzoo, MI: Medieval Institute Publications), 25–51.

Bailey, G. B. (1985). 'Late Roman Inland Signal Station, or Temple? Functional Interpretation at Walkington Wold', *Yorkshire Archaeological Journal* 57: 11–14.

Bailey, R. (2010). *Cheshire and Lancashire: The Corpus of Anglo-Saxon Stone Sculpture*, IX (Oxford: Oxford University Press).

——and Cramp, R. (1988). *Cumberland, Westmorland and Lancashire-north-of-the-Sands: The Corpus of Anglo-Saxon Stone Sculpture*, III, published for the British Academy (Oxford: Oxford University Press).

Baines, E. (1836). *A History of the County Palatine and Duchy of Lancaster*. 4 vols (London: Fisher and Son).

Baker, J. (2008). 'Old English *fæsten*', in O. Padel and D. Parsons (eds), *A Commodity of Good Names: Essays in Honour of Margaret Gelling* (Donington: Shaun Tyas), 333–44.

——(2011). 'Warriors and Watchmen: Place-Names and Anglo-Saxon Civil Defence', *Medieval Archaeology* 55: 258–67.

——(2012). 'What Makes a Stronghold? Reference to Construction Materials in Place-Names in OE *fæsten, burh* and (ge)*weorc*', in R. Jones and S. Semple (eds), *Sense of Place in Anglo-Saxon England* (Donnington: Shaun Tyas), 316–33.

——(in press). 'Meeting in the Shadow of Heroes? Personal Names and the Socio-Political Background of Assembly Places', in J. Carroll, A. Reynolds, and

B. Yorke (eds), *Power and Place in Later Roman and Early Medieval Europe* (Oxford: Oxford University Press).

Baker, J., Brookes, S., and Reynolds, A. (eds) (2013). *Landscapes of Defence in Early Medieval Europe*, Studies in the Early Middle Ages Series (Turnhout: Brepols Publishers).

Baker, J. and Brookes, S. (2015). 'Identifying Outdoor Assembly Sites in Early Medieval Britain', *Journal of Field Archaeology* 40.1: 3–21.

Baldwin Brown, G. (1915). *The Arts in Early England IV: Saxon Art and Industry in the Pagan Period* (London: John Murray).

Barclay, A. and Halpin, C. (1999). *Excavations at Barrow Hills, Radley, Oxfordshire*, Thames Valley Landscapes, 11 (Oxford: Oxford University Committee for Archaeology).

Barclay, G. J. (1983). 'Sites of the Third Millennium BC to the First Millennium AD at North Mains, Strathallan, Perthshire', *Proceedings of the Society of Antiquaries for Scotland* 113: 122–281.

Barfoot, J. F. and Price-Williams, D. (1976). 'The Saxon Barrow at Gally Hills, Banstead Down, Surrey', *Research Volume of the Surrey Archaeological Society* 3: 59–76.

Barford, P. M., Owen, W. G., and Britnell, W. J. (1986). 'Iron Spear-Head and Javelin from Four Crosses, Llandysilio, Powys', *Medieval Archaeology* 30: 103–6.

Barker, C. T. (1984). 'The Long Mounds of the Avebury Region', *Wiltshire Archaeological and Natural History Magazine* 79: 7–38.

Barker, E. E. (1947). 'Sussex Anglo-Saxon Charters', *Sussex Archaeological Collections* 86: 42–101.

—— (1948). 'Sussex Anglo-Saxon Charters', *Sussex Archaeological Collections* 87: 112–63.

—— (1949). 'Sussex Anglo-Saxon Charters', *Sussex Archaeological Collections* 88: 51–113.

Barnwell, P. S. (2005). 'Anglian Yeavering: A Continental Perspective', in P. Frodsham and C. O'Brien (eds), *Yeavering: People, Power and Place* (Stroud: Tempus Publishing Ltd).

Barrett, J. (1994). *Fragments from Antiquity* (Oxford: Blackwell Publishers Ltd).

Barrow, J. (2001). 'Chester's Earliest Regatta? Edgar's Dee-Rowing Revisited', *Early Medieval Europe* 10: 81–93.

Bartlett, J. E. and Mackey, R. W. (1973). 'Excavations on Walkington Wold, 1967–1969', *East Riding Archaeologist* 1(2): 1–93.

Bassett, S. (ed.) (1989). *The Origins of Anglo-Saxon Kingdoms* (Leicester: Leicester University Press).

Bateman, T. (1861). *Ten Years Digging in Celtic and Saxon Grave Hills, in the Counties of Derby, Stafford and York* (London: J. R. Smith).

Baudrillard, J. (1997). *Fragments: Cool Memories III. 1991–95* (London: Verso).

Beesley, T. (1855). 'The Rollright Stones', *Transactions of the North Oxfordshire Archaeology Society* 1: 61–73.

Bell, M. (1977). 'Excavations at Bishopstone', *Sussex Archaeological Collections* 115: 83–117.

Bell, T. (1998). 'Churches on Roman Buildings: Christian Associations and Roman Masonry in Anglo-Saxon England', *Medieval Archaeology* 42: 1–18.

—— (2005). *The Religious Use of Roman Structures in Early Medieval Britain*. BAR British Series, 390 (Oxford: Archaeopress).

Bender, B. (1998). *Stonehenge: Making Space* (Oxford: Berg).

—— Hamilton, S., and Tilley, C. (2007). *Stone Worlds: Narrative and Reflexivity in Landscape Archaeology* (Walnut Creek, CA: Left Coast Press).

Bergius, G. C. C. (2011). 'The Anglo-Saxon Stone Sculpture of Mercia as Evidence for Continental Influence and Cultural Exchange'. Unpublished PhD Thesis, Durham University.

Bhreathnach, E. (ed.) (2001). *Tara and the Medieval Kingdom of Brega: A Study in Kingship, Mythology and Landscape Dublin: Discovery Programme* (Dublin: Royal Irish Academy).

Biddle, M. (1976). 'The Archaeology of the Church: A Widening Horizon', in P. Addyman and R. Morris (eds), *The Archaeological Study of Churches*. CBA Research Report, 13 (London: CBA), 65–71.

Biggam, C. (ed.) (2003). *From Earth to Art: The Many Aspects of the Plant World in Anglo-Saxon England* (Amsterdam: Rodopi).

Biggs, F. and Hall, T. (1996). 'Traditions Concerning Jamnes and Mambres in Anglo-Saxon England', *Anglo-Saxon England* 25: 69–89.

Billard, C., Carré, F., Guillon, M., Treffort, C., Jagu, D., and Verron, G. (1996). 'L'Occupation funéraire des monuments mégalithiques pendant le haut Moyen-Age: Modalité et essai d'interprétation', *Bulletin de la Société préhistorique française* 93(3): 279–86.

Bintley, M. D. J. (2010). 'Trees and Woodland in Anglo-Saxon Culture'. Unpublished PhD Thesis, University of London.

—— (2013). 'Recasting the Role of Sacred Trees in Anglo-Saxon Spiritual History: The South Sandbach Cross "Ancestors of Christ" Panel in its Cultural Contexts', in M. Bintley and M. Shapland (eds), *Trees in Anglo-Saxon England: Literature, Lore and Landscape* (Oxford: Oxford University Press), 211–27.

Birch, W. de Gray (1885–93). *Cartularium Saxonicum: A Collection of Charters Relating to Anglo-Saxon History*. 3 vols (London: Charles J. Clark).

Blackburn, M. and Pagan, H. (1986). 'A Revised Check-List of Coin Hoards from the British Isles, *c*.500–1100', in M. A. S. Blackburn (ed.), *Anglo-Saxon Monetary History* (Leicester: Leicester University Press), 291–394.

Blackmore, H. P. (1894). 'On a Barrow near Old Sarum', *Salisbury Field Club Transactions* 1: 49–51.

Blair, W. J. (1988). 'Minster Churches in the Landscape', in D. Hooke (ed.), *Anglo-Saxon Settlements* (Oxford: Blackwell Publishers Ltd), 41–7.

—— (1992). 'Anglo-Saxon Minsters: A Topographical Review', in W. J. Blair and R. Sharpe (eds), *Pastoral Care Before the Parish* (Leicester: Leicester University Press), 226–66.

—— (1994). *Anglo-Saxon Oxfordshire* (Stroud: Alan Sutton Publishing).

—— (1995). 'Anglo-Saxon Pagan Shrines and their Prototypes', *Anglo-Saxon Studies in Archaeology and History* 8: 1–28.

—— (1997). 'Saint Cuthman, Steyning and Bosham', *Sussex Archaeological Collections* 135: 173–92.

—— (1998). 'Bampton: An Anglo-Saxon Minster', *Current Archaeology* 160: 124–30.

—— (1999). *The Bronze Age Barrows and Churchyard*. Bampton Research Paper 5, Oxford.

—— (2005). *The Church in Anglo-Saxon Society* (Oxford: Oxford Univesity Press).

—— (2009). 'The Dangerous Dead in Early Medieval England', in S. Baxter, C. Karkov, J. L. Nelson, and D. Pelteret (eds), *Early Medieval Studies in Memory of Patrick Wormald* (Farnham: Ashgate), 539–59.

Blair, W. J. (2013). 'Holy Beams: Anglo-Saxon Cult Sites and the Place-Name Element *Beām*', in M. Bintley and M. Shapland (eds), *Trees and Timber in the Anglo-Saxon World* (Oxford: Oxford University Press), 186–210.

Blake, N. F. (1977). 'The Dating of Old English Poetry', in B. S. Lee (ed.), *An English Miscellany Presented to W. S. Mackie* (New York: Oxford University Press), 14–27.

Bleach, J. (1997). 'A Romano-British (?) Barrow Cemetery and the Origins of Lewes', *Sussex Archaeological Collections* 135: 131–42.

Bolton, W. F. (1978). *Alcuin and Beowulf: An Eighth-Century View* (London: Edward Arnold).

Bonney, D. J. (1966). 'Pagan Saxon Burials and Boundaries in Wiltshire', *Wiltshire Archaeological and Natural History Magazine* 61: 25–30.

Bradley, R. J. (1980). 'Anglo-Saxon Cemeteries: Some Suggestions for Research', in P. Rahtz, T. Dickinson, and L. Watts (eds), *Anglo-Saxon Cemeteries 1979: The Fourth Anglo-Saxon Symposium at Oxford*. BAR British Series, 82 (Oxford: BAR), 171–8.

—— (1984a). 'Studying Monuments', in R. Bradley and J. Gardiner (eds), *Neolithic Studies: A Review of Some Current Research*. BAR British Series, 133 (Oxford: BAR), 61–6.

—— (1984b). *The Social Foundations of Prehistoric Britain: Themes and Variations in the Archaeology of Power* (London: Longman).

—— (1987a). 'Time Regained: The Creation of Continuity', *Journal of the British Archaeological Association* 140: 1–17.

—— (1987b). 'Stages in the Chronological Distribution of Hoards and Votive Deposits', *Proceedings of the Prehistoric Society* 53: 351–62.

—— (1993). *Altering the Earth*, Society of Antiquaries of Scotland Monograph Series, 8 (Edinburgh: Society of Antiquaries of Scotland).

—— (1998a). *The Significance of Monuments* (London: Routledge).

—— (1998b). *The Passage of Arms*, 2nd edn (Oxford: Oxbow Books Ltd).

—— (2000). *An Archaeology of Natural Places* (London: Routledge).

—— (2002). *The Past in Prehistoric Societies* (London: Routledge).

—— Chambers, R. A., and Halpin, C. E. (1984). *Barrow Hills, Radley 1983–4, Excavations: An Interim Report* (Oxford: Oxford Archaeology Unit).

Bradley, S. A. J. (1995). *Anglo-Saxon Poetry* (London: J. M. Dent).

Brassil, K. S., Britnell, W. J., and Owen, W. G. (1991). 'Prehistoric and Early Medieval Cemeteries at Tandderwen, near Denbugh, Clwyd', *Archaeological Journal* 148: 46–97.

Bratt, P. (1999). *Anundshög. Del 1, Delundersökning för datering: arkeologisk delundersökning av Anundshög, RAÄ 431, Långby, Badelunda socken, Västerås stad, Västmanland* (Stockholm: Stockholms Läns Museum).

Brenk, B. (1987). 'Spolia from Constantine to Charlemagne: Aesthetics versus Ideology', *Dumbarton Oaks Papers* 41: 103–9.

Briggs, K. (2010). 'Harrow', *Journal of the English Place-Name Society* 42: 43–62.

Brink, S. (2001). 'Mythologizing Landscape, Place and Space of Cult and Myth', in M. Stausberg (ed.), *Kontinuitäten und Brüche in der Religionsgeschichte. Festschrift für Anders Hultgard zu seinem 65. Geburtstag am 23. 12. 2002*, Ergänzungsbnd zum Reallexikon der Germanischen Altertumskunde, 31 (New York: Walter de Gruyter), 1–31.

Brooks, H. and Dennis, T. (2005). 'A Geophysical Survey at Coppins Farm, Alphamstone, Essex'. Unpublished Report, Essex County Council.

Brookes, S. J. (2007a). *Economics and Social Change in Anglo-Saxon Kent AD 400–900: Landscapes, Communities and Exchange*. BAR British Series, 431 (Oxford: Archaeopress).

—— (2007b). 'Walking with Anglo-Saxons: Landscapes of the Dead in Early Anglo-Saxon Kent', in S. Semple and H. Williams (eds), *Early Medieval Mortuary Practices: New Perspectives, Anglo-Saxon Studies in Archaeology and History* 14 (Oxford: Oxford University Press), 143–53.

—— (2011). 'The Lathes of Kent: A Review of the Evidence', in S. J. Brookes, S. Harrington, and A. Reynolds (eds), *Studies in Early Anglo-Saxon Art and Archaeology: Papers in Honour of Martin G. Welch*. BAR British Series, 527 (Oxford: Archaeopress), 156–70.

Brookes, S. J. (in press). 'Folk Cemeteries, Assembly and Territorial Geography in Early Anglo-Saxon England', in J. Carroll, A. Reynolds, and B. Yorke (eds), *Power and Place in Later Roman and Early Medieval Europe: Perspectives on Governance and Civil Organization* (London: British Academy).

—— and Harrington, S. (2010). *The Kingdom and People of Kent AD 400–1066: Their History and Archaeology* (Stroud: The History Press).

Brough, F. (1908). 'Corhampton', in W. Page (ed.), *The Victoria History of Hampshire and the Isle of Wight* (London: Archibald Constable and Co. Ltd), 246–54.

Brown, G., Field, D., and McOmish, D. (eds) (2005). *The Avebury Landscape: Aspects of the Field Archaeology of the Marlborough Downs* (Oxford: Oxbow Books Ltd).

Buckberry, J. and Hadley, D. (2007). 'An Anglo-Saxon Execution Cemetery at Walkington Wold, Yorkshire', *Oxford Journal of Archaeology* 26(3): 309–29.

Burl, A. (1979). *Prehistoric Avebury* (Yale: Yale University Press).

Butler, C. (1998). 'Rescue Archaeology in Mid-Sussex', *Current Archaeology* 156: 464–7.

Cam, H. and Crawford, O. G. S. (1935). 'The *Hoga* of Cutteslowe', *Antiquity* 9: 96–7.

Cambridge, E. (1984). 'The Early Church in County Durham: A Reassessment', *Journal of the British Archaeological Association* 137(1): 65–85.

Camden, W. (1610). *Britannia, or a Chorographicall Description of the Most Flourishing Kindomes, England, Scotland and Ireland, and the Llands Adjoining, out of the Depth of Antiqvitie: Beautified with Mappes of the Severall Shires of England: Written first in Latine by William Camden Clarenceux K. of A.* Translated newly into English by Philémon Holland Doctour in Physick. London.

Cameron, K. (1988). *English Place-Names*, 3rd edn (London: Batsford).

—— (1991). *The Place-Names of Lincolnshire, Part II*. EPNS, vol. 64/65 (Nottingham: EPNS).

—— (1992). *The Place-Names of Lincolnshire, Part III*. EPNS, vol. 66 (Nottingham: EPNS).

—— (1996). *The Place-Names of Lincolnshire, Part IV*. EPNS, vol. 71 (Nottingham: EPNS).

—— (2001). *The Place-Names of Lincolnshire, Part VI*. EPNS, vol. 77 (Nottingham: EPNS).

Campbell, A. (ed.) (1967). *De Abbatibus* (Oxford: Clarendon Press).

Campbell, E. (2007). *Continental and Mediterranean Imports to Atlantic Britain and Ireland, AD 400–800*, CBA Research Report, 157, (York: CBA).

Canham, A. S. (1890). 'Notes on the Archaeology of Crowland', *Journal of the British Archaeological Association* 46: 286–300.

Cantor, N. F. (1991). *Inventing the Middle Ages: The Lives, Works and Ideas of the Great Medievalists of the Twentieth Century* (Cambridge: The Lutterworth Press).

Capelle, T. (1971). *Studien über Elbgermanische Gräberfelder in der ausgehenden Latènezeit und der älteren römischen Kaiserzeit. Münstersche Beiträge zur Ur- und Frühgeschichte* 6 (Hildesheim: Lax).

Carelli, P. (1997). 'Thunder and Lightning, Magical Miracles: On the Popular Myth of Thunderbolts and the Presence of Stone Age Artefacts in Medieval Deposits', in H. Andersson, P. Carelli, and L. Ersgard (eds), *Visions of the Past: Trends and Traditions in Swedish Medieval Archaeology* (Lund: Central Board of National Antiquities), 393–417.

Carré, F. and Treffort, C. (2010). 'La Place des monuments dans l'environnement post-néolithique', in C. Billard, M. Guillon, and G. Verron (eds), *Les Sépultures collectives du néolithique récent-final de Val-de-Reuil et Porte-Joie* (Eure). Coll. ERAUL, 123 (Liège: Université de Liège), 341–51.

Carruthers, M. (1998). *The Craft of Thought* (Cambridge: Cambridge University Press).

Carver, M. O. H. (1992). 'The Anglo-Saxon Cemetery at Sutton Hoo: An Interim Report', in M. O. H. Carver (ed.), *The Age of Sutton Hoo* (Woodbridge: Boydell Press), 343–71.

——(1998). *Sutton Hoo, Burial Ground of Kings?* (Pennsylvania, PA: University of Pennsylvania).

——(2001). 'Why That, Why There, Why Then? The Politics of Early Medieval Monumentality', in H. Hamerow and A. MacGregor (eds), *Image and Power in the Archaeology of Early Medieval Britain: Essays in Honour of Rosemary Cramp* (Oxford: Oxbow Books), 1–22.

——(2002). 'Reflections on the Meaning of Anglo-Saxon Barrows', in S. Lucy and A. Reynolds (eds), *Burial in Early Medieval England and Wales*. Society for Medieval Archaeology Monograph, 17 (London: Society for Medieval Archaeology), 132–43.

——(2003). 'Introduction: Northern Europeans Negotiate their Future', in M. O. H. Carver (ed.), *The Cross Goes North: Processes of Conversion in Northern Europe* (York: Boydell Press), 3–14.

——(2005). *Sutton Hoo. A Seventh-Century Princely Burial Ground and its Context* (London: British Museum).

——(2008). *The Pictish Monastery at Portmahomack*. Jarrow Lecture 2008. Newcastle.

——(2009). 'Early Scottish Monasteries and Prehistory: A Preliminary Dialogue', *Scottish Historical Review* 88: 332–51.

——(2010). 'Agency, Intellect and the Archaeological Agenda', in M. O. H. Carver, A. Sanmark, and S. J. Semple (eds), *Signals of Belief Early England: Anglo-Saxon Paganism Revisited* (Oxford: Oxbow Books Ltd), 1–20.

——(2011). 'Intellectual Communities in Early Northumbria', in D. Petts and S. Turner (eds), *Early Medieval Northumbria: Kingdoms and Communities, AD 450–1100*, Studies in the Early Middle Ages, 24 (Turnhout: Brepols Publishers), 185–206.

——Sanmark, A., and Semple, S. (eds) (2010). *Signals of Belief in Early England: Anglo-Saxon Paganism Revisited* (Oxford: Oxbow Books Ltd).

Cessford, C. with Dickens, A., Dodwell, N., and Reynolds, A. (2007). 'Middle Anglo-Saxon Justice: The Chesterton Lane Corner Execution Cemetery and Related Sequence, Cambridge', *Archaeological Journal* 164: 192–226.

Chambers, R. A. (1978). 'A Secondary Burial on Shipton Barrow, Oxon', *Oxoniensia* 43: 253–5.

—— (1986). 'An Inhumation Cemetery at Castle Hill, Little Wittenham, Oxon., 1984–5', *Oxoniensia* 51: 45–8.

—— and McAdam, E. (2007). *Excavations at Barrow Hills, Radley, Oxfordshire*, ii. *The Romano-British Cemetery and Anglo-Saxon Settlement* (Oxford: Oxford Archaeology).

Champion, S. and Cooney, G. (1999). 'Naming the Places, Naming the Stones', in A. Gazin-Schwartz and C. Holtorf (eds), *Archaeology and Folklore* (London: Routledge), 196–211.

Charles-Edwards, T. (1976). 'Boundaries in Irish Law', in P. H. Sawyer (ed.), *Medieval Settlement, Continuity and Change* (London: Edward Arnold), 183–7.

—— (1989). 'Early Medieval Kingships in the British Isles', in S. Bassett (ed.), *The Origins of Anglo-Saxon Kingdoms* (Leicester: Leicester University Press), 28–39.

—— (2000). *Early Christian Ireland* (Cambridge: Cambridge University Press).

Chase, C. (1997). 'Opinions on the Date of Beowulf, 1815–1980', in C. Chase (ed.), *The Dating of Beowulf* (Toronto: University of Toronto Press), 3–8.

Cherry, B. and Pevsner, N. (1999). *The Buildings of England, Devon*, rev. repr. (Harmondsworth: Penguin Books).

Chester-Kadwell, M. (2009). *Early Anglo-Saxon Communities in the Landscape of Norfolk*. BAR British Series, 481 (Oxford: Archaeopress).

Christie, N. (2004). 'Landscapes of Change in Late Antiquity and the Early Middle Ages: Themes, Directions and Problems', in N. Christie (ed.), *Landscapes of Change: Rural Evolutions in Late Antiquity and the Early Middle Ages* (Aldershot: Ashgate), 1–38.

—— (2005). 'Charlemagne and the Renewal of Rome', in J. Story (ed.), *Charlemagne: Empire and Society* (Manchester and New York: Manchester University Press), 167–82.

Clarke, L. and Carlin, N. (2009). 'From Focus to Locus: A Window upon the Development of a Funerary Landscape', in M. B. Deevy and D. Murphy (eds), *Places along the Way: First Findings on the M3*. National Roads Authority Scheme Monograph Series, 5 (Dublin: National Roads Authority), 8–20.

Clarke, R. (1938–40). 'Norfolk in the Dark Ages', *Norfolk Archaeology* 27: 215–49.

Clayton, N. B. (1973). 'New Wintles, Eynsham, Oxon.', *Oxoniensia* 38: 382–4.

Clinch, G. (1908). 'Ancient Earthworks', in W. Page (ed.), *The Victoria County History of the County of Buckingham*, ii (London: Archibald Constable and Company Ltd), 22–3.

Coates, R. (1982). 'Friday's Church', *Sussex Archaeological Society Newsletter* 36: 277, 298.

—— (1989). *The Place-Names of Hampshire* (London: Batsford).

Cockayne, T. O. (1864–5). *Leechdoms, Wortcunning and Starcraft of Early England*. 3 vols (London: Longman, Green, Longman, Roberts and Green).

Coffey, G. (1904). 'On the Excavation of a Tumulus near Loughrea, Co. Galway', *Proceedings of the Royal Irish Academy* 25: 14–20.

Cohen, N. (2003). 'Boundaries and Settlement: The Role of the River Thames', in D. Griffiths, A. Reynolds, and S. Semple (eds), *Boundaries in Early Medieval Britain*, *Anglo-Saxon Studies in Archaeology and History* 12: 9–20.

Colgrave, B. (ed. and trans.) (1927). *The Life of Bishop Wilfrid by Eddius Stephanus* (Cambridge: Cambridge University Press).

Colgrave, B. (ed. and trans.) (1956). *Felix's Life of St Guthlac* (Cambridge: Cambridge University Press).

Collard, M. (1988). 'Excavations at Desborough Castle, High Wycomb, 1887', *Records of Buckinghamshire* 30: 15–41.

Collyer, H. C. (1895–6) 'Notes on the Opening of Some Tumuli on the South Downs', *Proceedings and Transactions of the Croydon Microscopical and Natural History Club* 4: 179–80.

Conder, E. (1893–5). 'Account of the Exploration of Lyneham Barrow, Oxford', *Proceedings of the Society of Antiquaries*, 2nd ser., 15: 404–10.

Connerton, P. (1989). *How Societies Remember* (Cambridge: Cambridge University Press).

Content, S. and Williams, H. (2010). 'Creating the Pagan English: From the Tudors to the Present Day', in M. O. H. Carver, A. Sanmark, and S. J. Semple (eds), *Signals of Belief in Early England: Anglo-Saxon Paganism Revisited* (Oxford: Oxbow Books Ltd), 181–200.

Cook, J. and Rowley, R. T. (eds) (1985). *Dorchester through the Ages* (Oxford: Oxford University Department for External Studies).

Cooney, G. and Grogan, E. (1991). 'An Archaeological Solution to the "Irish" Problem?', *Emania* 9: 33–43.

Cordier, G. (1985). 'Les Mérovingiens de Sublaines (Indre-et-Loire): Complément à l'étude anthropologique', *Revue Archéologique du Centre de la France* 24(2): 247–55.

Corney, M. (1997). 'New Evidence for the Romano-British Settlement by Silbury Hill', *Wiltshire Archaeological and Natural History Magazine* 90: 139–40.

—— (2001). 'The Romano-British Nucleated Settlements of Wiltshire', in P. Ellis (ed.), *Roman Wiltshire and After: Papers in Honour of Ken Annable* (Devizes: Wiltshire Archaeological and Natural History Society), 5–38.

Costen, M. (1994). 'Settlement in Wessex in the Tenth-Century: The Charter Evidence', in M. A. Aston and C. Lewis (eds), *The Medieval Landscape of Wessex*. Oxbow Monograph, 46 (Oxford: Oxbow Books Ltd), 97–107.

Cowley, D. C. (2003). 'Changing Places: Building Life-Spans and Settlement Continuity in Northern Scotland', in J. Downes and A. Ritchie (eds), *Sea Change: Orkney and Northern Europe in the Later Iron Age AD 300–800* (Balgavies, UK: Pinkfoot Press), 75–81.

Cramp, R. (1961). 'The Anglian Sculptured Crosses of Dumfriesshire', *Transactions of the Dumfriesshire Natural History and Antiquarian Society* 38: 9–20.

—— (2005). *Excavations at Wearmouth and Jarrow Monastic Sites*, i (Swindon: English Heritage).

—— (2006). *South West England: The Corpus of Anglo-Saxon Stone Sculpture*, vii (Oxford: Oxford University Press).

—— and Miket, R. (1982). *Catalogue of Anglo-Saxon and Viking Antiquities in the Museum of Antiquities, Newcastle upon Tyne* (Newcastle: Museum Publication).

Crawford, O. G. S. (1933). 'Some Recent Air Discoveries', *Antiquity* 7: 290–6.

Crewe, V. (2010). 'The Reuse of Prehistoric Monuments in Early to Middle Anglo-Saxon Settlements of the English Midlands'. Unpublished PhD thesis, University of Sheffield.

—— (2012). *Living with the Past: The Reuse of Prehistoric Monuments in Anglo-Saxon Settlements* BAR British Series, 573 (Oxford: Archaeopress).

Crook, B. (1953a). 'Appledram', in L. F. Salzman (ed.), *The Victoria History of the County of Sussex*, iv (London: Oxford University Press), 138–9.

—— (1953b). 'Pagham', in L. F. Salzman (ed.), *The Victoria History of the County of Sussex*, iv (London: Oxford University Press), 227–33.

Cubitt, C. (1995). *Anglo-Saxon Church Councils c.650–c.850* (London: Leicester University Press).

—— (2000). 'Sites and Sanctity: The Cult of Murdered and Martyred Royal Saints in Anglo-Saxon England Revisited', *Early Medieval Europe* 9(1): 53–83.

—— (2003). 'Introduction', in C. Cubitt (ed.), *Court Culture in the Early Middle Ages: The Proceedings of the First York Alcuin Conference* (Turnhout: Brepols Publishers), 1–15.

Cunliffe, B. W. (1973). 'The Middle Pre-Roman Iron Age, *c.400–c.*100 B.C.', in E. Crittall (ed.), *The Victoria History of the Counties of England: A History of Wiltshire*, i, pt. 2 (Oxford: Oxford University Press), 417–25.

—— (1978). *Iron Age Communities in Britain*, 2nd edn. (London: Routledge).

—— (1979). *Excavations in Bath, 1950–1975* (Bristol: Committee for Rescue Archaeology in Avon, Gloucestershire and Somerset).

Cunnington, M. E. (1911–12). 'Knap Hill Camp', *Wiltshire Archaeological and Natural History Magazine* 37: 42–65.

—— (1933–4). 'Wiltshire in Pagan Saxon Times', *Wiltshire Archaeological and Natural History Society Magazine* 46: 147–75.

—— and Goddard, E. (1934). *Catalogue of the Wiltshire Archaeological and Natural History Society at Devize*, ii (Devizes: Wiltshire Archaeological and Natural History Society).

Cunnington, W. (1885). 'Barrow at Ogbourne St Andrew', *Wiltshire Archaeological and Natural History Magazine* 22: 345–8.

Curwen, C. (1933). 'Excavations on Thundersbarrow Hill, Sussex', *Antiquaries Journal* 3: 109–33.

Dark, K. (1994a). *Discovery by Design: The Identification of Secular Elite Settlements in Western Britain, AD 400–700*. BAR British Series, 237 (Oxford: Tempus Reparatum).

—— (1994b) *Civitas to Kingdom: British Political Continuity 300–800* (Leicester: Leicester University Press).

Darling, M. with Gurney, D. (1993). *Caister-on-Sea: Excavations by Charles Green, 1951–55* (Gressenhall: East Anglian Archaeology).

Darvill, T. (1997). 'Landscapes and the Archaeologist', in K. Barker and T. Darvill (eds), *Making English Landscapes* (Oxford: Oxbow Books Ltd), 70–91.

—— (2004). 'Tynwald Hill and the "Things" of Power', in A. Pantos and S. Semple (eds), *Assembly Places and Practices in Medieval Europe* (Dublin: Four Courts Press), 217–33.

Deichmann, F. M. (1975). *Die Spolien in der spätantken Architektur* (Munich: Beck).

Dent, J. (1984). 'The Yorkshire Dykes', *Archaeological Journal* 141: 32–3.

Devlin, Z. (2007). *Remembering the Dead in Anglo-Saxon England: Memory Theory in Archaeology and History*. BAR British Series, 446 (Oxford: Archaeopress).

Dickinson, T. M. (1991). 'Material Culture as Social Expression: the Case of Saxon Saucer Brooches with Running Spiral Decoration', in H-J. Hässler (ed.), *Studien zur Sachsenforschung* 7: 39–70.

—— (2005). 'Symbols of Protection: The Significance of Animal-Ornamented Shields in Early Anglo-Saxon England', *Medieval Archaeology* 49: 109–63.

—— (2009). 'Medium and Message in Anglo-Saxon Animal Art: Some Observations on the Contexts of Salin's Style I in England', in S. Crawford and H. Hamerow with L. Webster (eds), *Form and Order in the Anglo-Saxon World, AD 600–1100*, *Anglo-Saxon Studies in Archaeology and History* 16: 1–12.

—— (2012). 'The Formation of a Folk District in the Kingdom of Kent: Eastry and its Early Anglo-Saxon Archaeology', in R. Jones and S. Semple (eds), *Sense of Place in Anglo-Saxon England* (Donington: Shaun Tyas), 147–67.

—— Fern, C., and Richardson, A. (2011). 'Early Anglo-Saxon Eastry: Archaeological Evidence and the Development of a District Centre in the Kingdom of Kent', *Anglo-Saxon Studies in Archaeology and History* 17: 1–86.

Dingwall, D. and Young, M. (1933). 'The Skeletal Material', in G. C. Dunning and R. E. M. Wheeler, 'A Barrow at Dunstable, Bedfordshire', *Archaeological Journal* 88: 210–17.

Dixon, F. (1849). 'On Bronze or Brass Relics, Celts etc. Found in Sussex', *Sussex Archaeological Collections* 2: 260–9.

Dolley, R. H. M. (1957). 'The Stockbridge Down Find of Anglo-Saxon Coins', *British Numismatic Journal* 28: 283–7.

Dooley Fairchild, S. (2012). 'Material Beliefs: A Critical History of Past and Contemporary Archaeological Approaches to Religion and Religious Change in Anglo-Saxon England'. Unpublished PhD thesis, Durham University.

Dornier, A. (1977). 'The Anglo-Saxon Monastery at Breedon-on-the-Hill, Leicestershire', in A. Dornier (ed.), *Mercian Studies* (Leicester: Leicester University Press), 155–68.

Down, A. and Welch, M. (1990). *Chichester Excavations Volume 7: Apple Down and the Mardens* (London: Phillimore).

Draper, S. (2006). *Landscape, Settlement and Society in Roman and Early Medieval Wiltshire*. BAR British Series, 419 (Oxford: BAR).

Drewett. P. (ed.) (1978). *Archaeology in Sussex to AD 1500*. CBA Research Report 29 (London: CBA).

—— Rudling, D., and Gardiner, M. (1988). *The South East to AD 1000* (London: Longman).

Driscoll, S. (1998). 'Picts and Prehistory: Cultural Resource Management in Early Medieval Scotland', *World Archaeology* 30(1): 142–58.

—— (2004). 'The Archaeological Context of Assembly in Early Medieval Scotland: Scone and its Comparanda', in A. Pantos and S. Semple (eds), *Assembly Places and Practices in Medieval Europe* (Dublin: Four Courts Press), 73–94.

—— (2010). 'Pictish Archaeology: Persistent Problems and Structural Solutions', in S. Driscoll, J. Geddes, and M. Hall (eds), *Pictish Progress: New Studies on Northern Britain in the Early Middle Ages* (Leiden: Brill), 245–80.

—— and Nieke, M. R. (eds). (1988). *Power and Politics in Early Medieval Britain and Ireland* (Edinburgh: Edinburgh University Press).

Dryden, H. E. L. (1897). 'The Dolmens at Rollright and Enstone', *Oxfordshire Archaeological Society Report* 40–51.

DuBois, T. A. (1999). *Nordic Religions in the Viking Age* (Pennsylvania, PA: University of Pennsylvania Press).

Duffey, J. E. (1977). 'The Inventive Group of Illustrations in the Harley Psalter'. Unpublished PhD thesis, Berkeley University.

Dugdale, W. (1656). *Antiquities of Warwickshire* (London: Thomas Warren).

Duignan, W. H. (1902). *Notes on Staffordshire Place-Names* (London: Henry Frowde).

Dumville, D. (1974). 'Some Aspects of the Chronology of the *Historia Brittonum*', *Bulletin of the Board of Celtic Studies* 25: 439–45.

—— (1977). 'Sub-Roman Britain: History and Legend', *History* 62: 177–92.

Dunning, G. C. and Wheeler, R. E. M. (1931). 'A Barrow at Dunstable, Bedfordshire', *Archaeological Journal* 88: 193–217.

Dyer, J. (1974). 'The Excavation of Two Barrows on Galley Hill, Streatley', *Bedfordshire Archaeological Journal* 9: 13–34.

Eagles, B. N. (1979). *The Anglo-Saxon Settlement of Humberside*. BAR British Series, 68 (Oxford: BAR).

—— (1986). 'Pagan Anglo-Saxon Burials at West Overton', *Wiltshire Archaeological and Natural History Magazine* 80: 103–20.

—— (1994). 'Evidence for Settlement in the 5th to 7th centuries AD', in M. Aston and C. Lewis (eds), *The Medieval Landscape of Wessex*, Oxbow Monograph, 46 (Oxford: Oxbow Books Ltd), 13–32.

—— (2001). 'Anglo-Saxon Presence and Culture in Wiltshire AD *c*.450–*c*.675', in P. Ellis (ed.), *Roman Wiltshire and After: Papers in Honour of Ken Annable* (Devizes: Wiltshire Archaeological and Natural History Society), 199–234.

Eaton, T. (2000). *Plundering the Past: Roman Stonework in Medieval Britain* (Stroud: Tempus Publishing Ltd).

Eckardt, H. and Williams, H. (2003). 'Objects without a Past? The Use of Roman Objects in Anglo-Saxon Graves', in H. Williams (ed.), *Archaeologies of Remembrance. Death and Memory in Past Societies* (New York: Kluwer Academic/Plenum Publishers), 141–70.

Edwards, H. (1986). 'Two Documents from Aldhelm's Malmesbury', *Bulletin of the Institute of Historical Research* 59: 1–19.

Edwards, N. (1990). *Archaeology of Early Medieval Ireland* (London: Routledge).

—— (ed.) (2009a). *The Archaeology of the Early Medieval Celtic Churches*, The Society for Medieval Archaeology Monograph, 29 (London: Maney and Sons).

—— (2009b). 'Rethinking the Pillar of Eliseg', *Antiquaries Journal* 89: 143–78.

—— et al. (2010). 'Report on Excavations at the Pillar of Eliseg, Denbighshire, Wales'. Unpublished Report: Bangor University.

Effros, B. (2001). 'Monuments and Memory: Repossessing Ancient Remains in Early Medieval Gaul', in M. De Jong, F. Theuws, and C. Van Rhijn (eds), *Topographies of Power in the Early Middle Ages* (Leiden: Brill), 93–118.

—— (2003). *Merovingian Mortuary Archaeology and the Making of the Middle Ages* (Berkeley and Los Angeles, CA: University of California Press).

Ekwall, E. (1960). *The Concise Oxford Dictionary of English Place-Names*, 4th edn (Oxford: Clarendon Press).

Elgee, F. and Elgee, H. W. (1933). *The Archaeology of Yorkshire* (Wakefield: S. R. Publishers).

Ellis, H. R. (1943). *The Road to Hel: A Study of the Conception of the Dead in Old Norse Literature* (Cambridge: Cambridge University Press).

Ellis-Davidson, H. R. (1950). 'The Hill of the Dragon', *Folklore* 61/4 (September): 169–85.

—— (1964). *Gods and Myths of Northern Europe* (London: Penguin Books Ltd).

—— and Webster, L. (1967). 'The Anglo-Saxon Burial at Coombe, Kent', *Medieval Archaeology* 11: 1–41.

Evans, A. (1895). 'The Rollright Stones and their Folklore', *Folklore* 6(1): 6–53.

Everitt, A. (1986). *Continuity and Colonization: The Evolution of Kentish Settlement* (Leicester: Leicester University Press).

Everson, P. and Stocker, D. (1999). *Lincolnshire: The Corpus of Anglo-Saxon Stone Sculpture*, v (Oxford: Oxford University Press).

—— —— (2011). *Custodians of Continuity? The Premonstratensian Abbey at Barlings and the Landscape of Ritual*, Lincolnshire Archaeological and Heritage Report Series, 11 (Lincoln: Lincoln Heritage Trust).

Evison, V. I. (1987). *Dover: Buckland Anglo-Saxon Cemetery* (London: HBMCE).

—— (1988). *An Anglo-Saxon Cemetery at Alton, Hampshire*, Hampshire Field Club and Archaeology Society Monograph, 4 (Winchester: Hampshire Field Club).

Faull, M. (1979). 'British Survival in Anglo-Saxon Yorkshire'. Unpublished PhD Dissertation, University of Leeds.

Fern, C. (2010). 'Horses in Mind', in M. O. H. Carver, A. Sanmark, and S. J. Semple (eds), *Signals of Belief in Early England: Anglo-Saxon Paganism Revisited* (Oxford: Oxbow Books Ltd), 128–57.

Field, N. and Parker Pearson, M. (2003). *Fiskerton: An Iron Age Timber Causeway with Iron Age and Roman Votive Offerings* (Oxford: Oxbow Books Ltd).

Finberg, H. P. R. (1964). *The Early Charters of Wessex*, Studies in English History, iii (Leicester: Leicester University Press).

Finn, C. (1997). ' "Leaving more than footprints": Modern Votive Offerings at Chaco Canyon Prehistoric Site', *Antiquity* 71: 169–78.

Fisher, I. (2005). 'Cross-Currents in North Atlantic Sculpture', in A. Mortensen and S. V. Arge (eds), *Viking and Norse in the North Atlantic: Select Papers from the Proceedings of the Fourteenth Viking Congress, Tórshavn, 19–30 July 2001*. Annales Scoietatis Scientiarum Færoensis Supplementum, XLIV (Tórshavn: Føroya Fróðskaparfelag), 160–6.

Fitzpatrick, A. (1984). 'The Deposition of La Tène Iron Age Metalwork in Watery Contexts in Southern England', in B. Cunliffe and D. Miles (eds), *Aspects of the Iron Age in Central Southern Britain* (Oxford: Oxford University Committee for Archaeology), 178–90.

FitzPatrick, E. (2004a). *Royal Inauguration in Gaelic Ireland c.1100–1600: A Cultural Landscape Study* (Woodbridge: Boydell Press).

—— (2004b). 'Royal Inauguration Mounds in Medieval Ireland: Antique Landscape and Tradition', in A. Pantos and S. Semple (eds), *Assembly Places and Practices in Medieval Europe* (Dublin: Four Courts Press), 44–72.

Flatman, J. (2010). 'Wetting the Fringe of Your Habit: Medieval Monasticism and Coastal Lifescapes', in H. Lewis and S. Semple (eds), *Perspectives in Landscape Archaeology*. BAR International Series, 2103 (Oxford: BAR), 66–77.

Forsberg, R. (1950). *A Contribution to a Dictionary of Old English Place-Names.* (Uppsala: Nomina Germanica).

Förster, M. (1902). 'Das lateinisch-altenglische Fragment der Apokryphe von Jamnes und Mambres', *Archiv für das Studium der neueren Sprachen und Literaturen* 108: 15–23.

Forward, E. (2008). 'Place-Names in the Whittlewood Area'. Unpublished PhD Thesis, University of Nottingham.

Foster, A. (2001). 'Romano-British Burials in Wiltshire', in P. Ellis (ed.), *Roman Wiltshire and After: Papers in Honour of Ken Annable* (Devizes: Wiltshire Archaeological and Natural History Society), 165–77.

Fowler, P. J. (2000). *Landscape Plotted and Pieced, Landscape History and Local Archaeology in Fyfield and Overton, Wiltshire* (London: The Society of Antiquaries of London).

—— and Blackwell, I. (1998). *An English Countryside Explored: The Land of Lettice Sweetapple* (Stroud: Tempus Publishing Ltd).

Fox, C. (1923). *The Archaeology of the Cambridge Region* (Cambridge: Cambridge University Press).

—— and Palmer, W. M. (1926). 'Excavations in the Cambridgeshire Dykes, v, Bran or Heydon Ditch. First Report', *Proceedings of the Cambridge Antiquarian Society* 27: 16–33.

Freeman, J. (1983). 'Avebury' and 'Ogbourne St. Andrew', in D. Crowley (ed.), *The Victoria History of the Counties of England: A History of Wiltshire*, xii (London: Oxford University Press), 86–104, 138–9.

Frodsham, P. and O'Brien, C. (2005). *Yeavering: People, Power and Place* (Stroud: Tempus Publishing Ltd).

Fry, D. K. (1987). 'The Cliff of Death in Old English Poetry', in J. M. Foley (ed.), *Comparative Research on Oral Traditions: A Memorial for Milman Parry* (Columbus: Slavonica), 211–33.

Fulk, R. D. (2004). 'On Argumentation in Old English Philology, with Particular Reference to the Editing and Dating of *Beowulf*', *Anglo-Saxon England* 32: 1–26.

—— Bjork, R. E., and Niles, J. D. (eds). (2008). *Klaeber's Beowulf and the Fight at Finnsburg* (Toronto: University of Toronto Press).

Gale, D. A. (1989). 'The Seax', in S. C. Hawkes (ed.), *Weapons and Warfare in Anglo-Saxon England*. Oxford University Committee for Archaeology Monograph, 21 (Oxford: Oxford University Committee for Archaeology), 71–84.

Gameson, F. and Gameson, R. (1996). 'Wulf and Eadwacer, The Wife's Lament, and the Discovery of the Individual in Old English Verse', in M. J. Toswell and E. M. Tyler (eds), *Studies in English Language and Literature: Papers in Honour of E. G. Stanley* (London: Routledge), 457–74.

Gardiner, M. (1988). 'Excavations at Testers, White Horse Square, Steyning, 1985', *Sussex Archaeological Collections* 126: 53–76.

—— (1990). 'An Anglo-Saxon and Medieval Settlement at Botolfs, Bramber, West Sussex', *Archaeological Journal* 147: 216–75.

Gardiner, M. (2003). 'Economy and Landscape Change in Post-Roman and Early Medieval Sussex, 450–1175', in D. Rudling (ed.), *The Archaeology of Sussex to AD 2000* (King's Lynn: University of Sussex), 151–60.

—— (2011). 'Late Anglo-Saxon Settlements', in H. Hamerow, D. Hinton, and S. Crawford (eds), *The Oxford Handbook of Anglo-Saxon Archaeology* (Oxford: Oxford University Press), 198–220.

—— and Rippon, S. (2007). *Medieval Landscapes* (Macclesfield: Windgather Press).

Gardner, W. (1904). 'Ancient Earthworks', in Anon. (ed.), *The Victoria History of the County of Warwick*, i (London: Archibald Constable and Co. Ltd), 345–406.

—— (1908). 'Ancient Earthworks', in W. Farrer and J. Brownbill (eds), *The Victoria History of the County of Lancaster*, ii (London: Archibald Constable and Co. Ltd), 507–60.

Garipzanov, I. H. (2008). *The Symbolic Language of Authority in the Carolingian World (c.751–877)* (Leiden: Brill).

Gazin-Schwartz, A. and Holtorf, C. (1999). ' "As Long as Ever I've Known it . . . ": on Folklore and Archaeology', in A. Gazin-Schwartz and C. Holtorf (eds), *Archaeology and Folklore* (London: Routledge), 3–20.

Geake, H. (1992). 'Burial Practice in Seventh- and Eighth-Century England', in M. Carver (ed.), *The Age of Sutton Hoo* (Woodbridge: Boydell Press), 83–94.

—— (1997). *The Use of Grave-Goods in Conversion-Period England c.600–850*. BAR British Series, 261 (Oxford: Archeopress).

—— (2002). 'Persistent Problems of Conversion-Period Burials in England', in S. Lucy and A. Reynolds (eds), *Burial in Early Medieval England and Wales*. Society for Medieval Archaeology Monograph, 17 (London: Society for Medieval Archaeology), 144–55.

Geary, P. (1994). *Phantoms of Remembrance: Memory and Oblivion at the End of the First Millennium* (Princeton, NJ: Princeton University Press).

—— (1999). 'Land, Language and Memory in Europe 700–1100', *Transactions of the Royal Historical Society*, 6th ser. 9: 169–84.

—— (2002a). *The Myth of Nations: The Medieval Origins of Europe* (Princeton, NJ: Princeton University Press).

—— (2002b). 'Oblivion between Orality and Textuality in the Tenth Century', in G. Althoff, J. Fried, and P. Geary (eds), *Medieval Concepts of the Past: Ritual, Memory, Historiography* (Cambridge: Cambridge University Press), 111–38.

Gelling, M. (1953). *The Place-Names of Oxfordshire, Part I*. EPNS, vol. 23 (Cambridge: Cambridge University Press).

—— (1954). *The Place-Names of Oxfordshire, Part II*. EPNS, vol. 24 (Cambridge: Cambridge University Press).

—— (1961). 'Place-Names and Anglo-Saxon Paganism', *University of Birmingham Historical Journal* 8: 7–25.

—— (1973). *The Place-Names of Berkshire, Part I*. EPNS, vol. 49 (London: Cambridge University Press).

—— (1974). *The Place-Names of Berkshire, Part II*. EPNS, vol. 50 (Cambridge: Cambridge University Press).

—— (1976). *The Place-Names of Berkshire, Part III*. EPNS, vol. 51 (Cambridge: Cambridge University Press).

—— (1988). *Signposts to the Past*, 2nd edn (Chichester: Phillimore).

—— (1998). 'Place-Names and Landscape', in S. Taylor (ed.), *The Uses of Place-Names*, St John's House Papers, no. 7 (Edinburgh: Scottish Cultural Press), 75–100.

—— and Cole, A. (2000). *The Landscape of Place-Names* (Stamford: Shaun Tyas).

—— and Foxall, H. D. G. (1990). *The Place-Names of Shropshire*. EPNS, 62/63 (Cambridge: Cambridge University Press).

Gerrard, C. M. (2003). *Medieval Archaeology: Understanding Traditions and Contemporary Approaches* (London: Routledge).

—— (2007). 'Not all Archaeology is Rubbish: The Elusive Life Histories of Three Artefacts from Shapwick, Somerset', in M. Costen (ed.), *People and Places: Essays in Honour of Mick Aston* (Oxford: Oxbow Books Ltd), 166–80.

—— (2009a). 'The Society for Medieval Archaeology: The Early Years (1956–62)', in R. Gilchrist and A. Reynolds (eds), *Reflections: Fifty Years of Medieval Archaeology*, Society for Medieval Archaeology Monograph, 30 (Leeds: Society for Medieval Archaeology), 23–46.

—— (2009b). 'Tribes and Territories: 50 Years of Medieval Archaeology in Britain', in R. Gilchrist and A. Reynolds (eds), *Reflections: Fifty Years of Medieval Archaeology*, Society for Medieval Archaeology Monograph, 30 (Leeds: Society for Medieval Archaeology), 79–112.

Gibson, C. and Murray J. (2003). 'An Anglo-Saxon Settlement at Godmanchester, Cambridgeshire', *Anglo-Saxon Studies in Archaeology and History* 12: 183–90.

Gilchrist, R. (1994). *Gender and Material Culture: The Archaeology of Religious Women* (London: Routledge).

—— (1995). *Contemplation and Action: the Other Monasticism* (Leicester: Leicester University Press).

—— and Reynolds, A. (eds) (2009). *Reflections: Fifty Years of Medieval Archaeology*, Society for Medieval Archaeology Monograph, 30 (Leeds: Society for Medieval Archaeology).

Gillings, M. and Pollard, J. (2004). *Avebury* (London: Duckworth).

—— Pollard, J. Wheatley, D., and Peterson, R. (2008). *Landscape of the Megaliths: Excavation and Fieldwork on the Avebury Monuments, 1997–2003* (Oxford: Owbow Books).

Gittos, H. (2011). 'Christian Sacred Spaces and Places', in H. Hamerow, D. Hinton, and S. Crawford (eds), *The Oxford Handbook of Anglo-Saxon Archaeology* (Oxford: Oxford University Press), 824–44.

Glass, H., Booth, P., Champion, T., Garwood, P., Munby, J., and Reynolds, A. (2011). *Tracks through Time: The Archaeology of the Channel Tunnel Rail Link* (Oxford: Oxford Archaeology.

Goddard, E. H. (1913–14). 'A List of the Prehistoric, Roman, and Pagan Saxon Antiquities in the County of Wiltshire, Arranged under Parishes', *Wiltshire Archaeological and Natural History Magazine* 38: 153–378.

Goldberg, E. J. (2006). *The Struggle for Empire: Kingship and Conflict under Louis the German, 817–876* (Ithaca, NY: Cornell University Press).

Gordon, C. A. (1960). *Professor James Garden's Letters to John Aubrey 1692–1695, Miscellany of the Third Spalding Club*. 3 vols (Aberdeen: Third Spalding Club), 1–56.

Gould, I. C. (1908a). 'Ancient Earthworks', in W. Page (ed.), *The Victoria History of the County of Hereford* (London: Archibald Constable and Company Ltd), 199–287.

—— (1908b). 'Ancient Earthworks', in W. Page (ed.), *The Victoria History of the County of Kent* (London: Archibald Constable and Company Ltd), 389–445.

Gover, J. E. B., Mawer, A., and Stenton, F. M. (1931). *The Place-Names of Devon, Part I.* EPNS, vol. 8 (Cambridge: Cambridge University Press).

—— Mawer, A., and Stenton, F. M. (1932). *The Place-Names of Devon, Part II.* EPNS, vol. 9 (Cambridge: Cambridge University Press).

—— Mawer, A., and Stenton, F. M. (1939). *The Place-Names of Wiltshire.* EPNS, vol. 16 (Cambridge: Cambridge University Press).

—— Mawer, A., Stenton, F. M., and Houghton, F. T. S. (1936). *The Place-Names of Warwickshire.* EPNS, vol. 13 (Cambridge: Cambridge University Press).

Gravestock, P. (1999). 'Did Imaginary Animals Exist?', in D. Hassig (ed.), *The Mark of the Beast* (New York and London: Routledge), 119–40.

Green, B., Rodgerson, A., and White, S. G. (1987). *The Anglo-Saxon Cemetery at Morning Thorpe, Norfolk* (Gressenhall: Norfolk Archaeology Unit).

Green, M. (1999). 'Back to the Future: Resonances of the Past in Myth and Material Culture', in A. Gazin-Schwarz and C. Holtorf (eds), *Archaeology and Folklore* (London: Routledge), 48–62.

Greenhalgh, M. (1989). *The Survival of Roman Antiquities in the Middle Ages* (London: Duckworth and Co.).

Greenwell, W. and Rolleston, G. (1877). *British Barrows* (Oxford: Clarendon Press).

Grierson, P. and Blackburn, M. A. S. (1986). *Medieval European Coinage 1: The Early Middle Ages* (Cambridge: Cambridge University Press).

Griffith, A. F. (1915). 'Anglo-Saxon Cemetery at Alfriston', *Sussex Archaeological Collections* 57: 197–210.

—— and Salzmann. L. F. (1914). 'An Anglo-Saxon Cemetery at Alfriston, Sussex', *Sussex Archaeological Collections* 56: 16–53.

Griffiths, B. (1996). *Aspects of Anglo-Saxon Magic* (Hockwold-cum-Wilton: Anglo-Saxon Books).

Griffiths, D. (2006). '*Maen Achwyfan*, and the Context of Viking Settlement in North-East Wales', *Archaeologia Cambrensis* 155: 143–62.

Grinsell, L. V. (undated). *Stanton Drew Stone Circles, Somerset* (London: Ministry of Works, Ancient Monuments and Historic Buildings).

—— (1934). 'Sussex Barrows', *Sussex Archaeological Collections* 75: 216–75.

—— (1935–6). 'An Analysis and List of Berkshire Barrows. Parts I & II'. *Berkshire Archaeological Journal* 40: 20–58.

—— (1939). 'Wayland's Smithy, Beahild's Byrigels, and Hwittuc's Hlaew: A Suggestion', *Transactions of the Newbury and District Field Club* 8: 136–9.

—— (1953). *The Ancient Burial-Mounds of England*, 2nd edn (London: Methuen and Co). Ltd.

—— (1957). 'Archaeological Gazetteer', in R. B. Pugh (ed.), *The Victoria History of the Counties of England, Wiltshire*, i, pt. 1 (London: Institute of Historical Research), 21–279.

—— (1967). 'Barrow Treasure, in Fact, Tradition, and Legislation', *Folklore* 78: 10–16.

—— (1973). 'Witchcraft at Some Prehistoric Sites', in V. Newall (ed.), *The Witch Figure* (London: Routledge & Kegan Paul), 72–9.

—— (1976a). *The Folklore of Prehistoric Sites in Britain* (London: Newton Abbot, David Charles).

—— (1976b). 'The Legendary History and Folklore of Stonehenge', *Folklore* 87: 5–20.

—— (1986). 'The Christianisation of Prehistoric and Other Pagan Sites', *Landscape History* 8: 27–37.

—— (1991a). 'Barrows in the Anglo-Saxon Land Charters', *Antiquaries Journal* 71: 47–63.

—— (1991b). 'Wayland the Smith and his Relatives: A Legend and its Topography', *Folklore* 102(2): 235–6.

Grundy, G. B. (1919). 'The Saxon Land Charters of Wiltshire', 1st ser., *Archaeological Journal* 76: 143–301.

—— (1920). 'Saxon Land Charters of Wiltshire (Second Series)', *Archaeological Journal* 77: 8–126.

—— (1921). 'The Saxon Land Charters of Hampshire with Notes on Place and Field Names', *Archaeological Journal* 78: 55–173.

—— (1924). 'The Saxon Land Charters of Hampshire with Notes on Place and Field Names', *Archaeological Journal* 81: 31–126.

—— (1926). 'The Saxon Land Charters of Hampshire with Notes on Place and Field Names', *Archaeological Journal* 83: 91–253.

—— (1927a). 'The Saxon Land Charters of Hampshire with Notes on Place and Field Names', *Archaeological Journal* 84: 160–340.

—— (1927b). 'Saxon Charters of Worcestershire', *Birmingham Archaeological Society Transactions and Proceedings* 52: 1–183.

—— (1935). *The Saxon Charters and Field Names of Somerset* (Taunton: Somerset Archaeology and Natural History Society).

—— (1935–6). *The Saxon Charters and Field-Names of Gloucestershire* (Gloucester: Council of the Bristol and Gloucestershire Archaeological Society).

Gunstone, A. J. H. (1992). *South-Eastern Museums. Ancient British, Anglo-Saxon, and Later Coins to 1279.* Sylloge of Coins of the British Isles, 42 (Oxford: Oxford University Press and Spink and Sons Ltd).

Hadley, D. (2001). *Death in Medieval England: An Archaeology* (Stroud: Tempus Publishing Ltd).

—— (2002). 'Burial Practices in Northern England in the Later Anglo-Saxon Period', in S. Lucy and A. Reynolds (eds), *Burial in Early Medieval England and Wales.* Society for Medieval Archaeology Monograph 17 (London: Society for Medieval Archaeology), 209–28.

Hall, A. (2002). 'The Structure of the Wife's Lament', *Leeds Studies in English* 33: 1–29.

—— (2006). 'Are There Any Elves in Anglo-Saxon Place-Names?', *Nomina: Journal for the Society of Place-Name Studies in Britain and Ireland* 29: 61–80.

—— (2007a). *Elves in Anglo-Saxon England. Matters of Belief, Health, Gender and Identity* (Woodbridge: Boydell and Brewer).

—— (2007b). 'Constructing Anglo-Saxon Sanctity: Tradition, Innovation and Saint Guthlac', in D. Strickland (ed.), *Images of Sanctity: Essays in Honour of Gary Dickson.* Visualising the Middle Ages, 1 (Leiden: Brill), 207–35.

Hall, R. and Whyman, M. (1996). 'Settlement and Monasticism at Ripon, North Yorkshire, from the 7th to the 11th centuries AD', *Medieval Archaeology* 40: 62–150.

Halliday, S. (2006). 'Into the Dim Light of History: More of the Same or All Change?', in A. Woolf (ed.), *Landscape and Environment in Dark Age Scotland*. St John's House Papers. St Andrews: Committee for Dark Age Studies, 11–28.

Halsall, G. (1989). 'Anthropology and the Study of Pre-Conquest Warfare and Society: The Ritual War in Anglo-Saxon England', in S. Chadwick Hawkes (ed.), *Weapons and Warfare in Anglo-Saxon England* (Oxford: Oxford University Committee for Archaeology), 155–78.

——(1992). 'The Origins of the Reihengräberzivilisation: Forty Years on', in J. F. Drinkwater and H. Elton (eds), *Fifth-Century Gaul: A Crisis of Identity?* (Cambridge: Cambridge University Press), 196–207.

——(1995). *Settlement and Social Organisation: The Merovingian Region of Metz* (Cambridge: Cambridge University Press).

——(2000). 'The Viking Presence in England? The Burial Evidence', in D. Hadley and J. Richards (eds), *Cultures in Contact: Scandinavian Settlement in England in the Ninth and Tenth Centuries* (Turnhout: Brepols Publishers), 259–76.

——(2006). 'Villas, Territories and Communities in Merovingian Northern Gaul', in W. Davies, G. Halsall, and A. Reynolds (eds), *People and Space in the Middle Ages, 300–1300* (Turnhout: Brepols Publishers), 209–31.

——(2010). *Cemeteries and Society in Merovingian Gaul: Selected Studies in History and Archaeology, 1992–2009* (Leiden: Brill).

Halsall, M. (1981). *The Old English Rune Poem: A Critical Edition* (Michigan: University of Toronto Press).

Hamerow, H. (1993). *Excavations at Mucking 2: The Anglo-Saxon Settlement*. English Heritage Research Report, 21. (London: English Heritage in association with the British Museum Press).

——(2002). *Early Medieval Settlements: The Archaeology of Rural Communities in North-West Europe 400–900* (Oxford: Oxford University Press).

——(2004). 'The Archaeology of Early Anglo-Saxon Settlements: Past, Present and Future', in N. Christie (ed.), *Landscapes of Change* (Aldershot: Ashgate), 301–16.

——(2011a). 'Overview: Rural Settlement', in H. Hamerow, D. Hinton, and S. Crawford (eds), *The Oxford Handbook of Anglo-Saxon Archaeology* (Oxford: Oxford University Press), 119–27.

——(2011b). 'Anglo-Saxon Timber Buildings and their Social Context', in H. Hamerow, D. Hinton, and S. Crawford (eds), *The Oxford Handbook of Anglo-Saxon Archaeology* (Oxford: Oxford University Press), 128–55.

——Hayden, C., and Hey. G. (2007). 'Anglo-Saxon and Earlier Settlement near Drayton Road, Sutton Courtenay, Berkshire', *Archaeological Journal* 164: 109–96.

Hamilton, D., Pitts, M., and Reynolds, A. (2007). 'A Revised Date for the Early Medieval Execution at Stonehenge', *Wiltshire Archaeological and Natural History Magazine* 101: 202–3.

Harding, A. F. (1981). 'Excavations in the Prehistoric Ritual Complex near Milfield, Northumberland', *Proceedings of the Prehistoric Society* 47: 87–135.

Härke, H. (1997a). 'The Nature of Burial Data', in C. Kjeld Jensen and K. Høilund Nielsen (eds), *Burial and Society* (Århus: Århus University Press), 19–27.

—— (1997b). 'Early Anglo-Saxon Social Structure', in J. Hines (ed.), *The Anglo-Saxons from the Migration Period to the Eighth Century: An Ethnographic Perspective* (Woodbridge: Boydell Press), 125–60.

—— (2011). 'Anglo-Saxon Immigration and Ethnogenesis', *Medieval Archaeology* 55: 1–28.

—— and Williams, H. (1997). 'Angelsächsische Bestattungsplatze und altere Denkmaler: Bemerkungen zur zeitlichen Entwicklung und Deutung des Phänomens'. *Archäologische Informationen* 20(1): 25–7.

Harrington, S. (2006). 'Soft Furnished Burial: An Assessment of the Role of Textiles in Early Anglo-Saxon Inhumations, with Particular Reference to East Kent', in S. Semple and H. Williams (eds), *Anglo-Saxon Studies in Archaeology and History* 14: 110–16.

—— and Welch, M. (2014). *The Early Anglo-Saxon Kingdoms of Southern Britain: Beyond the Tribal Hidage* (Oxford: Oxbow Books Ltd).

Hart, C. R. (1966). *The Early Charters of Eastern England* (Leicester: Leicester University Press).

Harte, J. (1995). 'The Power of Lonely Places', *Mercian Mysteries* 23: 8–13.

Hartridge, R. (1977–8). 'Excavations at the Prehistoric and Romano-British Site on Slonk Hill, Shoreham, Sussex', *Sussex Archaeological Collections* 116: 69–141.

Hase, P. H. (1994). 'The Church in the Wessex Heartlands', in M. Aston and C. Lewis (eds), *The Medieval Landscape of Wessex* (Oxford: Oxbow Books Ltd), 47–82.

Haselgrove, C., et al. (1990). 'Stanwick, North Yorkshore, Part 3: Excavations on the Earthworks Sites 1981–86', *Archaeological Journal* 147: 1–90.

Haslam, J. (ed.) (1984). *Anglo-Saxon Towns in Southern England* (Chichester: Phillimore).

—— (1987). 'Market and Fortress in the Reign of Offa', *World Archaeology* 19(1): 76–93.

Haughton, C. A. and Powlesland, D. (1999). *West Heslerton: The Anglian Cemetery*. 2 vols. Landscape Research Centre Monograph 1 (Yedingham: Landscape Research Centre).

Hawkes, C. F. C. (1940a). 'La Tene I Brooches from Deal, Preston Candover, and East Dean', *Antiquaries Journal* 20: 276–9.

—— (1940b). 'A Saxon Spear-Head and Scramasax from the Disputed Long Barrow at Preston Candover, Hampshire', *Antiquaries Journal* 20: 279–80.

Hawkes, J. (2003a). '*Iuxta Morem Romanorum*: Stone and Sculpture in Anglo-Saxon England', in C. Karkov and G. Brown (eds), *Anglo-Saxon Styles* (New York: State University Press), 69–100.

—— (2003b). 'The Plant-Life of Early Anglo-Saxon Art', in C. Biggam (ed.), *From Earth to Art* (Amsterdam: Rodpoi), 263–86.

Hawkes, S. C. (1986). 'The Early Anglo-Saxon Period', in G. Briggs, J. Cook, and T. Rowley (eds), *The Archaeology of the Oxford Region* (Oxford: Oxford University Department for External Studies), 64–108.

—— (1989). 'The South-East after the Romans: Saxon Settlement', in V. Maxfield (ed.), *The Saxon Shore: A Handbook*. Exeter Studies in History, 25 (Exeter: University of Exeter), 78–95.

Hayman, G. N. (1991–2). 'Further Excavations at the Former Goblin Works, Ashstead (TQ 182 567)', *Surrey Archaeological Collections* 81: 1–18.

Hayman, G. N. and Reynolds, A. (2005). 'An Anglo-Saxon Execution Cemetery at Staines, Surrey', *Archaeological Journal* 162: 215–55.

Heaney, S. (trans.) (1999). *Beowulf: A New Translation* (London: Faber and Faber).

Hearne, T. (ed.). (1774). *Joannis Lelandi Antiquarii Collectanea*, 2nd edn (privately published).

Hellström, J. A. (1996). *Vägar till Sveriges kristnande* (Stockholm: Atlantis).

Higham, N. J. (1993). *The Kingdom of Northumbria AD 350–1100* (Stroud: Alan Sutton Ltd).

Hill, D. (1978). 'Trends in the Development of Towns during the Reign of Æthelred II', in D. Hill (ed.), *Ethelred the Unready*. BAR British Series, 59 (Oxford: BAR), 213–26.

—— (1981). *An Atlas of Anglo-Saxon England* (Oxford: Blackwell).

—— and Rumble, A. (eds.) (1996). *The Defence of Wessex* (Manchester: Manchester University Press).

Hill, F. (1962). 'The Borough of Old Salisbury', in E. Crittall (ed.), *The Victoria History of the Counties of England: A History of Wiltshire*, (London: Oxford University Press), 51–65.

Hill, N. G. (1937). 'Excavations on Stockbridge Down 1935–6', *Proceedings of the Hampshire Field Club* 13: 247–59.

Hillier, G. (1855). 'Excavations on Brightstone and Bowcombe Downs, Isle of Wight', *Journal of the British Archaeological Association* 11: 34–40.

Hills, C. (2003). *The Origins of the English* (London: Duckworth).

—— (2009). 'Early Historic Britain', in J. Hunter and I. Ralston (eds), *The Archaeology of Britain* (London: Routledge), 219–40.

—— Penn, K., and Rickett, R. (1984). *The Anglo-Saxon Cemetery at Spong Hill, North Elmham. Part III: Catalogue of Inhumations*. East Anglian Archaeology Report, no. 21 (Norfolk: Norfolk Archaeology Unit, Norfolk Museums Service).

Hinchcliffe, J. (1975). 'Excavations at Grim's Ditch, Mongwell, 1974', *Oxoniensia* 40: 122–35.

—— (1986). 'An Early Medieval Settlement at Cowage Farm, Foxley, Near Malmesbury', *Archaeological Journal* 143: 240–59.

Hines, J. (1984). *The Scandinavian Character of Anglian England in the Pre-Viking Period*. BAR British Series, 124 (Oxford: BAR).

—— (1997). 'Religion: the Limits of Knowledge', in J. Hines (ed.), *The Anglo-Saxons from the Migration Period to the Eighth Century* (Woodbridge: Boydell Press), 375–401.

Hingley, R. (1996). 'Ancestors and Identity in the Later Prehistory of Atlantic Scotland: the Reuse and Reinvention of Neolithic Monuments and Material Culture', *World Archaeology* 28(2): 231–43.

Hinton, D. (1978). 'Late Anglo-Saxon Treasure and Bullion', in D. Hill (ed.), *Ethelred the Unready*. BAR British Series, 59 (Oxford: BAR), 135–58.

Hodges, C. C. (1905). 'Anglo-Saxon Remains', in W. Page (ed.), *The Victoria History of the Counties of England: A History of the County of Durham*, vol. I (London: Constable and Company Ltd).

Hollis, S. (1998). 'The Minster-in-Thanet Foundation Story', *Anglo-Saxon England* 27: 41–64.

Holtorf, C. J. (1997). 'Christian Landscapes of Pagan Monuments: A Radical Constructivist Perspective', in G. Nash (ed.), *Semiotics of Landscape: Archaeology of Mind*. BAR International Series, 661 (Oxford: Archaeopress), 80–8.

—— (1998a). 'Monumental Past. Interpreting the Meanings of Ancient Monuments in Later Prehistoric Mecklenburg-Vorpommern (Germany)'. Unpublished PhD, University of Wales <http://citd.scar.utoronto.ca/CITDPress/Holtorf/5.2.7.html>.

—— (1998b). 'The Life-History of Megaliths in Mecklenburg-Vorpommern (Germany)', *World Archaeology* 30(1): 23–38.

—— and Williams, H. (2006). 'Landscapes and Memories', in D. Hicks and M. Beaudray (eds), *Cambridge Companion to Historical Archaeology* (Cambridge: Cambridge University Press), 235–54.

Hooke, D. (1980–1). 'Burial Features in West Midland Charters', *Journal of the English Place-Name Society* 13: 1–40.

—— (1987). 'Two Documented Pre-Conquest Christian Sites Located upon Parish Boundaries', *Medieval Archaeology* 31: 96–101.

—— (1990). *Worcestershire Anglo-Saxon Charter-Bounds* (Woodbridge: Boydell Press).

—— (1994). *Pre-Conquest Charter-Bounds of Devon and Cornwall* (Woodbridge: Boydell Press).

—— (1998). *The Landscape of Anglo-Saxon England* (Leicester: Leicester University Press).

—— (2003). 'Trees in the Anglo-Saxon Landscape: The Charter Evidence', in C. P. Biggam (ed.), *From Earth to Art: The Many Aspects of the Plant World in Anglo-Saxon England* (Amsterdam: Rodopi), 17–40.

—— (2010). 'The Nature and Distribution of Early Medieval Woodland and Wood-Pasture Habitats', in H. Lewis and S. Semple (eds), *Perspectives in Landscape Archaeology*. BAR International Series, 2103 (Oxford: Archaeopress), 55–65.

Hope-Taylor, B. (1977). *Yeavering: An Anglo-British Centre of Early Northumbria*. Department of the Environment Archaeological Reports, 7 (London: HMSO).

Hoskins, W. G. (1955). *The Making of the English Landscape* (London: Hodder and Stoughton).

Hough, C. (1996). 'An Old English Etymon for Modern English Drake, "Male Duck"', *Neophilologus* 80(4): 613–15.

—— (2001). 'Place-Name Evidence for an Anglo-Saxon Animal Name: OE *pohha/ *pocca "fallow deer"', *Anglo-Saxon England* 30: 1–14.

Howe, J. M. (1997). 'The Conversion of the Physical World: The Creation of Christian Landscape', in J. Muldoon (ed.), *Varieties of Religious Conversion in the Middle Ages* (Gainesville: University Press of Florida), 63–78.

Howe, N. (2000). 'An Angle on this Earth: Sense of Place in Anglo-Saxon England', *Bulletin of the John Rylands University Library of Manchester*, 82/1 (Spring), 3–27.

—— (2002). 'The Landscape of Anglo-Saxon England: Inherited, Invented, Imagined', in J. Howe and M. Wolfe (eds), *Inventing Medieval Landscapes: Senses of Place in Western Europe* (Gainsville: University Press of Florida), 91–112.

—— (2004). 'Looking for Home in Anglo-Saxon England', in N. Howe (ed.), *Home and Homelessness in the Medieval and Renaissance World* (Notre Dame: University of Notre Dame Press), 143–64.

Hume, K. (1974). 'The Concept of the Hall in Old English Poetry', *Anglo-Saxon England* 3: 63–74.

Hume, K. (1980). 'From Saga to Romance: The Use of Monsters in Old Norse Litera-ture', *Studies in Philology* 77: 1–25.

Hunter, M. (1974). 'German and Roman Antiquity and the Sense of the Past in Anglo-Saxon England', *Anglo-Saxon England* 3: 29–50.

Hutton, R. E. (1993). *The Pagan Religions of the Ancient British Isles'* (hardback, 1991), (Oxford: Blackwells).

Ingold, T. (2000). *The Perception of the Environment: Essays on Livelihood, Dwelling and Skill* (London: Routledge).

Innes, M. (2000). 'Introduction: Using the Past, Interpreting the Present, Influencing the Future', in Y. Hen and M. Innes (eds), *The Uses of the Past in the Early Middle Ages* (Cambridge: Cambridge University Press), 1–8.

Jacobs, N. (1977). 'Anglo-Danish Relations and Poetic Archaism and the Date of *Beowulf*: A Reconsideration of the Evidence', *Poetica* (Tokyo) 8: 23–43.

Jacobsson, M. (1997). *Wells, Meres, and Pools: Hydronomic Terms in the Anglo-Saxon Landscape*. Studia Anglistica Upsaliensia, 98 (Uppsala: Acta Universitatis Upsaliensis).

James, H. (1992). 'Early Medieval Cemeteries in Wales', in N. Edwards and A. Lane (eds), *The Early Church in Wales and the West. Recent Work in Early Christian Archaeology, History and Place-Names* (Oxford: Oxbow Books Ltd), 90–104.

Jamison, C. (1908a). 'Great Kimble', in W. Page (ed.), *The Victoria County History of the County of Buckingham*, ii (London: Archibald Constable and Company Ltd), 298–302.

—— (1908b). 'Stone', in W. Page (ed.), *The Victoria County History of the County of Buckingham*, ii (London: Archibald Constable and Company Ltd), 307–11.

Janes, D. (2000). 'The World and its Past as Christian Allegory in the Early Middle Ages', in Y. Hen and M. Innes (eds), *The Uses of the Past in the Early Middle Ages* (Cambridge: Cambridge University Press), 102–13.

Jenkinson, A. V. (1925). 'West Wycombe', in W. Page (ed.), *The Victoria County History of the County of Buckinghampshire*, iii (London: St Catherine Press), 135–40.

Jennings, D, (1908). 'Cholesbury', in W. Page (ed.), *The Victoria County History of the County of Buckingham*, ii (London: Archibald Constable and Company Ltd), 334–5.

—— (1925). 'Edlesborough', in W. Page (ed.), *The Victoria County History of the County of Buckinghampshire*, iii (London: St Catherine Press), 350–61.

Jewell, R. H. I. (1986). 'The Anglo-Saxon Friezes at Breedon-on-the-Hill', *Archaeologia* 108: 95–115.

Johnson, M. (1999). *Archaeological Theory: An Introduction* (Oxford: Blackwells).

—— (2007). *Ideas of Landscape* (Oxford: Blackwell).

Jolly, K. (1996). *Popular Religion in Late Saxon England* (Chapel Hill, NC: University of North Carolina Press).

Jones, P. (2010). *Roman and Medieval Staines: The Development of the Town* (Staines: Spoilheap Monograph).

Jones, R. and Semple, S. (eds) (2012a). *Sense of Place in Anglo-Saxon England* (Donington: Shaun Tyas).

—— (2012b). 'Making Sense of Place in Anglo-Saxon England', in R. Jones and S. Semple (eds), *Sense of Place in Anglo-Saxon England* (Donington: Shaun Tyas), 1–15.

Keay, S. J. (1988). *Roman Spain* (Berkerley and Los Angeles: University of California Press).

Keiller, A. and Piggott, S. (1939). 'The Chambered Tomb in Beowulf', *Antiquity* 13: 360–1.

Kelly, D. B. (1962). 'Ditton', *Archaeologia Cantiana* 7: 204–5.

Kelly, S. E. (1998). *Charters of Selsey. Anglo-Saxon Charters VI* (Oxford: Oxford University Press).

Kemble, J. M. (1839–48). *Codex Diplomaticus Aevi Saxonici.* 6 vols (London: Sumptibus Societatis).

—— (1855). 'On Mortuary Urns Found at Stade-on-the-Elbe, and Other Parts of North Germany, Now in the Museum of the Historical Society of Hanover', *Archaeologia* 36: 270–83.

Kempson, E. G. H. (1955). 'The Anglo-Saxon Name for Avebury Circle', *Wiltshire Archaeological and Natural History Magazine* 56: 60–1.

Kendrick, T. D. (1938). *Anglo-Saxon Art to AD 900* (London: Methuen).

Ker, N. R. (1957). *Catalogue of Manuscripts Containing Anglo-Saxon* (Oxford: Clarendon Press).

Keynes, S. and Lapidge, M. (ed. and trans.) (1983). *Alfred the Great: Asser's Life of Alfred and other Contemporary Sources* (London: Penguin Books Ltd).

Kiernan, K. (1997). 'The Eleventh-Century Origin of Beowulf and the Beowulf Manuscript', in C. Chase (ed.), *The Dating of Beowulf* (Toronto: University of Toronto Press), 9–22.

Kinsley. A. G. (1993). *Broughton Lodge: Excavations on the Romano-British Settlement and Anglo-Saxon Cemetery at Broughton Lodge, Willoughby-on-the-Wolds, Nottinghamshire 1964–8.* Nottingham Archaeological Monographs 4 (Nottingham: Department of Classical and Archaeological Studies).

Kitson, P. (1995). 'The Nature of Old English Dialetical Distributions, Mainly as Exhibited in Anglo-Saxon Charter Boundaries', in J. Fisiak (ed.), *Medieval Dialectology* (Berlin and New York: Mouton de Gruyter), 43–135.

—— (2008). 'Fog on the Barrow-Downs', in O. Padel and D. Parsons (eds), *A Commodity of Good Names: Essays in Honour of Margaret Gelling* (Donington: Shaun Tyas), 382–94.

Kjølbye-Biddle, B. (1995). 'Iron Bound Coffins and Coffin-Fittings from the Pre-Norman Cemetery', in M. O. H. Carver (ed.), *Excavations at York Minster I, from Roman Fortress to Norman Cathedral* (London: HMSO), 489–521.

Knapp, B. and Ashmore, W. (1999). 'Archaeological Landscapes: Constructed, Conceptualized, Ideational', in W. Ashmore and B. Knapp (eds), *Archaeologies of Landscape Contemporary Perspectives* (Oxford: Blackwell Publishers Ltd), 1–30.

Knocker, G. M. (1957). 'Early Burials and an Anglo-Saxon Cemetery at Snell's Corner near Horndean, Hampshire', *Proceedings of the Hampshire Field Club* 19: 117–70.

Lambrick, G. (1988). *The Rollright Stones: Megaliths, Monuments and Settlement in the Prehistoric Landscape.* English Heritage Archaeological Report, 6 (London: HBMCE).

Lane, T. (1988). 'Some Cropmarks in Crowland', *Archaeology in Lincolnshire 1987–1988,* (Fourth Annual Report of the Trust for Lincolnshire Archaeology), 8.

Lang, J. T. (1981). 'A Viking Age Spear-Socket from York', *Medieval Archaeology* 25: 157–60.

—— (1991). *York and Eastern Yorkshire. Corpus of Anglo-Saxon Stone Sculpture,* vol. 3 (Oxford: Oxford University Press).

Lapidge, M. (1997). 'The Comparative Approach', in K. O'Brien (ed.), *Reading Old English Texts* (Cambridge: Cambridge University Press), 20–38.

Lapidge, M. (2000). 'The Archetype of *Beowulf*', *Anglo-Saxon England* 29: 5–42.

Laughton, G. A. and Locke, A. A. (1908). 'Cheriton with Beauworth', in W. Page (ed.), The *Victoria History of Hampshire and the Isle of Wight*, x (London: Archibald Constable), 311–13.

Lavelle, R. (2005). 'Why Grateley? Reflections on Anglo-Saxon Kingship in a Hampshire Landscape', *Proceedings of the Hampshire Field Club and Archaeological Society* 60: 154–69.

Lee, A. (1998). 'Symbolism and Allegory', in R. E. Bjork and J. Niles (eds), *A Beowulf Handbook* (Nebraska: University of Nebraska), 233–54.

Leech, R. (1981). *Historic Towns in Gloucestershire* (Bristol: Committee for Rescue Archaeology in Avon, Gloucestershire and Somerset).

Leeds, E. T. (1913). *The Archaeology of the Anglo-Saxon Settlements* (Oxford: Clarendon Press).

—— (1923). 'A Saxon Village near Sutton Courtenay, Berkshire', *Archaeologia* 73: 147–92.

—— (1927). 'A Saxon Village at Sutton Courtenay, Berkshire; Second Report', *Archaeologia* 76: 59–80.

—— (1936). *Early Anglo-Saxon Art and Archaeology* (Oxford: Clarendon Press).

—— (1939). 'Anglo-Saxon Remains', in L. Salzman (ed.), *The Victoria History of the County of Oxford*, i (London: Oxford University Press).

—— (1947). 'A Saxon Village at Sutton Courtney, Berkshire; Third Report', *Archaeologia* 112: 73–94.

Lees, C. A. and Overing, G. R. (2006). 'Anglo-Saxon Horizons: Places of the Mind in the Northumbrian Landscape', in C. A. Lees and G. R. Overing (eds), *A Place to Believe in: Locating Medieval Landscapes* (Pennsylvania, PA: Pennsylvania State University Press), 1–26.

Leone, A. (2007). *Changing Townscapes in North Africa from Late Antiquity to the Arab Conquest* (Bari: Edipuglia).

—— (2013). *The End of the Pagan City: Religion, Economy and Urbanism in Late Antique North Africa* (Oxford: Oxford University Press).

Leslie, R. F. (ed.) (1988). *Three Old English Elegies* (Exeter: University of Exeter).

Lethbridge, T. C. (1938). 'Anglo-Saxon Remains', in L. F. Salzman (ed.), *The Victoria County History of the County of Cambridgeshire and the Isle of Ely* (London: Oxford University Press), 305–34.

—— and Palmer, W. M. (1929). 'Excavations in the Cambridgeshire Dykes, VI, Bran Ditch, Second Report', *Proceedings of the Cambridge Antiquarian Society* 30: 78–93.

Levy, J. (1982). *Social and Religious Organisation in Bronze Age Denmark: An Analysis of Ritual Hoard Finds*. BAR International Series, 124 (Oxford: BAR).

Leyser, K. (1994). 'Ritual, Ceremony and Gesture: Ottonian Germany', in K. Lesyer, *Communications and Power in Medieval Europe* (ed. T. Reuter). 2 vols (London: Hambledon Press), 7–17.

Liddle, D. M. (1933). 'Excavations at Meon Hill', *Proceedings of the Hampshire Field Club* 12: 126–62.

Liebermann, F. (1913). *The National Assembly in the Anglo-Saxon Period* (Halle: Max Niemeyer).

Lipscomb, G. (1831–47). *History and Antiquities of the County of Buckingham.* 8 vols (London: John Bowyer).

Loveluck, C. (1996). 'The Development of the Anglo-Saxon Landscape: Economy and Society "On Driffield", East Yorkshire, 400–750 AD', *Anglo-Saxon Studies in Archaeology and History* 9: 25–48.

—— (2005). 'Rural Settlement Hierarchy in the Age of Charlemagne', in J. Story (ed.), *Charlemagne: Empire and Society* (Manchester: Manchester University Press), 230–58.

Lovett, E. H. (1893–6). 'Report on the Opening of a Round Barrow and Supposed Saxon Burial, on the South Downs near Arundel', *Proceedings and Transactions of the Croydon Microscopical and Natural History Club* 4: 82–3.

Lowther, A. W. G. (1931). 'The Saxon Cemetery at Guildown, Guildford, Surrey', *Surrey Archaeological Collections* 39: 1–50.

Loyn, H. R. (1984). *The Governance of Anglo-Saxon England 500–1087.* The Governance of England I (gen. ed. A. L. Brown) (London: Edward Arnold).

Luce, R. H. (1979). *The History of the Abbey and Town of Malmesbury* (Malmesbury: The Friends of Malmesbury Abbey).

Lucy, S. (1992). 'The Significance of Mortuary Ritual in the Political Manipulation of Landscape', *Archaeological Review from Cambridge* 11(1): 93–105.

—— (1998). *The Early Anglo-Saxon Cemeteries of East Yorkshire.* BAR British Series, 272 (Oxford: BAR).

—— (1999). 'Changing Burial Rites in Northumbria AD 500–750', in J. Hawkes and S. Mills (eds), *Northumbria's Golden Age* (Stroud: Sutton Publishing Ltd), 12–43.

—— (2000). *The Anglo-Saxon Way of Death* (Stroud: Sutton Publishing Ltd).

—— (2002). 'Burial Practice in Early Medieval Eastern England: Constructing Local Identities, Deconstructing Ethnicity', in S. Lucy and A. Reynolds (eds), *Burial in Early Medieval England and Wales.* Society for Medieval Archaeological Monograph 17 (London: Society for Medieval Archaeology), 72–87.

—— (2005). 'Early Medieval Burial at Yeavering: A Retrospective', in P. Frodsham and C. O'Brien (eds), *Yeavering. People, Power and Place* (Stroud: Tempus Publishing Ltd), 127–44.

—— Tipper, J., and Dickens, A. (2009). *The Anglo-Saxon Settlement and Cemetery at Bloodmoor Hill, Carlton Colville, Suffolk.* East Anglian Archaeology Monograph 131 (Cambridge: Cambridge Archaeological Unit).

Lund, J. (2005). 'Thresholds and Passages: The Meanings of Bridges and Crossings in the Viking Age and Early Middle Ages', *Viking and Medieval Scandinavia* 1: 109–37.

—— (2008). 'Banks, Borders and Bodies of Water in a Viking Age Mentality', *Journal of Wetland Archaeology* 8: 51–70.

—— (2010). 'At the Water's Edge', in M. O. H. Carver, A. Sanmark, and S. J. Semple (eds), *Signals of Belief Early England: Anglo-Saxon Paganism Revisited* (Oxford: Oxbow Books Ltd), 49–66.

Lutz, M. (1950). 'La 'Villa' Gallo-Romaine et la nécropole mérovingienne de Berthelming (Moselle)', *Revue Archaeologique de L'Est et du Centre-Est* I: 180–4.

Lysons, D. 1792–6. *The Environs of London: Being an Historical Account of the Towns, Villages and Hamlets within Twelve Miles of that Capital*, vol. 2, pt 3 (London: A. Strahan, for T. Cadell, Jr and W. Davies).

McCullagh, R. (1989). 'Excavation at Newton, Islay', *Glasgow Archaeological Journal* 15: 23–51.

McInnes, I. J. (1964). 'A Class II Henge in the East Riding of Yorkshire', *Antiquity* 38: 218–19.

Mackie, W. S. (ed. and trans.) (1934). *The Exeter Book, Part II: Poems IX–XXXII*. Early English Text Society, orig. ser., 194 (London: Oxford University Press).

Macmahon, P. (2001). *The Archaeology of Wiltshire's Towns: An Extensive Urban Survey* (Trowbridge: Wiltshire County Archaeological Service).

McNamee, M. B. (1960). '"Beowulf": An Allegory of Salvation?', *Journal of English and Germanic Philology* 59(2): 190–207.

Maldonado, A. D. (2011). 'Christianity and Burial in Late Iron Age Scotland, AD 400–650'. Unpublished PhD thesis, University of Glasgow.

Malim, T. (1993). 'An Investigation of Multi-Period Cropmarks at Manor Farm, Harston', *Proceedings of the Cambridgshire Antiquarian Society* 82: 11–54.

——and Hines, J. (1998). *The Anglo-Saxon Cemetery at Edix Hill (Barrington A), Cambridgeshire: Excavations 1989–1991 and a Summary Catalogue of Material from 19th Century Interventions* (York: CBA).

Manby, G. T. (1985). *Thwing: Excavation and Field Archaeology in East Yorkshire*. Yorkshire Archaeology Society: Prehistoric Research Section.

Manwaring, J. P. (1900). 'Ford and its Church', *Sussex Archaeological Collections* 43: 105–57.

——(1912). 'Chithurst and its Church', *Sussex Archaeological Collections* 55: 98–107.

Mattingly, H. (ed. and trans.) (1970). *Agricola and Germania* (London: Penguin).

Maurin, L. (1971). 'Le Cimetiere merovingien de Neuvicq-Montguyon (Charente-Maritime)', *Gallia* 29: 151–89.

Mawer, A. and Stenton, F. M. (1927). *The Place-Names of Worcestershire*. EPNS, vol. 4 (Cambridge: Cambridge University Press).

————(1929–30). *The Place-Names of Sussex. Parts I and II*. EPNS, vol. 6 (Cambridge: Cambridge University Press).

————(1936). *The Place-Names of Warwickshire*. EPNS, vol. 8 (Cambridge: Cambridge University Press).

Meaney, A. L. (1964). *A Gazetteer of Early Anglo-Saxon Burial Sites* (London: Allen and Unwin).

——(1981). *Anglo-Saxon Amulets and Curing Stones*. BAR British Series, 96 (Oxford: BAR).

——(1993). 'Gazeteer of Hundred and Wapentake Meeting-Places of the Cambridge Region', *Proceedings of the Cambridge Antiquarian Society* 82: 67–92.

——(1995). 'Pagan English Sanctuaries, Place-Names and Hundred Meeting-Places', *Anglo-Saxon Studies in Archaeology and History* 8: 29–42.

——(1997). 'Hundred Meeting-Places in the Cambridge Region', in A. R. Rumble and A. D. Mills (eds), *Names, Places and People: An Onomastic Miscellany in Memory of John McNeal Dodgson* (Stamford: Paul Watkins), 195–240.

——(2001). 'Felix's *Life of Guthlac*: Hagiography and/or Truth', *Proceedings of the Cambridgeshire Antiquarian Society* 90: 29–48.

——(2005). 'Felix's *Life of Guthlac*: History or Hagiography?', in D. Hill and M. Worthington (eds), *Æthelbald and Offa: Two Eighth-Century Kings of Mercia*. BAR British Series, 383 (Oxford: BAR), 75–84.

Mercer, E. (1964). 'The Ruthwell and Bewcastle Crosses', *Antiquity* 38: 268–76.

Metcalf, D. M. (1984). 'Twenty-Five Notes on Sceatta Finds', in D. Hill and D. M. Metcalf (eds), *Sceattas in England and on the Continent*. BAR British Series, 128 (Oxford: BAR), 193–205.

—— (1993–4). *Thrymsas and Sceattas in the Ashmolean Museum, Oxford*. 3 vols (London: Royal Numismatic Society and Ashmolean Museum).

—— (1998). *An Atlas of Anglo-Saxon and Norman Coin Finds 973–1086*. Royal Numismatic Society Special Publication, no. 32 (Oxford: Ashmolean Museum).

—— and Jonsson, K. (1980). 'A Hoard from Early in the Reign of Æthelred II Found at Spettisbury Rings Hillfort, Dorset', *British Numismatic Journal* 50: 132–3.

Miket, R. (1980). 'A Restatement of Evidence from Bernician Anglo-Saxon Burials', in P. Rahtz, T. M. Dickinson, and L. Watts (eds), *Anglo-Saxon Cemeteries 1979*. BAR British Series, 82 (Oxford: BAR), 289–305.

Miller, T. (trans.) (1891). *The Old English Version of Bede's Ecclesiastical History of the English People*. Early English Text Society, orig. ser., 96 (London: Oxford University Press).

Millett, M. and James, S. (1983). 'Excavations at Cowdery's Down, Basingstoke, Hampshire, 1978–81', *Archaeological Journal* 140: 151–279.

Mills, A. D. (1998). *A Dictionary of English Place-Names*, 2nd edn (Oxford: Oxford University Press).

Mitchell, B. (1995). *An Invitation to Old English and Anglo-Saxon England* (Oxford: Blackwell Publishers Ltd).

Mitchell, J. (2001). 'The High Cross and Monastic Strategies in Eighth-Century Northumbria', in P. Binsky and W. Noel (eds), *New Offerings, Ancient Treasures: Studies in Medieval Art for George Henderson* (Stroud: Sutton), 88–114.

Moralee, J. (2006). 'The Stones of Theodore: Disfiguring the Pagan Past in Christian Gerasa', *Journal of Early Christian Studies*, 14(2): 183–215.

Morris, C. A. (1983). 'A Late Saxon Hoard of Iron and Copper-Alloy Artefacts from Nazeing, Essex', *Medieval Archaeology* 27: 27–40.

Morris, J. (1962). 'The Anglo-Saxons in Bedfordshire', *Bedforshire Archaeological Journal* 1: 58–76.

Morris, R. (1989). *Churches in the Landscape* (London: J. Dent and Sons Ltd).

—— (2008). *Journeys from Jarrow: Jarrow Lecture 2004* (Jarrow: Jarrow Parish Council), 1–31.

—— (2011). 'Local Churches in the Anglo-Saxon Countryside', in H. Hamerow, D. Hinton, and S. Crawford (eds), *The Oxford Handbook of Archaeology* (Oxford: Oxford University Press), 172–97.

—— and Roxan, J. (1980). 'Churches on Roman Buildings', in W. Rodwell (ed.), *Temples, Churches and Religion: Recent Research in Roman Britain, Vol. I*. BAR British Series, 77 (Oxford: BAR), 175–210.

Mortimer, J. R. (1905). *Forty Year's Researches in British and Saxon Burial Mounds of East Yorkshire* (London: A. Brown and Sons).

Mortimer, R. and Regan, R. (2001). 'Chesterton Lane Corner, Cambridge: Archaeological Excavations at Anglian Water Sewage Shaft M5'. Cambridge Archaeological Unit Unpublished Assessment Report, 420.

Musty, J. (1969). 'The Excavation of Two Barrows, One of Saxon Date, at Ford, Laverstock, Near Salisbury, Wiltshire', *Antiquaries Journal* 49: 98–117.

Myres, J. N. L. (1986). *The English Settlements* (Oxford: Clarendon Press).

Nairn, I. and Pevsner, N. (1965). *The Buildings of England, Sussex*, repr. (Harmondsworth: Penguin Books).

Nelson, J. (1951). 'The Medieval Churchyard and Wayside Crosses of Warwickshire', *Transactions of the Birmingham Archaeological Society* 68: 74–88.

Nenk, B. S., Margeson, S., and Hurley, M. (1995). 'Cheshire: Wervin, Chapel House Farm, 21', *Medieval Archaeology* 39: 190–1.

Neville, R. C. (1852). 'Account of Excavations near the Fleam Dyke, Cambridgeshire, April, 1952', *Archaeological Journal* 9: 226–30.

Newman, C. (1997). *Tara: An Archaeological Survey* (Dublin: Royal Irish Academy).

Newman, J. (1980). *West Kent and the Weald*, 2nd edn (Harmondsworth: Penguin Books).

—— (1983). *North-East and East Kent*, 3rd edn (Harmondsworth: Penguin Books).

Newman, R. (1984). 'The Problems of Rural Settlement in Northern Cumbria in the Pre-Conquest Period', in M. Faull (ed.), *Studies in Late Anglo-Saxon Settlement* (Oxford: Department for External Studies, Rewley House), 155–76.

Niles, J. D. (2003). 'The Problem of the Ending of the Wife's Lament', *Speculum* 78: 110–70.

—— (2007). *Beowulf and Lejre* (Tempe, AZ: ACMRS).

North, R. (1997). *Heathen Gods in Old English Literature* (Cambridge: Cambridge University Press).

O'Brien, C. (2011). 'Yeavering and Bernician Kingship: A Review of Debate on the Hybrid Culture Thesis', in D. Petts and S. Turner (eds), *Early Medieval Northumbria. Kingdoms and Communities, AD 450–1100,* Studies in the Early Middle Ages 24 (Turnhout: Brepols Publishers), 207–20.

O'Brien, E. (1999). *Post-Roman Britain to Anglo-Saxon England: Burial Practices Reviewed*. BAR British Series, 289 (Oxford: BAR).

Ó'Carragáin, T. (2010). *Churches in Early Medieval Ireland: Architecture, Ritual and Memory* (New Haven, CT, and London: Yale University Press).

O'Neill, H. (1977). 'Salmonsbury, Boughton-on-the-Water: Some Aspects of Archaeology in Boughton Vale', *Transactions of the Bristol and Gloucestershire Archaeology Society* 95: 11–23.

—— and Grinsell, L. V. (1960). 'Gloucestershire Barrows', *Transactions of the Bristol and Gloucestershire Archaeological Society* 79(1): 5–143.

Oakley, K. P. (1933). 'The Pottery from the Romano-British Site on Thundersbarrow Hill', *Antiquaries Journal* 13: 134–51.

Okasha, E. (1993). *Corpus of Early Christian Inscribed Stones of South-West Britain* (London and New York: Leicester University Press).

—— (1995). 'Literacy in Anglo-Saxon England: The Evidence from Inscriptions', *Anglo-Saxon Studies in Archaeology and History* 8: 69–74.

Orton, F. (1999). 'Northumbrian Sculpture (the Ruthwell and Bewcastle Monuments): Questions of Difference', in J. Hawkes and S. Mills (eds), *Northumbria's Golden Age* (Stroud: Sutton), 216–26.

—— (2003). 'Rethinking the Ruthwell and Bewcastle Monuments: Some Deprecation of Style: Some Consideration of Form and Ideology', in C. Karkov and G. Brown (eds), *Anglo-Saxon Styles* (New York: State University Press), 31–68.

—— (2006). 'At the Bewcastle Monument, in Place', in C. A. Lees and G. R. Overing (eds), *A Place to Believe In: Locating Medieval Landscapes* (Pennsylvania, PA: Pennsylvania State University Press), 29–66.

—— Wood, I., and Lees, C. (2007). *Fragments of History: Rethinking the Ruthwell and Bewcastle Monuments* (Manchester: Manchester University Press).

Ozanne, A. (1962–3). 'The Peak Dwellers', *Medieval Archaeology* 6–7: 15–52.

Page, R. I. (1999). *An Introduction to English Runes*, 2nd edn (Woodbridge: Boydell Press).

Page, W. (1902). *The Victoria History of the County of Hertford*, i (London: Archibald Constable).

Palliser, D. M. (1976). *The Staffordshire Landscape* (London: Hodder and Stoughton).

Palmer, W. M., Leaf, C. S., and Lethbridge, T. C. (1931). 'Further Excavations at the Bran Ditch', *Proceedings of the Cambridgeshire Antiquarian Society* 32: 54–6.

Pantos, A. (2002). 'Assembly Places in the Anglo-Saxon Period: Aspects of Form and Location'. Unpublished DPhil Thesis, University of Oxford.

—— (2004a). 'The Location and Form of Anglo-Saxon Assembly-Places: Some "Moot Points"', in A. Pantos and S. Semple (eds), *Assembly Places and Practices in Medieval Europe* (Dublin: Four Courts Press), 155–80.

—— (2004b). '*In medle oððe an þinge*: The Old English Vocabulary of Assembly', in A. Pantos and S. Semple (eds), *Assembly Places and Practices in Medieval Europe* (Dublin: Four Courts Press), 181–201.

—— and Semple, S. J. (2004). 'Introduction', in A. Pantos and S. Semple (eds), *Assembly Places and Practices in Early Medieval Europe* (Dublin: Four Courts Press), 11–23.

Parker Pearson, M. (1982). 'Mortuary Practices, Society and Ideology: An Ethnoarchaeological Study', in I. Hodder (ed.), *Symbolic and Structural Archaeology* (Cambridge: Cambridge University Press), 99–113.

—— (1993). 'The Powerful Dead: Archaeological Relationships between the Living and the Dead', *Cambridge Archaeological Journal* 3(2): 203–29.

—— (1999). *The Archaeology of Death and Burial* (Texas: Texas A&M University Press).

—— (2005). 'The Stonehenge Riverside Project: Interim Report 2005'. Unpublished Report.

Passmore, D. and Waddington, C. (2009). *Managing Archaeological Landscapes in Northumberland*. Till–Tweed Studies I (Oxford: Oxbow Books Ltd).

Peake, H. J. E. (1935). 'Excavation on the Berkshire Downs', *Transactions of the Newbury and District Field Club* 7(2): 90–108.

Peddie, J. (1999). *Alfred: Warrior King* (Stroud: Sutton).

Pennant, T. (1773). *A Tour in Wales*, repr. (London: T. Hughes, 1998).

Petts, D. (2000). 'Burial and Religion in Sub-Roman and Early Medieval Britain: AD 400–800'. Unpublished PhD thesis, University of Reading.

—— (2002). 'Cemeteries and Boundaries in Western Britain', in S. Lucy and A. Reynolds (eds), *Burial in Early Medieval England and Wales*. Society for Medieval Archaeology Monograph 17 (London: Society for Medieval Archaeology), 24–46.

—— (2004). 'Burial in West Britain AD 400–800: Late Antique or Early Medieval?', in R. Collins and J. Gerrard (eds), *Debating Late Antiquity in Britain AD 300–700*. BAR British Series, 365 (Oxford: Archaeopress), 77–87.

—— (2009). *The Early Medieval Church in Wales* (Stroud: The History Press).

—— (2011). *Pagan and Christian: Religious Change in Early Medieval Europe* (London: Bloomsbury Press).

Petts, D. and Turner, S. (eds) (2011). *Early Medieval Northumbria* (Leiden: Brill).

Pevsner, N. (1951). *The Buildings of England, Cornwall* (Harmondsworth: Penguin Books).

—— (1958a). *The Buildings of England, Shropshire* (Harmondsworth: Penguin Books).

—— (1958b). *The Buildings of England, North Somerset and Bristol* (Harmondsworth: Penguin Books).

—— (1963). *The Buildings of England, Herefordshire* (Harmondsworth: Penguin Books).

—— (1966). *The Buildings of England, Yorkshire, North Riding* (Harmondsworth: Penguin Books).

—— (1968). *The Buildings of England, Worcestershire* (Harmondsworth: Penguin Books).

—— (1973). (Revised by B. Cherry.) *The Buildings of England, Northamptonshire*, 2nd edn (Harmondsworth: Penguin Books).

—— (1974). *The Buildings of England, Staffordshire* (Harmondsworth: Penguin Books).

—— (1991). *The Buildings of England, Lancashire* (Harmondsworth: Penguin Books).

—— (1996). (Revised by E. Radcliffe.) *The Buildings of England, Essex* (Harmondsworth: Penguin Books).

—— (1999). *The Buildings of England, Gloucestershire* (Harmondsworth: Penguin Books).

—— and Cherry, B. (1975). *The Buildings of England, Wiltshire*, 2nd edn (Harmondsworth: Penguin Books).

—— and Harris, J. (1964). *The Buildings of England, Lincolnshire* (Harmondsworth: Penguin Books).

—— and Lloyd, D. (1967). *The Buildings of England, Hampshire* (Harmondsworth: Penguin Books).

—— and Wedgwood, A. (2000). *The Buildings of England, Warwickshire* (Harmondsworth: Penguin Books).

—— and Williamson, E. (1994). *The Buildings of England. Buckinghampshire*, 2nd edn (Harmondsworth: Penguin Books).

Pewsey, S. and Brooks, A. (1993). *East Saxon Heritage: An Essex Gazetteer* (Stroud: Alan Sutton Publishing Ltd).

Pietri, C. (1983). 'Grabinschrift II (Lateinisch)', *Reallexikon für Antike und Christentum* 12: 514–90.

Piggott, S. (1948). 'The Excavations at Cairnpapple Hill, West Lothian, 1947–1948', *Proceedings of the Society of Antiquaries of Scotland* 82: 68–123.

Pitt, J. M. (1999). 'Wiltshire Minster *Parochiae* and West Saxon Ecclesiastical Organisation'. Unpublished PhD Thesis, King Alfred's College, Winchester.

Pitt Rivers, Lt General, A. (1892). *Excavations in Bokerly Dyke and Wansdyke, Dorset and Wiltshire*. 1888–91 (Privately printed).

—— (1898). *Excavations on Cranbourne Chase near Rusholme on the Borders of Dorset and Wiltshire 1893–1896*, i (London: Harrison and Sons).

Pitts, M., Bayliss, A., McKinley, J., Boylston, A., Budd, P., Evans, J., Chenery, C., Reynolds, A., and Semple, S. (2002). 'An Anglo-Saxon Decapitation and Burial at Stonehenge', *Wiltshire Archaeological and Natural History Magazine* 95: 131–46.

Pluskowski, A. (2006a). *Wolves and Wilderness in the Middle Ages* (Woodbridge: Boydell Press).

—— (2006b). 'Harnessing the Hunger: Religious Appropriations of Animal Predation in Early Medieval Scandinavia', in A. Andrén, K. Jennbert, and C. Raudvere (eds), *Old Norse Religion in Long-Term Perspectives* (Lund: Nordic Academic Press), 119–23.

—— (2010). 'Animal Magic', in M. O. H. Carver, A. Sanmark, and S. Semple (eds), *Signals of Belief in Early England: Anglo-Saxon Paganism Revisited* (Oxford: Oxbow Books Ltd), 103–27.

—— and Patrick, P. (2003). 'How Do You Pray to God? Fragmentation and Variety in Early Medieval Christianity', in M. O. H. Carver (ed.), *The Cross Goes North: Processes of Conversion in Northern Europe. AD 300–1300* (Woodbridge: Boydell and Brewer), 29–58.

Pohl, W. (2000). 'Memory, Identity and Power in Lombard Italy', in Y. Hen and M. Innes (eds), *The Uses of the Past in the Early Middle Ages* (Cambridge: Cambridge University Press), 9–28.

Pollard, J. and Reynolds, A. (2002). *Avebury: The Biography of a Monument* (Stroud: Tempus Publishing Ltd).

Pollington, S. (2000). *Leechcraft: Early English Charms, Plant-lore and Healing* (Norfolk: Anglo-Saxon Books).

—— (2008). *Anglo-Saxon Burial Mounds: Princely Burials in the 6th and 7th Centuries* (Norfolk: Anglo-Saxon Books).

Powell, W. R. (ed.) (1963). *Victoria County History of Essex*, iii (London: Oxford University Press).

Powlesland, D. (1999). 'The Anglo-Saxon Settlement at West Heslerton, North Yorkshire', in J. Hawkes and S. Mills (eds), *Northumbria's Golden Age* (Stroud: Sutton Publishing Ltd), 55–65.

—— Lyall, D., Hopkins, G., Donoghue, D., Beck, M., Harte, A., and Stott, D. (2006). 'Beneath the Sand: Multi-Sensor Studies within the Archaeological Landscape of the Vale of Pickering, North Yorkshire, England', *Archaeological Prospection* 13: 291–9.

Price, N. (2002). *The Viking Way* (Uppsala: University of Uppsala Press).

Pull, J. H. (1929). 'The Blackpatch Excavations', *South-Eastern Naturalist* 34: 29–30.

—— (1932). *The Flint Miners of Blackpatch* (London: Williams and Norgate Ltd).

Rahtz, P. (1970). 'A Possible Saxon Palace near Stratford-upon-Avon', *Antiquity* 44: 137–43.

Rattue, J. (2001). *The Living Stream: Holy Wells in Historical Context* (Woodbridge: Boydell and Brewer).

Rauer, C. (2000). *Beowulf and the Dragon: Parallels and Analogues* (Cambridge: Brewer).

—— (2001). 'Dragons', in J. Blair, S. Keynes, and D. Scragg (eds), *The Blackwell Encyclopaedia of Anglo-Saxon England* (Oxford: Blackwell Publishers Ltd), 145.

Read, C. H. (1895). 'On Excavations in a Cemetery of South Saxons on Highdown, Sussex', *Archaeologia* 54: 369–82.

Reaney, P. H. (1943). *The Place-Names of Cambridgeshire and the Isle of Ely*. EPNS, vol. 19 (Cambridge: Cambridge University Press).

—— (1960). *The Origin of English Place-Names* (London: Routledge & Kegan Paul).

Reynolds, A. (1997). 'The Definition and Ideology of Anglo-Saxon Execution Sites and Cemeteries', in G. de Boe and F. Verhaeghe (eds), *Death and Burial in Medieval Europe*, vol. 2 (Zelik: Instituut voor het Archeologisch Patrimonium), 33–41.

—— (1998). 'Anglo-Saxon Law in the Landscape: An Archaeological Study of the Old English Judicial System'. Unpublished PhD thesis, University of London.

—— (1999). *Later Anglo-Saxon England: Life and Landscape* (Stroud: Tempus Publishing Ltd).

—— (2001). 'Avebury: A Late Anglo-Saxon *burh*?'. *Antiquity* 75 (287): 29–30.

—— (2002). 'Burials, Boundaries and Charters in Anglo-Saxon England: A Reassessment', in S. Lucy and A. Reynolds (eds), *Burial in Early Medieval England and Wales*. Society for Medieval Archaeology Monograph 17 (London: Society for Medieval Archaeology), 171–94.

—— (2003). 'Boundaries and Settlements in Later 6th to 11th Century England', in D. Griffiths, A. Reynolds, and S. Semple (eds), *Boundaries in Early Medieval Britain*, Anglo-Saxon Studies in Archaeology and History 12 (Oxford: Oxford University School of Archaeology), 97–139.

—— (2008). 'The Emergence of Anglo-Saxon Judicial Practice: The Message of the Gallows', *Anglo-Saxon* 2: 1–62.

—— (2009a). *Anglo-Saxon Deviant Burial Customs* (Oxford: Oxford University Press).

—— (2009b). 'Meaningful Landscapes: An Early Medieval Perspective', in R. Gilchrist and A. Reynolds (eds), *Reflections: 50 Years of Medieval Archaeology 1957–2007*. Society for Medieval Archaeology Monograph, 30 (Leeds: Maney), 409–34.

—— and Langlands, A. (2006). 'Social Identities on the Macro Scale: A Maximum View of Wansdyke', in W. Davies, G. Halsall, and A. Reynolds (eds), *People and Space in the Middle Ages, 300–1300*. Studies in the Early Middle Ages, 28 (Turnhout: Brepols Publishers), 13–44.

—— and Semple, S. J. (2011). 'Anglo-Saxon Non-Funerary Weapon Depositions', in S. Brookes, S. Harrington, and A. Reynolds (eds), *Studies in Early Anglo-Saxon Art and Archaeology: Papers in Honour of Martin G. Welch*. BAR British Series, 527 (Oxford: Archaeopress), 40–8.

Richards, J. (1999). 'Anglo-Saxon Settlements of the Golden Age', in J. Hawkes and S. Mills (eds), *Northumbria's Golden Age* (Stroud: Sutton Publishing Ltd), 44–54.

Rigold, S. E. and Metcalf, D. M. (1984). 'A Revised Check-List of English Finds of Sceattas', in D. Hill and D. M. Metcalf (eds), *Sceattas in England and on the Continent*. BAR British Series, 128 (Oxford: BAR), 245–68.

Rippon, S. (2004). 'Making the Most of a Bad Situation? Glastonbury Abbey and the Exploitation of Wetland Resources in the Somerset Levels', *Medieval Archaeology* 48: 91–130.

Roach, L. (2011). 'Public Rites and Public Wrongs: Ritual Aspects of Diplomas in Tenth- and Eleventh-Century England', *Early Medieval Europe* 19(2): 182–203.

Roberts, J. (ed. and trans.) (1979). *The Guthlac Poems of the Exeter Book* (Oxford: Clarendon Press).

—— (2001). 'Hagiography and Literature: The Case of Guthlac of Crowland', in M. P. Brown and C. A. Farr (eds), *Mercia: An Anglo-Saxon Kingdom in Europe* (London: London University Press), 69–86.

Robertson, A. J. (1939). *Anglo-Saxon Charters* (Cambridge: Cambridge University Press).

Robinson, P. (2002). 'The Treasure Act', *Trilithon, Newsletter of the Wiltshire Archaeological and Natural History Society* 46: 3.

Rodwell, W. (1981). *The Archaeology of the English Church* (London: Batsford).

—— (1984). 'Churches in the Landscape: Aspects of Topography and Planning', in M. Faull (ed.), *Studies in Late Anglo-Saxon Settlement* (Oxford: Oxford University Press), 1–23.

—— (1986). 'Saint Mary's Priory, Les Écréhous, Jersey: A Reappraisal', *Bulletin Société Jersiaise* 24: 225–31.

—— and Rodwell, K. (1977). *Historic Churches: A Wasting Asset*. CBA Research Report, 19 (London: CBA).

—— —— (1982). 'St Peter's Church, Barton-upon-Humber', *Antiquaries Journal* 62: 283–315.

Rollason, D. (2003). *Northumbria 500–1100: The Creation and Destruction of a Kingdom* (Cambridge: Cambridge University Press).

Rolleston, G. (1870). 'On the Character and Influence of the Anglo-Saxon Conquest of England, as Illustrated by Archaeological Research', *Notices of the Proceedings at the Meetings of the Royal Institution* 6: 116–19.

Rome Hall, G. (1876). 'On Ancient British Remains near Birtley and Barrasford, North Tyne', *Archaeologia Æliana* 7: 3–19.

Roymans, N. (1995). 'The Cultural Biography of Urnfields and the Long-Term History of a Mythical Landscape', *Archaeological Dialogues* 2(1): 2–24.

—— and Kortland, F. (1999). 'Urnfield Symbolism, Ancestors and the Land in the Lower Rhine Region', in F. Theuws and N. Roymans (eds), *Land and Ancestors: Cultural Dynamics in the Urnfield Period and the Middle Ages in the Southern Netherlands* (Amsterdam: Amsterdam University Press), 33–62.

Salzman, L. F. (1931). 'The Rapes of Sussex', *Sussex Archaeological Collections* 72: 28.

—— (1951). *The Victoria History of the County of Warwick*, iv *Knightlow Hundred*. University of London Institute of Historical Research (London: Oxford University Press).

Sanmark, A. (2004). *Power and Conversion: A Comparative Study of Christianization in Scandinavia*. OPIA 34 (Uppsala: Uppsala University Press).

—— (2009). 'Administrative Organisation and State Formation: A Case Study of Assembly Sites in Södemanland, Sweden', *Medieval Archaeology* 53: 205–41.

—— (2010). 'Living On: Ancestors and the Soul', in M. O. H. Carver, A. Sanmark, and S. Semple (eds), *Signals of Belief in Early England: Anglo-Saxon Paganism Revisited* (Oxford: Oxbow Books Ltd), 158–80.

—— and Semple, S. J. (2008). 'Places of Assembly: New Discoveries in Sweden and England', *Fornvännen* 103(4): 245–59.

—— —— (2010). 'The Topography of Outdoor Assembly Sites in Europe with Reference to Recent Field Results from Sweden', in H. Lewis and S. J. Semple, *Perspectives in Landscape Archaeology*. BAR International Series, 2103 (Oxford: BAR), 107–19.

—— —— (2011). *Tingsplatsen som arkeologiskt problem*. Etapp 3: Anundshög. TAP Field Report, no. 3.

Sawyer, P. H. (1968). *Anglo-Saxon Charters: An Annotated List and Bibliography*. London Royal Historical Society Guides and Handbooks, no. 8 (London: Royal Historical Society).

—— (1978). *From Roman Britain to Norman England* (London: Methuen).

Sayer, D. and Williams, H. (eds) (2010). *Mortuary Practices and Social Identities in the Middle Ages* (Exeter: Exeter University Press).

Scaife, R. G. and Burrin, P. J. (1983). 'Floodplain Development and the Vegetational History of the Sussex High Weald and Some Archaeological Implications', *Sussex Archaeological Collections* 121: 1–10.

Scarre, C. (2002a). 'A Place of Special Meaning: Interpreting Prehistoric Monuments through Landscape', in B. David and M. Wilson (eds), *Inscribed Landscapes: Marking and Making Place* (Honolulu: University of Hawaii Press), 154–75.

—— (2002b). 'Coast and Cosmos: The Neolithic Monuments of Northern Brittany', in C. Scarre (ed.), *Monuments and Landscape in Atlantic Europe* (London: Routledge), 84–102.

—— (2007). *The Megalithic Monuments of Britain and Ireland* (London and New York: Thames & Hudson).

—— (2011). *Landscapes of Neolithic Brittany* (Oxford: Oxford University Press).

Schama, S. (1995). *Landscape and Memory* (New York: Knopf).

Schweiso, J. (1979). 'The Anglo-Saxon Burials', in G. J. Wainwright (ed.), *Mount Pleasant, Dorset, Excavations 1970–1971*. Reports of the Research Committee of the Society of Antiquaries of London, no. 37 (London: Thames & Hudson), 181–3.

Scott, E. (1993). *A Gazetteer of Roman Villas in Britain* (Leicester: University of Leicester Press).

Scragg, D. (ed. and trans.) (1992). *The Vercelli Homilies and Related Texts*. Early English Text Society Original Series 300 (Oxford and New York: English Text Society).

Scull, C. (1991). 'Post-Roman Phase 1 at Yeavering: A Re-Consideration', *Medieval Archaeology* 35: 51–63.

Scull, C. J. and Harding, A. H. (1990). 'Two Early Medieval Cemeteries at Milfield, Northumberland', *Durham Archaeological Journal* 6: 1–29.

Semple, S. J. (1994). 'St James' Church, Avebury: A Structural Analysis and a Consideration of the Church in its Landscape Context'. Unpublished BA dissertation, University of London.

—— (1998). 'A Fear of the Past: The Place of the Prehistoric Burial Mound in the Ideology of Middle and Later Anglo-Saxon England', *World Archaeology* 30(1): 109–26.

—— (2003a). 'Burials and Political Boundaries in the Avebury region, North Wiltshire', *Anglo-Saxon Studies in Archaeology and History* 12: 72–91.

—— (2003b). 'Illustrations of Damnation in Late Anglo-Saxon Manuscripts', *Anglo-Saxon England* 32: 31–45.

—— (2004). 'Locations of Assembly in Early Anglo-Saxon England', in A. Pantos and S. Semple (eds), *Assembly Places and Practices in Medieval Europe* (Dublin: Four Courts Press), 135–54.

—— (2007). ''Defining the OE *Hearg*: A Preliminary Archaeological and Topographic Examination of *Hearg* Place Names and their Hinterlands', *Early Medieval Europe* 15(4): 364–85.

—— (2008). 'Polities and princes AD 400–800: new perspectives on the funerary landscape of the South Saxon kingdom', *Oxford Journal of Archaeology* 27(4), 407–29.

—— (2009). 'Recycling the Past: Ancient Monuments and Changing Meanings in Early Medieval Britain', in M. Aldrich and R. J. Wallis (eds), *Antiquaries and Archaists, the Past in the Past, the Past in the Present* (Reading: Spire Books Ltd).

—— (2010). 'In the Open Air', in M. O. H. Carver, A. Sanmark, and S. J. Semple (eds), *Signals of Belief: Anglo-Saxon Paganism Revisited* (Oxford: Oxbow Books Ltd), 21–48.

—— (2011). 'Sacred Spaces and Places in Pre-Christian and Conversion Period Anglo-Saxon England', in H. Hamerow, D. A. Hinton, and S. Crawford (eds), *The Oxford Handbook of Anglo-Saxon Archaeology* (Oxford: Oxford University Press), 742–63.

—— (forthcoming (a)). 'Excavations at Scutchmer's Knob, East Hendred, Berkshire', *South Midlands Archaeological Journal*.

—— (forthcoming (b)). Temples and Heathen Groves.

—— (forthcoming (c)). Plants and Magic in Anglo-Saxon England.

—— and Langlands, A. (2001). 'Swanborough Tump', *Wiltshire Archaeological and Natural History Magazine* 94: 239–42.

—— and Sanmark, A. (2013). 'Assembly in North West Europe: Collective Concerns for Early Societies', *European Journal of Archaeology* 16/3: 518–42.

Sheahan, J. J. and Whellan, T. (1856). *History and Topography of the City of York: The Ainsty Wapentake and the East Riding of Yorkshire*. 2 vols (Beverley: Privately printed).

Sheldon, J. (1978). 'The Environmental Background', in P. L. Drewett (ed.), *Archaeology in Sussex to AD1500: Essays for Eric Holden*. CBA Research Report, no. 29 (London: CBA), 3–7.

Shephard, J. (1979a). 'Anglo-Saxon Barrows of the Later Sixth and Seventh Centuries AD'. Unpublished PhD dissertation, University of Cambridge.

—— (1979b). 'The Social Identity of the Individual in Isolated Barrows and Barrow Cemeteries in Anglo-Saxon England', in B. Burnham and J. Kingsbury (eds), *Space, Hierarchy and Society: Interdisciplinary Studies in Social Area Analysis*. BAR International Series, no. 59 (Oxford: BAR), 47–79.

Sheppard, T. (1906a). 'An Anglo-Saxon Grave in East Yorkshire, and its Contents', *The Antiquary* 42: 333–8.

—— (1906b). 'An Anglo-Saxon Grave in East Yorkshire, and its Contents', *Hull Museum Publications* 33, June: 10–18, p. xvii.

—— (1907). 'Local Archaeological Notes', *East Riding Antiquarian Society Transactions* 14: 74–7.

—— (1909). 'Some Anglo-Saxon Vases in the Hull Museum', *East Riding Antiquarian Society Transactions* 16: 50–70.

—— (1919). 'Our German Ancestors: Being an Account of the Anglo-Saxon Remains Found in East Yorkshire (reprinted from *Transactions of the Hull Scientific and Field Naturalists Club*, 4, Part 6)', *Hull Museum Publications* 117: 299–320.

Sherley-Price, L. (trans.) (1968). *Bede: A History of the English Church and People*, 2nd edn (Harmondsworth: Penguin Books).

Sherlock, S. and Simmons, M. (2008). 'A Seventh-Century Royal Cemetery at Street House, North-East Yorkshire, England', *Antiquity* 82 (316), Project Gallery, June 2008 <http://antiquity.ac.uk/projgall/sherlock/index.html> (accessed 22 March 2013).

Shore, T. W. (1892). *The History of Hampshire* (London: Penguin Books).

Shore, T. W. (1893). 'The Candover Valley and its Prehistoric Inhabitants', *Papers and Proceedings of the Hampshire Field Club* 2: 283–94.

Simpson, J. (1978). 'Fifty British Dragon Tales: An Analysis', *Folklore* 89(1): 79–93.

——(1986). 'God's Visible Judgements: The Christian Dimension of Landscape Legends', *Landscape History* 8: 53–8.

Sims-Williams, P. (1990). *Religion and Literature in Western England, 600–900* (Cambridge: Cambridge University Press).

Sisam, K. (1953). 'Anglo-Saxon Royal Genealogies', *Proceedings of the British Academy* 39: 287–348.

Smith, A. H. (1928). *The Place-Names of the North Riding of Yorkshire*. EPNS, vol. 5 (Cambridge: Cambridge University Press).

——(1937). *The Place-Names of the East Riding of Yorkshire and York*. EPNS, vol. 14 (Cambridge: Cambridge University Press).

——(1956). *English Place-Name Elements*. 2 vols. EPNS, vols 25–6 (Cambridge: Cambridge University Press).

——(1961a). *The Place-Names of the West Riding of Yorkshire, Part I*. EPNS, vol. 30 (Cambridge: Cambridge University Press).

——(1961b). *The Place-Names of the West Riding of Yorkshire, Part II*. EPNS, vol. 31 (Cambridge: Cambridge University Press).

——(1961c). *The Place-Names of the West Riding of Yorkshire, Part III*. EPNS, vol. 32 (Cambridge: Cambridge University Press).

——(1961d). *The Place-Names of the West Riding of Yorkshire, Part IV*. EPNS, vol. 35 (Cambridge: Cambridge University Press).

——(1964–5). *The Place-Names of Gloucestershire*. Vols. I–IV. EPNS, vols 38–41 (Cambridge: Cambridge University Press).

Smith, R. A. (1908). 'Anglo-Saxon Remains', in W. Page (ed.), *The Victoria History of the County of Stafford*, i (London: Archibald Constable and Company Ltd), 199–216.

——(1912a). 'The Excavation by Canon Greenwell FSA, in 1908, of an Anglo-Saxon Cemetery at Uncleby, East Riding of Yorkshire', *Proceedings of the Society of Antiquaries* 24: 146–58.

——(1912b). 'Anglo-Saxon Remains', in W. Page (ed.), *The Victoria County History of the Counties of England, Yorkshire*, ii (London: Constable and Company), 73–108.

Sopp, M. (1999). *Die Wiederaufnahme älter Bestattungsplätze in den nachfolgenden vor- und frügeschichtlichen Perioden in Norddeutschland* (Bonn: Habelt).

Speake, G. (1989). *A Saxon Bed Burial on Swallowcliffe Down* (London: HBMCE).

Stanley, E. G. (1975). *The Search for Anglo-Saxon Paganism* (Cambridge: D. S. Brewer).

——(1979). 'Two Old English Poetic Phrases Insufficiently Understood for Literary Criticism: Þing gehegan and seonoþ gehegan', in D. G. Calder (ed.), *Old English Poetry: Essays in Style* (Cambridge: Brewer), 67–9.

——(2000). *Imagining the Anglo-Saxon Past: 'The Search for Anglo-Saxon Paganism' and 'Anglo-Saxon Trial by Jury'*, 2nd edn (Cambridge: Brewer).

Stenton, F. M. (1941). 'The Historical Bearing of Place-Name Studies: Anglo-Saxon Heathenism', *Transactions of the Royal Historical Society* (4th ser.) 23: 1–24.

——(1955). *The Latin Charters of the Anglo-Saxon Period* (Oxford: Clarendon Press).

——(1971). *Anglo-Saxon England*, 3rd edn (Oxford: Clarendon Press).

Stevens, J. (1884). 'On the Remains Found in an Anglo-Saxon Tumulus at Taplow, Bucks', *Journal of the British Archaeological Association* 40: 61–71.

Stevenson, J. H. (1980). 'Overton', in D. A. Crowley (ed.), *A History of Wiltshire, The Victoria History of the Counties of England*, for The University of London Institute of Historical Research, xi (London: Oxford University Press) 181–202.

Stiegemann, C. and Wemhoff, M. (1999). *Kunst und Kultur der Karolingerzeit, Karl der Große und Papst Leo III. In Paderborn*, 6: 18 (Mainz: Verlag Phillipp von Zabern).

Stockdale, J. (1978 [1872]). *Annales Cærmoelenses: or Annals of Cartmel*, repr. (Beckermet: Michael Morn).

Stocker, D. (1993). 'The Early Church in Lincolnshire: A Study of the Sites and their Significance', in A. Vince (ed.), *Pre-Viking Lindsey*. Lincoln Archaeological Studies 1 (Lincoln: City of Lincoln Archaeology Unit), 101–22.

—— with Everson, P. (1990). 'Rubbish Recycled: A Study of the Reuse of Stone in Lincolnshire', in D. Parsons (ed.), *Stone: Quarrying and Building in England* AD *43–1525* (Chichester: Phillimore), 83–101.

—— and Everson, P. (2003). 'The Straight and Narrow Way: Fenland Causeways and the Conversion of the Landscape in the Witham Valley, Lincolnshire', in M. O. H. Carver (ed.), *The Cross Goes North: Processes of Conversion in Northern Europe*, AD *300–1300* (York: York Medieval Press with Boydell Press), 271–88.

—— Went D., and Farley, M. (1995). 'The Evidence for a Pre-Viking Church Adjacent to the Anglo-Saxon Barrow at Taplow, Buckinghamshire', *Archaeological Journal* 152: 441–51.

Stocking, R. L. (2000). *Bishops, Councils, and Concensus in the Visigothic Kingdom 589–633* (Michigan: Ann Arbor).

Stoertz, C. (1997). *Ancient Landscapes of the Yorkshire Wolds* (Swindon: RCHME).

Stone, J. F. S. (1932). 'Interments on Roche Court Down, Winterslow', *Wiltshire Archaeological and Natural History Magazine* 45: 568–82.

Stukeley, W. (1743). *Abury, a Temple of the British Druids, with Some Others, Described* (London: Privately printed).

Sumner, H. (1913). *The Ancient Earthworks of Cranborne Chase* (London: Chiswick Press).

Swanton, M. (1973). *The Spear-Heads of the Anglo-Saxon Settlements* (London: Royal Archaeological Institute).

—— (1974). *A Corpus of Anglo-Saxon Spear Types*. BAR British Series, 7 (Oxford: BAR).

Swanton, M. J. (ed.) (1996). *The Anglo-Saxon Chronicle* (London: J. M. Dent and Sons).

Sykes, N. and Carden. R. F. (2011). 'Were Fallow Deer Spotted (OE **pohha/*pocca*) in Anglo-Saxon England? Reviewing the Evidence for *Dama dama dama* in Early Medieval Europe', *Medieval Archaeology* 55: 138–62.

Taylor, A., and Denton, B. (1977). 'Skeletons on Wandlebury Hillfort. TL 495533', *Proceedings of the Cambridge Antiquarian Society*, 67: p. xi.

Taylor, H. M. and Taylor, J. (1965). *Anglo-Saxon Architecture*, i–ii (Cambridge: Cambridge University Press).

Taylor, J. and Taylor, H. M. (1963). 'The Anglo-Saxon Church at Edenham', *Journal of the British Archaeological Association* (3rd ser.) 26: 6–10.

Temple, E. (1976). *Anglo-Saxon Manuscripts 900–1066* (London: Harvey Miller).

Tempel, W-D. (1982). 'Zur Gliederung des gemischtbelegten Friedhofs der Volkerwan-derungszeit von Barchel, Gem. Oerel', *Studien zur Sachsenforschung* 4: 315–21.

Thäte, E. (1993). 'Die Orientierung frühgeschichtlicher Bestattungen an älteren Denk-mälern im sächsich-angel-sächsischen Raum'. Unpublished MA dissertation, Univer-sity of Münster.

—— (1996). 'Alte Denkmäler und frügeschichtliche Bestattungen: Ein sächsisch-angelsächsischer Totenbrauch und seine Kontinuität', *Archäologische Informationen* 19(1&2): 105–16.

—— (2007). *Monuments and Minds: Monument Reuse in Scandinavia in the Second Half of the First Millennium AD*. Acta Archaeological Lundensia Series in 4°, no. 27 (Lund: Lund University).

Theuws, F. (2009). 'Grave Goods, Ethnicity, and the Rhetoric of Burial Rites in Late Antique Northern Gaul', in T. Derks and N. Roymans (eds), *Ethnic Constructs in Antiquity: The Role of Power and Tradition* (Amsterdam: Amsterdam University Press), 283–320.

Thomas. C. (1993). *Tintagel: Arthur and Archaeology* (London: English Heritage).

Thompson, V. (2002). 'Constructing Salvation: A Homiletic and Penitential Context for Late Anglo-Saxon Burial Practice', in S. Lucy and A. Reynolds (eds), *Burial in Early Medieval England and Wales*. Society for Medieval Archaeology Monograph 17 (London: Society for Medieval Archaeology), 229–40.

—— (2003). 'The View from the Edge: Dying, Power and Vision in Late Saxon England', in D. Griffiths, A. Reynolds, and S. Semple (eds), *Boundaries in the Anglo-Saxon World*, *Anglo-Saxon Studies in Archaeology and History* 12 (Oxford: Oxford Com-mittee for Archaeology), 92–7.

—— (2004). *Dying and Death in Later Anglo-Saxon England* (Woodbridge: Boydell Press).

Tilley, C. (1994). *A Phenomenology of Landscape: Places, Paths and Monuments* (Oxford: Berg).

—— (1996). 'The Power of Rocks: Topography and Monument Construction on Bod-min Moor', *World Archaeology* 28(2): 161–76.

—— (2004). *The Materiality of Stone: Explorations in Landscape Phenomenology* (Oxford: Berg).

Tolley, C. (2009). *Shamanism in Norse Myth asnd Magic*. 2 vols. Folklore Fellows' Communications, 296 and 297 (Helskinki: Folklore Fellow's Communications).

—— (2013). 'What is a "World Tree", and Should We Expect to Find One Growing in Anglo-Saxon England?', in M. Bintley and M. Shapland (eds), *Trees and Timber in the Anglo-Saxon World* (Oxford: Oxford University Press), 177–85.

Toop, N. (2011). 'Northumbria in the West: Considering Interaction through Monu-mentality', in D. Petts and S. Turner (eds), *Early Medieval Northumbria: Kingdoms and Communities, AD 450–1100*. Studies in the Early Middle Ages, 24 (Turnhout: Brepols Publishers), 85–111.

Turner, S. (2006). *Making a Christian Landscape: The Countryside in Early Medieval Cornwall, Devon and Wessex* (Exeter: Exeter University Press).

—— Semple, S., and Turner, A. (2013). *One Monastery in Two Places: Wearmouth and Jarrow in Their Landscape Context* (London: English Heritage).

Tweddle, D. with M. Biddle and B. Kjølby-Biddle (1995). *South-East England: The Corpus of Anglo-Saxon Stone Sculpture*, iv (Oxford: Oxford University Press).

Ucko, P. J., Hunter, M., Clark, A., and David, A. (1991). *Avebury Reconsidered from the 1660s to the 1990s* (London: Unwin Hyman Ltd).

Ulmschneider, K. (2000). *Markets, Minsters, and Metal-Detectors*. BAR British Series, 307 (Oxford: Archaeopress).

—— (2011). 'Settlement Hierarchy', in H. Hamerow, D. Hinton, and S. Crawford (eds), *The Oxford Handbook of Anglo-Saxon Archaeology* (Oxford: Oxford University Press), 156–71.

Urbanczyk, P. (2003). 'The Politics of Conversion in North Central Europe', in M. O. H. Carver (ed.), *The Cross Goes North: Processes of Christian Conversion in Northern Europe* (York: Boydell Press), 15–28.

Urtāns, J. (2008). *Ancient Cult Sites of Semigallia*. CCC Papers, 11 (Rīgā: Tapals/Gotland University).

Vinycomb, J. (1906). *Ficticious and Symbolic Creatures in Art* (London: Chapman and Hall).

Wailes, B. (1982). 'The Irish Royal Sites in History and Archaeology', *Cambridge Medieval Celtic Studies* 3: 1–29.

Walker, J. (2010). 'In the Hall', in M. O. H. Carver, A. Sanmark, and S. Semple (eds), *Signals of Belief Early England: Anglo-Saxon Paganism Revisited* (Oxford: Oxbow Books Ltd), 83–102.

Walsham, A. (2011). *The Reformation of the Landscape: Religion, Identity and Memory in Early Modern Britain and Ireland* (Oxford: Oxford University Press).

Ward, S. (2008). *Chester: A History* (London: Phillimore).

Wardell, J. (1849). 'Antiquities and Works of Art Exhibited', *Archaeological Journal* 6: 401–2.

Warhurst, A. (1955). 'The Jutish Cemetery at Lyminge', *Archaeologia* 50: 383–406.

Warner, R. (1988). 'The Archaeology of Early Historic Irish Kingship', in S. Driscoll and M. R. Nieke (eds), *Power and Politics in Early Medieval Britain and Ireland* (Edinburgh: Edinburgh University Press), 47–68.

—— (1994). 'On Crannógs and Kings', *Ulster Journal of Archaeology* 57: 61–9.

—— (2004). 'Notes on the Inception and Early Development of the Royal Mound in Ireland', in A. Pantos and S. Semple (eds), *Assembly Places and Practices in Early Medieval Europe* (Dublin: Four Courts Press), 27–43.

Watkin, D. A. (1956). 'Abbey of Malmesbury', in R. B. Pugh and E. Crittall (eds), *The Victoria History of the Counties of England: A History of Wiltshire*, iii (London: Oxford University Press), 210–30.

Watkin, J. and Mann, F. (1981). 'Some Late Anglo-Saxon Finds from Lilla Howe, N. Yorks and their Context', *Medieval Archaeology* 25: 153–7.

Waton, P. V. (1982). 'Man's Impact on the Chalkland: Some New Pollen Evidence', in M. Bell and S. Limbrey (eds), *Archaeological Aspects of Woodland Ecology*. BAR International Series, 146 (Oxford: BAR), 75–92.

Webber, M. (1999). 'The Roman, Anglo-Saxon and Medieval Coffins', in C. Heighway and R. Bryant (eds), *The Golden Minster: The Anglo-Saxon Minster and Later Medieval Priory of St Oswald at Gloucester*. CBA Research Report, 117 (York: CBA), 207–18.

Webster, L. (1992). 'Death's Diplomacy: Sutton Hoo in the Light of Other Male Princely Burials', in C. Neuman de Vegvar and R. Farrell (eds), *Sutton Hoo: Fifty Years After* (Oxford, OH: Miami University Press), 75–81.

—— (1999). 'The Iconographic Programme of the Franks Casket', in J. Hawkes and S. Mills (eds), *Northumbria's Golden Age* (Stroud: Sutton Publishing Ltd), 227–46.

—— and Cherry, J. (1972). 'Hunsbury Hill', *Medieval Archaeology* 16: 158–9.

—— —— (1975). 'Bedhampton', *Medieval Archaeology* 19: 222.

Wedderburn, L. M. and Grime, D. (1984). 'The Cairn Cemetery at Garbeg, Drumnadrochit', in J. Friell and W. Watson (eds), *Pictish Studies: Settlement, Burial and Art in Dark Age Northern Britain*. BAR British Series, 125 (Oxford: Archaeopress), 151–68.

Welch, M. (1983). *Early Anglo-Saxon Sussex*. 2 vols. BAR British Series, 112 (Oxford: BAR).

—— (1985). 'Rural Settlement Patterns in the Early and Middle Anglo-Saxon Periods', *Landscape History* 7: 13–25.

—— (1989). 'The Kingdom of the South Saxons: The Origins', in S. Bassett (ed.), *The Origins of Anglo-Saxon Kingdoms* (Leicester: Leicester University Press), 75–83.

—— (1992). *Anglo-Saxon England* (London: Batsford).

Wentersdorf, K. (1981). 'The Situation of the Narrator in the Old English *Wife's Lament*', *Speculum* 56: 492–516.

Wheeler, M. (1954). *The Stanwick Fortifications, North Riding of Yorkshire*, Reports of the Research Committee of the Society of Antiquaries of London No. XVII (Oxford: Oxford University Press).

White, R. and Barker, P. (1995). *Wroxeter: Life and Death of a Roman City* (Stroud: Tempus Publishing Ltd).

Whitelock, D. (1955). *English Historical Documents I c.500–1042* (London: Eyre and Methuen).

—— Brett, M., and Brooke, C. N. L. (1981). *Councils and Synods with Other Documents Relating to the English Church, I. AD 871–1204* (Oxford: Clarendon Press).

Whitfield, N. (2007). 'A Suggested Function for the Holy Well?', in A. J. Minnis (ed.), *Text, Image, Interpretation: Studies in Anglo-Saxon Literature and its Insular Context in Honour of Éamonn Ó Carragáin* (Turnhout: Brepols Publishers), 495–514.

Whitley, J. (2002). 'Too Many Ancestors', *Antiquity* 76: 119–26.

Whittle, A. (1997). *Sacred Mound Holy Rings* (Oxford: Oxbow Books Ltd).

Whymer, J. J. (1996). *Barrow Excavations in Norfolk, 1984–88*. East Anglian Archaeology 77 (Dereham: Norfolk Museums Service and Norfolk Archaeology Unit).

Wickham, C. (2005). *Framing the Middle Ages: Europe and the Mediterranean 400–800* (Oxford: Oxford University Press).

Wickham-Crowley, K. M. (2006). 'Living on the *Ecg*: The Mutable Boundaries of Land and Water in Anglo-Saxon Contexts', in C. A. Lees and G. R. Overing (eds), *A Place to Believe In: Locating Medieval Landscapes* (Pennsylvania, PA: Pennsylvania State University Press), 85–110.

Wilkinson, K., Barber, L., and Bennell, M. (2002). 'The Examination of Six Dry Valleys in the Brighton Area: The Changing Environment', in D. Rudling (ed.), *Downland Settlement and Landuse: The Archaeology of the Brighton Bypass*, University College London Field Archaeology Unit Monograph 1 (London: University College London).

Williams, H. (1996). 'Placing the Dead in Ancient Landscapes'. Unpublished MA thesis, University of Reading.

—— (1997). 'Ancient Landscapes and the Dead: The Reuse of Prehistoric and Roman Monuments as Early Anglo-Saxon Burial Sites', *Medieval Archaeology* 41: 1–32.

—— (1998a). 'Ancestral and Supernatural Places in Early Anglo-Saxon England', *At the Edge* 9 (March): 1–9.

—— (1998b). 'Monuments and the Past in Early Anglo-Saxon England', *World Archaeology* 30(1): 90–108.

—— (1998c). 'Identities and Cemeteries in Roman and Early Medieval Archaeology', in C. Forcey and R. Witcher (eds), *TRAC 98 Proceedings of the Eighth Annual Theoretical Roman Archaeology Conference, Leicester* (Oxford: Oxbow Books Ltd), 96–108.

—— (1999). 'Placing the Dead: Investigating the Location of Wealthy Barrow Burials in Seventh Century England', in M. Rundkvist (ed.), *Grave Matters: Eight Studies of First Millenium AD Burials in Crimea, England and Southern Scandinavia*. BAR International Series, 781 (Oxford: BAR), 57–86.

—— (2001). 'Death, Memory and Time: A Consideration of the Mortuary Practices at Sutton Hoo', in C. Humphrey and W. M. Ormrod (eds), *Time in the Medieval World* (Woodbridge: York Medieval Press), 35–72.

—— (2002). 'Cemeteries as Central Places: Landscape and Identity in Early Anglo-Saxon England', in B. Hardh and L. Larsson (eds), *Central Places in the Migration and Merovingian Periods*. Papers from the 52nd Sachsensymposion (Lund: Almqvist), 341–62.

—— (2003). 'Introduction', in H. Williams (ed.), *Archaeologies of Remembrance: Death and Memory in Past Societies* (New York: Kluwer Academic/Plenum Publishers), 1–24.

—— (2004). 'Assembling the Dead', in A. Pantos and S. Semple (eds), *Assembly Places and Practices in Medieval Europe* (Dublin: Four Courts Press), 109–34.

—— (2006a). *Death and Memory in Early Medieval Britain* (Cambridge: Cambridge University Press).

—— (2006b). 'Digging Saxon Graves in Victorian Britain', in R. Pearson (ed.), *The Victorians and the Ancient World: Archaeology and Classicism in Nineteenth-Century Culture* (Cambridge: Cambridge Scholars Press), 61–80.

—— (2006c). 'Heathen Graves and Victorian Anglo-Saxonism: Assessing the Archaeology of John Mitchell Kemble', *Anglo-Saxon Studies in Archaeology and History* 13: 1–18.

—— (2011). 'Remembering Elites: Early Medieval Stone Crosses as Commemorative Technologies', in S. Kleingärtner, S. Pedersen, and L. Matthes (eds), *Arkæologi i Slesvig, Archäologie in Schleswig. Sonderband, Det 61. Internationale Sachsensymposion 2010, Haderslev, Danmark*, Neumünster: Wachholtz.

—— and Sayer, D. (2009). ''Halls of Mirrors': Death and Identity in Medieval Archaeology', in D. Sayer and H. Williams (eds), *Mortuary Practices and Social Identities in the Middle Ages* (Exeter: Exeter University Press), 1–22.

Wilson, D. (1992). *Anglo-Saxon Paganism* (London: Routledge).

Wilson, D. M. (1964). *Anglo-Saxon Ornamental Metalwork, 700–1100* (London: British Museum).

—— (1965). 'Some Neglected Late Anglo-Saxon Swords', *Medieval Archaeology* 9: 32–54.

Wilson, D. M. and Hurst, D. G. (eds) (1969). 'Yorkshire: Cowlam, Kemp Howe', *Medieval Archaeology* 13: 241.

Wingrave, W. (1931). 'An Anglo-Saxon Burial on Hardown Hill', *Proceedings of the Dorset Archaeological and Natural History Society* 53: 247–9.

Wood, I. (2006). 'Bede's Jarrow', in C. A. Lees and G. R. Overing (eds), *A Place to Believe In: Locating Medieval Landscapes* (Pennsylvania, PA: Pennsylvania State University Press), 67–84.

Woodwark, T. H. (1924). *The Crosses on the North York Moors* (Whitby: Whitby Literary and Philosophical Society).

Woolf, A. (2003). 'The Britons: from Romans to Barbarians', in H-W. Goetz, J. Jamut, and W. Pohl (eds), *Regna and Gentes: the Relationship between Late Antique and Early Medieval Peoples and Kingdoms in the Transformation of the Roman World* (Leiden: Brill), 345–80.

Wormald, P. (1978). 'Bede, *Beowulf*, and the Conversion of the Anglo-Saxon Aristocracy', in R. T. Farrell (ed.), *Bede and Anglo-Saxon England: Papers in Honour of the 1300th Anniversary of the Birth of Bede*. BAR British Series, 46 (Oxford: BAR), 32–95.

——(1983). 'Bede, the *Bretwaldas* and the Origins of the *gens Anglorum*', in P. Wormald, D. Bullough, and R. Collins (eds), *Ideal and Reality in Frankish and Anglo-Saxon Society: Studies Presented to J. M. Wallace-Hadrill* (Oxford: Blackwell Publishers Ltd), 99–129.

——(1986). 'Charters, Law and the Settlement of Disputes in Anglo-Saxon England', in W. Davies and P. Fouracre (eds), *The Settlement of Disputes in Early Medieval Europe* (Cambridge: Cambridge University Press), 149–68.

——(1999). *The Making of English Law: King Alfred to the Twelfth Century, Vol. 1: Legislation and its Limits* (Oxford: Blackwell Publishers Ltd).

Wright, T. (1841). *The History of Ludlow and its Neighbourhood*, i (Ludlow: Privately printed).

——(1855). 'Treago, and the Large Tumulus at St Weonard's', *Archaeologia Cambrensis* (3rd ser.) 1: 161–74.

Yeoman, P. A. (1986). 'Excavations at the Prebendal Court, Aylesbury, 1985', *South Midlands Archaeology* 16: 37–8.

Yoffee, N. (ed.) (2007). *Negotiating the Past in the Past: Identity, Memory and Landscape* (Arizona: Arizona University Press).

Yorke, B. (1990). *Kings and Kingdoms of Early Anglo-Saxon England* (London: Routledge).

——(1995). *Wessex in the Early Middle Ages* (Leicester: Leicester University Press).

——(2006). *The Conversion of Britain 600–800* (Harlow: Pearson Education Limited).

Young, R. J. C. (2008). *The Idea of English Ethnicity* (Oxford: Blackwell Publishers Ltd).

Youngs, S., Clarke, J., and Barry, T. (1986). 'Medieval Britain and Ireland in 1985, no. 25: St Buryan, St Berian's Church', *Medieval Archaeology* 30: 124–6.

Zadora-Rio, E. (2003). 'The Making of Churchyard and Parish Territories in the Early Medieval Landscape of France and England in the 7th–12th Centuries: A Reconsideration', *Medieval Archaeology* 47: 1–19.

Index

Locators in *italic* refer to colour plates. Those in **bold** refer to photographs. Those suffixed with *fig* or *tab* refer to figures or tables respectively.